Philip Melanchthon: *Summary of Moral Philosophy*

Early Modern Natural Law

VOLUME 7

The titles published in this series are listed at *brill.com/emnl*

Philip Melanchthon: *Summary of Moral Philosophy*

And Other Writings on Politics, Ethics, and Law

Edited and translated by

Alexander Batson

BRILL

ISSN 2589-5982
ISBN 978-90-04-77473-5
ISBN 978-90-04-77474-2 (PDF)
DOI https://doi.org/10.1163/9789004774742

Library of Congress Control Number: 2026949714

Brill and Koninklijke Brill BV are part of De Gruyter Brill.
www.degruyterbrill.com

Questions about General Product Safety Regulation: productsafety@degruyterbrill.com

Cover illustration: Hunter-gatherer mosaic illustration, from William MacKenzie's National Encyclopaedia (1891). Digitally enhanced by Rawpixel. Public domain image, used with permission. Lucas Cranach d.J. Bildnis Philipp Melanchthon, 1551. Ludwig Roselius Museum, Bremen. Photo: © Ludwig Roselius Museum, Bremen

Contents

Acknowledgements

Editing and translating a large book like this is impossible without ample help from others. I extend my sincere thanks to Knud Haakonssen, Laura Beck Varela, and Frank Grunert, the editors of the "Early Modern Natural Law: Studies and Sources" series in which this book appears. Knud especially provided much-needed editorial guidance in shepherding this large project. I am also extremely grateful to the reviewers, who showed an extraordinary diligence and generosity in providing detailed comments on the essays and translation. This project is much improved as a result of their comments.

I am grateful to my former professors, Bruce Gordon and Jim Whitman, for providing invaluable advice as I planned this project. I have incurred a special debt to two friends. Layne Hancock's constant interest, keen eye for theological and philosophical detail, and willingness to read anything spurred me to finish the book. Jamie Dunn, a master of Melanchthon's work as well as sixteenth-century Lutheran intellectual culture, provided extremely detailed and incredibly helpful comments on the translations. I cannot thank those two enough.

Because Melanchthon possessed seemingly infinite knowledge of ancient and medieval sources across all disciplines, it is impossible for any one modern scholar to immediately recognize all of his references and precise terms. For this reason, I found myself constantly sending emails and texts to friends and colleagues as I tried to track down the various sources of Melanchthon's thought or sharpen a certain translation. For help in these matters, I am grateful to a host of colleagues. Mads Langballe Jensen and Tomás Valle helped me with details about Melanchthon's life and work. Volker Leppin provided some helpful references about sixteenth-century Wittenberg. Tom Ward, Jordan Lavender, and Reid Comstock helped me understand the nuances of some Latin theological terms. Nick Barden tracked down some stray references to Renaissance legal culture, and Wim Decock and Noel Lenski helped me unravel some arcane legal terms. Aaron Pratt provided valuable guidance on the bibliographical material, and Stephen Lahey gave some helpful suggestions about Melanchthon's knowledge of Wycliffe. Finally, Mirko Canevaro and Naomi Campa ran their expert eyes over Melanchthon's *Collatio* and his description of Athenian law. On that subject, I found myself far outside of my own expertise, and I am grateful for their assistance.

I would also like to thank the Wittenberg Center for Reformation Studies for its financial support of this project. I am grateful to the Yale University History Department, and to the School of Civic Leadership at University of Texas at Austin for providing me an institutional home as I worked on the manuscript. The preface to the *Comparison of the Chief Attic and Roman Legal Actions* contains material previously published as "Sinai and the Areopagus: Philip Melanchthon, Natural Law, and the Beginnings of Athenian Legal History in the Shadow of the Schmalkaldic War", *Journal of the History of Ideas* 85.4 (October 2024): 713–748. I am grateful to the *Journal of the History of Ideas* and the University of Pennsylvania Press for their permission to reproduce it here.

I began this project back in 2018, before I started my PhD at Yale University. After completing a Masters Degree at Yale, I went back to my hometown of Powdersville, South Carolina, where I worked on a tree farm for a year. Every morning before work, I would translate Melanchthon's Latin before heading off to a day of driving tractors, digging holes, pruning trees, and clearing brush. I am grateful to my friends and co-workers back on the farm, and especially to Quintin Hall, Bill Gaddis, Taylor Willimon, Connor Perkins, Manuel Villegas, and Tom Merritt. Those friends, and that work, will always live fondly in my memory.

The final person who deserves my gratitude is also the reason why I worked on that farm back in 2018. I moved back home for that year to convince my then-girlfriend to marry me. I hoped to prove to her that I would give up anything—even my career ambitions—for her. She is now my wife. Even if this book had never appeared, it would have been worth it. To Carly, I am grateful for more love and support than I could ever deserve. And to Carly, I am most of all thankful for little Owen, to whom this book is dedicated. May he grow up to be, as Melanchthon was fond of saying, a *vir doctus et pius*.

Abbreviations

1546a/1546b	editor's abbreviations for two separate 1546 Strasbourg editions of the *PME*. See p. 53 below.
ASD	*Opera omnia Desiderii Erasmi, Recognita et Adnotatione Critica Instructa Notisque Illustrata*. Amsterdam: Elsevier, 1969–.
C	Justinian's Codex. *Codex Iustinianus*. ed. Paul Krüger. Berlin: Weidmann, 1877.
Claus	Helmut Claus, *Melanchthon-Bibliographie, 1510–1560*. 4 vols. Gütersloh: Gütersloher Verlagshaus, 2014.
CR	*Corpus Reformatorum* / Philipp Melanchthon, *Opera quae supersunt omnia*. ed. Karl Gottlieb Brettschneider and Heinrich Ernest Bindseil. 28 vols. Halle: Schwetschke et Filium, 1834–1860.
CTC	*Catalogus translationum et commentariorum: Mediaeval and Renaissance Latin Translations and Commentaries: Annotated Lists and Guides*. ed. Paul Oskar Kristeller, F. Edward Cranz, Virginia Brown, and Greti Dinkova-Bruun. 11 vols. Washington, D.C., Catholic University of America Press, 1960–.
D	Justinian's Digest. *Digesta Iustiniani Augusti*. ed. Theodor Mommsen. Berlin: Weidmann, 1870.
EDE	*Ethicae doctrinae elementa*. (Melanchthon's re-writing of the *Philosophiae Moralis Epitome*, published first in 1550 and in many editions thereafter).
Inst	Justinian's Institutes. *Iustiniani Institutiones*. ed. Paul Krüger. Berlin: Weidmann, 1867.
LCL	Loeb Classical Library. Cambridge, MA: Harvard University Press, 1912–.
MBW	*Melanchthons Briefwechsel: Kritische und Kommentierte Gesamtausgabe im Auftrag der Heidelberger Academie der Wissenschaften*. ed. Heinz Scheible. Stuttgart: Fromann-Holzboog, 1997–.
MD	*Melanchthon deutsch*. ed. Michael Beyer et al. 7 vols. Leipzig: Evangelische Verlagsanstalt, 2011–.
MWA	*Melanchthons Werke in Auswahl*. ed. Robert Stupperich. 7 vols. Gütersloh: C. Bertelsmann, 1951–1975.
Muller, *DLGTT*	*Dictionary of Latin and Greek Theological Terms, Drawn Principally from Protestant Scholastic Theology*, ed. Richard A. Muller. 2nd edition. Grand Rapids, MI: Baker Academic, 2017.
NE	Aristotle, *Nicomachean Ethics*

NPNF	*A Select Library of Nicene and Post-Nicene Fathers of the Christian Church*, ed. Philip Schaff and Henry Wace. 28 vols. in 2 series. 1886–1889.
PG	*Patrologia Graeca*. ed. J.-P. Migne. 161 vols. Paris: 1857–1886.
PL	*Patrologia Latina*. ed. J.-P. Migne. 221 vols. Paris: 1844–1864.
PME	*Philosophiae moralis epitome*
USTC	*Universal Short Title Catalogue* (ustc.ac.uk)
VD16	*Verzeichnis der im deutschen Sprachbereich erschienenen Drucke des XVI. Jahrhunderts* (vd16.de)
VD17	*Verzeichnis der im deutschen Sprachraum erschienenen Drucke des 17. Jahrhunderts.* (vd17.de)
WA	Martin Luther. *D. Martin Luthers Werke: kritische Gesamtausgabe*. Weimar: Hermann Böhlau, 1883–2009.

Philip Melanchthon: The Founder of Protestant Natural Law?

Natural law was central to the philosophy of the Protestant Reformer Philip Melanchthon (1497–1560). No concept was more critical to his understanding of political and moral life than the idea that God had endowed all human beings, Christian and pagan alike, with natural knowledge of the divine commandments. In Melanchthon's view, foundational principles concerning the external and civic life of man—that is, everything outside of the realm of the Gospel, grace, and revelation—were available to all men through divinely implanted knowledge. As a result, he believed that moral philosophy, political thought, and jurisprudence were all products of nature and reason, not grace and revelation. To put things in Lutheran terms, these subjects belonged to the realm of the Law, not the Gospel. Melanchthon, relying heavily on this concept of natural law, was the first Protestant thinker to construct a systematic approach to moral philosophy. This volume presents for the first time in English the most important political and ethical works of "The Moral Philosopher [*Ethiker*] of the Reformation",[1] as Wilhelm Dilthey called Melanchthon.

As readers will soon gather from the texts in this volume, natural law shaped virtually every aspect of Melanchthon's ethical thought. His *Summary of Moral Philosophy* presented a framework of moral philosophy in which natural law provided the basis for understanding virtue, ordering human life towards God, and ensuring justice among men. That work was first published in 1538 but is translated here from the revised version of 1546 (published several times between 1540 and 1546). In the 1530 commentary on Aristotle's *Politics*, Melanchthon sought to establish political life on the basis of nature in conjunction with divine ordination. In the other three works, the 1532/34 *Prefaces* to Hesiod, the 1540 *Preface* to Xenophon, and the 1546 *Comparison of the Chief Attic and Roman Legal Actions*, Melanchthon illustrated how knowledge of the natural law beamed forth in the brilliant pagan writers and societies of ancient Greece and Rome.

In an excellent recent monograph on Melanchthon's political thought, Mads Langballe Jensen has identified the reformer as "the first Protestant natural law

1 Wilhelm Dilthey, "Melanchthon und die erste Ausbildung des natürlichen Systems in Deutschland", in *Wilhelm Diltheys gesammelte Schriften, II. Band: Weltanschauung und Analyse des Menschen seit Renaissance und Reformation* (1929), pp. 162–202. Quote on p. 193.

 HTTPS://DOI.ORG/10.1163/9789004774742-002

theorist".[2] In its plainest sense, this assertion is correct. Melanchthon was the first Protestant to write systematic treatises on natural law and to afford it a central place in his moral and political thought, although he was not the only Protestant to discuss the subject. While modern scholarship largely acknowledges that natural law plays some role in Martin Luther's thought, Luther himself provides little extended treatment of the topic.[3] The same can be said for John Calvin; scholars generally agree that Calvin had a concept of natural law, although his works on the topic are far from systematic, and the place of the concept in his theology is disputed.[4] But while scholars might debate the place of natural law in Luther or Calvin, it is a simple fact that it was absolutely essential to Melanchthon's political and moral vision, a fact quickly gathered from the writings presented here.

Yet in another sense, identifying Melanchthon as the first Protestant natural lawyer raises an important question. He may have been the first Protestant to afford natural law a central place in his work, but what, if anything, was specifically Protestant about his treatment of the subject? This Introduction investigates that question and argues that Melanchthon was a "Protestant" natural lawyer, but only in certain qualified senses.

In one way, Melanchthon's own conception of natural law resists any definition that seeks to label it as specifically "Protestant". He believed that all people, whether Christian, Catholic, Protestant, or even pagan, could access the divinely implanted truths of natural law and build those truths up into a sophisticated system of moral philosophy. As proof of this, Melanchthon (in a way not so different from his Catholic contemporaries) drew upon a wide variety of ancient and medieval sources, including Greek philosophy, Roman law, and

2 See Mads Langballe Jensen, *A Humanist in Reformation Politics: Philipp Melanchthon on Political Philosophy and Natural Law* (2020), p. vii.

3 For natural law in Luther and Lutheranism, see the variety of treatments in *Natural Law: A Lutheran Reappraisal*, ed. Robert C. Baker and Roland Cap Ehlke (2011) and the literature cited in Antti Raunio, "Divine and Natural Law in Luther and Melanchthon" in *The Lutheran Reformation and the Law*, ed. Virpi Mäkinen (2006), pp. 21–61, esp. pp. 21–25. For the classic article on natural law in the Reformation more broadly, see John T. McNeill, "Natural Law in the Teaching of the Reformers", *Journal of Religion* 26 (1946): 168–182. For a more recent perspective, see Sarah Mortimer, *Reformation, Resistance, and Reason of State (1517–1625)* (2021), esp. pp. 63–88.

4 For three fairly recent treatments, see David S. Sytsma, "John Calvin on the Intersection of Natural, Roman, and Mosaic Law", *Perichoresis* 20.2 (2022): 19–41; Alexander Batson, "Calvin and Equity" in *The Oxford Handbook of Calvin and Calvinism*, ed. Bruce Gordon and Carl Trueman (2021): pp. 74–87; and Irena Backus, "Calvin's Concept of Natural and Roman Law", *Calvin Theological Journal* 38 (2003): 7–26.

even medieval theology and canon law. Accordingly, Melanchthon's concept of natural law and moral philosophy was not narrowly Protestant, nor was it even specifically Christian—he believed that these subjects were available to all humans by virtue of their status as creatures made in God's image. As he understood it, Melanchthon did not develop a Christian theory of natural law, but a theory of natural law that was *useful* for Christians as they sought to navigate the complicated realities of moral, civic, and political life. Melanchthon's own understanding of his work complicates the idea that he crafted a "Protestant" theory of natural law.

But in other ways, Melanchthon's natural law theory certainly was distinctly Protestant. In structural terms, his theory was predicated upon the specifically Lutheran distinction between Law and Gospel. This allowed him to assert the theoretical separation between moral philosophy (a subcategory of Law) and the Gospel. Epistemologically speaking, Melanchthon posited that all men could understand matters of the Law through nature and reason. These truths included the duties of humanity towards God and towards each other in the external realm of human life. In contrast, matters of the Gospel, including man's interior disposition towards God and the Christian message of salvation and forgiveness, could only be accessed by revelation in the Bible.

Further, Melanchthon's natural law theory was specifically Protestant in its contemporary applications. Melanchthon used the idea of natural law to address the political challenges raised in the sixteenth-century Holy Roman Empire by the new reality of religious pluralism. By the 1530s and 40s, when Melanchthon wrote these works, Protestants and Catholics held concretely disparate definitions of true religion. As a result, a host of political questions followed: What was the role of the prince in enforcing true religion and punishing false worship? What should be the relationship of the Church and the State? And what options were left for adherents of a minority religion in the case of religiously motivated persecution or warfare? Melanchthon applied his concept of natural law at moments of political crisis as he attempted to answer all of these questions in a way that would carve out enduring political protections for the Lutheran faith.

Finally, Melanchthonian natural law and moral philosophy was distinctly Protestant in that it exercised a considerable influence on the development of Protestant university and intellectual culture for at least a century after his death. Melanchthon's daily life was occupied in the teaching and training of students, and nearly all of his works indicate some pedagogical purpose. He became known as the *Praeceptor Germaniae* ("Teacher of Germany") for his vast influence in shaping German education. In the texts presented here, readers will find repeated references to students and the benefits that Melanchthon thought his works could offer them. In this sense, Melanchthon laid the groundwork for what would become a distinctly Protestant way of teaching and writing about natural law and moral philosophy. Yet his great influence in this area still needs further investigation. As we shall see at the end of this Introduction, modern scholars have attended to Melanchthon's influence on Protestant universities both in personal and institutional terms, but a comprehensive examination of his legacy in later Protestant moral thought and natural law is still missing.

The aim of this book is to make Melanchthon's thought available to the non-specialist reader. Accordingly, a full discussion of his natural law theory must be preceded by a consideration of Melanchthon's status (or often, lack of status) in scholarship about the history of natural law, moral philosophy, and political thought. There follows a brief overview of the texts translated in this volume, but for more detailed information about the individual texts, the reader is referred to the individual introductions at the head of each translation. After that, I give a concise overview of Melanchthon's life and career that will situate his intellectual work in the eventful and tumultuous context of Reformation-era Germany. After these introductory sections, the essay turns to Melanchthon's theory of natural law and the question of his status as a "Protestant" natural lawyer.

Melanchthon's Place in the History of Natural Law

Melanchthon's standing in the broader historiography of natural law is disputed. On the one hand, specialists on Melanchthon and the Reformation more broadly have emphasized the immense role that the natural law played in the reformer's thought.[5] Scholarship on early modern legal history has also empha-

5 The literature is vast, but see the helpful treatments in Clemens Bauer, "Melanchthons Naturrechtslehre", *Archiv für Reformationsgeschichte* 42 (1951): 64–100; Guido Kisch, *Melanchthons Rechts- und Soziallehre* (1967); Sachiko Kusukawa, *The Transformation of Natural Philosophy: The Case of Philip Melanchthon* (1995); Christoph Strohm, "Zugänge zum Naturrecht bei Melanchthon" in *Der Theologe Melanchthon*, ed. Günter Frank (2000), pp. 339–356; Charlotte Methuen, "Lex Naturae and Ordo Naturae in the Thought of Philip Melanchthon", *Reformation and Renaissance Review* 3 (2000): 110–125; Isabelle Deflers, *Lex und ordo: Eine rechtshistorische Untersuchung der Rechtsauffassung Melanchthons* (2005); Mads Langballe Jensen, *A Humanist in Reformation Politics: Philipp Melanchthon on Political Philosophy and Natural Law* (2019). For a brief introduction to the major themes and literature, see Christoph Strohm, "Jurisprudenz" in *Philipp Melanchthon: Der Reformator zwischen Glauben und Wissen: Ein Handbuch*, ed. Günter Frank, with Axel Lange (2017), pp. 495–506.

sized Melanchthon's outsize role in developing Protestant jurisprudence.[6] On the other hand, Melanchthon usually occupies a more limited role in general histories of natural law, early modern ethics, and moral philosophy. Scholars in those fields have traditionally focused on the Protestant natural lawyers of the seventeenth century, such as Hugo Grotius, Samuel Pufendorf and John Locke.[7] If the Reformation features in such works, the attention is devoted mainly to Luther and Calvin.

Melanchthon also plays a limited role in the grand narratives of early modern political thought, where Luther and Calvin again occupy the Reformation-era spotlight. For example, in Quentin Skinner's monumental *The Foundations of Modern Political Thought*, Melanchthon appears largely in discussions of obedience and resistance theory. While resistance was certainly an important topic in Melanchthon's thought, Skinner's neglect of the reformer's broader ideas about moral philosophy and natural law lead to statements such as "[T]he Lutheran vision of man's relationship with God had undermined any attempt to base the conduct of politics on the foundations of natural law."[8] The texts presented here present a serious challenge to that interpretation of Lutheran political thought.

In other cases, Melanchthon has been ignored altogether. For example, Sheldon Wolin's *Politics and Vision* devotes a chapter each to Luther and Calvin but does not treat Melanchthon. In a recent wide-ranging history of political theory, the chapter on the Reformation focuses on Luther, Calvin, and more radical reformers, while referring to Melanchthon as "Luther's aide and disciple" and only mentions him in passing in the discussion of resistance theory.[9] History of political thought written from the Straussian perspective has largely followed

---

6 See Harold Berman, *Law and Revolution II: The Impact of the Protestant Reformations on the Western Legal Tradition* (2003), pp. 77–88, 111–124; John Witte, *Law and Protestantism: The Legal Teachings of the Lutheran Reformation* (2009), pp. 121–140; Paolo Astorri, *Lutheran Theology and Contract Law in Early Modern Germany (ca. 1520–1720)* (2019), pp. 55–59, 173–178, 346–353.

7 See, for example, Alasdair MacIntyre, *A Short History of Ethics* (1966); Jerome B. Schneewind, *The Invention of Autonomy: A History of Modern Moral Philosophy* (1997); Richard Tuck, *The Rights of War and Peace: Political Thought and the International Order from Grotius to Kant* (1999); Knud Haakonssen, *Natural Law and Moral Philosophy: From Grotius to the Scottish Enlightenment* (2012); and "Early Modern Natural Law Theories" in *The Cambridge Companion to Natural Law Jurisprudence*, ed. George Duke and Robert P. George (2017), pp. 76–102.

8 See Skinner, *The Foundations of Modern Political Thought, Volume II: The Reformation* (1978), here p. 139. For other discussions of Melanchthon, see pp. 65–71, 99, 202–204, 217, 231.

9 See Wolin, *Politics and Vision: Continuity and Innovation in Western Political Thought*. Expanded edition (2004). See Alan Ryan, *On Politics: A History of Political Thought: From Herodotus to the Present* (2012), pp. 327, 341.

the same pattern.[10] The obvious exception has been German scholarship, where Melanchthon has played an important role in intellectual histories.[11]

In short, despite the fact that he developed a concept of natural law in much more detail than any contemporary reformer, Melanchthon has historically remained a peripheral figure in English scholarship on the history of natural law and Western political theory, apart from a few exceptions.[12] Fortunately, this situation has begun to change in recent years. Mads Langballe Jensen has recently written a fine intellectual history which analyses Melanchthon's theory of natural law as a "combative concept" which the reformer used in the political and confessional struggles in which he was engaged. Similarly, Sarah Mortimer's recent survey of Reformation political thought has treated Melanchthon as one of the chief natural law theorists of the Reformation era.[13] Additionally, a recent English translation of Melanchthon's *Commentary on Proverbs* by Derek Cooper and Timothy J. Wengert indicates scholarly interest in making Melanchthon's ethical works available in English.[14]

These recent developments point to a renewed interest in Melanchthon's political and moral thought. Yet still, a problem remains: Melanchthon's major writings on these subjects have historically been inaccessible to Anglophone audiences. The English translations used to teach Reformation political and moral thought have usually been limited to small selections of Luther, Calvin,

10 In *History of Political Philosophy*, ed. Leo Strauss and Joseph Cropsey, 3rd ed. (1987), the essays on the sixteenth century cover Machiavelli, Luther and Calvin, and Richard Hooker.

11 For a few influential treatments, see Karl von Kaltenborn, *Die Vorläufer des Hugo Grotius auf dem Gebiete des ius naturae et gentium im Reformationszeitalter* (1848), vol. I, pp. 211–217; Dilthey, "Melanchthon und die erste Ausbildung"; Merio Scattola, *Das Naturrecht vor dem Naturrecht. Zur Geschichte des* "ius naturae" *im XVI. Jahrhundert* (1999); and Horst Dreitzel, "Von Melanchthon zu Pufendorf: Versuch über Typen und Entwicklung der philosophischen Ethik im protestantischen Deutschland zwischen Reformation und Aufklärung" in *Spätrenaissance-Philosophie in Deutschland 1570–1650* (2007). For a comprehensive overview of German scholarship on this question, see Günter Frank, *Die theologische Philosophie Philipp Melanchthons (1497–1560)* (1995), pp. 11–36.

12 For a few English works that do include Melanchthon in the broader narrative of moral philosophy and natural law, see Terence Irwin, *The Development of Ethics: Volume 1: From Socrates to the Reformation* (2007), pp. 744–774 and Annabel S. Brett, *Changes of State: Nature and the Limits of the City in Early Modern Natural Law* (2011), pp. 62–89. T.J. Hochstrasser treats Melanchthon as the founder of Protestant Aristotelianism that lies in the background of Enlightenment theories of natural law in *Natural Law Theories in the Early Enlightenment* (2004).

13 See Jensen, *A Humanist in Reformation Politics* and Mortimer, *Reformation, Resistance, and Reason of State*, esp. pp. 72–79.

14 Philip Melanchthon, *Commentary on Proverbs*. Trans. and ed. by Derek Cooper and Timothy J. Wengert (2023).

and more radical tracts on pacifism and separatism. To take just one example, the excellent Cambridge series, "Texts in the History of Political Thought", includes a volume on Calvin and Luther and one on the Anabaptists before transitioning to later sixteenth-century figures such as Richard Hooker.[15] Later sixteenth-century Calvinist works on monarchomachy and tyrannicide, especially those penned in France, have occasionally merited translation as well.[16] In contrast, German moral and political thought from the first and second generations of the Reformation have remained largely inaccessible except to specialists.[17] Outside of dedicated Melanchthon readers by Ralph Keen, Sachiko Kusukawa, and Christine F. Salazar, Melanchthon's own sophisticated writings about natural law, moral philosophy, and political life have remained almost entirely unavailable in English. And when these works have been rendered into English, the picture of his moral thought is still fragmented; the translations are almost entirely excerpts of longer texts, or full translations of shorter, minor texts.[18] For this reason, this volume presents a full translation of Melanchthon's major moral-philosophical textbook, along with several other shorter, previously untranslated works on ethics and politics.

While the goal of this book is to make Melanchthon's works available for historians of natural law and political thought, the texts included here may also be of interest to modern theologians and seminarians. Scholars of Protestant theology and ethics should find in Melanchthon's moral philosophy an interesting challenge to some of the dominant scholarly assumptions in their own fields.

---

15 See *Luther and Calvin on Secular Authority*, ed. Harro Höpfl (1991); *The Radical Reformation*, ed. Michael G. Baylor (1991), and Richard Hooker, *Of the Laws of Ecclesiastical Polity*, ed. Arthur Stephen McGrade (1989).

16 See, for example, *Brutus: Vindiciae Contra Tyrannos: Or, Concerning the Legitimate Power of a Prince over the People, and of the People over a Prince*, ed. George Garnett (1994).

17 A salutary exception is the recently published *A Global Sourcebook in Protestant Political Thought, Volume I: 1517–1660*, ed. Matthew Rowley and Marietta van der Tol (London: Routledge, 2024), which includes translations of two brief works by Melanchthon among many other texts.

18 See Ralph Keen, ed., *A Melanchthon Reader* (1988), which contains the first book of Melanchthon's commentary on Aristotle's *Nicomachean Ethics* as well as a 1532 manuscript, the *Epitome ethices* ("Summary of Ethics"), which was an important precursor to the *Summary of Moral Philosophy*. Christine F. Salazar has translated the prefatory epistle to the *Summary of Moral Philosophy* in Kusukawa, ed. *Melanchthon: Orations on Philosophy and Education* (2012), pp. 139–143. The 1550 *Ethicae doctrinae elementa* is available in an excellent Latin edition and modern German translation in *Philipp Melanchthon: Ethicae Doctrinae Elementa et Enarratio Libri quinti Ethicorum*, ed. Günter Frank and Michael Beyer (2008), and John Monfasani has rendered brief selections of the *EDE* into English in *Cambridge Translations of Renaissance Philosophical Texts. Volume 1: Moral Philosophy*, ed. Jill Kraye (1997), pp. 108–119.

For example, one grand narrative holds that natural law largely faded from Protestant theology in the twentieth century, due largely to the concept's disavowal by prominent Protestant theologians including, above all, Karl Barth.[19] Scholars working in related disciplines will find in Melanchthon a stimulating attempt to integrate Protestant theology with the concepts of natural law.[20]

Melanchthon's writings also challenge the narrative, common in some historiographies of Christian ethics, that the focus on salvation by faith alone rendered Protestantism inimical to any rational inquiry into moral philosophy.[21] In the *Summary of Moral Philosophy*, we see Melanchthon not only establish moral philosophy on the grounds of natural law, but we see him erect a sophisticated system of virtue ethics from natural human moral knowledge. The *Summary* is a work about natural law, but it is just as prominently a work about virtue. Relatedly, Melanchthon's deep debt to Aristotle may surprise those whose understanding of Reformation attitudes towards Aristotle is predominantly shaped by Luther's famous fulmination that "In short, all of Aristotle is to theology as darkness is to light."[22] Despite numerous recent scholarly works which have reconstructed a vast history of Protestant Aristotelianism, the myth that the Reformation amounted to a rejection of Aristotle is still stubbornly

---

19 See for example Barth's debate with Emil Brunner over natural theology and natural law, specifically his essay "Nein! Antwort an Emil Brunner", translated into English in *Natural Theology: Comprising "Nature and Grace" by Professor Dr. Emil Brunner and the reply "No!" by Dr. Karl Barth*, translated by Peter Fraenkel (2002). Indeed, Barth himself identified Melanchthon's theology as a crucial wrong turn in introducing natural law as a source of authority in later Protestant theology. For more on Barth, see Christoph Strohm, "Melanchthon et l'éthique réformée. Le probleme du statut de droit naturel" in *Crossing Traditions: Essays on the Reformation and Intellectual History: in Honour of Irena Backus*, ed. Maria-Cristina Pitassi and Daniela Solfaroli Camillocci (2017), pp. 467–491, here pp. 467–468.

20 In fact, recent theological scholarship has argued for the importance of natural law in the Protestant tradition. See Stephen J. Grabill, *Rediscovering the Natural Law in Reformed Theological Ethics* (2006); David VanDrunen, *Natural Law and the Two Kingdoms: A Study in the Development of Reformed Social Thought* (2010); Jennifer Herdt, "Natural Law in Protestant Christianity" in *The Cambridge Companion to Natural Law Ethics*, ed. Tom Angier (2019), pp. 155–178.

21 See, for example, Servais Pinckaers, *The Sources of Christian Ethics*, trans. Noble, 3rd ed. (1995), pp. 280–286.

22 See Luther, WA I.226. "Breviter, totus Aristoteles ad theologiam est Tenebrae ad lucem." Several accounts, many of them from Catholic theologians, have read Protestantism through Luther's anti-Aristotelianism and asserted that the entire Reformation was opposed to Aristotle and his teleological account of human virtue. For a classic account, see Jacques Maritain, *Trois Réformateurs: Luther—Descartes—Rousseau* (1925), pp. 42–49. For a more recent version of this argument, see Brad S. Gregory, *The Unintended Reformation: How a Religious Revolution Secularized Society* (2012), pp. 180–234.

persistent.[23] Melanchthon's works decisively demonstrate that the Philosopher remained an important voice in Protestant thought from the first decades of the Reformation.

Varying Interpretations of Melanchthon's Moral Philosophy

When scholars have devoted attention to Melanchthon, the nature and legacy of his natural law theory have been subject to varying interpretations. There are a number of wide open questions in the scholarship. What is Melanchthon's place in the broader history of natural law? Was he a medieval theological figure or a forerunner of the new natural law theories of the seventeenth century? To what degree was Melanchthon's moral philosophy distinctively Protestant, or even distinctively Christian? Was he in any sense a precursor of any of the major figures of the fractious natural law of the seventeenth century, in which case who?

Generally, there have been two sides to the debate: those who see Melanchthon as the founder of a naturalistic ethics which was separated from theology, and those who see him as the founder of the theological Protestant scholastic tradition. Scholars in the former camp have understood Melanchthon as a figure who points towards the new world of anti-Orthodox seventeenth-century natural law. Because of Melanchthon's strict division between the Gospel and moral philosophy, Wilhelm Dilthey viewed him as the founder of Germany's first naturalistic system of *Wissenschaft*, and as such considered him to be a transitional figure between medieval scholasticism and the natural jurisprudence of the seventeenth century.[24] Dilthey saw Melanchthon as a progenitor of the rationalism and secularism brought on by the Enlightenment. This idea of Melanchthon as a transitional figure has been prominent in older German-language scholarship, with authorities such as Hans Kelsen, Werner Elert, and

---

23 Manfred Svensson's *The Aristotelian Tradition in Early Modern Protestantism* (2024) provides the fullest discussion of Protestant Aristotelianism, as well as a helpful overview of the historiography on pp. 1–18. For a shorter version of the argument, see Svensson, "Aristotelian Practical Philosophy from Melanchthon to Eisenhart: Protestant Commentaries on the Nicomachean Ethics 1529–1682", *Reformation & Renaissance Review* 21.3 (2019): 218–238. For an excellent treatment of the reception of Aristotle's *Ethics* specifically within German Lutheranism, see James J. Dunn, "The Reformation of Virtue: The Teaching of Aristotle's *Ethics* at Wittenberg and Helmstedt (1502–1648)". Unpublished Ph.D. diss., Yale University (2023).

24 See Dilthey, "Melanchthon und die erste Ausbildung".

Guido Kisch echoing Dilthey's interpretation.[25] Karl von Kaltenborn presented Melanchthon as a "forerunner" (*Vorläufer*) of Hugo Grotius, and Merio Scattola has placed Melanchthon as an important precursor to Grotius, suggesting that Grotius himself, instead of being the father of modern natural law, was more of a liminal figure between premodern and modern approaches to the subject.[26]

In contrast, scholars such as Günter Frank have insisted that Melanchthon's ethical system rested upon theological concepts, and thus could not be the foundation of a purely naturalistic system of moral philosophy.[27] According to this line of thinking, Melanchthon's natural law was founded upon ideas of God's existence and God's justice, and was rooted in the Lutheran conception of the order of the creation. This essentially theological interpretation of Melanchthon's ethics has been adopted by scholars to argue that Melanchthon represented the theological tradition of Protestant orthodoxy from which Grotius, Pufendorf, and other seventeenth-century natural lawyers departed.[28] Melanchthon's extensive legacy in Lutheran and Reformed scholasticism offers another avenue to support this viewpoint. Still other scholars have sought to chart a course between these two poles. As Ralph Keen puts it, "Melanchthon has not developed a system that could be called philosophical or theological ethics: his ethics is both, and it is the synthesis achieved that gives his work interest."[29]

One aim of this volume is to provide scholars with some of the key primary texts that are critical to investigating the nature and legacy of Melanchthonian natural law. As Nicole Kuropka has noted, much of Melanchthon scholarship has traditionally combed over many of the same sources, above all the various editions of the *Loci Communes*, although, fortunately, more recent scholarship has begun to break that trend.[30] It is my hope that this volume will enable scholars

25 See Kelsen, *Die philosophischen Grundlagen der Naturrechtslehre und des Rechtspositivismus* (1928), p. 37; Werner Elert, *Morphologie des Luthertums. Zweiter Band: Soziallehren und Sozialwirkungen des Luthertums*, 2nd edition (1958), p. 351; and Kisch, *Melanchthons Rechts- und Soziallehre*, pp. 125–126. See also Michael Stolleis, "Reichspublizistik—Politik—Naturrecht im 17. und 18. Jahrhundert", in *Staatsdenker in der frühen Neuzeit*, 3rd edition, ed. Michael Stolleis (1995).

26 See von Kaltenborn, *Die Vorläufer*, vol. I, pp. 211–217, and Scattola, *Das Naturrecht*, esp. pp. 215–217.

27 See "Melanchthon—der 'Ethiker der Reformation'" and *Die theologische Philosophie*, pp. 140–158.

28 For this view, see T.J. Hochstrasser, *Natural Law Theories*, with references to Melanchthon on pp. 3, 20, 33, and 83; and Dreitzel, "Von Melanchthon zu Pufendorf."

29 Keen, *Divine and Human Authority in Reformation Thought: German Theologians on Political Order 1520–1555* (1997), p. 190.

30 See Kuropka, *Philipp Melanchthon: Wissenschaft und Gesellschaft. Ein Gelehrter im Dienst*

to resolve these questions about Melanchthon's distinctive theory of natural law and its place in the history of political thought and natural jurisprudence.

On the Selection of Texts in This Volume

While each of the writings in this collection is prefaced by a brief introduction which explains the context and contents of each individual text, here I sketch briefly how they relate to Melanchthon's overall conception of natural law. Because the *Summary of Moral Philosophy* is the most comprehensive treatment of Melanchthon's moral philosophy, it is placed at the beginning of the volume. The other works are arranged in chronological order, beginning with the 1530 commentary on the *Politics* and proceeding to the 1532 and 1534 *Prefaces to Hesiod*, then the 1540 *Preface* to Xenophon, then the 1546 *Comparison of the Attic and Roman Legal Actions*. While these works may be read in chronological order, I suggest that readers begin with the first *Preface* to Hesiod, which succinctly summarizes Melanchthon's conception of natural law.

The *Summary of Moral Philosophy* was Melanchthon's first major ethical textbook. The *Summary* was originally published in 1538 and heavily revised in 1540. The second version was published throughout the early 1540s until two final, virtually identical editions were printed in Strasbourg in 1546. The present translation is based on the second version of the text. The *Summary* contains Melanchthon's most extensive explanation of the natural law. Melanchthon begins the work by separating moral philosophy from the Gospel, asserting that moral truth is universally available to all persons through divinely-implanted knowledge of the natural law. Thus, moral philosophy was a rational project which was built upon certain universally known natural principles, i.e., principles that required no recourse to Scripture (although, as we shall see later, Melanchthon believed that moral philosophy did not disagree with the truths of Scripture).

Because Melanchthon held that the natural law was available to all peoples, he drew heavily upon classical pagan sources and used the foundations of natural law, together with classical Greek and Roman developments of that law, to work out theories of virtue and human ends. In the second book, he drew upon the same sources to answer more specific questions about justice, including the nature of contracts and the legality of political resistance. Both in its explicit

der Kirche (1526–1532) (2002), pp. 1–3. Kuropka's book, as well as the work of Mads Langballe Jensen and Sarah Mortimer, have incorporated a much wider variety of sources.

content and its methodology, the *Summary of Moral Philosophy* illustrates how Melanchthon founded his moral and political thought upon natural law.

The other texts in this volume likewise treat classical pagan sources. The second translation, the *Commentaries on Some Books of Aristotle's Politics*, was first printed in 1530. Published in the aftermath of the brutal 1525 Peasants' War, during which (in Melanchthon's view, at least), radical zealots had twisted the evangelical ideals of Christian freedom into an anarchic disregard for political authority, the *Commentaries* sought to ground government on the foundation of reason and human nature. For Melanchthon, Aristotle's theory of politics as an integral part of human nature avoided fanatical anarchy as well as a stricter view of authority as a merely punitive divine ordination. While Melanchthon still asserted the divine foundation of government, Aristotle's view of man as a political animal who is naturally inclined towards political community allowed Melanchthon to establish a positive vision of civic life which affirmed both a divine and a natural basis for politics.

The next texts, the 1532 and 1534 *Prefaces* to Hesiod, provide the most straightforward introduction to Melanchthon's conception of natural law. These two *Prefaces* assert that the ancient Greek poet Hesiod revealed the teachings of natural law through his *Works and Days*. Here readers could see an example of how the law of nature was impressed upon the minds of the virtuous pagans. In Melanchthon's view, Hesiod's knowledge of morals was just as natural as his knowledge of physical phenomena such as astronomy, weather, and agriculture. Hesiod perfectly demonstrated how moral philosophy was intimately connected with the natural order of the cosmos.

The 1540 *Preface* to Xenophon's works provides an alternative perspective on the moral life. It does not explicitly discuss natural law but is an ode to the study of history and the ways that history shapes moral and political judgment. This *Preface* is included to illustrate that, while natural law was central to Melanchthon's moral thought, he did not think about ethical matters exclusively through the categories of natural jurisprudence. Following one of the main lines of humanist moral thought, the reformer also highlighted the importance of wisdom for responding to circumstance and the vicissitudes of life. For Melanchthon, the study of ancient texts cultivated the character, knowledge, and prudence to navigate the capricious winds of fortune.

The final translation in this volume, the 1546 *Comparison of the Chief Attic and Roman Legal Actions*, is a highly unusual text. At first glance, the text is, as the title suggests, a parallel comparison of the Attic and Roman legal actions—that is, the various types of suits and accusations that could be brought in ancient courts. Melanchthon organized the actions under the headings of the Ten Commandments, which he saw as the summary of the natural and divine law. For example, under the heading "You shall not kill", Melanchthon includes the corresponding ancient actions against assault and murder. As this organization implies, he saw the Athenian and Roman laws as concrete historical instantiations of the natural law. The overall message of the work, then, is that there are certain transhistorical legal standards—i.e. the natural law—which are enshrined in the Decalogue and have been implemented throughout history. Besides this concrete illustration of the natural law in history, the *Comparison* was also a remarkably original contribution to ancient history. It was the first attempt by any European scholar to reconstruct the laws of ancient Athens in a systematic manner.[31]

Melanchthon's Life

Born in 1497 in the town of Bretten, in southwestern Germany, Philip Melanchthon (born Schwarzerdt) quickly distinguished himself as an intellectual prodigy.[32] After earning his baccalaureate from Heidelberg and his masters' degree from Tübingen in record time, in 1518 he was appointed professor at Wittenberg at twenty-one years old. He soon busied himself with revolutionizing the university curriculum. Beginning with his inaugural lecture entitled *De corrigendis adolescentiae studiis* ("On Correcting the Studies of Youth"), Melanchthon announced his vision for a humanist educational agenda centred around a deep study of classical authors and directed towards moral and intellectual cultivation.[33] Although Melanchthon is best known for his theological contributions to the Reformation, he continued to teach moral philosophy and classical Greek and Roman writers throughout his life, and until his death remained the University of Wittenberg's star humanist scholar. Melanchthon's educational reforms, as well as his productivity in writing textbooks such as the *Summary of Moral Philosophy*, gave him an immense reputation as an educator and earned him the nickname *Praeceptor Germaniae*: "The Teacher of Germany".

---

31 For this argument, see Alexander Batson, "Sinai and the Areopagus: Philip Melanchthon, Natural Law, and the Beginnings of Athenian Legal History in the Shadow of the Schmalkaldic War", *Journal of the History of Ideas* 85.4 (2024): 713–748.

32 The most detailed modern biography of Melanchthon is Heinz Scheible's *Melanchthon: Vermittler der Reformation: Eine Biographie* (2016). The English biographies are now quite dated, but still provide a helpful introduction to Melanchthon's life. See Clyde Leonard Manschreck, *Melanchthon: The Quiet Reformer* (1958) and Michael Rogness, *Philip Melanchthon: Reformer without Honor* (1969).

33 This speech can be found in CR 11.15–25, and is translated in Keen, *A Melanchthon Reader* (1988), pp. 47–57.

Melanchthon was a prolific author. His collected works span eighteen massive volumes in the nineteenth-century *Corpus Reformatorum* edition. While today he is mostly regarded as a theologian, especially for his masterpieces such as the *Loci Communes* and the 1530 Augsburg Confession, Melanchthon published on an immense variety of topics. He penned translations of or commentaries on myriad classical writers, including well-known figures such as Homer and Demosthenes as well as more obscure ones such as the Greek poet Theognis.[34] In 1518, he published a Greek grammar which became widely used in German schools. He wrote commentaries on Aristotle's *De anima*, he edited the monumental historical work *Carion's Chronicle*, and he gave orations on a vast variety of topics.[35] Melanchthon was also highly engaged in writing on politics and moral philosophy. In addition to the texts in this volume, Melanchthon published several commentaries on Aristotle's *Nicomachean Ethics* and Cicero's *De officiis*, each of which appeared in multiple substantively different versions.[36]

Melanchthon was also a prodigious letter writer, and he cultivated extensive networks of colleagues and friends in Wittenberg, in Germany, and throughout all of Europe. He earned admiration from prominent humanists such as Desiderius Erasmus and Johannes Reuchlin. One of his closest friends was the humanist scholar Joachim Camerarius (1500–1574), who went on to pen his own influential commentaries on Aristotle's *Politics* and *Ethics* and wrote a biography of Melanchthon after his death.[37] Many of Melanchthon's students became prominent scholars in their own right.[38] For example, after studying with Melanchthon at Wittenberg, the German humanist Hieronymus Wolf (1516–1580) edited Isocrates and Demosthenes and was a foundational figure in Byzantine studies.[39]

---

34 Scholars have recently begun to pay closer attention to Melanchthon's Greek scholarship and the role that it played in his broader theological and political thinking. See, for example, Asaph Ben-Tov, *Lutheran Humanists and Greek Antiquity: Melanchthonian Scholarship between Universal History and Pedagogy* (2009); Micha Lazarus, "Tragedy at Wittenberg: Sophocles in Reformation Europe", *Renaissance Quarterly* 73.1 (2020): 33–77; and William Weaver, *Homer in Wittenberg: Rhetoric, Scholarship, Prayer* (2023).

35 Readers can get a sense of the range of Melanchthon's interests from perusing the orations translated by Christine F. Salazar in *Philip Melanchthon: Orations on Philosophy and Education*, ed. Sachiko Kusukawa (1999).

36 For a good overview of the Aristotle commentaries, see Kuropka, *Philipp Melanchthon: Wissenschaft und Gesellschaft*, pp. 275–283. For the works on Cicero's *De officiis*, see CR 16.529–680.

37 For Camerarius' commentaries, see Svensson, *The Aristotelian Tradition*, pp. 64–65.

38 See, for example, the collection of essays in *Melanchthon in seinen Schülern*, ed. Heinz Scheible (1997).

39 For Wolf, see Batson, "Isocrates and the Persian Turks. Ottoman Invasions and Confessional

Likewise, the theologian Martin Chemnitz (1522–1586) and the historian David Chytraeus (1531–1600) had been Melanchthon's pupils, as had the natural lawyer Niels Hemmingsen (1513–1600) and the humanist scholar Johannes Caselius (1533–1613).

Like his friend and colleague Martin Luther, Melanchthon played a leading role in the German Reformation from its earliest years. He was present at decisive events such as the 1529 Diet of Speyer and the 1529 Marburg Colloquy, where his sharp theological mind and conciliatory disposition lent themselves to high-stakes negotiations. In his theological work, particularly the *Loci Communes*, Melanchthon was the great systematiser of Lutheran thought. Perhaps the document with the longest legacy was the *Augsburg Confession*, which Melanchthon penned for presentation before Emperor Charles V at the 1530 Diet of Augsburg. This document is still one of the foundational statements of faith for Lutheran churches today. Due to his reputation for theological genius and his diplomatic disposition, Melanchthon also filled a prominent role as an international liaison for German Protestantism, corresponding with foreign potentates such as King Henry VIII of England and Francis I of France.[40] Famously, in the mid-1530s, Henry VIII even attempted to bring Melanchthon to England as a theological adviser, but Melanchthon never made the journey.

While Melanchthon had been a prominent reformer since the beginning of the evangelical movement, the years 1546–1548 were a decisive turning point for his status within the broader Reformation. Luther died in February 1546, leaving a massive gap in leadership for the German evangelical cause. Melanchthon was the obvious heir, and he immediately asserted himself as a figurehead in his response to the critical challenge of that year: the Schmalkaldic War. As the war broke out in summer of 1546, Melanchthon became one of the chief minds behind Lutheran resistance theory, most prominently with his revisions to Justus Menius' *Von der Notwehr Unterricht*.[41] Of the texts in the present volume, the *Summary of Moral Philosophy* and the *Comparison of the Chief Attic and Roman Legal Actions* contain material directly pertinent to this war. The *Sum-*

Conflict in the Classical Scholarship of Hieronymus Wolf", forthcoming in the *Journal of the Warburg and Courtauld Institutes*.

40 For Melanchthon's correspondence with foreign rulers, see Irene Dingel, "Melanchthon's Paraphrases of the Augsburg Confession, 1534 and 1536, in the Service of the Smalcald League", in *Philip Melanchthon: Theologian in Classroom, Confession, and Controversy*, ed. Irene Dingel, Robert Kolb, Nicole Kuropka, and Timothy J. Wengert (2012), pp. 104–122.

41 For Melanchthon's work on this document, see Luther D. Peterson, "Justus Menius, Philipp Melanchthon, and the 1547 Treatise, *Von der Notwehr Unterricht*", *Archiv für Reformationsgeschichte* 81 (1990): 138–157.

mary provides explicit arguments for resistance against tyranny, some of which had already appeared in the 1538 edition, while the *Comparison* highlights the natural law themes that undergirded Melanchthonian resistance theory in the mid-1540s. As the prefaces to those works point out, readers must keep in mind that much of Melanchthon's moral and political philosophy was forged in the leadup to a disastrous war.

For the Protestants, at least, the Schmalkaldic War was indeed a disaster. In April 1547, Charles V's troops crushed the Protestant Schmalkaldic Armies at the Battle of Mühlberg. Shortly thereafter, Charles captured Wittenberg while Melanchthon and his family sought refuge in exile. The Protestants had been defeated and were now at the mercy of the Emperor. In May 1548, Charles passed the Augsburg Interim, which codified substantial restrictions on Protestant worship and essentially reinstated Catholic Christianity, with small concessions to the Lutherans. In that year, Melanchthon worked to strike a compromise, and he drafted his own proposal, the Leipzig Interim in 1548. While the document did assert some elements of the Lutheran faith, Melanchthon was willing to compromise on what he considered *adiaphora* (indifferent matters), such as the reinstatement of bishops. Neither the Emperor nor the more unyielding Lutherans accepted the proposal. The Leipzig Interim was a failure, and Melanchthon's attempt to compromise for the sake of peace led to heavy criticism from a significant faction of Lutherans.

Following the Interim, the Lutherans split into two camps: the Philippists, who sided with Melanchthon, and the Gnesio-Lutherans ("True Lutherans"), who believed that Melanchthon had betrayed the original principles of the Lutheran reformation. From the Augsburg Interim until his death in 1560, Melanchthon's life was largely consumed in these conflicts. In a brief note that he wrote only days before he died, the reformer listed reasons not to fear death. Alongside "You will depart from sins", Melanchthon scribbled, "You will be freed from trials, and from the fury of the theologians."[42] Following the fallout from the Interim, Melanchthon's legacy within Lutheranism became increasingly complicated. Yet despite these intra-Lutheran disputes, Melanchthon continued to exercise a significant influence on Protestant thought for the next century and beyond, as we shall see at the end of this essay.

---

42 CR. 9.1098.

Melanchthon's Concept of Natural Law

Against this biographical background we can turn to Melanchthon's theory of natural law and ask whether he was, in any meaningful sense, a "Protestant" natural lawyer. From at least the late 1520s, when he returned to Cicero's and Aristotle's moral-philosophical works, an emphasis on the natural law dominated his moral and political thought.[43] And while the details of his natural law thinking developed between the late 1520s and the mid-1540s, it is possible to identify some overarching characteristics.[44] Because this volume deals with Melanchthon's political and moral philosophy, the treatment here will focus on the role of the natural law in those areas. The role of the natural law in Melanchthon's theological works—for example, its role in revealing sin and accusing sinners—would require a separate essay.[45]

Melanchthon's theory of natural law was distinctly Protestant in that it was predicated upon a sharp division between the parts of human life that were governed by the revelation of the Gospel, and those which were governed by the Law, that is, natural law and moral philosophy. As he wrote on the first page of the *Summary*, "Above all else, it is necessary at first to distinguish among genera of doctrine: namely the Gospel, the law of God, and philosophy."[46] The matters which were revealed in the Bible about man's interior relationship with God—repentance, regeneration, salvation, and forgiveness—all belonged to the Gospel. In Melanchthon's view, natural law did indeed include general religious precepts commanding humans to believe in God and obey him. However, the specifically Christian content of the Gospel could not be derived from natural reason; it was the province of the Bible and the Word: "For without the Word of God, reason has not determined that God forgives our sins, and it does

43 See Bauer, "Melanchthons Naturrechtslehre", pp. 80–82.

44 Mads Langballe Jensen's *A Humanist in Reformation Politics* is highly recommended for its detailed examination of how Melanchthon developed his conception of natural law in response to concrete political crises. For Melanchthon's view of natural law in the early 1520s, see Clemens Bauer, "Die Naturrechtsvorstellungen des jüngeren Melanchthon" in Bauer, *Gesammelte Aufsätze zur Wirtschafts- und Sozialgeschichte* (1965), pp. 266–276. For a straightforward account of the development of Melanchthon's moral thought, see Nicole Kuropka, "Melanchthon und die Ethik", *Zeitschrift für Theologie und Kirche* 113.3 (2016): 235–257.

45 For an extended treatment of natural law in Melanchthon's theological texts, particularly in the 1559 *Loci Communes*, see Bauer, "Melanchthons Naturrechtslehre", pp. 64–78. For the development of Melanchthon's theological concept of the law more broadly, see Timothy Wengert, *Law and Gospel: Philip Melanchthon's Debate with John Agricola of Eisleben over "Poenitentia"* (1997).

46 See p. 65 below.

not discern that sins are remitted freely. These things are entirely outside of the scope of reason and are foreign to philosophy."[47]

On the other hand, Melanchthon understood issues of human moral and civil life as belonging to the domain of moral philosophy, which was in turn founded upon the natural law. Questions about human morality—What is justice? What is virtue?—could be answered through reasoning applied to innate human knowledge of the natural law. The same was true of questions about politics, constitutions, and governments. As we shall see below, for Melanchthon, the proper guide in these matters was not the Bible, but the divinely implanted knowledge of the natural law and the exposition of that law through reason. As Melanchthon defined it in the opening lines of the *Summary*, moral philosophy "is the knowledge of the precepts concerning all honourable actions which reason understands to be appropriate to human nature and to be necessary in a civil manner of life, having investigated the sources of these precepts with art and demonstrations, insofar as this can be done."[48] In other words, moral philosophy was the explication of the law of nature through a scientific method of investigation. In this way, Melanchthon's moral philosophy was distinctly Protestant. By separating moral philosophy from religion, Melanchthon presented a distinct way of thinking about ethics which mirrored the fundamental Lutheran polarity between Law and Gospel. In fact, as Heinz Scheible has observed, this was the fundamental framework in which Melanchthon approached all issues of practical philosophy.[49]

While the division between Law and Gospel reflected a fundamental principle of Lutheran theology, it was also a useful distinction, as it allowed Melanchthon to develop several fruitful areas of political thought. He could clarify the disparate roles of the Magistrate and the Church, mirroring Luther's concept of the Two Kingdoms (although Melanchthon does not use these terms in the texts translated here). This again led him to emphasize the concept of calling and to stress each person's moral responsibility in his own vocational sphere. And as the end of this essay will discuss, Melanchthon put this framework to use in solving the most pressing topics of Protestant political thought in the sixteenth century: the defence of true religion through armed resistance and the contested role of the magistrate in defining the nature of that true religion.

---

47 See p. 65 below.

48 See pp. 64–65 below.

49 See Scheible, "Die Bedeutung der Unterscheidung von Gesetz und Evangelium für die theologische Ethik und Praktische Theologie am Beispiel Melanchthons" in *Christentum und Spätmoderne. Ein internationaler Diskurs über Praktische Theologie und Ethik*, ed. W. Gräb et al. (2000), pp. 93–100.

In this sense, Melanchthon's natural law thinking was specifically Protestant in that it addressed a new set of problems that had not existed in medieval Latin Christendom. It was a Protestant theory for a new Protestant age.

A Moral Philosophy Useful for Christians

While Melanchthon drew a sharp distinction between Law and Gospel, this did not mean that he saw any substantive disagreement between Christianity and rational moral philosophy (which was part of the Law). His concept of law included natural law, divine law, the Decalogue, and moral philosophy, and these categories were closely connected and often overlapped in his thought. The *Comparison of the Chief Attic and Roman Legal Actions* illustrates this well; in the preface, Melanchthon writes that "Law is the one chief ruler of human life. It is the eternal wisdom in the divine mind and the unchanging rule of justice which God poured into the minds of men. And he willed that a light be born within us, and afterwards, on Mount Sinai, he proclaimed [it] with a brilliant testimony, so that we might know that it is truly the divine standard for life."[50] God's law as revealed on Sinai (i.e. the Decalogue) was identical with his law as revealed in the hearts of all men (i.e. the natural law). In the *Summary*, Melanchthon stated this principle even more bluntly: "[T]he law of nature truly is the law of God."[51]

While Melanchthon drew a strict line between moral philosophy and the Gospel, by no means did he bifurcate religion from political and moral life. Regarding the external actions of human life (but importantly, *not* regarding the inner disposition of the heart towards God), Melanchthon saw no meaningful difference between the moral teachings of the Scriptures and those of the natural law. The purpose of Melanchthon's division between the Gospel and moral philosophy, then, was not to assert some discrepancy in content between God's commands and the commands of nature. Rather, it was to highlight the different ways in which humans acquired knowledge in either of these spheres.

The major difference between natural law and the morality of the Scriptures was not one of substance, but of epistemology. While Christians might recognize the truths of the divine law more readily than others due to their knowledge

50 See p. 311 below.

51 See p. 67 below. For the overlap between the divine law and the natural law, see also Bernd-Rüdiger Kern, "Philipp Melanchthon als Interpret des Naturrechts" in *Werk und Rezeption Philipp Melanchthons in Universität und Schule bis ins 18. Jahrhundert*, ed. Günther Wartenberg and Markus Hein (1999), pp. 147–160, here pp. 149–150.

of the Bible, Scripture was not necessary for moral knowledge. In matters of external morals, the pagans had inborn knowledge of the natural law, too. But a major question arises here. If Christians had access to the moral knowledge contained in the Bible, which did not depart from the precepts of natural law, then what was the use of moral philosophy? In the *Summary*, Melanchthon lists several benefits of the discipline. It sharpens moral judgment and cultivates a certain moderation of soul, it elucidates the sources and interpretations of civil laws, it cultivates oratorical eloquence, and it helps theologians think clearly about politics.[52] Moral philosophy was "the explication of the law of nature" and "a long treatment and meditation in seeking causes, considering the order of nature, and contemplating the beauty of virtue".[53] In other words, moral philosophy was a sophisticated intellectual tool for working out the subtler implications of natural moral knowledge and its application to fields like law, oratory, and politics.

Günter Frank has argued that Melanchthon's moral philosophy was inherently theistic, as it rested upon the core theological beliefs of God's existence, goodness, and justice.[54] However, the fact that Melanchthon believed that some knowledge of God was contained in the natural law does not mean that this was, in any meaningful sense, a "Protestant" moral philosophy. In fact, it should not even be referred to as a "Christian" moral philosophy. The idea behind Melanchthon's concept of natural law, as it is presented in the *Summary of Moral Philosophy*, is that natural law is available to all people—Christian or otherwise—and that it is a natural human discipline common to the entire human race. In Melanchthon's own understanding, moral philosophy was not specifically Protestant or even Christian; it was broadly human. Thus, he sought to develop not a Christian moral philosophy, but a moral philosophy that was *useful for* Christians.

Notitia and *Ars*: The Process of Moral-Philosophical Investigation in the *Summary*

How then did Melanchthon go about developing his system of moral philosophy? Melanchthon classified that discipline, alongside geometry, medicine, architecture, and other fields, as one of the many *artes*, or branches of human

52 See pp. 68–70 below.
53 See p. 68 below.
54 See Frank, "Melanchthon—der 'Ethiker der Reformation'", pp. 72–75.

knowledge. In Melanchthon's view, each *ars* began from foundational principles which he termed *notitiae*, or "notions", which God had impressed upon the human heart and were common to all people.[55] As he wrote in the *Summary of Moral Philosophy*, the natural laws were "notions [*notitiae*] divinely imprinted upon the soul."[56]

Practically, the *notitiae* were certain obvious truths about the world. For example, in the case of mathematics, a *notitia* could be the idea that "a sum is greater than any of its parts". In moral philosophy, *notitiae* included foundational moral precepts such as prohibitions against harming others and the necessity of keeping promises. In Melanchthon's view, each *ars* was developed as human beings took the *notitiae* as building blocks and then used reason to elaborate these principles into broader systems in a process of reasoning which he termed a *demonstratio*. As he writes in the *Summary*, "For just as other arts have their first principles and demonstrations which cannot be overturned, so in moral philosophy there are certain practical principles from which firm demonstrations arise."[57]

Therefore, any firm conclusion which moral philosophy develops from the *notitiae* is as certain and true as the divine or natural law: "All true demonstrations in moral philosophy are properly the law of nature or law of nations. And because these demonstrations are, without doubt, divine ordinations established in nature, or notions of the divine ordination in nature, then the natural law [*ius naturale*] is rightly said to be the divine law [*ius divinum*] …"[58] As several scholars have argued, one of Melanchthon's chief claims to originality in the history of natural law is his focus on the idea that God has impressed the natural law into men's souls through the *notitiae*.[59] As Christoph Strohm puts it, Melanchthon's connection between the natural law and the *imago dei* "anthropocentrizes" and "subjectivizes" the natural law.[60]

Thus, Melanchthon's conception of morality and politics was based on natural law in the sense that men could have knowledge of the divine commandments through the *notitiae*, or the light of nature, which God had implanted in

55 See Jensen, *A Humanist in Reformation Politics*, pp. 112–115.

56 See p. 108 below.

57 See p. 66 below.

58 See p. 118 below.

59 See Dilthey, "Melanchthon und die erste Ausbildung", p. 171; Scattola, "Notitia naturalis de Deo et de morum gubernatione: die Naturrechtslehre Philipp Melanchthons und ihre Wirkung im 16. Jahrhundert", in *Melanchthon und die Marburger Professoren (1527–1627)*, ed. Barbara Bauer, (1999), vol. 2, pp. 865–882, esp. pp. 877–878.

60 See Strohm, "Zügange", p. 341. Strohm's German terms are "Anthropozentrierung" and "Subjektivierung".

the souls of men. That is, humans naturally know that things such as murder, theft, and adultery are wrong. But there is a second sense in which nature played a major role in Melanchthon's philosophy. Besides direct natural knowledge of the divine law, he also believed that moral truths could be derived from philosophical and empirical investigations of the "causes" and "effects" of human nature. Investigation into man's causes, in the traditional Aristotelian sense of the word, could reveal important metaphysical information about human life.[61] For example, recognizing that God the Creator was the ultimate cause of human life leads to the idea that "reverence towards God is the primary virtue."[62] At the same time, observation of the "effects" of man—here Melanchthon means the common and observable functions of human nature—offered clues to the divine law as well. Human proclivities towards self-defence, procreation, and the rearing of children all provided empirical evidence for discerning man's nature and purpose.

It may seem surprising that a Lutheran thinker provided such a robust epistemological foundation for ascertaining the moral purposes of human life. Because Protestants stressed the corrupting power of human sin, did it not then follow that human reason was compromised and incapable of discerning moral truths apart from Scripture? Not in Melanchthon's view. Certainly, he believed that sin's power was quite formidable; but he largely confined its effects to matters of internal disobedience. That is, sin affected the human relationship with the divine and prevented interior righteousness before God.

Melanchthon did not, however, believe that sin meaningfully obscured ethical knowledge as it related to external life. Because human nature contained the *notitiae*, the seeds of moral philosophy, Christians as well as non-Christians could act rightly in matters of external morals and civic life by following the dictates of reason. In Melanchthon's view, sin might dim the light of nature, and in certain extreme cases, men could approach a savagery that entirely perverted these moral intuitions. In stressing the need for moral education, Melanchthon admitted that total ignorance in the depths of barbarism, such as that which characterized the ancient Scythians, had "covered up and nearly extinguished even the common judgment of nature."[63] Yet aside from these rare outliers, Melanchthon believed that no human, no matter how depraved, could totally erase this natural knowledge of good and evil.

---

61 For the connection between Aristotelianism and natural law, see Manfred Svensson, "The Aristotelian Conception of Natural Law and Its Reception in Early Protestant Commentaries on the Nicomachean Ethics", *Perichoresis* 20.2 (2022): 3–18.

62 See p. 107 below.

63 See p. 84 below.

The Sources of Melanchthon's Moral Philosophy: Ancient Philosophy, Roman Law, Medieval Theology

One major consequence of Melanchthon's deep faith in human knowledge of the divinely-implanted *notitiae* was his elevation of non-Christians—and in particular, the enlightened Greek and Roman pagans—to be authoritative voices on moral and political philosophy. Of course, trust in the authority of classical antiquity was common to humanists all over Europe in the sixteenth century. But Melanchthon's faith in antiquity grew right out of his core beliefs about human nature and the nature of moral philosophy. Because he believed that true knowledge of the natural law was imprinted upon all human beings, Melanchthon valued the ancient pagans as wise interpreters of the law of nature. As he wrote in the 1532 *Preface* to Hesiod, "[T]hose things which the learned pagans have derived from common sense and the judgment of nature and have passed on in their writings are *no less divine commandments* than those things which appear on the stone tablets of Moses." (emphasis added).[64]

But the ancients were not Melanchthon's only sources. He drew from a standard set of classical, medieval, theological, and juristic sources that were common to writers of his age, regardless of confession. There was nothing particularly Protestant about Melanchthon's use of Aristotle, Cicero, Roman law, canon law and medieval theology; all of these could and did appear in the writings of contemporary Catholic natural lawyers such as Francisco Vitoria or Domingo de Soto. As one of the preeminent scholars of his age, Melanchthon may have drawn from a slightly wider source base than some of his contemporaries, but in his use and selection of ancient and medieval sources, he was firmly within the bounds of contemporary European humanism.

While there is no room to explore fully the origins of Melanchthon's moral thought here, we can identify a number of familiar elements.[65] Aristotle was particularly influential, and the Philosopher's impact upon the *Summary of Moral Philosophy* is more obvious than that of any other author. Martin Luther famously attacked Aristotle's *Ethics* as "the worst enemy of grace", although his own position on the Philosopher was more nuanced and less influential than it may appear at first glance.[66] In contrast, Melanchthon praised Aristotle for his clarity and directness. In his 1537 *Oration on Aristotle*, Melanchthon

64 See p. 280 below.

65 For eclecticism in this period more broadly, see Richard A. Muller, "Reformation, Orthodoxy, 'Christian Aristotelianism', and the Eclecticism of Early Modern Philosophy", *Nederlands Archief Voor Kerksgeschiedenis / Dutch Review of Church History* 81.3 (2001): 306–325.

66 See Svensson, *The Aristotelian Tradition*, pp. 44–50. For Luther's quote, see WA I.226.

claimed that the Philosopher "employs two things that bring light to teaching, namely method and accuracy of speech."[67] Melanchthon, ever concerned with pedagogy, believed that Aristotle's chief value was in his directness and his application of a reliable intellectual method. As he wrote in the *Commentaries on Aristotle's Politics*, "Aristotle is the greatest creator of method."[68] Aristotle's clarity and methodical rigor would help students avoid the errors of scholastic "sophistry", with its obscure vocabulary and labyrinthine arguments.

Melanchthon also borrowed heavily from Aristotle's content. In the *Commentaries on Aristotle's Politics*, he used the philosopher's treatments of society, authority, servitude, and economic life to craft his own interpretation of those subjects. Similarly, the *Summary of Moral Philosophy* often follows Aristotle explicitly, drawing upon his definition of virtue and his treatment of justice. That work's organization also followed Aristotle; the first book loosely mirrors the topics of the first three books of the *Nicomachean Ethics*, and the second book draws deeply from Aristotle's discussion of justice in book V of the *Ethics*.

The printing history of these texts illustrates how closely Melanchthon connected them with Aristotle. Throughout the 1540s, the *Summary* was frequently printed with various commentaries on parts of Aristotle's *Ethics*. In reprints in 1531 and 1541, the *Politics* commentary was followed by a discussion of Book V of the *Nicomachean Ethics*, on justice. And even the *Comparison* was included in a 1548 volume which also contained commentaries on the *Nicomachean Ethics*.[69] Melanchthon was deeply Aristotelian in terms of both content and method.

In a seminal 1951 article on Melanchthon's moral philosophy, Clemens Bauer claimed that the 1538 *Summary of Moral Philosophy* inaugurated "the second epoch of Christianisation [*Verchristlichung*] of Aristotle in western intellectual history after the first took place in high scholastic philosophy."[70] Bauer was correct about the importance of Melanchthon's work in crafting a Protestant integration of Christianity and Aristotelian philosophy, but we must be careful here. Melanchthon would not have understood himself to be "Christianising" the classics. Such a claim implies that there were significant differences between pagan and Christian teachings. This is not how Melanchthon saw things, at least in reference to the external moral and political facets of human life. As he wrote

67 A translation of Melanchthon's 1537 oration on the life of Aristotle can be found in Kusukawa, *Melanchthon: Orations on Philosophy and Education*, pp. 204–211. The quote here is from p. 210.

68 See p. 254 below.

69 For all of these editions, see the printing histories of the respective works below.

70 Bauer, "Melanchthons Naturrechtslehre", p. 93.

in his 1525 introduction to Cicero's *De officiis*, "Religion has no disagreement with the manner of civic life described by Cicero."[71] In Melanchthon's view, there was little to "Christianise" in Cicero or Aristotle's moral teachings; these writers simply reflected the truths of God's natural law. In Melanchthon's mind, the ancients did not need to be made Christian, at least not in their moral and political philosophy. The ancient Greeks and Romans merely explicated the inborn truth known to all humans.

However, Melanchthon did believe that the ancients had missed certain points about the relationship between God and human morality. Following Aristotle, Melanchthon agrees that "the action of virtue is the end of man."[72] However, this was only partly correct; the full truth, according to Melanchthon, is "that virtue, in itself, is not the highest thing in which the mind should find its satisfaction, but that [virtue] should be directed to something still higher, to the knowledge and obedience of God."[73]

Melanchthon solved this tension by affirming the validity of Aristotle's argument while conceding that "the knowledge of God is not fully illuminated in man's [i.e., Aristotle's] corrupted nature."[74] In Melanchthon's view, problems like these were understandable errors which could be corrected, not reasons to reject pagan philosophy. For Melanchthon, the genius of the ancients lay in the fact that they had constructed a true and correct system of moral philosophy by their investigation into the *notitiae* which God had planted within them. Again, in Melanchthon's view, moral philosophy was not specifically Christian; it belonged to Aristotle and Cicero as much as it did to his fellow Lutheran pastors. But regardless of its sources, moral philosophy was useful for Christian moral and civic life.

While Melanchthon explicitly championed the approach of Aristotle's Peripatetic school, he also drew from other ancient philosophical traditions. In particular, Melanchthon's idea of innate knowledge of natural law was influenced by his reading of Cicero.[75] And although he rejected much of Stoic philosophy in the *Summary*, Stoic natural law was also influential upon his philosophy; in the 1559 edition of the *Loci Communes*, the *notitiae* were explicitly identified with the Stoic notion of *koinai ennoiai*, or "common conceptions."[76]

71 CR 16.629.
72 See p. 75 below.
73 See p. 74 below.
74 See p. 74 below.
75 See Dilthey, "Melanchthon und die erste Ausbildung", p. 171–177 and Strohm, "Zugänge", pp. 341–346.
76 See CR 21.711.

Melanchthon also used ancient literature in other ways. As a good humanist, he believed that classical literature and history provided a wealth of exemplary characters and stories. As a result, the *Summary* is replete with accounts of figures like Achilles, Alexander the Great, and Julius Caesar as a way to illustrate moral concepts. But Melanchthon could also be remarkably original in his reading of sources. As explained in the preface to the *Comparison* below, Melanchthon was highly innovative in scouring Greek oratory, history, and drama for historical information about ancient Athenian law, thus becoming the first European scholar to reconstruct the laws of ancient Athens.

Roman law, too, was central to the way that Melanchthon approached moral philosophy. Unlike Calvin, Melanchthon had no official law degree, although he had close relationships with a number of lawyers, including the Basel jurist Bonifacius Amerbach and the Wittenberg professor Hieronymus Schurff.[77] Nevertheless, Roman law appeared throughout Melanchthon's moral writings and provided the language of his fundamental moral principles. The legal phrases "harm no one" (*neminem laedere*), "keep your promises" (*pacta sunt servanda*), and "render to each his own" (*suum cuique tribuere*) appear repeatedly in these texts. Seeking to unravel knotty questions about usury, contracts, and property, he was quick to invoke Roman lawyers as authoritative sources. For him, Roman law contained the most penetrating of the ancient insights into morality, not least because he believed that Roman law was an incredibly detailed and sophisticated exposition of natural law. In his 1553 oration, "On the Dignity of the Doctrine of the Laws and Jurists", Melanchthon asserted that "Just as the other arts are constructed from the divine notions, partly from demonstrations, and partly from probable reason ... so the Roman laws have been derived in good order from the natural notions, which are the rays of divine wisdom briefly summarized in the Decalogue."[78] Moreover, Melanchthon saw Roman law, which was in the process of being implemented throughout Germany in the early sixteenth century, as a tool of cultivation and civilization. Following the chaos of the Peasants' War in 1525, Melanchthon viewed the universal acceptance of Roman law in Germany as a path towards peace and order.[79]

---

77 See Kern, "Philipp Melanchthon als Interpret", p. 147. For Schurff's influence on Melanchthon, see Kisch, *Melanchthons Rechts- und Soziallehre*, pp. 149–156.

78 See CR 12.22. The Latin title of the oration is *Oratio de dignitate doctrinae legum et Iurisconsultorum*. For Melanchthon's identification of Roman law with natural law, see Kisch, *Melanchthons Rechts- und Soziallehre*, pp. 116–126.

79 See Isabelle Deflers, *Lex und ordo*, pp. 151–159 and James Q. Whitman, *The Legacy of Roman Law in the German Romantic Era: Historical Vision and Legal Change* (1990), pp. 3–40 for Melanchthon's view of the Roman law as an impartial instrument of peace. For the con-

There were, of course, specifically Christian, biblical, and medieval elements to Melanchthon's concept of natural law. Most obviously, Melanchthon's concept of divinely inborn *notitiae* closely echoed St. Paul's assertion that "When the gentiles, who do not possess the law, by nature do what the law requires, these, though not having the law, are a law to themselves. They show that what the law requires is written on their hearts" (Romans 2:14–15). Melanchthon also relied upon medieval Christian sources. He drew freely from medieval canon law, repeatedly citing the Decretum (ca. 1139) and the Decretals (1234). Yet while Melanchthon valued these sources, he also examined them with a critical eye. For example, in discussing the doctrine of private property in the Decretum, he dismissed a "poorly written epigraph" while maintaining that the text correctly affirmed the idea that God had created private property. Melanchthon also read widely in the medieval canon law commentary tradition. For example, on the thorny topic of contracts and usury, he cited the works of Henry of Segusio (Hostiensis, c. 1200–1271) and Nicolò de Tedeschi (Panormitanus, 1386–1445). While Luther had been famously hostile to canon law, going so far as to burn some canonists' textbooks in December 1520, Melanchthon found in it a helpful source of moral and legal analysis, too useful to be discarded.[80]

Scholars generally agree that Melanchthon owed much to medieval scholastic theories of natural law.[81] However, in the works in this volume, he provides almost no direct attributions to individual thinkers, although he frequently cites the shadowy figures of "the theologians". In the rare cases that he mentions medieval theologians by name, it is to critique their ideas, as he does William of Ockham (c. 1287–1347) and John Wycliffe (c. 1330–1384) in the *Commentaries on Aristotle's Politics*. The major exception is the Paris theologian Jean Gerson (1363–1429), whom Melanchthon had studied under his teacher Jacob Wimpfeling.[82] Melanchthon cites Gerson approvingly several times in these texts,

---

tested reception of Roman law in Germany, see Gerald Strauss, *Law, Resistance, and the State: The Opposition to Roman Law in Reformation Germany* (1986).

80 Richard Helmholz has made this point about the persistence of canon law in post-Reformation England in his excellent *Roman Canon Law in Reformation England* (2004).

81 See Bernd-Rüdiger Kern, "Philipp Melanchthon als Interpret des Naturrechts" in *Werk und Rezeption Philipp Melanchthons in Universität und Schule bis ins 18. Jahrhundert*, ed. Markus Hein and Günther Wartenberg (1999), p. 159; Methuen, "Lex Naturae", esp. pp. 123–125; Scattola, *Das Naturrecht*, pp. 29–35. For a comparison between Melanchthon's natural law theory and that of Aquinas and other medieval scholastics, see Scattola, "Notitia naturalis".

82 Wimpfeling had been responsible for printing the first edition of Gerson's works in Strasbourg in 1488. For Gerson's influence on Melanchthon, see Jensen, *A Humanist in Reformation Politics*, pp. 12–13, 127–133.

and it is possible that Gerson's was the only medieval theological natural law theory to which Melanchthon had direct access.[83] A deep study of the medieval sources of Melanchthon's natural law theory would be a welcome addition to scholarship.

Melanchthon drew from a vast variety of sources to think about moral philosophy, and this eclecticism was an essential feature of his own educational background.[84] In 1508–1509, as a boy at the Pforzheim Latin school, he had fallen under the intellectual influence of the great humanist Johann Reuchlin. Then, as a student at Heidelberg and Tübingen, Melanchthon had been exposed to a wide range of sources. While Melanchthon had taken his baccalaureate degree at Heidelberg in the *via antiqua*, at Tübingen the influence of the *via moderna* won him over.[85] At Tübingen, he studied Greek and Aristotle with Georg Simler and theology with Wendelin Steinbach, who had edited the theologian Gabriel Biel's commentary on Lombard's *Sentences*.[86] Melanchthon's unusually voracious intellectual appetites can be evidenced from his studies with Johannes Stöffler, from whom Melanchthon acquired an impressive knowledge of astronomy and mathematics.[87] Nor was his education limited to classroom studies; for a time at Heidelberg he lived with the prominent professor of theology Pallas Spangel, and at Tübingen he read Hesiod with the future reformer Johannes Oecolampadius.

Melanchthon's eclecticism was by no means accidental but, rather, a necessary consequence of his understanding of moral philosophy. Because he had established moral philosophy on the foundation of reason and natural law, Melanchthon had quite consciously authorized the use of myriad ancient, medieval, and contemporary sources in moral philosophy. If all men possessed the natural *notitiae* of moral knowledge, then all the sources supplied by his own humanist background were valid, the works of classical antiquity above all else.

83 See Bauer, "Melanchthons Naturrechtslehre", p. 98.

84 For varying interpretations of Melanchthon's "eclecticism", see Frank, *Die theologische Philosophie*, pp. 15–29.

85 Heinz Scheible, "Melanchthons Werdegang" in *Aufsätze zu Melanchthon* (2010), pp. 28–45, here p. 36.

86 See Jensen, *A Humanist in Reformation Politics*, p. 13.

87 Heinz Scheible, *Melanchthon: Vermittler der Reformation*, pp. 24–27.

Melanchthonian Natural Law and Reformation Politics in the 1530s and 1540s

While Melanchthon was one of the Reformation's first-rate thinkers, he also had a keen eye for politics, and he developed his conceptions of natural law and moral philosophy in the crucible of political life.[88] One of Melanchthon's greatest challenges was producing a system of natural law that was coherent and helpful amidst the vicissitudes of the 1530s and 1540s.[89] Because Melanchthon put his theory of natural law to work trying to solve some of the most pressing political and confessional problems of the Reformation era, it is in the realm of political thought that we can most confidently say that he constructed a genuinely "Protestant" natural law. As we shall see below, he used the concept of natural law to devise politically viable solutions to two concrete problems of the Reformation era: 1) the possibility of armed resistance in defence of true religion, and 2) the magistrate's responsibility for enforcing true religion in a confessionally-divided Germany. Here, as Jensen has argued, Melanchthonian natural law was a response "to the specific political, philosophical, religious, and theological challenges which he faced".[90] And by virtue of Melanchthon's role as one of the most prominent Protestant reformers, and arguably the intellectual leader of the German evangelical movement, this makes his natural law theory particularly Protestant in its concrete political applications.

One of the major political questions of the 1530s and 40s concerned the possibility of armed resistance against the Catholic Holy Roman Emperor Charles V, should he decide to use the force of imperial arms to tamp down the Protestant religion. This possibility loomed throughout those two decades, and it eventually became reality with the outbreak of the Schmalkaldic War in the summer of

88 For Melanchthon's involvement with politics and diplomacy, see Günther Wartenberg, "Melanchthon als Politiker" in *Der Theologe Melanchthon*, ed. Frank (2000), pp. 153–168; Timothy J. Wengert, "Philip Melanchthon and a Christian Politics", *Lutheran Quarterly* 17.1 (2003): 29–62; Dingel, "Melanchthon's Paraphrases of the Augsburg Confession, 1534 and 1536, in the Service of the Smalcald League"; and "Melanchthon's Efforts for Unity between the Fronts: the Frankfurt Recess", in *Philip Melanchthon: Theologian in Classroom, Confession, and Controversy* (2012).

89 James Estes has argued that the early 1530s mark a turning point in Melanchthon's political thought, as the political pressures of these two decades led Melanchthon to develop his "mature" thought with a special emphasis on the magistrate's role in enforcing true religion for the glory of God. See *Peace, Order, and the Glory of God: Secular Authority and the Church in the Thought of Luther and Melanchthon, 1518–1559* (Leiden, 2005), pp. 93–133.

90 Jensen, *A Humanist in Reformation Politics*, p. ix.

1546. Religious warfare presented a serious problem for Melanchthon's bifurcation between the Gospel and moral philosophy because it brought the question of confessional identity into the realm of politics and war. If political resistance was to be predicated upon oppression of true religion, then determinations about the nature of true religion would become political topics and not just part of the domain of the Gospel. When Protestants had to take concrete political and military action to defend their interpretation of religion, Melanchthon's boundaries between moral philosophy and the Gospel encountered intense pressure.

Melanchthon's approach to resistance theory developed throughout the 1530s and 1540s. In the 1530 *Commentaries on Aristotle's Politics*, written in the aftermath of the chaos and violence of the 1525 Peasants' War, he had rejected the possibility of violent resistance, arguing instead for civil disobedience in the face of religious persecution. In the early 1530s, he had begun to change his mind on this issue, and by the first edition of the *Summary*, in 1538, he argued that citizens could exercise self-defence against tyrannical rulers who assaulted them directly.[91] By 1546 Melanchthon became the chief architect of Protestant resistance theory with works such as *De licita defensione* and his revisions on Justus Menius' *Von der Notwehr Unterricht*, unreservedly justifying resistance against violent attempts to quell evangelical religion.[92]

Melanchthon's resistance theory echoed the broader natural law framework of politics and morals which he had laid out in the *Summary*. Unlike other Lutherans, Luther among them, who had turned to apocalyptic and religious rhetoric to justify Protestant defensive warfare (Luther had referred to the Pope as a *Beerwolf*, or "werewolf"), Melanchthon justified resistance on the basis of natural law's concept of self-defence against outrageous and violent offenses (in his original terms, an *atrox ac notoria iniuria*).[93] In his mind,

91 For Melanchthon's acceptance of resistance in certain circumstances in the 1530s, see Jensen, *A Humanist in Reformation Politics*, pp. 150–156 and Diethelm Böttcher, *Ungehorsam oder Widerstand: Zum Fortleben des mittelalterlichen Widerstandsrechtes in der Reformationzeit (1529–1530)* (1991), pp. 82–98.

92 For *De licita defensione*, which was likely written sometime in 1546, see CR 6.150–155. The 1547 Latin translation of Melanchthon's revised version of Menius' *Von der Notwehr Unterricht* can be found in a modern Latin-German edition edited by Hans-Otto Schneider, *Politischer Widerstand als Protestantische Option: Philipp Melanchthon und Justus Menius:* Von der Notwehr *(1547)* (2014). For Melanchthon's revisions of Menius' work, see Peterson, "Justus Menius, Philipp Melanchthon".

93 For Melanchthon's shift towards natural law resistance theory, see Robert von Friedeburg, *Self-Defence and Religious Strife*, pp. 56–70 and Jensen, *A Humanist in Reformation Politics*, pp. 139–187. For the role of the *Comparison of the Chief Attic and Roman Legal Actions* in

Charles V's attacks against Protestant religion certainly counted as this type of offence, and so resistance was justified. One did not have to adjudicate between Catholic and Lutheran doctrines in order to see that Charles' attack on the Schmalkaldic League violated the natural law. Melanchthon's confessionally neutral appeals to natural law were partially intended to preserve the overarching framework of his political philosophy by removing the issue of resistance from the realm of religion and locating it squarely within the political realm, which was governed by natural law.[94] In basing a resistance theory upon natural law, rather than explicitly confessional or even apocalyptic foundations, Melanchthon managed to preserve his distinction between philosophy and the Gospel.

A related political topic challenged Melanchthon's Law-Gospel framework: the *cura religionis*, or the role of the magistrate in enforcing true religion. This was one of the critical problems of Reformation political theory prior to the 1555 Peace of Augsburg. In Melanchthon's context, the question was this: When Protestant princes such as John Frederick of Saxony or Philip of Hesse were confronted with the possibility of enforcing the true Protestant religion in their own realms or bowing to opposition from the Emperor and the Catholic church, what should they do?

There is no room here to fully explore the development of Melanchthon's thought on this issue. The question of the magistrate's role in establishing true religion, and the magistrate's responsibility to enforce the first table of the Decalogue, has been one of the most-discussed topics in Reformation-era political thought.[95] Examining only the texts in this volume, however, we can see that by 1539, Melanchthon openly endorsed the idea that the magistrate should use political power to establish true religion. In that year he had published a tract entitled *De officio principum* ("On the Duty of Princes"), which was included in the revised editions of the *Summary of Moral Philosophy* under the heading, "Whether Princes Should Change Impious Worship When Bishops or Higher Lords Fail to Act or Forbid [Them From Acting]".[96] The beginning of the tract gave a clear answer: "Princes and magistrates should eradicate impious wor-

Melanchthon's resistance theory, see the introduction to that work in this volume, as well as Batson, "Sinai and the Areopagus: Philip Melanchthon, Natural Law, and the Beginnings of Athenian Legal History in the Shadow of the Schmalkaldic War", *Journal of the History of Ideas* 85.4 (2024): 713–748.

94 For this point, see Jensen, *A Humanist in Reformation Politics*, 184.

95 For an excellent treatment, see James M. Estes, *Peace, Order, and the Glory of God*. Jensen also treats this problem in *A Humanist in Reformation Politics*, pp. 97–138.

96 See pp. 134–154 below. For this tract, see Estes, *Peace, Order*, pp. 135–177.

ship and see to it that true doctrine is taught and godly worship is established in the churches."[97] In other words, magistrates should take an active role in establishing evangelical religion.

Theoretically, the tract's argument was founded upon the idea that the magistrate, as the guardian of the Decalogue, should enforce both the first and second tables of the Decalogue. Concretely, this meant that the magistrate should establish evangelical churches, provide stipends for ministers, and set up a system of Protestant education. On this last point, Melanchthon even proposed dissolving monasteries and reallocating their endowments to fund Protestant schools. In all of these cases, the magistrate was required to use his political authority to further the cause of true religion. But there was a tension here. It might be consistent with Melanchthon's natural law theory of politics to say that magistrates ought to enforce the entirety of the natural law—including the first table of the Decalogue—by preventing idolatry and blasphemy. But then a new problem arose: some authority had to make determinations about what counted as true religion or idolatry and blasphemy.

Melanchthon outlined a lengthy solution to this problem in the *Summary of Moral Philosophy*, marshalling a host of arguments that justify the magistrate's enforcement of true religion. He asserted that the prince had authority to intervene in ecclesiastical affairs because, although he occupied the office of prince, he was also a member of the Church. If the church was led by bad pastors, then it fell to the "healthier part of the Church" to correct this situation.[98] Thus, princes, as the "chief members" of the Church, alongside the other "healthier parts", were responsible for using the tools at their disposal to remedy things. Another, syllogistic argument came from natural law: "The proper and chief end of human society is to make God known. The magistrate is the guardian of human society. Therefore, all the more should he be the guardian of this chief end, for in every action, the proper end should be principally sought and protected."[99]

Yet another argument relied on ancient examples. Melanchthon suggested that princes should follow Constantine's example in calling and participating in church councils. Accordingly, Melanchthon argued that "From these things, it can be sufficiently understood that the inquiry concerning doctrine pertains to the Church, that is, to the presbyters and princes. But once a matter has been investigated and adjudicated, the princes then become the guardians of external

97 See p. 134 below.
98 See p. 138 below.
99 See p. 140 below.

discipline and executors of the synod's decision, meaning that they prohibit idolatrous worship, blasphemy, and impious dogma and they punish those who profess [such things]."[100]

In Melanchthon's vision of politics, princes were not the sole arbiters of doctrine, but they did play a role in defining the nature of true religion. And after doctrinal questions had been settled by a consultation of the pastors, teachers, and princes, it became the prince's task to support that religion and punish outward departures from it. In an environment with two or more legitimate confessional choices, the prince took a very active role in determining and enforcing true religion. Ultimately, Melanchthon's theory offered a practical solution to the divisions of sixteenth-century Germany. After the 1555 Peace of Augsburg, which established the principle that each prince should determine the confessional policy of his own territory (later known as *cuius regio, eius religio*), Melanchthon's principles had essentially become political reality.

What all of this illustrates is that when Melanchthon's theory came into contact with the exigencies of the German political situation, his strict division between the Gospel and moral philosophy was subject to immense pressures. Yet, as Jensen has illustrated, Melanchthon's grounding of politics upon the natural law provided him with a highly flexible and capacious way of thinking about political life that could react to the rapidly-changing state of German princely politics.[101]

The Afterlife of Melanchthon's Natural Law

The most obvious sense in which Melanchthon can rightly be called the first Protestant natural lawyer—or even the founder of Protestant natural law—was in his enormous institutional influence on subsequent Protestant education. Through his university reforms and textbooks, Melanchthon, who was known as the *Praeceptor Germaniae* ("Teacher of Germany"), did more than any other Reformation figure to establish the educational and institutional foundations for Protestant intellectual culture which dominated northern European universities for the following century. Paul Oskar Kristeller wrote that Melanchthon "had more influence on many aspects of Lutheran Germany than Luther himself and ... was responsible for the humanistic tradition of the German Protestant

---

100 See p. 173 below.

101 Jensen, *A Humanist in Reformation Politics*, pp. 2–10, 188–191.

schools down to the nineteenth century."[102] Wilhelm Dilthey claimed that he "became the greatest organizing force in Protestant Germany at the time."[103]

In contrast to Luther, Melanchthon possessed a brilliantly systematic mind, and systems foster strong institutions. The very things that make Luther so readable today—his verve, wit, and flowing prose—frustrate those who desire a more ordered and logical treatment from one of the giants of Protestant theology. Whereas Luther's works were often occasional, and usually written as penetrating treatises on individual subjects ("The Freedom of a Christian" and "On Good Works" are excellent examples), he rarely wrote in a programmatic way. It was in the task of systematisation where Melanchthon shone as a theologian and moral philosopher. He was able to assimilate the grand theological insights of the Lutheran Reformation into a coherent system that could be passed down for generations in churches and universities. Thus, Melanchthon's primary influence in the creation of a Protestant natural law tradition must be sought in those who followed in his methodological footsteps, as well as those who were trained in the intellectual traditions and institutions which he shaped.

As readers will see below, scholars have developed a fairly robust picture of the educational and institutional legacy of Melanchthon's moral philosophy. Scholars also have a firm grasp of his personal impact on the numerous theologians and moral philosophers who studied under him and went on to teach and write in various capacities. Undoubtedly, the pieces published in the present volume are critical to understanding Melanchthon's legacy. What is still needed, however, is a detailed explanation of Melanchthon's intellectual legacy—an insightful study of the afterlife of Melanchthon's key ideas such as the *notitiae*, or his particular conception of natural law or the ancient pagans' knowledge of the divine law. A book-length study examining Melanchthon's intellectual influence would be a much-needed addition to scholarship, but it will suffice here to trace his institutional legacy in Protestant university culture.

Unsurprisingly, Melanchthon's afterlife was longest and strongest in German Lutheranism. Following his death, the reformer's *Ethicae doctrinae elementa*, the 1550 revision of the *Summary of Moral Philosophy*, was the subject of commentaries until the end of the seventeenth century. His student Viktorin Strigel (1524–1569) and Strigel's student Christoph Pezel (1539–1604) both produced commentaries on the *Ethicae doctrinae elementa*.[104] Scholars such as the Stras-

102 See Kristeller, *Renaissance Thought: The Classic, Scholastic, and Humanist Strains* (1961), p. 87.

103 Dilthey, "Melanchthon und die erste Ausbildung", p. 164.

104 Strigel's and Pezel's works are listed below in the introduction to the *Summary of Moral*

bourg professor Theophilus Golius (d. 1600) expounded upon Melanchthon's esteem for pagan moral philosophy in the realm of politics and civic morality.[105] The humanist scholar Hubert van Giffen (ca. 1533–1604) in his commentary on the *Nicomachean Ethics* pointed readers to Melanchthon's *Summary* to learn about natural law.[106] Melanchthon also shaped future discussions about particular moral doctrines; for example, as Risto Saarinen has shown, the reformer's teaching on "heroic virtue" remained important well into the seventeenth century.[107] Moreover, despite the complications in Melanchthon's legacy engendered by the conflict between Philippists and Gnesio-Lutherans at the end of his life, a specifically Philippist strain of natural law persisted into the early seventeenth century.[108] Of course, after Melanchthon, the tradition of Protestant natural law and Aristotelian ethics continued to evolve, often in ways that diverged significantly from Melanchthon's own writings.[109] Yet Melanchthon's moral philosophy remained an integral element of Lutheran university circles for over a century.

Melanchthon's works became influential in Lutheran jurisprudence as well. His teachings were adopted by contemporary Lutheran jurists including Johann Oldendorp (1480–1567), Johannes Eisermann (ca. 1485–1588), Johann Apel (1486–1536), and Konrad Lagus (ca. 1499–1546).[110] Oldendorp, one of the famous Lutheran jurists at the newly-founded Protestant University of Marburg, echoed Melanchthon in his 1539 treatise on natural law, where he claimed that "Law is a natural notion which God has implanted within us for discerning just from

---

Philosophy. For Strigel, see Günter Frank, "Fragmentierung und topische Neuordnung der aristotelischen Ethik in der frühen Neuzeit: Ethik bei Viktorin Strigel und Abraham Scultetus" in *Späthumanismus und reformierte Konfession*, ed. Christoph Strohm, Joseph S. Freedman, and Herman J. Selderhuis (2006), pp. 153–167.

105 See Jill Kraye, "Melanchthon's Ethics Commentaries and Textbooks" in *Classical Traditions in Renaissance Philosophy*, ed. Jill Kraye (2002), chapter VII (pp. 1–12), esp. 7–9.

106 *Commentarii in decem libros Ethicorum Aristotelis ad Nicomachum* (Frankfurt, 1608), p. 405.

107 "Die heroische Tugend in der protestantischen Ethik. Von Melanchthon zu den Anfängen der finnischen Universität Turku." In *Melanchthon und Europa. 1 Teilband: Skandinavien und Mittelosteuropa*, ed. Günter Frank and Martin Treu (2001), pp. 129–138.

108 For Philippist natural law and the reactions against it, see Scattola, *Das Naturrecht*, pp. 77–90.

109 See Svensson, *The Aristotelian Tradition*, esp. pp. 180–182.

110 For Oldendorp and Eisermann, see Witte, *Law and Protestantism*, pp. 140–175. For Apel, see Berman, *Law and Revolution*, pp. 113–118. For Lagus, see Hans Erich Troje, "Konrad Lagus (ca. 1500–1546): Zur Rezeption der Loci-Methode in der Jurisprudenz" in *Melanchthon in seinen Schülern*, ed. Heinz Scheible (1997), pp. 255–284. For Melanchthon's broader influence upon Lutheran jurisprudence, see Kisch, *Melanchthons Rechts- und Soziallehre*, pp. 67–73.

unjust."[111] Melanchthon's moral works were standard reading for jurists in this tradition; direct citations of Melanchthon appear in the works of Oldendorp and the German jurist Benedikt Winkler (d. 1646).[112] In particular, Melanchthon's method of dividing a particular subject into *loci*, or topics, became an influential organizational tool for this new school of Lutheran jurisprudence. This fact is illustrated by the titles of some representative works: Apel's 1535 *Method of Dialectical Reason Applied to Jurisprudence* and Lagus' 1543 *Methodical Treatment of Both Types of Law* (i.e., civil and canon law) illustrate the primacy of Melanchthonian method.[113] Melanchthon's legal teachings spread beyond Germany as well; his student Niels Hemmingsen expounded upon Melanchthonian natural law in Denmark.[114] Nor were Melanchthon's legal works quickly forgotten. Later jurists recognized the originality of his *Comparison of the Chief Attic and Roman Legal Actions*, which was reprinted well into the seventeenth century.[115]

The reformer's influence on law and moral philosophy stretched well beyond the confines of northern European Lutheranism. Melanchthon exercised an especially strong influence on Reformed theology from its very roots; John Calvin and his successor Theodore Beza both held Melanchthon in high esteem.[116] This fact shaped the reformer's favourable reception in Reformed orthodoxy, where

---

111 Oldendorp, *Iuris naturalis, gentium, et civilis eisagōgē* (Cologne, 1539), fol. [a7]v: "Lex est notitia naturalis a Deo nobis insita, ad discernendum aequum ab iniquo." Melanchthon frequently refers to the law of nature in this way. Compare, for example, with Melanchthon's phrase in his commentary on Aristotle's *Nicomachean Ethics* in CR 16.385, where he refers to the origin of natural law as "[N]otitia in mentibus humanis nobiscum nascens, et divinitus insita."

112 See the selections in Karl von Kaltenborn, *Die Vorläufer*, vol. II, esp. pp. 13, 29, and 77.

113 See Apel, *Methodica Dialectices Ratio ad Iurisprudentiam Accomodata* (Nuremberg, 1535) and Lagus, *Iuris Utriusque Methodica Traditio* (Frankfurt, 1543).

114 See Witte, *Law and Protestantism*, pp. 139–140, Mads Langballe Jensen, "'Without Prophetic and Apostolic Voices': Niels Hemmingsen's *On the Law of Nature According to a Demonstrative Method*", in *Sacred Polities, Natural Law and the Law of Nations in the 16th–17th Centuries*, ed. Hans Blom (Leiden, 2022), pp. 56–76, as well as Tarald Rasmussen, "Skandinavien" in *Philip Melanchthon: Der Reformator zwischen Glauben und Wissen*, ed. Frank and Lange (2017), pp. 647–658. Hemmingsen's tract *De lege naturae apodicta methodus* (Wittenberg, 1563) has been translated into English as *On the Law of Nature: A Demonstrative Method*, ed. and trans. by E.J. Hutchinson, introduction by E.J. Hutchinson and Korey D. Maas (2018).

115 See Konrad Rittershausen, *Commentarius novus in quatuor libros institutionum imperialium divi Justiniani* (Strasbourg, 1618), pp. 788–796, reprinted 1649, and Christian Woldenberg, *Principia Juris Romani, i.e. leges Draconis et Solonis, leges Romuli, et leges XII. Tabularum* (Rostock, 1668), pp. 50–62.

116 See Christoph Strohm, "Melanchthon-Rezeption in der Ethik des frühen Calvinismus" in *Melanchthon und der Calvinismus*, ed. Günter Frank and Herman J. Selderhuis (2005), pp. 135–157, here pp. 135–139.

he influenced major figures such as the Dutch theologian Gisbertus Voetius (1589–1676).[117] More specifically, Melanchthon decisively shaped the teaching of Reformed ethics. As Christoph Strohm has demonstrated, the first systematic formulation of a specifically Calvinist moral philosophy, the *Ethices Christianae libri tres* of Lambert Daneau (c. 1530–1595), was heavily influenced by Melanchthon's *Summary of Moral Philosophy*.[118] Melanchthon's conception of natural law was particularly influential; his concept of *notitiae*, or innate ideas, was also adopted by the Danzig polymath Bartholomaeus Keckermann (ca. 1572–1609) as well as the German theologian Heinrich Alting (1583–1644).[119] Keckermann's student Johann Heinrich Alsted (1588–1638) also picked up Melanchthon's natural law theory in his 1630 *Encyclopaedia septem tomis distincta*.[120]

Melanchthon also exercised a massive influence on the institutions of Reformed education, with several of his students teaching in important Reformed universities. For example, Otto Werdmüller (1513–1552), who had taken a master's degree under Melanchthon at Wittenberg in 1538 (the year the *Summary* was first published) and went on to teach moral philosophy in Zürich, directly cited the *Summary* in his own ethics textbook, where he referred to "Philip Melanchthon, my teacher, most worthy of every honour."[121] From 1567–1569, the aforementioned Viktorin Strigel, freshly converted to the Reformed faith, even took a post as ethics professor at Heidelberg.[122]

In some cases, Melanchthon was even directly involved in shaping Reformed universities. The 1558 statutes of Heidelberg University, which Melanchthon had helped develop (and which were retained after the university became Reformed three years later), listed Aristotle's *Nicomachean Ethics* as a foundational text for the study of moral philosophy and Melanchthon's own ethical works were

117 See Andreas J. Beck, "Melanchthon und die reformierte Scholastik" in *Melanchthon und die Reformierte Tradition*, ed. Andreas J. Beck (2016): pp. 107–128 and "Zur Rezeption Melanchthons bei Gisbertus Voetius (1589–1676), namentlich in seiner Gotteslehre", in *Melanchthon und der Calvinismus*, Melanchthon Schriften der Stadt Bretten 9, ed. Günter Frank and Herman J. Selderhuis (2005), pp. 317–342.

118 See Strohm, "Melanchthon-Rezeption", pp. 147–149 and Strohm, *Ethik im frühen Calvinismus. Humanistische Einflüsse, philosophische, juristische und theologische Argumentationen sowie mentalitätsgeschichtliche Aspekte am Beispiel des Calvin-Schülers Lambertus Danaeus* (1996), pp. 240–256.

119 See Beck, "Melanchthon und die reformierte Scholastik", p. 186.

120 See Strohm, *Melanchthon-Rezeption*, p. 156.

121 See Luca Baschera, "Shaping Reformed Aristotelianism: Otto Werdmüller's Evaluation of the Nicomachean Ethics in *De dignitate, usu et methodo philosophiae moralis* (1545)" in *Following Zwingli: Applying the Past in Reformation Zurich*, ed. Luca Baschera, Bruce Gordon, and Christian Moser (2016), pp. 210–231. The quote is on p. 225, n. 64.

122 See Strohm, "Melanchthon-Rezeption", p. 140.

part of the curriculum. Through the end of the sixteenth century, his commentaries on Aristotle's *Ethics* were frequently taught at the leading Reformed universities at Geneva, Heidelberg, and Leiden.[123] In Lutheran and Reformed circles alike, Melanchthon was arguably the single most influential figure on sixteenth-century Protestant moral philosophy.

Melanchthon was also well-received in England, even if his moral philosophy was less influential across the Channel than it was on the continent. During his lifetime, English Protestants held him in high regard. Henry VIII's fascination with Melanchthon and insistence that the reformer visit England are well known. During the reign of Edward VI, Thomas Cranmer even invited Melanchthon to replace the late Martin Bucer as Regius Professor of Divinity at Cambridge, which the reformer declined.[124] Yet despite the fact that Melanchthon never set foot in England, his ethical thought (not to mention his theology) had a significant impact there. There was clearly an appetite for his ethical works, evidenced by the fact that portions of the *Summary of Moral Philosophy* were translated into English and published in London in 1550 and 1570.[125] Robert E. Stillman has even uncovered the influence of Melanchthonian natural law ideas in the anti-tyranny works of the English poet Philip Sidney (1554–1586).[126]

While the picture of Melanchthon's legacy in the moral philosophy of sixteenth-century Protestant university culture is fairly clear (at least on the institutional level, if not the intellectual level), the question of his influence on later seventeenth-century natural law is more difficult to discern. By the era which produced the works of Grotius, Pufendorf, or Leibniz, Melanchthon's direct influence had faded. In the sixteenth century, his ethical textbooks were standard reading in Lutheran and Reformed universities, but they were phased out in the seventeenth. Nevertheless, even in the mid-to-late seventeenth century, he was still a revered figure and was cited approvingly by authorities such as Johann Heinrich Boecler, the great commentator upon Grotius' *De Iure Belli ac Pacis*, and Valentin Alberti, the Orthodox Lutheran divine.[127]

---

123 See Donald W. Sinnema, "The Discipline of Ethics in Early Reformed Orthodoxy", *Calvin Theological Journal* 28 (1993): 10–44.

124 See Anthony Milton, "A Tale of Two Melanchthons: Melanchthon and English Protestantism 1560–1660" in Beck, ed., *Melanchthon und die Reformierte Tradition* (2016), pp. 129–138, here p. 130.

125 See the printing history of the *Summary* on p. 56 below.

126 See Robert E. Stillman. "The Truths of a Slippery World: Poetry and Tyranny in Sidney's 'Defence'". *Renaissance Quarterly* 50 (2002): 1287–1319.

127 See Boecler, *In Hugonis Grotii jus belli et pacis commentatio* (Strasbourg, 1663), Vol. I, pp. 4,

Conclusion

This essay has considered Melanchthon's conception of moral philosophy, his division between Law and Gospel, his ancient and medieval sources, the political applications of his work, and his lengthy legacy in Protestant intellectual culture. In light of these subjects, we have seen that assessing Melanchthon's status as the central figure of early Protestant natural law requires a complex investigation into the ways in which his moral philosophy was distinctly "Protestant". Still, it is hard to disagree that Melanchthon was the first Protestant natural lawyer, and that as such, he represents an important yet often-forgotten aspect of Protestant intellectual history, with relevance for the broader history of natural law, moral philosophy, and political thought.

Yet, as we have seen, many central questions about the reformer's theory of natural law and its legacy remain open. Was Melanchthon a forerunner of one side or the other in the division that occurred in Protestant natural law in the decades after Grotius? In what ways was he operating within a broader sixteenth-century humanist and scholastic tradition of thinking about natural law, and to what extent was his theory unique and idiosyncratic? Which medieval natural law theories did Melanchthon know, and what intellectual debts did he owe to these theories? Finally, was his impact on later Lutheran and Reformed intellectual history largely a matter of institutional and practical influence, or did the form and content of Melanchthon's moral philosophy persist throughout the late sixteenth and early seventeenth centuries? These are, without doubt, large and difficult questions. This volume is an invitation to those who are keen to wrestle with them.

113, 235. For Boecler, Alberti, and Melanchthon's legacy in Protestant natural law, see Jensen, *A Humanist in Reformation Politics*, pp. 194–198.

Notes on Text and Translation

On references to Latin texts: To provide readers with quick access to the Latin texts of these works, I have included cross-references to two different sets of sources: 1) the early modern Latin prints, and 2) the nineteenth-century editions of the *Corpus Reformatorum*. Throughout the text, any marginal reference beginning with a page or signature number (e.g., p. 25, sig. Aij^{r}) is a reference to the early modern printed work from which I translate. The preface of each text clarifies the specific early modern edition from which I have translated.

Throughout the text, any marginal reference with volume and column numbers (e.g., 16.21, 3.1004, 18.321) is a reference to the *Corpus Reformatorum*. The first number is the volume number and the second number is the column number.

On footnotes: The footnotes in this volume are primarily used to trace Melanchthon's biblical, classical, legal, and theological references. Like most writers of his day, he did not follow modern citation practices. His quotations and allusions sometimes include an author's name, and sometimes they do not. In some cases, the notes in the CR editions have been extremely helpful; in other cases, I have had to track down the citations myself. In the footnotes, I have identified all of the references that I have been able to trace definitively. In some cases, Melanchthon's quotation is too vague, or too paraphrased, to be traced to a concrete source.

I have also used the footnotes to explain the content of Melanchthon's work. These explanatory notes are intended to provide historical context, discuss difficult terms, draw connections to other Melanchthonian texts, and explain ambiguous passages. As this volume is already quite lengthy, I have cited secondary literature in the footnotes only sparingly.

On capitalisation: In general, I have followed Melanchthon's own usage in capitalising nouns such as "Church", "Republic", and "Gospel".

On Greek terms: In order to make the volume more accessible to non-specialist readers, I have transliterated Greek terms instead of providing Greek text. In a few rare cases I have included Greek text to demonstrate precise variants in the editions.

On paragraphs: This translation generally inserts paragraph breaks whenever Melanchthon's printed editions do. However, to aid the reader by avoiding the

 HTTPS://DOI.ORG/10.1163/9789004774742-003

multi-page paragraphs which are common in early modern print, I have frequently added additional paragraph breaks whenever he transitions to a new idea.

On Roman law citations: Melanchthon, in accordance with contemporary practice, cites Roman laws by the words of the chapter, title, and heading. Because these are extremely cumbersome for modern readers, I have translated these citations into modern numerical citations (i.e. D.1.1.2, etc.). Following current scholarly practice, I have abbreviated the Digest as D., the Codex as C., and the Institutes as Inst. (i.e. D.1.1.2, C.2.3.4, Inst. 4.2.8). For these texts, I have referred to the nineteenth-century Berlin edition of the *Corpus juris civilis*, ed. Theodor Mommsen and Paul Krüger.

On canon law citations: Melanchthon occasionally cites from the canon law collections of the Decretum [ca. 1139] and the Decretals [1234]. When referencing Gratian's Decretum, I have cited the *distinctiones* in the following manner: Decretum Dist.9, c.3 = Decretum, distinction 9, canon 3. I have cited the *causae* in a similar way (i.e. Decretum Ca.23.2.1 = Decretum, causa 23, question 2, canon 1). Although there were many collections of decretals in medieval canon law, any citation to the Decretals in this text refers to the 1234 collection assembled under Pope Gregory IX, known commonly as the Decretals; the *Liber Extra*; or the *Liber extravagantium decretalium*. I cite this work in the following way: Decretals 5.19.8 = Decretals, book 5, title 19, chapter 8. I have used the following texts:

Decretum Magistri Gratiani, ed. Emil Friedberg. In *Corpus Iuris Canonici*, volume I. Reprint. (Graz: Akademische Druck- u. Verlagsanstalt, 1959). Original, Leipzig: Bernhard Tauchnitz, 1879.

Liber extravagantium decretalium, ed. Emil Friedberg. In *Corpus Iuris Canonici*, volume II. Reprint. (Graz: Akademische Druck- u. Verlagsanstalt, 1959). Original, Leipzig: Bernhard Tauchnitz, 1881.

On medieval legal citations: Whenever he cites medieval jurists such as Baldus or Panormitanus, I have referred the reader to the relevant passages in the most readable and accessible early modern printed editions, even if they postdate Melanchthon.

On classical citations: In order to facilitate easy access for readers, I cite classical works according to the numbering of the widely available Loeb Classical Library series (abbreviated LCL). The only exceptions are the works of Plato and Plutarch, which I have cited by Stephanus numbers. For Aristotle, I have included both the Loeb numbering and Bekker numbering. Unless otherwise noted, translations of Melanchthon's Greek citations are my own. For a few particularly difficult passages, I have reproduced existing English translations and have acknowledged this in the footnotes.

I have tried to trace his classical references as accurately as possible. In cases where he cites a particular author (i.e., "as Pausanias writes", etc.), I have cited the relevant passages. In other cases, where certain anecdotes or vague references appear in a variety of classical sources, a solid attribution is much more difficult. In these cases, I have suggested likely or possible references in the footnotes. I have only cited classical works which he possibly could have accessed (i.e., not those which were edited or printed for the first time after his works were published).

On biblical citations: Throughout these texts, Melanchthon constantly quotes Scripture. He rarely gives explicit attributions. When he does, he usually mentions the book of the Bible only and very rarely cites individual chapters. To aid the reader in identifying these citations, I have filled out his biblical citations in the text to meet modern style in square brackets (i.e., Deuteronomy 2:[17], John [1:12], [Proverbs 23:5]). In citing the Psalms, I have followed the numbering of modern Protestant Bibles like the NRSV.

The reader should be aware that Melanchthon's Latin biblical quotations almost never match up with the Vulgate text. Much of this is probably attributable to his citing these texts from memory. However, the citations occasionally differ so much that an alternate explanation may be needed. For example, he may be remembering the biblical text in Greek and mentally translating into Latin. Certainly, he read the New Testament in Greek, and several times in the *Summary*, he references original Greek terms in the New Testament, although he never quotes extended biblical passages in Greek. In translating these inexact quotations, I have tried to preserve his distinctive phrasing as well as render the biblical quotations in a recognizable form to modern English readers. In cases of significant divergence, I have referenced the biblical passages with "cf."

On patristic sources: Melanchthon occasionally cites early Christian writers such as Ambrose, Augustine, and John Chrysostom. I generally refer the reader to the *Patrologia Latina* and *Patrologia Graeca*. When there are reliable, scholarly, modern English editions, I refer the reader to those.

On technical Latin terms: One of the challenges of translating Melanchthon, who was a master of so many disciplines, is rendering his technical Latin terms into modern English. While I have attempted to provide a readable English translation, there are some cases in which the technical Latin legal, philosophical, or theological terms will be relevant and helpful to the reader. In such cases, I have included the original Latin terms in square brackets, although I have tried to minimize such insertions. In general, to aid the reader in looking up certain technical words or phrases, I have included nouns and adjectives in the nominative form, regardless of the case in which they appear in the original Latin sentences. When these words are parts of longer phrases where the original case is relevant to the syntax, or if the Latin case is particularly relevant for understanding the translation, I have included these Latin terms in the form and case in which they appear in the text.

Translations of Particular Terms:

Affectus: I have translated this term as "passion." While in modern English, that term usually has a negative connotation (i.e., murder as a crime of passion, or lust as a passion), in moral philosophy, the term can have a more neutral meaning. In this text, Melanchthon argues that the passions can be both good or bad, and insists against the Stoics that the passions are actually necessary for cultivating virtue. Thus, the passions are morally ambivalent; they can prompt a person towards virtue or vice. In this text, Melanchthon defines a passion explicitly as an "impulse [*motus*] by which a sense or the will pursues or flees from something presented to it." (see p. 95 below.)

Ars: I have translated this term as "art", but Melanchthon's term encompasses much more than our idea of visual or musical arts. For Melanchthon, an *ars* is an advanced and conventional discipline of human knowledge or practice, such as politics, law, medicine, architecture, or mathematics. In Melanchthon's thought, the basic principles of an *ars* are available through natural reason, and human beings use reason to build upon these principles and construct sophisticated *artes*. For example, the *ars* of law begins from some natural presuppositions about justice which are then built up into complex legal systems. So the principle, available to all humans by nature, that one should not harm others, becomes the basis of sophisticated laws about murder, assault, theft, etc.

Causa/Effectus: In keeping with the philosophical usage of the term, I have translated *causa* as "cause" (i.e. final cause, efficient cause, etc.), except in the occasional cases where the term is used more generally to mean something like "source" or "origin." *Effectus* refers to the observable operations or tendencies of a certain nature (i.e., the *effectus* of human nature are to procreate, care for children, and defend itself against unjust harm). *Effectus* are generally understood as operations stemming from a thing's *causae*. To highlight the causal relationship, I have rendered *effectus* as "effect."

Demonstratio: Melanchthon uses this term to refer to the process of reasoning from fundamental, naturally known principles, or *notitiae* (see below). Thus, moral philosophy begins from the *notitiae* inborn within human beings, and proceeds through the operations of reason in constructing *demonstrationes* which build out the complexities of moral philosophy. I have usually translated this as "demonstrations", which should be understood as containing this technical definition. Occasionally, the term also means something like "logical proofs."

Doctrina: Melanchthon generally uses this term to refer to a broad concept of instruction and discipline by which a person develops their moral, spiritual, and intellectual faculties. I have largely translated it "doctrine" to keep the sense of the Latin term and to emphasize Melanchthon's idea of doctrine as a body of knowledge acquired through education and study. In some cases, however, Melanchthon uses the term to refer more specifically to the concrete process of education. In these cases, I have translated it "instruction", "training", or "education".

Genus/Species: In most cases, Melanchthon uses these terms in the strict Aristotelian sense of a *genus* as a category of thing containing several *species* which are distinguished by their differentiating properties (*differentia*). In cases where this technical sense of the terms is relevant, I have retained the Latin terms. In other cases, when the sense of the terms is less explicitly technical, I have translated the terms as "category", "kind", or "type" to render the translation more accessible to modern English readers.

Homo/humanus: In translating this term, I have tried to render the most common and natural English equivalents. For this reason, some translations render *homo* as "man" in keeping with the general conventions of theological and philosophical writing from before the mid-20th century (i.e., *finis hominis* = "the end of man"). At other times, I have rendered *homo/humanus* as "human" whenever that is the more natural English equivalent (i.e. *natura hominis* = "human nature" and *genus humanum* = "human race").

Ius: This term, like German *Recht* or Spanish *derecho*, can mean either "right" or "law." Melanchthon uses the term in both ways, and in his discussion of *ius* among the Roman jurists, he even explicitly highlights the flexibility of the term. I have translated this term as either "right" or "law" according to its context; i.e. *ius naturae* = "law of nature", *ius gentium* = "law of nations", but *ius suum cuique tribuere* = "render to each his right." Melanchthon also uses *ius* in a subjective sense, i.e. *ius recipiendi certos reditus* = "the right to receive certain revenues." In passages where Melanchthon uses the term in multiple senses, I have also included *ius* in square brackets after the translation when helpful.

Moralis/ēthikos: Melanchthon uses the Latin term *moralis* and the Greek term *ēthikos* interchangeably to refer to the sphere of external human moral action. Moreover, Melanchthon occasionally refers to moral philosophy by the Latinised term *ethice*. For instance, an earlier version of the *Philosophiae moralis epitome* was entitled *Epitome ethices*, and a later edition was entitled *Ethicae doctrinae elementa*.

To highlight the connection between the Greek term *ēthikos* and the subject of moral philosophy in the *PME*, and to avoid giving the sense of a disparity between the two terms, I have translated the Greek term *ēthikos* as "moral" and included the Greek term in brackets.

***Motus*:** This is a flexible term which Melanchthon uses in discussing moral psychology. At the most general level, *motus* refers to an impulse, and in the context of moral philosophy, it generally refers to an impulse of the heart. I have generally translated the term as "impulse". In some cases, as when Melanchthon refers to the *motus* of fear, anger, or love, the term is basically interchangeable with the English word "emotion" or "affection" (the latter especially in reference to positive emotions) and I have sparingly translated it as such when the context demands it. In Melanchthon's usage, an *affectus* (passion) is a specific type of *motus*. As a result, the terms are occasionally used interchangeably. In a few rare instances, Melanchthon refers more specifically to the physical processes behind the emotions, that is, literally the movements of the heart, or the heartbeat and pulse. In these cases, I have translated as "movement" or "motion."

***Notitia*:** This is one of the most important terms in Melanchthon's thought. Melanchthon uses the plural *notitiae* to refer to those natural notions which God has implanted in human nature and which impart fundamental knowledge about good and evil (as well as the other arts such as geometry, mathematics, and architecture). The *notitiae*, or natural notions, thus constitute the foundational principles of moral philosophy and the other arts, since reason uses the *notitiae* as the starting point for deriving more sophisticated principles, proofs, and demonstrations of moral philosophy. In the plural, I have translated this term as "notions". Melanchthon occasionally uses the term *notitia* in the singular, and in these cases, it usually signifies the more general idea of "knowledge".

Officium: Melanchthon uses this word in two main senses. The first is an *officium* as a "duty" owed according to natural, divine, or civil law. The second is in the sense of "office", as in the "office of the magistrate". I have generally translated the word as "duty" or "office", according to context. On rare occasions, Melanchthon means something like "service", as in the section on contracts (see p. 173 of the 1546 *PME*), where he refers to the "*officium mutuationis*", or "the service of borrowing".

Ratio probabilis: Probable reason (*ratio probabilis*) was an important medieval and Renaissance category of thought. Because much of human life involves acting upon knowledge that is not absolutely verifiable, the category of "probable reason" was used to analyse propositions that were likely, but not certain, to be true. Melanchthon frequently appeals to this category of thinking, particularly in reference to legal judgments, where absolute certainty was almost always impossible.

Storgē: Melanchthon often uses this Greek term (especially in the phrase *storgai phusikai*) to refer to the natural affections or impulses which lead humans and animals to procreate and raise their offspring. In his *Erotemata dialectices* (see CR 13.541–542), he defines the term as "natural benevolence" [*naturalis benevolentia*]. In *The Summary of Moral Philosophy*, Melanchthon refers to the natural affections towards procreation and rearing of children, self-preservation, and self-defence against unjust violence.

CHAPTER 1

Summary of Moral Philosophy

1 Introduction

The *Summary of Moral Philosophy*, which first appeared in 1538, was the first systematic ethical textbook that Melanchthon published.[1] In this text, Melanchthon carved out a distinct discipline of moral philosophy which was separate from the religious domain of the Gospel. In the first part of the work, Melanchthon addresses fundamental topics of moral philosophy: the end of man; the nature of virtue; the relationships among the passions, will, and reason; and the division of the virtues. In the second part, he turns his focus to the virtue of justice and the concrete questions of justice in sixteenth-century European society. The result is the first systematic attempt by any Protestant thinker to establish a system of moral philosophy on the basis of natural law.

The *Summary* grew out of Melanchthon's previous commentaries on Aristotle. As Melanchthon reveals in the preface to this work, "Thus, since I already expounded upon Aristotle's *Ethics*, I have also added this commentary in which I follow not only Aristotle's opinions, but his method too."[2] Indeed, the *Summary* was the culmination of Melanchthon's intense interest in ancient moral philosophy throughout the previous decades.[3] At only twenty-one years old, in 1518, he expressed his desire to produce a new edition of Aristotle's works in collaboration with scholars such as Johann Reuchlin, Willibald Pirckheimer, and Johannes Oecolampadius, although the work never appeared.[4] Soon after his arrival in Wittenberg, Melanchthon began to demonstrate a certain scepticism about Aristotle's philosophy, which can almost certainly be attributed to Luther's influence.

However, following the disturbances of the Peasants' War in 1525, Melanchthon began to turn back to Aristotle's political and ethical thought. In 1527, Melanchthon decided to lecture on Aristotle's *Nicomachean Ethics*, and soon

1 The 1532 *Epitome ethices* was not published until the nineteenth century, and the previous commentaries on Aristotle's *Nicomachean Ethics* were, as the name suggests, more commentaries than they were independent, systematic approaches to moral philosophy.

2 See p. 61 below.

3 For this turn to Aristotle, see Nicole Kuropka, *Philipp Melanchthon: Wissenschaft und Gesellschaft*, pp. 23–31, 176–183, 239–244.

4 See Frank, *Ethicae doctrinae elementa*, p. XXIX.

 HTTPS://DOI.ORG/10.1163/9789004774742-004

after he began to produce commentaries on Aristotle's practical philosophy.[5] In 1529, he had published a commentary on Aristotle's *Nicomachean Ethics*, and in 1530 he published a commentary on the *Politics* (which is translated into English for the first time in this volume).[6] In 1532, he lectured on Aristotle at Wittenberg, during which time he also drafted a manuscript entitled *Epitome ethices*, which was only printed in 1893 after it was discovered by the German scholar Hermann Heineck.[7] Melanchthon's moral philosophical project finally came to fruition in the 1538 *Philosophiae moralis epitome*, reprinted in 1538 and twice in 1539. In 1540, Melanchthon heavily revised the work and inserted several new sections. This second version was printed eight times from 1540 to 1546 and is the basis of the translation in this volume (more on this below in "A Note on the Text").

In the *Summary*, Melanchthon constructed a Lutheran system of moral philosophy which was built upon Aristotle in many ways. For one, the *Summary* largely mirrored the organization of Aristotle's *Nicomachean Ethics*. Book I follows Aristotle's discussion of virtue in books I–III of the *NE* and even includes an extended analysis of Aristotle's definition of virtue as "a disposition concerning choice, consisting in a mean with respect to us, according to some principle, that is, as a wise man judges."[8] The second book of the *Summary* follows Aristotle's discussion of justice in book V of the *NE*. Most notably, some of Melanchthon's definitions (i.e. his descriptions of virtue and the passions) and his division of categories (i.e., commutative vs. distributive justice) are largely taken directly from Aristotle, with occasional changes. Yet while the *Summary* bore clear Aristotelian influences, it was more than a mere commentary on the Greek philosopher, as the more particular discussions on law and justice reveal in the second half of the work. Aristotle offered Melanchthon a foundation for

5 For Melanchthon's changing attitudes towards Aristotle in the 1520s, see Jill Kraye, "Melanchthon's Ethics Commentaries and Textbooks" in *Classical Traditions in Renaissance Philosophy*, ed. Jill Kraye (London: Routledge, 2002), chapter VII (pp. 1–12), esp. pp. 4–7 and Frank, *Ethicae doctrinae elementa*, pp. XXIX–XXX. For Melanchthon's decision to teach the *Ethics* in 1527, see MBW 580.

6 These two works are *In Ethica Aristotelis commentarius Philipp. Melanchtho.* (Wittenberg: Josef Klug, 1529) and *Commentarii in aliquot politicos libros Aristotelis* (Wittenberg: Josef Klug, 1530).

7 Ralph Keen has translated part of the Aristotle *Ethics* commentary and the entirety of the *Epitome ethices* in *A Melanchthon Reader* (New York: Peter Lang, 1988), pp. 179–238. The manuscript *Epitome ethices* was first published in 1893 by Hermann Heineck, under the title *Die Aelteste Fassung von Melanchthons Ethik*. Ed. Hermann Heineck (1893). Melanchthon mentions his 1532 lectures on Aristotle in CR 2.579–580.

8 See p. 101 below.

thinking about moral philosophy, but Melanchthon took that foundation and constructed his own edifice of moral philosophy.

Melanchthon begins the work by asserting the fundamental distinction between moral philosophy and the Gospel. While the Gospel treated eternal spiritual matters such as forgiveness of sins, eternal life, and the gift of the Spirit, moral philosophy treated matters of external ethics. As Melanchthon defined it, "Moral philosophy is that part of divine law which teaches about external actions."[9] The Gospel was the domain of God's direct revelation through Christ and through the Scriptures, while moral philosophy was available to all men through reason. In this division, Melanchthon framed Protestant moral thought in the defining Lutheran categories of Law and Gospel, which formed the basis of Melanchthon's entire intellectual project.[10]

However, despite the fact that moral philosophy dealt with external behaviour and not the internal matters of the heart, Melanchthon asserted that moral philosophy was essential for Christians as they navigate the ethical and political quandaries of life in a fallen world. In the first book of the *Summary*, Melanchthon follows Aristotle in asserting the value of virtue in human life. However, whereas Aristotle had pointed to virtue as the end of man, Melanchthon directs virtue to a still higher end, namely the glory of God, arguing that "One should seek virtue for God's sake, that is, in order to render to God that obedience which is owed to him and to illustrate God's glory, that is, to invite others to the knowledge of God."[11] Thus, Melanchthon presented a view of human morality that was compatible with Aristotelian ethics while directing human beings to the final end of glorifying God.

Melanchthon also favoured Aristotle because the philosopher was a viable alternative to the other ancient schools of philosophy such as Epicureanism and Stoicism. Much of book I is dedicated to refuting these philosophies. Melanchthon sharply criticized Epicureanism, which he closely associated with the Italian humanist philosopher Lorenzo Valla, as a philosophy which upended the order of goods, placing pleasure above virtue. He applied a more measured approach to his critique of Stoicism. While he praised the Stoics' emphasis on the divine (i.e., that "men were created for the sake of the gods") and utilized their category of *adiaphora* in his own theological writings, Melanchthon also

---

9 See p. 65 below.

10 For this point, see Heinz Scheible, "Die Bedeutung der Unterscheidung von Gesetz und Evangelium für theologische Ethik und Praktische Theologie am Beispiel Melanchthons" in *Christentum und Spätmoderne. Ein internationaler Diskurs über Praktische Theologie und Ethik*, ed. W. Gräb et al. (2000), pp. 93–100.

11 See pp. 86–87 below.

critiqued the Stoics on two major points. First, they denied the freedom of human will, and second, they denied that any human passions could be good. Melanchthon opposed this second point especially because it invalidated his concept of the *storgai phusikai*, that is, the natural affections, like a father's love towards his children. Thus, a Stoic denial of all passions would erase an important part of divinely endowed human goodness and an important source of moral virtue. In the *Summary*, Stoicism and Epicureanism constitute the extreme poles of philosophical error which serve to highlight the correct course of Aristotle's philosophy. In response, Melanchthon encourages his readers to "repudiate the Stoics and Epicureans and to embrace the Peripatetic [i.e. Aristotelian] school."[12]

The remainder of Book I of the *Summary* addresses various implications of this theory of ethics, with topics ranging from the freedom of the will and influence of the passions to a careful reading of Aristotle's definition of virtue. After delineating the virtues at the end of the first book, in book II Melanchthon focuses on the virtue of justice and its concrete applications in human society. Following Aristotle's analysis in Book V of the *Nicomachean Ethics*, Melanchthon delineates categories of universal and particular justice as well as distributive and commutative justice. He also treats the definition of justice from Roman law, and then addresses a number of thorny legal problems, including the relationship between strict law and equity and the status of ignorance as a legal excuse.

The latter part of Book II of the *Summary* addresses contract law. Although this may seem an odd choice for a text about moral philosophy, Melanchthon believed that a right understanding of contract law, like the other branches of Roman jurisprudence which were being adopted across Germany in his age, were integral to living a moral life in human society. He saw contracts as a tool for inculcating in citizens the "duties of the virtues and mutual love." He even went so far as to call contracts "sacraments" [*sacramenta*], which teach the major lesson that "we should care about the interest of others as well as our own interest".[13] The *Summary* concludes with brief treatments of the virtues of truthfulness, beneficence, gratitude, and friendship (the 1538/1539 version only treated truthfulness).

While the *Summary* was largely about moral philosophy, it also touched upon political topics which were becoming increasingly controversial in the early 1540s, as military conflict between Charles V and the German Protestant

12 See p. 62 below.
13 See p. 183 below.

princes became inevitable. Book II contains some of the most explosive claims in the entire work. In the second version of the text Melanchthon inserted a tract which argued that rulers must use their political authority to eliminate idolatry and establish true religion. This was aimed at Protestant princes and was highly controversial for its claim that they should ignore "higher lords" (i.e., the Emperor) as well as Church hierarchies as they instituted the Reformation in their own territories. The work then moves on to a section which asserted the rights of private citizens to defend themselves against an openly tyrannical ruler.

These two sections illustrate that by the end of the 1530s and certainly by 1540, Melanchthon had begun to consider, at least theoretically, the concrete political steps that princes and citizens could take against tyrants who refused to allow or even persecuted the true Protestant faith. Although he was careful to distinguish the Gospel from moral and political philosophy, this did not mean that politics and religion had nothing to do with each other. Melanchthon conceived of the end of man as an ultimately religious one—to know and to glorify God—which was obvious to all people through reason. Thus, the purpose of politics was not just to protect citizens' physical well-being; a good ruler was responsible for instituting and protecting true religion as well. Put another way, the ruler was the guardian of both the first and second tables of the law. Working from these presuppositions, Melanchthon justified self-defence on the basis of natural law and laid a foundation for Protestant military action in the Schmalkaldic War (1546–1547), a conflict which would end in a crushing defeat for the Protestants. Thus, the 1546 *Summary*, presented here in English translation for the first time, represents Melanchthon's political and moral philosophy in the critical moment right before the Schmalkaldic War.

2 A Note on the Text

The numerous editions of the *Philosophiae moralis epitome* (*PME*) can be divided into two main versions (for a list of all known editions, see the "Printing History" section below). The first version of the text was printed in Strasbourg in 1538 by Krafft Müller, and reprinted in that same year by Sébastien Gryphe in Lyon. In 1539, two more printings appeared, one in March by Müller, and another in September in Leipzig by Michael Blum.[14] These four editions had

14 There were actually two Michael Blum editions, but the only difference was a corrected date on the title page. See Claus 1539.31.1 and 1539.31.2.

only minor orthographic and typographic variants. The one major change was that, while the 1538 editions contained the *PME* alone, the 1539 volumes also contained a separate work: Melanchthon's commentary on the fifth book of Aristotle's *Nicomachean Ethics*. He had finished drafting the first version of the *PME* by 30 April, 1537. On that date, he revealed to Joachim Camerarius that he had sent the draft to the printer, Krafft Müller.[15] In June, he turned to teaching the fifth book of Aristotle's *Ethics*, and by October, at which point Müller had not yet printed the work, Melanchthon mentioned plans for returning to the *Epitome* and adding his discussion of the fifth book.[16] Apparently, Müller eventually produced the original draft sometime in 1538, and only in 1539 did he add the work on book V of the *Ethics*.

In February 1540, Melanchthon published a revised and updated version of the *PME* with Krafft Müller in Strasbourg. While the overall structure of the book was roughly the same, the second version was heavily revised and extensive parts rewritten. The extent of these changes is noticeable on the very first page, as Melanchthon's answer to the question, "What is Moral Philosophy?" was entirely rewritten in 1540.

Another major alteration was the insertion into book II of the tract *"De officio principum"* ("On the Duty of the Prince", included below under the heading "Whether Princes Should Change Impious Worship ..."). This essay, which addressed the prince's duty to change false worship practices and institute true religion, was originally published as a separate tract.[17] James Estes has called this work "the longest and most detailed discussion of the *cura religionis* of Christian magistrates that Melanchthon would ever publish."[18] The tone is much more pugnacious than the rest of the *PME*, and the insertion in the 1540 edition reflects Melanchthon's increasing awareness, in the buildup to the Schmalkaldic War, that Protestant political thought had to account for the role of state power in establishing evangelical religion in the face of deep-seated opposition to evangelical reforms.

Aside from the addition of this lengthy tract, book II of the 1540 edition shared largely the same organization as the first version of the *PME*, although the content was substantially revised and some of the subheadings were

15 CR 3.359 / MBW 1897.

16 CR 3.378, 3.419.

17 *De officio principum, quod mandatum Dei praecipiat eis tollere abusus Ecclesiasticos* (Wittenberg: Josef Klug, 1539). This was first printed as a separate tract in 1539 and reprinted several times thereafter. For more information on this text, see Ralph Keen, "Defending the Pious: Melanchthon and the Reformation in Albertine Saxony, 1539", *Church History* 60.2 (1991): 180–195.

18 Estes, *Peace, Order*, p. 136.

changed. In general, the sections before "May Private Citizens Kill Tyrants?" contained heavy revisions in the 1540 version. The sections after that subheading, however, were virtually untouched until the very end of the volume, where another major change appears. At the very end, Melanchthon added discussions of beneficence, gratitude, and friendship to truthfulness, the only virtue treated at the end of the 1538 and 1539 editions. The editions of 1540 and 1546 were also printed with two other separate works: a commentary on Aristotle's *Nicomachean Ethics* as well as a short treatise entitled "*De arbore consanguinitatis et affinitatis* (On the Tree of Consanguinity and Affinity)". The 1546 editions also included some additional prefaces and poems, as well as an additional short treatise entitled "*De contractibus*" (On Contracts).[19] These additional works are not translated here.

Melanchthon's revised and expanded version of the *PME* was printed seven more times: once separately in 1541, once in the 1541 Basel *opera omnia*, twice in 1542, once in 1544, and twice in 1546. The 1540, 1542 Strasbourg, 1544, and both 1546 editions of the *PME* even share the same collation and pagination. Readers should be aware that the two 1546 editions (both by Krafft Müller) appear nearly identical but can be distinguished by the punctuation in the title: One printing reads "*Item,*" while the other reads "*Item.*" The spacing of the text on the title pages is also slightly different. There are minor orthographic and typographical discrepancies between these two texts, suggesting that they were, in fact, two separate typesettings. Readers should note that the edition in the *Corpus Reformatorum* is based on the "*Item.*" edition; the editors of that volume appear not to have known of the other 1546 Müller ("*Item,*") edition. In what follows, I refer to the "*Item.*" edition as "1546a" and the "*Item,*" edition as "1546b". However, it is unclear which edition came first, and the a/b labelling implies no determination about chronology. 1546b does contain more errors than 1546a, but one could draw conflicting conclusions from this: Perhaps 1546b was an earlier typesetting that was later corrected, or perhaps 1546b contains errors because it was hastily re-set due to unexpectedly high demand after the publication of 1546a.

2.1 Text for This Translation

Because the first and second versions of the *PME* are so different, creating a critical edition that accounted for both the 1538–1539 and 1540–1546 texts would be a futile exercise; an editor would basically need to create two different trans-

19 This was a different tract than the section of the *PME* below entitled "On Contracts."

lations. The present translation is based on the second version of the text (i.e., the 1540/1546), which includes Melanchthon's substantial revisions as well as the tract *De officio principum*. To give a sense of the disparities between the two versions, an appendix at the end of the *Summary* provides a translation of the section on virtues according to the natural law from the 1538/1539 editions but omitted in the latter version. The footnotes also flag discrepancies between the section headings of the 1538 and 1540/46 editions.

The revised version is the basis for the modern editions of the Latin texts of *Philosophiae moralis epitome* (see CR 16.21–164 and MWA III.149–301), providing an easy way to compare the present translation with the original. I have translated the *Summary* primarily from the 1546a Strasbourg edition, but I have compared it closely with the 1540 and 1546b editions. Aside from the fact that the 1546 editions include more numerous marginal headings (which I have inserted in this translation), these three editions are virtually identical, even down to the page numbers. The vast majority of discrepancies are either orthographic or typographical errors (e.g., "*referant*" instead of "*referrant*", etc.) and thus have no real impact on the translation. In most of these cases, I have not indicated variants of this type in the footnotes. In the rare cases that textual variants impact the meaning, I have flagged this in the footnotes and made editorial decisions about which reading is the most likely. The footnotes in the *Corpus Reformatorum* provide a good (but not entirely comprehensive) account of the differences, although the editors of the *Corpus Reformatorum* apparently were not aware that there were two separate 1546 Müller editions and had access only to 1546a.

3 Bibliography of Editions of the *Summary*

The following list includes the extant Latin editions of Melanchthon's *Summary of Moral Philosophy* from its *editio princeps* in 1538 to the final printing in 1546. I have attempted to provide a comprehensive bibliography for the *Summary* as well as for the other texts in this volume. The bibliographies of the *Corpus Reformatorum* have provided a useful starting point, as has Ralph Keen's *Checklist of Melanchthon Imprints Through 1560*. Helmut Claus's *Melanchthon-Bibliographie* is by far the most comprehensive bibliography of Melanchthon's writings.[20] I have also identified each of the entries by the numbers in the

20 For Keen, see *A Checklist of Melanchthon Imprints through 1560* (1988). For Claus, see *Melanchthon-Bibliographie 1510–1560*. 4 vols. (2014).

Universal Title Short Catalogue (USTC) and the *Verzeichnis der im deutschen Sprachbereich erschienenen Drucke des 16 Jahrhunderts* (VD16) or *Verzeichnis der im deutschen Sprachraum erschienenen Drucke des 17 Jahrhunderts* (VD17). I have drawn much of the bibliographical information from Claus' work and corroborated with the USTC and VD16 databases. While the bibliographies of the CR, Keen, and Claus rarely include entries after Melanchthon's death in 1560, the bibliographic contribution of this volume is largely the inclusion of materials after 1560.

3.1 Sixteenth Century Editions of the *Philosophiae moralis epitome*

1538. *Philosophiae Moralis Epitome, Phillippo* [sic] *Melanchthone autore, Nunquam antea excusa.* (Strasbourg: Kraft Müller, March 1538). [Claus 1538.57 / VD 16 M 3961 / USTC 683927].

1538. *Philosophiae Moralis Epitome, Philippo Melanchthone autore.* (Lyon: Sébastien Gryphe). [Claus 1538.30 / USTC 147492].

1539. *Philippi Melanchthonis Moralis Philosophiae Epitome. Item in quintum librum Ethicorum Arist: Commentarius, recognitus a Philippo & in quibusdam locis omnino renovatus.* (Strasbourg: Kraft Müller, March 1539). [Claus 1539.69 / VD16 M 3963 / USTC 683821].

1539. *Philippi Melanchthonis Moralis Philosophiae Epitome. Item in quintum librum Ethicorum Aristotelis Commentarius, recognitus a Philippo et in quibusdam locis omnino renovatus* (Leipzig: Michael Blum, Sept. 1539). [Claus 1539.31.1 / VD16 M 3962 / USTC 683822]. See also Claus 1539.31.2, which is identical except for a corrected date at the end of the volume.

1540. *Philippi Melanchthonis Philosophiae moralis epitome libri duo emendati et aucti. Nam tres virtutes additae, Quintus Aristotelis totus immutatus, accessit etiam tractatus De autoritate principum, & alter De arbore consanguinitatis et affinitatis, & index copiosus.* (Strasbourg: Kraft Müller, February 1540). [Claus 1540.86 / VD16 ZV 10686 / USTC 683826].

1541. *Moralis philosophiae epitome. Philippi Melancht.* (Lyon: Sébastien Gryphe). [Claus 1541.61 / USTC 140238].

1541. *Operum Philippi Melancthonis* [sic] *tomi quinque, quorum Catalogos sequentes paginae indicabunt* (Basel: Johann Herwagen, August 1541), Vol. IV.199–265 [Claus 1541.9, VD16 ZV 18396]. See also VD16 ZV 10690 and VD16 M 2330.

1542. *Philippi Melanchthonis Philosophiae moralis Epitomes libri duo emendati & aucti. Nam tres virtutes additae, Quintus Aristotelis totus immutatus, accessit etiam tractatus De autoritate principum, et alter De arbore consanguinitatis et affinitatis, & index copiosus.* (Strasbourg: Kraft Müller, March 1542). [Claus 1542.72 / VD16 ZV 10694 / USTC 683827].

1542. *Moralis philosophiae epitome. Philippi Melanchth.* (Lyon: Sébastien Gryphe, 1542) [Claus 1542.51 / USTC 157483].

1544. *Philippi Melanchthonis Philosophiae moralis Epitomes libri duo emendati & aucti. Nam tres virtutes additae, Quintus Aristotelis totus immutatus, accessit etiam tractatus De autoritate principum, & alter De arbore consanguinitatis et affinitatis, & index copiosus.* (Strasbourg: Kraft Müller, September 1544). [Claus 1544.78 / VD16 ZV 10698 / USTC 683823].

1546. *Philippi Melanthonis Philosophiae moralis Epitomes Libri duo emendati et aucti. Item.* [!] *Enarratio aliquot librorum Ethicorum Aristotelis, Primi, Secundi, Tertij, et Quinti, ad intelligendum Aristotelem utilis. Eodem Philip. Melant. autore.* (Strasbourg: Kraft Müller, March 1546). [Claus 1546.95 / VD16 M 3964 / USTC 683835]. Referred to below as "1546a".

1546. *Philippi Melanthonis Philosophiae Moralis Epitomes Libri duo emendati & aucti. Item,* [!] *Enarratio aliquot librorum Ethicorum Aristotelis, Primi, Secundi, Tertii, & Quinti, ad intelligendum Aristotelem utilis. Eodem Philip. Melant. Autore.* (Strasbourg: Kraft Müller, March 1546). [Claus 1546.96 / VD16 M 3965 / USTC 683834]. This edition is almost identical to the above (Claus 1546.95). In addition to minor textual variants, they can be distinguished by the punctuation after "Item" in the title. Referred to below as "1546b"

3.2 Excerpts of the *Philosophiae Moralis Epitome* Were Also Translated into English

1550. *A civile nosgay wherin is contayned not onelye the offyce and dewty of all magestrates and Judges but also of of* [sic] *all subiectes with a preface concernynge the lyberty of Justice in this our tyme newly collected an gethered out of latyn and so translated in to the Inglyshe tonge by J.G.* Translated by John Goodale. (London: Robert Wyer for John Goodale). [Claus 1550.50 / USTC 504509]. Translation includes excerpts from book II on justice.

1570. *Whether it be a mortall sinne to transgresse civil lawes which be the commaundementes of civill magistrates. The iudgement of Philip Melancton in his epitome of morall philosophie. The resolution of D. Hen. Bullinger, and D. Rod Gualter, of D. Martin Bucer, and D. Peter Martyr, concernyng thapparrel of ministers, and other indifferent thinges.* (London: Richard Jugge). [USTC 507185]. Includes a translation of the section "Is it a Mortal Sin to Violate Civil Laws, that is, the Edicts of the Civil Magistrates?"

3.3 The *Ethicae doctrinae elementa*: A Further Revision of the *Philosophiae moralis epitome*

Melanchthon produced another work of moral philosophy following the *PME*. This revision roughly followed the *PME* in organization but usually appeared under the title *Ethicae doctrinae elementa* (*EDE*). It was a rewriting of the *PME* (the first page of the 1550 edition of the work reads "*Epitome philosophiae moralis repetita anno 1548*") but is sufficiently different that it should be considered a separate work. In fact, the editors of the *Corpus Reformatorum* include the *EDE* as a separate work in CR 16.165–276. This work was first published in 1550 and was reprinted around twenty times throughout the rest of the century.[21]

It is important to highlight the *EDE* because, while it must be considered a separate work from the *PME*, the close relationship can easily lead to confusion. For example, the following two books are actually editions of the *EDE*, despite having titles extremely similar to the *PME*:

1556. *Philippi Melanthonis Philosophiae moralis libri duo ad usum studiosorum paulo quam ante accomodatiores. Item, Enarratio aliquot librorum Ethicorum Aristotelis ad intelligentiam reliquorum ejusdem authoris scriptorum mire conducens, scilicet primi, secundi, tertii et quinti.* (Strasbourg: Blasius Fabricius). [VD16 ZV 25475 / USTC 683836].

1559. *Philippi Melanthonis Philosophiae moralis libri duo, ad usum studiosorum paulo quam ante accommodatiores. Item, enarratio aliquot librorum Ethicorum Aristotelis, ad intelligentiam reliquorum eiusdem authoris scriptorum mire conducens, scilicet primi, secundi, tertij, et quinti.* (Strasbourg: Paul Messerschmidt). [VD16 M 3966 / USTC 683792].

Further, two commentaries on Melanchthon's moral philosophy appeared later in the century.[22] From the titles, they appear to be commentaries on the *PME*, but they are actually commentaries on the *EDE*:

21 For more detailed bibliographical information, see Frank, *Ethicae Doctrinae*, p. XXII, fn. 20.

22 For Strigel as a commentator in the Melanchthonian tradition of moral philosophy, see Günter Frank, "Fragmentierung und topische Neuordnung der aristotelischen Ethik in der frühen Neuzeit: Ethik bei Viktorin Strigel und Abraham Scultetus" in *Späthumanismus und reformierte Konfession*, ed. Christoph Strohm, Joseph S. Freedman, and Herman J. Selderhuis (2006), pp. 153–167.

1580. Victorinus Strigel. *In epitomen philosophiae moralis Philippi Melanchthonis. Hypomnemata Victorini Strigelii. Excepta de ore ipsius in praelectionibus publicis: quibus in academia Lipsensi ante annos quindecim, ratione docendi ad captum juventutis scholasticae accommodata, illustravit initia doctrinae ethicae. Nunc primum contexta & in lucem edita, opera & studio, Christophori Pezelii Sacrae Theologiae Doctoris*. (Neustadt an der Weinstrasse: Matthaeus Harnisch, 1580). [VD16 S 9604 / USTC 665640].
The above work was reprinted in 1580 [VD16 S 9603 / USTC 665642]; 1582 [VD16 S 9605 / USTC 665639]; and 1590 [VD16 S 9606 / USTC 665641].

1589. Christoph Pezel. *Epitome philosophiae moralis sive Ethice Philippi Melanchthonis: Duobus libris, seu partibus distincta: cum explicationibus ad discentium usum accommodatis: & in Gymnasio Bremensi traditis a Christophoro Pezelio, sacrae theologiae doctore*. (Zerbst: Bonaventura Faber, 1589). [VD16 M 3967 / USTC 653025].

Judging by the printing and reception history, the *EDE* may be considered Melanchthon's final revision of his moral philosophical project. It certainly had the widest reception in Germany after Melanchthon's death. However, the *PME* deserves a translation for two major reasons. First, the *EDE* is already available to modern audiences in a Latin edition and German translation by Frank and Beyer.[23] Second, the *EDE* was published in revised form in 1550, two years after the Augsburg Interim. As a result of the unfavourable political situation, Melanchthon had removed the more controversial portions of his political philosophy. For example, the 1550 edition of the *EDE*, while preserving many of the discussions of justice in book II from the *PME*, entirely omits those headings having to do with resistance theory—namely the subheading "May Private Citizens Kill Tyrants?" and the entire tract on the magistrate's duty to enforce true religion, entitled *De officio principum*. Thus, the *PME*, unlike the *EDE*, represents Melanchthon's moral and political thought at the moment right before his most explosive political ideas were swept away by the crisis of the Schmalkaldic War and the Interim.[24]

---

23 *Philipp Melanchthon: Ethicae Doctrinae Elementa et Enarratio Libri quinti Ethicorum* (2008).

24 For a good discussion of the changes between the 1546 *Summary* and the 1550 *Ethicae doctrinae elementa*, see James J. Dunn, "The Reformation of Virtue", pp. 176–189.

3.4 Other Translations of Melanchthon's Ethical Works

This volume presents the first translation of the entire *Philosophiae moralis epitome* into English. However, some of Melanchthon's other ethical works have appeared in a variety of modern editions and translations. See the following:

Keen, Ralph, ed. *A Melanchthon Reader*. (New York: Peter Lang, 1988). Includes the first book of the 1546 commentary on Aristotle's *Nicomachean Ethics* (pp. 179–201) and a translation of the 1532 manuscript *Epitome ethices* (pp. 203–238).

Kraye, Jill, ed. *Cambridge Translations of Renaissance Philosophical Texts*. Volume 1: Moral Philosophy. (Cambridge: Cambridge University Press, 1997). This includes selections of Book I of the *EDE* translated into English by John Monfasani (pp. 108–119).

Frank, Günter, with Michael Beyer, eds. *Philipp Melanchthon: Ethicae Doctrinae Elementa et Enarratio Libri quinti Ethicorum*, ed. Günter Frank with Michael Beyer. (Stuttgart-Bad Cannstatt: Frommann-Holzboog, 2008). This work is a Latin edition and German translation of the *EDE*.

Sachiko Kusukawa, ed. *Melanchthon: Orations on Philosophy and Education*. Translated by Christine F. Salazar. (Cambridge: Cambridge University Press, 2012). Includes the dedicatory epistle to the *PME* (pp. 139–143).

4 Edition

Preface

MBW 1890 / CR 3.360 / sig. Aij^{r}

Philip Melanchthon to Christian Brück of Wittenberg:[25]

Among other charges, the accusation against Socrates was that, since he had reoriented the studies of men towards arguments about morality, he abandoned inquiry into nature and rejected natural philosophy.[26] Xenophon decisively refutes this unfair accusation and claims that Socrates had not led men away from natural philosophy, but rather had added to it a more learned doctrine of morals which had been neglected by others, for indeed this [moral] component, most useful for life, also required its own method and art.[27] For although common precepts about morals are broadly recognized, and many of them are born within us, | still, an art and a certain sig. Aij^{v} more learned doctrine are surely needed for discerning many duties, for comprehending the true distinction between just and unjust actions, and for understanding the sources of those actions. One must investigate human nature and consider the order of the parts and which function nature assigns to each of them, and then one should seek the proper causes of actions. Socrates himself, when he discusses providence in Xenophon, gathers and points out the traces of divinity in nature in order to argue not only that there is a God, but that God cares for human affairs.[28] The origins of such arguments lie in natural philosophy.

Therefore, echoing Xenophon's defence of Socrates, when we teach this part of philosophy about morals, | we intend not to lure the youth away sig. Aiij^{r} from the rest of philosophy, but rather to invite them to it. From the very beginning of this work, I have reminded my readers that the doctrine of morals requires an art, and that it is like a stream trickling down from natural philosophy. Therefore, let them consider that no one can become a master of this field without the other parts of philosophy. Moreover, since

---

25 Christian Brück (latinised as "Pontanus") was the son of the influential jurist Gregor Brück, the most prominent legal figure in the early German Reformation. This preface has been previously translated in *Melanchthon: Orations on Philosophy and Education*, ed. Kusukawa, pp. 139–143.

26 Here, Melanchthon's term is *physica* (elsewhere, occasionally *physice*, a more direct transliteration from the Greek). Since this was a broad term that included all inquiries into the natural world, "natural philosophy" is a more accurate rendering than "physics".

27 See Xenophon, *Memorabilia* I.1.11–16.

28 Xenophon, *Memorabilia* I.4.1–19.

this field contains the sources of law and justice, and jurists as well as theologians borrow many precepts from it whenever they discuss morals and the civic manner of life, it must be carefully elaborated, as its vast utility certainly demands, if we seek not the shadow of an art, but solid doctrine, sig. Aiij^v and it must be truly joined to the rest of philosophy. | Accordingly, following this principle, in this *Summary* (although I have tried not to wander too far 3.361 astray), in many places I still have often referred back | to arguments from natural philosophy in order to show by example that these disputations about morals are "maimed and mutilated"[29] without the rest of philosophy.

Further, in this way, I assert that morals cannot even become gentler, nor can that which is properly called "moral" [*ēthikon*], namely moderation and sweetness, even come into being unless common teachings are united with liberal doctrine,[30] which, having refined and habituated us, will allow us to see the true causes of duties, moderate all our actions by reason, and ornament them with a certain kindness and elegance. The power of this subject is so great that, if an ordinary nature is trained and conditioned in this way, sig. Aiiij^r it will become not only much | sweeter in its private manner, but also more moderate and diligent in the weightiest matters of the Republic. For "how many tempests, how many mighty storms"[31] do fools sometimes stir up, for no other reason than that they have not trained themselves with this type of doctrine? They are, as the Greeks say, "without principles" [*anēthopoiētoi*]. Thus, since I already expounded upon Aristotle's *Ethics*, I have also added this commentary in which I follow not only Aristotle's opinions, but his method too.[32] It is true that I have added certain disputations which are more applicable to our own times, which I have indeed collected because I judged them to be profitable to morals, and because they form judgments about many common affairs. They also prepare the students to study civil sig. Aiiij^v law and that part of the doctrine of theology | which contains precepts about civic duties.

I know that some admire other sects. Indeed, some regard the Stoics as if they were demigods. Although Valla[33] furiously inveighs against the

29 *"mutilas et truncatas"*, cf. Aulus Gellius, *Attic Nights* XVII.9.12.

30 *Liberalis doctrina*, that is, humanist studies of the type that Melanchthon taught.

31 A reference to Cicero, *Pro Caelio* XXIV (59).

32 A reference to Melanchthon's 1529 *In Ethica Aristotelis commentarius*. The 1529 edition covered the first two books of the *NE*, but Melanchthon expanded the work throughout the 1530s. See CR 16.277–416 for this work.

33 Lorenzo Valla (c. 1406–1457), an Italian humanist famous for translating ancient Greek authors such as Thucydides into Latin and for proving that the *Donation of Constantine* was a forgery. In 1431, he completed a complex defence of Epicurean philosophy

other philosophers, he still openly praises Epicurus. But I, who have been deeply engaged in these controversies over sects for a long time, having often "turned their arguments upside down", as Plato commands, strongly exhort you students to repudiate the Stoics and Epicureans and to embrace the Peripatetic school.[34] For when the Epicureans and Stoics are zealously defended, and, I might say, broadly advertised, one must mix in much sophistry, according to that [saying] of Euripides, "An unjust argument, diseased in itself, demands wise medicine."[35] Furthermore, false opinions are harmful to morals | and the sophistic style is pernicious in many ways: it corrupts judgment, leads souls away from love and zeal for propriety and plain truth, and shapes one's character to love monstrous opinions | and to strive to obscure matters instead of explaining them. sig. Av^r 3.362

In Aristotle, however, method rules the disputation and, one might say, forces it into certain boundaries, lest it depart from proofs and the correct path. In this way, [method] arrives at true beliefs and explains them properly and in order. Accordingly, because of its true propositions and its model of method, the Peripatetic school is more useful. Aristotle himself says to reject opinions which are of no use for life or morals. So then, many Stoic [opinions] are like this, namely their opinions concerning *apatheia*, Fate, and many others. | When someone boasted that he had listened to Carneades for many years, another man replied that the important point was not how long he had listened to the philosopher, but whether he had heard Carneades as an old man. For later in life, Carneades did not design his lectures for ostentation or applause, but for use and the explanation of things, or, as Plutarch says, "for what is useful and of common interest".[36] Therefore, because in selecting a type [*genus*] of doctrine, one should choose whatever is right, true, simple, sure, well-developed, and useful for life, I think that tender young minds should be instructed chiefly with Aristotle's teaching, which surpasses the other sects in these qualities. And what of the fact that Aristotle's *Ethics* should also be cherished for this sig. Av^v

entitled *De voluptate* (On Pleasure), which was revised over the next two decades as *De vero falsoque bono* (On True and False Good) or *De vero bono*.

34 cf. Plato, *Gorgias* 511A. Aristotle founded the Peripatetic school of Greek philosophy.

35 Euripides, *Phoenician Women* lines 471–472.

36 See Plutarch, *Moralia* 791B. Carneades (214–129/8 BCE) was a member and eventually head of the Athenian Academy, the school which Plato had founded. Carneades was famous as a major figure in philosophical scepticism.

reason: that he alone saw and understood that the virtues are means [*medi-*
sig. [Avi]r *ocritates*]? With this definition, he most wisely | advises that the impulses of souls must be restrained and bent towards moderation.

So then, although I did not have the time to perfect this little book, nevertheless, I did not oppose those who were insisting on its publication because I have included things that are very useful. However, since in my disputations I have often imitated the narrow and childlike formulations of the dialecticians, I have decided to set out the examples of method and dialectical precepts in these more pleasant subjects as well. And I think this manner of teaching is helpful in the schools, for it accustoms the mind to fitness in explaining things, which is a characteristic most necessary in great and weighty matters.

To you, then, my Pontanus, I have dedicated these little commentar-
sig. [Avi]v ies. First, since | I owe so much to your father, a most illustrious man, I thought that this token of my fondness for you would delight him. In addition, because I think so highly of your talent, I especially wanted to write to you to remind you and your peers, our students, that this genus of doctrine is most applicable to the young. For truly, no one can even comprehend how praiseworthy and beautiful is the moderation of character which we
3.363 properly call "moral" [*ēthikēn*], unless | their souls are trained up from youth in this liberal doctrine and they learn to restrain and rule their impulses. Moreover, this beauty can be more easily grasped when, admonished by teachings, we also see concrete examples in which distinguished virtue
sig. [Avij]r shines. Truly, you | have a most perfect example in your own family, namely your father's surpassing virtue and moderation in every duty. To his excellence of character are added the doctrine of many great arts, eloquence adorned with every oratorical honour, and knowledge of governing the Republic, but how much does his crowning honour—that is to say, his actions—add to all these gifts? For he displays a singular moderation and elegance in every endeavour, lending to the other ornaments of his character even more dignity and grace. But although nature's influence is great, still he could not have attained this moral [*ēthikēn*] elegance without letters and a variety of doctrine. You see how greatly he burns with zeal for the highest
sig. [Avij]v arts. To the science of law, in which he excels, he adds so much | study of Christian doctrine that he comprehends it extremely well and cultivates it with the deepest piety. And what great devotion he has to understanding the history of every age! Thus, just as Homer proclaims the richness and abundance of Ulysses' speech such that he compares it to the winter snows, so the eloquence of your father Gregor, cultivated with great richness and variety of doctrine, has earned the highest admiration among all learned

men.[37] The harmony and moderation in his character, which we call "moral" [*ēthikēn*], wondrously magnifies such great plaudits. Indeed, whenever I look at him, it seems that I am beholding one of those ancient heroes who held first place in the Republic on account of their wisdom, learning, eloquence, political skill, moral gravity, and | elegance—a character like the sig.
ones we read about: Laelius, Crassus, or Cicero at Rome, and Pericles and [Aviij]r
others at Athens.

Therefore, my Pontanus, look upon your father, study him intently with all your mind and soul, and when you learn to understand that most beautiful model of morals, strive to imitate him. For although his example is common to everyone, it should still move your soul more powerfully on account of your close relationship. May the gravity of your father's name spur you on! For I believe that certain seeds of these same virtues are planted in you, and you should nurture, enliven, and mould them with art and reason. | At the same time, consider that your father could not have attained 3.364
such honour, no matter how powerful his nature, unless he had polished it with letters and a variety of doctrine. | Therefore, apply every power of your sig.
talent and soul to this doctrine, the most ardent study of which you witness [Aviij]v
in your own home. And indeed, since the Republic should also exhort you to do this with greater diligence, since it has need of these arts and letters for which your father has destined you, prepare yourself with every effort of your soul, so that someday your talents can be of use to the Republic, and you may add your own great services to those of your father.

Farewell. Wittenberg, 1537.[38]

Book I 16.21 / p. 1

What Is Moral Philosophy?

[Moral philosophy] is the knowledge of the precepts concerning all honourable[39] actions which reason understands to be appropriate to human nature and to be necessary in a civil manner of life, having investigated the sources of these precepts with art and demonstrations, insofar as this can

37 Homer, *Iliad* III.221–222.

38 The 1538 and 1539 editions include here a prefatory poem from the German humanist Melchior Acontius (Melchior Foltz, ca. 1515–1569).

39 The adjective here is *honestus*, that is, morally good and upright. In this translation, it has been rendered as "honourable" to signal the distinctiveness of the term.

be done.[40] But the most erudite definition is this: Moral philosophy is that part of divine law which teaches about external actions.[41]

What Is the Difference between Philosophy and the Gospel?

Above all else, it is necessary at first to distinguish among genera of doctrine: namely the Gospel, the law of God, and philosophy. For the confusion of these genera produces horrible errors. However, a comparison is illustrative for understanding each genus, and the true merits of philosophy become apparent in this comparison. For this is the solid and chief merit
p. 2 of moral philosophy: | to understand what is truly part of the divine law and, as Paul says in Romans 1, "The righteousness of God." But one should diligently consider that the Gospel is entirely a different genus of doctrine
16.22 than is philosophy. | For the Gospel's particular subject is the promise by which God, on account of Christ, promises to us the free remission of sins, reconciliation, and the gift of the Holy Spirit and of eternal life. And this promise was divinely revealed, not discovered by reason, just as John [1:18] says: "The Son, who is in the bosom of the Father, he has declared it to us."[42] For without the word of God, reason has not determined that God forgives our sins, and it does not discern that sins are remitted freely. These things are entirely outside of the scope of reason and are foreign to philosophy.

The righteousness of God

The Gospel

Moreover, the law of God is the doctrine which commands us how we should be and what works should be performed before God and men. In other words, it is the doctrine requiring perfect obedience before God. It is not, however, the promise of free remission of sins, nor does it judge that we are pleasing to God when we do not satisfy the law. Now, he who understands the distinction between Law and Gospel will easily compre-

The Law of God

40 For Melanchthon, "demonstrations" (*demonstrationes*), also rendered in this text as "proofs", are the logical outworkings of the first principles (*notitiae*) known by natural reason. In Melanchthon's understanding, every art or discipline, whether it be morals, medicine, or geometry, is made up of demonstrations built upon a foundation of the *notitiae*.

41 Readers may get a sense of the differences between the first and second versions of the *PME* by comparing the text above to the opening lines of the 1538 edition (p. 1): "What is moral philosophy? It is the knowledge of the law of nature and of the conclusions which follow from that in demonstrations, concerning morals and all honourable human actions. For that reason, the precepts about morals have been recalled back to method, or the form of a science or art, so that, whenever the sources are understood, and whenever we have demonstrations, it is possible to judge which precepts are firm, certain, and immutable, and which actions are necessarily required in a man."

42 1546b: *vobis* ("to you").

hend to which genus philosophy belongs, for philosophy is an entirely different type of doctrine than the Gospel. For philosophy teaches nothing about the remission of sins, nor does it show how God approves the unworthy. Otherwise, philosophy is part of divine law. | For brilliant men p. 3
have studied the law of nature itself and arranged it in order. Moreover, it is the case that the law of nature is truly | the law of God concerning 16.23
those virtues which reason understands. For the divine law is impressed upon the minds of men, but in this weakness of nature it has been obscured such that that one cannot fully see those precepts which command adherence to the will of God and order perfect obedience of the heart. But judgment concerning honourable external actions remains, and is born with us, and ultimately it is itself the law of nature and part of the divine law.

Human nature has no greater gift than this knowledge, that is, the distinction between good and evil. In all of nature, this is the most obvious evidence of God, which testifies that humans do not exist by chance, but that they have their origin from some eternal mind which distinguishes between good and evil. And if human nature were perfect, then God would indeed shine through in this knowledge [*notitia*] and the human mind, better endowed with this clear knowledge, would be a much brighter image of God. Great is the dignity of man, because human minds are like a mirror which brilliantly reflects the wisdom of God, namely the wisdom of law. For God especially intended that he be made known through man.

Therefore, great is the merit of moral philosophy, because it is the wisdom of God and part of the divine law, even if it is not the Gospel. But let it be known that philosophy is not merely | every opinion of every p. 4
man, but certain notions [*notitiae*] which are either demonstrations [*demonstrationes*] or their parts, that is, principles or conclusions. For just as other arts have their first principles and demonstrations which cannot be overturned, so in moral philosophy there are certain practical principles from which firm demonstrations arise. And just as arts are the explication of nature, in the same way, demonstrations in moral philosophy are the explication of human nature, as we will show below. Therefore, we should reject those Academics who seek to remove the merit of certainty from the arts, although philosophy, like medicine, sometimes takes up probable arguments, and it falls to the practitioners to judge how far they hold. For those arguments which are at odds with principles should be rejected outright.

May Christians Use This Doctrine?

One may use the divine law or the law of nature; therefore, one may also use moral philosophy [*Ethica*].

I respond: It is clear that moral philosophy is the explication of the law of
nature. Moreover, the law of nature truly is the law of God. See Romans 1.
16.24 Therefore, just as one may use the law of nature or the law of God, | one
may also use philosophy insofar as it pertains to the external and civil manner of life. For we do not use the term "philosophy" to refer to everyone's invented opinions; rather, we [give that name] to propositions which have demonstrations, as has been said.

I. God demands tutelage.

First, then, [this claim] is beyond doubt because God requires and com-
p. 5 mands | tutelage [*paedagogia*], namely so that men may be constrained by
external discipline and become accustomed to honourable morals. Likewise, [he requires tutelage] to instruct men, just as the scripture says: [Galatians 3:24] "The law is the tutor [*paedagogus*],"[43] and God ordains this tutelage with rewards, just as the text says [Exodus 20:12]: "Honor your father and mother, so that you might live long in the land," and he punishes licentiousness. Therefore, this tutelage should not be held in contempt.

II. We owe obedience to the laws of the magistrates, with which this philosophy agrees.

Second, Scripture commands us to obey the laws of the magistrates [Romans 13:1]. Moreover, philosophy agrees with the laws of the magistrates, because both genera arise from the law of nature, just as Aristotle cites the saying of Alcidamas, who claims that philosophy is "the bulwark of the law".[44] Therefore, Christians may use philosophy just as they use the civil laws.

III. One may use the truth in all things, including in this doctrine.

Third, it is clear that truth, that is, the demonstrations of any art, is a gift of God, or a certain light divinely implanted in nature. Therefore, just as one may use truth in arithmetic and geometry, one may also use truth or demonstrations in the doctrine of morals.

IV. Pious yet coarse men may use the law of God and of nature, and hence they may also use this doctrine.

Fourth, there is no doubt that both the pious, if they are coarse like boys,
and other ignorant people should be taught about the law, lest they perform actions apart from the word of God and contrary to natural judgment. Ignorance produced many such acts among the barbarians, such as incestuous desires and other things which, for the sake of example, are told in the descriptions of Cyclopes and Centaurs. And the nature of man is
p. 6 inclined towards license, and it chafes | at the chains of the law, just as we

---

43 In ancient Greece and Rome, the *paedagogus* was the tutor, often a slave, who accompanied young boys from the age of six or seven until puberty. He was a chaperone who was responsible for the physical safety and good behaviour of the boys as well as for imparting some rudimentary instruction.

44 Aristotle, *The Art of Rhetoric* III.3.4 (1406b.11–12).

see men, acting rashly in morals and in religion as if they had forgotten the word and the law, obey their desires, ambition, wrath, hate, avarice, and lust. Moreover, ignorance nourishes and confirms this rashness in men. Therefore, there is no doubt that all ignorant and unlearned men should be taught about the law, just as Paul [2 Tim. 3:16] says: "All scripture is divinely breathed and useful for teaching, rebuking, etc." And when the law is explained, the law of nature should also be demonstrated | because it is 16.25
also cited and approved in the scriptures, as in Romans 1 and 2.

Governing one's morals is a good work among the pious.

So then, learned philosophy is properly and truly the explication of the law of nature, and therefore just as the pious may use the law of God or the law of nature, they may also use moral philosophy, insofar as it pertains to external morals. Moreover, when the pious combine their faith and knowledge of Christ, alongside their fear of God, with this diligence in governing morals, they also present this [diligence] on behalf of Christ and direct it to Christ's glory. In this way, these morals become good works and worship of God. And here, one should learn the old rule which teaches that sins against the law of nature are mortal sins, just as they are done contrary to the express commands of God. From these things, it is clear that Christians may use this doctrine of morals, and that it is useful and dignified, because the law of nature is a light divinely implanted in our souls, and a certain vestige and testimony of God in our nature, and it far surpasses all other arts. | p. 7

What Are the Benefits of This Doctrine?[45]

I. It contributes towards the discipline and tutelage which God requires.

There are many. The first is that [this doctrine] contributes towards the discipline and tutelage which God requires, as has been said above, just as the laws of the magistrates contribute [toward those things]. For this purpose, philosophy is actually more useful, since it is not contained in short statements like the laws are. Rather, it is a long treatment and meditation in seeking causes, considering the order of nature, and contemplating the beauty of virtue. It invites the soul in and renders it more refined, just as the saying goes, "Study produces character."[46] And accordingly, these virtues are properly called "moral" [*ēthikai*]. For moral character [*ēthos*] does not mean fleeting or haphazard impulses, but a certain gentleness and refinement of soul which peacefully moderates the actions, etc. A verse of Menander

Moral character [*ēthos*]

45 1538: "For what is [this doctrine] beneficial?"

46 Ovid, *Heroides* XV.83.

describes this refinement: "How pleasant is goodness tempered with prudence."[47] Just like lions and horses, barbarians and uncultured men often have excellent natural dispositions, but they lack the refinement imparted by doctrine, which renders the soul sweeter and gentler, skilfully bends a person toward decorum in a variety of circumstances, and strives to temper actions with a certain grace. This moderation is properly "moral" [*ēthikē*],
16.26 and | no one can truly attain it unless he is polished by liberal doctrine and
p. 8 erudition. |

Second, there is no doubt that moral philosophy [*ethice*] is useful for the jurists because it contains the sources of law, that is, the primary demonstrations from which the entire doctrine of law is constructed, so to speak. It is the learned man's task to see to what extent the laws have their causes in nature, and [to see] to what extent that very political doctrine, which the jurists proclaim, is an art, and a certain one at that. It is commonly said: "That which disagrees with nature does not have the force of law", and as Aristotle most gracefully wrote, "There is one best constitution: the one which agrees with nature," that is, which does not depart from the law of nature.[48] But in order to judge these things which disagree with nature, some more accurate explication of the law of nature is needed, like the one offered to us in moral philosophy [*in ethicis*].

II. It is beneficial to jurists because it contains the sources of law, and from here are often gathered interpretations and relaxations of the laws, and method itself is helpful.

Moreover, in legal judgments and in interpretation of laws, people often take up arguments, interpretations, and relaxations of the laws from this philosophy, as happens in contracts. Likewise, regarding deeds which are done out of deception or under duress, and in contracts and punishments, the method observed here also helps students then be able to explicate many questions of the law with greater dexterity. Therefore, there is no doubt that students of law should be prepared by this doctrine, and that training in these disputations is greatly beneficial for them.

Certainly, that one speech, *On the Crown*, sufficiently teaches how many things orators should take from [moral philosophy].[49] It contains many remarkable passages taken from a certain more learned doctrine about the duty of a good citizen, and about how considerations of what is honourable
p. 9 should be preferred to private gain. | And because those who plead cases
should be instructed with a great wealth of moral sayings, as they are called, they need this philosophy, for those who are ignorant of method produce

III. It benefits orators, who take many excellent adornments from it.

47 Melanchthon gives this quote in Latin and Greek. I have only translated it once to avoid redundancy.

48 cf. *Nicomachean Ethics* (hereafter *NE*) V.7.5 (1135a.5).

49 That is, Demosthenes' *On the Crown*.

many absurd beliefs, and they adopt ones wrongly handed down by others.

IIII. It is useful for theologians in their treatment of political topics.

Indeed, most of all, this philosophy offers a clear benefit to theologians when it is treated with erudition and prudence. For although the Gospel has its own subject matter which is distinct from law and philosophy, as has been said above, still the theologian must often speak about the dignity of civil affairs, about political laws, about magistrates and governments, and about those morals which are necessary in this civic manner of life. This doctrine will greatly assist him in speaking about such things, as many

It accustoms to method

writings of this age attest. | Yet even if there were no other benefits, there 16.27
is still great profit in being made accustomed to method. Those who are trained in this genus [i.e., moral philosophy] see a model for explaining the virtues, and comparison is useful since it demonstrates the extent to which Christian doctrine agrees with philosophy, and the extent to which it does not. But the theologian should see to it that he does not improperly mix that part which is specific to the Gospel with these civic disputes. Instead, let him keep and preserve the distinction between both parts, which he will be able to do more easily if he rightly recognizes each genus.

That knowledge should be sought for its own sake.

Finally, if the knowledge of the nature of jewels, | plants, animals, and the p. 10
motions of the heavens is worthy and delightful to good minds, how much more should we seek the knowledge of our own souls and of those things which are the most outstanding and beautiful in all of nature? Specifically, I mean how nature itself calls us towards virtue, and how human minds are imprinted with virtue's causes and notions [*notitiae*], which have produced all the laws of the states and govern every honourable duty.

What Are the Differences among the Laws of the Magistrates, Collections of Moral Maxims, and Entire Disputations of the Philosophers?[50]

The laws of the magistrates and collections of moral maxims contain bare precepts without causes and arguments.[51] In contrast, philosophy seeks the demonstrations and causes of these precepts which are placed in nature. Moreover, just as in the other arts, the principal matters, i.e. those contain-

50 1538: "What are the differences among the laws of the magistrates and moral philosophy, or collections of moral maxims [*parainetikous libellos*]?"

51 What I have translated as "collections of moral maxims" is, in Latin, *paraenetici libelli*. Melanchthon here refers to short works of ethical instruction, like the Decalogue and works by the Greek poets Hesiod and Phocylides, in contrast to extended moral-philosophical treatises.

ing the "what" [*to hoti*], are taught first, and afterwards one inquires into the
causes, or the "why" [*dioti*], in the same way, in the doctrine of morals, it is
advantageous to learn first the collections of maxims, including most prom-
inently the Decalogue, and then other [authors] of this type, like Hesiod or
Phocylides.[52] After this, the demonstrations are more easily understood. But
in order to better understand the "what", a liberal education and training
containing many exercises should be added to doctrine so that repeated use
p. 11 would sharpen judgment, just as | Plato says: "One must be trained correctly
from a young age."[53] Indeed, for this reason, the divine law contains not just
16.28 various exercises and ceremonies; it also includes political punishments |
and calamities common to the human race by which God admonishes and
coerces us. As Psalm [32:9] teaches, this is the reason why God imposes
such calamities on the human race: "With bridle and rein he controls their
mouths."

What Is the End of Man?

Thus far, we have provided a preface about this genus of doctrine in
order to distinguish it from the Gospel and to be able to understand the
extent to which it may be proven and what its benefits are. Now let us
start upon the doctrine itself. So then, the very first question concerns
the end, for just as natural philosophy [*physica*] seeks the other causes
of man, so moral philosophy in particular seeks the end of man. There-
fore, moral doctrine is necessary for understanding the nature of man,
because complete knowledge of anything, insofar as it may be attained,
demands an investigation into all causes. Moreover, it is the task of the
learned man to consider here that moral doctrine arises from natural phil-
osophy, because the question of causes pertains first to natural philosophy.
Therefore, just as it is necessary, regarding other things and animals, to
p. 12 investigate the end, or the function, or the | purpose for which things
were created, so it is of the highest importance to investigate this about
the human race: For what purpose or end was this distinguished nature
created? This question concerning the end is the beginning of moral phil-
osophy.

---

52 This distinction between *to hoti* (the what) and *dioti* (the reason why) is drawn from Aristotle's *Posterior Analytics* I.13 (78a.22).

53 Likely a reference to Plato, *Republic* 377a or *Laws* 729a–c.

The end of man according to philosophy is the same as that according to the law: To know and obey God.

Argument

Moreover, below, we shall demonstrate from whence the dissensions among the philosophers about the end have arisen. But first, I shall lay out what should be believed by those who do philosophy rightly and wisely. Because moral philosophy is part of the law of God, as has been said above, the end of man according to the divine law and according to true philosophy are one and the same: namely to know God, to obey him, to illustrate and display his glory, and to preserve human society for God's sake. For the image of God is impressed upon man so that God would be visible and recognizable in it. For the image should display the archetype. Therefore, the end of man is to know God and to display his glory. So then, just as other natures have keen and powerful impulses towards their own ends, just as the sun quickly hastens to complete its own fixed course, in the same way it was proper for humans to have the most ardent impulses to fulfil this end, that is, to illustrate the knowledge of God and to obey God.

Nothing could be thought to be more beautiful than this human nature, if the firm and bright knowledge of God shone forth in it and if there was such
harmony | that all of man's powers obeyed God. But after human nature 16.29
was corrupted | by original sin [*morbum originis*], this knowledge of God p. 13
was obscured and disobedience followed suit. However, that end for which we were created still remains, and some knowledge of the law remains, and reason sees that the knowledge [*notitia*] of God is stamped upon man alone. As a result, [reason] understands that God is the creator, that he is just and punishes wickedness, and that he should be obeyed primarily. Therefore, the end of man should be the same according to both the law of God and true and erudite philosophy.

Therefore, the Stoics correctly said that other things were created for the sake of men, but men [were created] for the sake of the gods, that is, so that God would be revealed through men, so that we would promote the knowledge and justice of God in human society, and so that God would be known in both of these things. Some verses of the poets advise the same thing, like the one that Paul cites in Acts [17:28]. But according to the Gospel, the end is to acknowledge Christ the son of God, to accept the mercy which he offers, and to glorify and obey God. For as it was said above, there is a distinction between the Law and the Gospel. Yet still, in the Gospel, Christ is announced as the end so that in him, God might be apprehended and truly known. Therefore, even though the Gospel preaches about the knowledge of Christ, it still also includes the end which is set forth in the law.

The end of man according to the Gospel is to acknowledge Christ the son of God.

Now, at this point, keen minds may wonder: "What does the knowledge of this end require?" This end should never be abandoned. Every delib-

eration, every action should be directed toward it, and the soul should
p. 14 strive with every effort and impulse | to attain and honour this end. In this way, we should struggle with our entire heart to know God and to obey him, and to display his glory, just as Christ [Matt. 5:16] says: "Let your light shine before men, so that the heavenly Father might be glorified." In prayer, the first thing that we ask concerns this end: "hallowed be"—that is, be truly acknowledged—"thy name and thy word".[54] And there is a most weighty verse from Gregory Nazianzen: "Make God the beginning and end of all."[55]

Here, one should consider how great human weakness is, since it does not contemplate or seek this end as it should. Conversely, [one should consider] how much open fury there is to destroy this end, as if it were even possible to erase it from nature. Such is the madness of Epicurus, and images of this
16.30 kind are also set forth in poetry, as when Euripides' Cyclops says: |

> "I tremble at no deity in heaven,
> But I offer sacrifices to the greatest of the Gods, my belly,
> And I ignore the rest of the Gods."[56]

Thus, when the poets attribute the contempt of God to such persons who have fallen so far from human nature, they show that this vice particularly fights against human nature. But Epicurean philosophy is in fact nothing else than the voice of the Cyclops.

Arguments about the end of man

Now I will include, in the form of syllogisms, the arguments which have been set down above concerning the end of man.

First, the archetype should be seen and displayed through the image. I.
p. 15 Man is the image of God. | Therefore, man is God's image for this reason: so that God would be displayed through him.

Second, the knowledge imprinted on nature is not implanted in minds II.
in vain. The knowledge about God is implanted in man alone. Therefore, man was created specifically to illustrate and propagate this knowledge.

Third, just as in nature the effects are governed by their own causes, III.
so is it necessary that a creature obeys its creator. The mind recognizes

54 A reference to the Lord's Prayer (Matthew 6:9–13). Melanchthon inserts the phrase "and thy word", which is not in the biblical text.

55 Gregory of Nazianzus (c. 330–c. 389), Byzantine theologian and one of the Cappadocian Fathers along with Basil the Great and Gregory of Nyssa. Melanchthon here paraphrases PG vol. 37, col. 908.

56 A Latin paraphrase of Euripides, *Cyclops*, lines 320, 334, 335.

that we come from God, and indeed it sees that obedience is required and disobedience is punished. Therefore, we should obey God primarily.[57]

How Does Aristotle Speak about the End [of Man]?[58]

According to Aristotle, the end is the action of virtue.

Because the knowledge of God is not fully illuminated in man's corrupted nature, Aristotle speaks a little differently about the end of man. For he established that the end of man in general is the right action of the highest faculty in man, that is, the action of virtue, or virtue itself.[59] For he seeks the end from the order and worthiness of the faculties, but if he had inquired into the degrees of actions, he would have found that the best and highest action is to acknowledge God and to obey him, and he would have seen that virtue should be directed towards this end, namely, towards the knowledge of God. Therefore, although that end which we have established above has been established in a correct and philosophic manner, still we will not refute Aristotle's opinion here, lest this subtlety distract the young. But in the meantime, let the students | consider that man is not his own end, but p. 16
that men are created for the sake of God, and that virtue, in itself, is not the highest thing in which the mind should find its satisfaction, but that [virtue] should be directed to something still higher, to the knowledge and obedience of God.

Up to this point, the discussion has been about the chief end, yet there are also other less important ends which accompany virtue. | One may also 16.31
rightly pursue these in their own place, and ends can be joined together, provided that the principal end is not deserted. In fact, it is beneficial that our souls are imprinted with the idea that punishments do not happen to the wicked by chance, but that punishments and rewards are divinely rendered, such that, when we consider the ordination of God, we know that these ends are certain, for God promises rewards for virtue according to that verse [Leviticus 18:5]: "Whoever does these things will live by them." And [Exodus 20:12]: "Honor your father and mother, that you may live long

57 The 1538 edition includes a section here entitled "What is the Use of this Teaching about the End?"

58 Instead of this section and the following section on Aristotle, the 1538 section is entitled "What is the Use of This Precept about the End [of Man]?"

59 See Aristotle, *NE* I.7.15–16 (1098a.16–18). The highest faculty [*suprema potentia*] which Melanchthon references here is the rational nature of man, in contrast to his biological life (which he shares with plants and animals) and his sentience (which he shares with animals). See *NE* I.7.12–15 (1097b.33–1098a.15).

in the land." And on the other hand, it is clear that God carries away to punishment those who commit external wrongs, such as murderers, tyrants, perjurers, and people contaminated by shameful lusts. Yet obeying God freely is not incompatible with expecting a reward or obeying out of fear of punishment, especially if one looks principally to the will of God and seeks
p. 17 utility in second place and less principally. |

What Is the Argument behind Aristotle's Opinion?

The proper action of any nature is that nature's end. The action of virtue is the proper action of man. Therefore, the action of virtue is the end of man. This is an apt demonstration taken from principles of natural philosophy. So then, students should take note here that, after having inspected nature, this argument is taken from reasoning about ends. And since it is derived from true and firm principles of natural philosophy, which are divinely ordained in nature, [this argument] should be recognized as the law of God. For it is for this very reason that the laws of nature are divine laws: because they have been divinely ordained in nature.

What Should One Think about the Opinion of Epicurus, Who Argues That Pleasure Is the End of Man?

It is not useful to morals or to the republic to accustom one's character to defending monstrous and absurd opinions. For it is a sign of a distorted nature to delight in paradoxes which are remote from the common judgments of good and prudent men. This phenomenon arises mostly from petulance or a certain perversity of nature, and then its example is harmful, too, since those who are accustomed in this way then destroy law, religion, and the arts. However, it is characteristic of a noble soul to love simple truth, to flee from absurd opinions which have been disproven by the judgments
p. 18 of good and prudent men, and wholeheartedly | to hate sophistry, which
16.32 some occasionally use to conjure up false opinions, misusing their talents. |
Therefore, Valla is rightly excoriated; for although he ferociously cursed all the other philosophers, he preferred Epicurus alone, who plainly plays the fool (just as he does in all the other parts of philosophy) such that, in his opinion on pleasure, he strays very far from true reasoning and from that end for which human nature was created. For this reason, I will refute the arguments of the Epicureans, which I have diligently assembled.

First. The end is that action to which a nature brings itself voluntarily and without coercion. Arguments of the Epicureans.

Humans are driven to pleasure voluntarily and with the strongest impulse, [but] they can barely be coerced into virtue. Therefore pleasure, not virtue, is the end of man.

The philosophers cannot easily refute this argument because philosophy does not recognize the source of the great disagreement between reason and the appetites in human nature. However, Christian doctrine shows the causes of this disagreement and testifies that the nature of man is vicious and corrupt. Therefore, according to Christian doctrine, there is a simple response to the minor premise, namely that it is only accidental [*per accidens*][60] that in this case, nature, in this corruption, does not obey reason. For if nature were whole, perfect obedience and harmony would exist among all faculties, and the entire nature would be driven towards virtue by a certain perpetual impulse. Therefore, let the students consider here | how p. 19
much philosophical clarity the comparison of Christian doctrine adds, and [consider] which genus seems more pleasant by comparison. Philosophy acknowledges and confesses that there is a horrible weakness in human nature, and that there is a rift between reason and the appetites, even if it does not recognize the cause. But Christian doctrine illustrates the causes.

Moreover, the philosophers can respond to the minor premise in this way: The minor premise should be denied because it is not the entire nature which is driven towards pleasure, but only the lower and brutish part. Indeed, reason or judgment of the mind, which is the higher part, rebukes and condemns the appetites which do not obey, and it has determined that virtue is something more excellent, even if pleasure does not accompany it.

The second argument. Nature desires its own preservation above all else. Pleasure is the preservation of nature; virtue is its destruction, just as Socrates | and other similar great men were forced to their deaths on account 16.33
of virtue. Therefore, pleasure is the end of man.

There is a most fitting response to the minor premise. It is true that pleasure is accidentally [*per accidens*] the preservation of nature. But on the other hand, virtue is in itself [*per sese*] the preserver of nature, because it harms no one and protects others. But pleasure harms others in many ways; in order to look out for itself, it refuses to make an effort towards the common defence and it desires the resources and spouses of others. Moreover, the fact that virtue is not the preservation of nature happens accidentally [*per accidens*] in this | human wickedness. For Seneca's virtue p. 20

60 That is, human nature disobeys reason because of an accidental quality of human nature, namely its corruption. The contrast highlights that nature does not, in itself [*per se*], incline towards pleasure and away from reason.

was not, in itself [*per se*], the cause why he was killed, but [the cause was] the unjust desire and cruelty of a tyrant, who is an enemy of virtue. Again, virtue is the preservation of the species because all good men's labours are directed towards the preservation of common society. On the contrary, pleasure dissolves the entire species so long as each man looks out only for himself.

The third argument. The end should be the ultimate thing in which a nature is satisfied, such that it requires nothing more. A nature which has achieved virtue by a right and legitimate appetite nevertheless still seeks pleasure, that is, safety and preservation. Therefore, virtue is not the ultimate good.

I respond: The minor premise should be denied, for although nature rightly seeks safety, nevertheless, it does not seek it as the highest and principal good, but as a useful good [*bonum utile*], which is an inferior degree [of good] which reason understands indeed to be necessary, but still less excellent than virtue. And virtue should not be abandoned even if it does not result in useful goods, although it most justly deserves them. For example, Themistocles, Scipio, and similar men most meritorious in the republic certainly deserved the amplest rewards, but those most excellent men still judge that one must act rightly even if rewards do not follow. For although Valla strongly argues that all men are motivated by utility and the desire
p. 21 for glory, and | virtue itself says in Xenophon, "the sweetest song is praise of oneself," this is not contrary to right opinion.[61] I grant that glory and the conveniences of life should be sought, but not principally. Reason also seeks these things with a right appetite, but virtue, as the superior end, governs this appetite. That is, utility should not be preferred to virtue, and virtue
16.34 should be retained | even if rewards do not materialize, or even if hardships must be endured, etc. In this way, the sacred scriptures promise rewards and punishments, but they still intend that God be obeyed principally for his own sake. And when the godly do this, they may also seek protection, conveniences of life, or other rewards. For the scriptures promise these for three reasons:

Why rewards are promised.

First, so that we may understand that these things are gifts of God, and, for that reason, that they are also necessary in their own place, and we should recognize that they are to be expected from God.

Second, so that we would exercise faith in seeking these goods and better understand the goodness of God.

61 cf. Xenophon, *Hiero* I.14.

Third, so that we would habituate ourselves to obedience by this tutelage and be restrained by fear of punishments.

The fourth argument. It is better to seek two goods joined together, which constitutes a more excellent good. Virtue and pleasure are the two conjoined goods, for Epicurus wants to join these two. Therefore, virtue and pleasure are the end, not virtue without pleasure. | p. 22

I respond to the major premise. The major premise is true, provided that one preserves the dignity of each good, or the order of goods, that is, so long as virtue is understood to be the principal [good] and is sought for its own sake. So then, one may still seek the fruit [of virtue], provided that the principal good[62] be retained even if [this fruit] does not materialize. Further, if the order of goods is not preserved, the major premise is false precisely on the ground that the principal good is destroyed.

Now I come to the minor premise. Epicurus does not preserve the order of goods, but instead thinks that pleasure is the ultimate good such that he rejects the seeking of virtue that does not generally result in pleasure. That is, having inverted the order [of goods], he places pleasure above all. Therefore, this combination [of virtue and pleasure] does not produce a greater good, but instead it destroys virtue. This is the correct response to this argument, which demonstrates that it is indeed possible to seek two conjoined goods, but in such a way that we do not embrace a lesser good as the principal good. Thus, even the Christian rightly seeks the conveniences of life, but in such a way that he still preserves the principal good even if these conveniences do not follow. Hence, it is easy to understand that pleasure should not be sought as the highest or principal good.

The fifth argument. Christ promises the highest good. Christ promises eternal life and happiness. Therefore, that happiness is the highest good.

I respond to the minor premise, that eternal life is principally a new and
perpetual knowledge of God and | obedience to him. Christ principally 16.35
promises these goods, just as he | claims in John [17:3]: “This is eternal life, p. 23
that they would know you, the true God, and the one whom you have sent, Jesus Christ.” And thus, in the Gospel, we see the true restoration of that end for which man was particularly created, namely that men would recognize God with clear sight, celebrate him, and obey him, just as it was said above. Further, other goods also accompany this highest good: perpetual life and eternal happiness. But in order for us to see the chief end of man, and to distinguish knowledge of God from bodily tranquillity, God subjects the

62 1540: *bonum*. 1546: *donum* (“gift”).

The pious are subjected to afflictions

pious in this life to the harshest afflictions, and he wants the chief end to be retained internally even when bodily tranquillity does not materialize. And he attests that these very afflictions are a training which incites us towards understanding the chief end. Therefore, even if certain dabblers accommodate Epicurus' words on pleasure to the doctrine of tranquillity of the conscience or perpetual joy, these ideas are actually contrary to each other, and sophistic tricks of this sort impede one's judgment.

Arguments against Epicurus's theory

Thus far, I have refuted the arguments which Epicurus' theories seem to support, and from these solutions one may easily evaluate similar arguments. But in the meantime, some strong arguments which overturn Epicurus' opinion should be brought into view. For this purpose, I have collected the following five arguments:

First. The action proper to any given nature is the end of that nature. The
p. 24 action of virtue is proper to man. Therefore, virtue is the end of man. |

Second. The human mind contains the natural and immutable judgement that there is a God and that obedience is owed to him on account of his will, even if rewards or punishments do not follow. Therefore, pleasure is not the end, but knowing and obeying God is. So then, although Epicurus foolishly derides this reasoning, nevertheless, one should ask what right reason demonstrates, not what Epicurus audaciously invented. For it is absolutely disgraceful for a philosopher to dissent from the natural judgment of reason and the law of nature. But Epicurus tries to abolish that judgment of nature and of conscience which clamours in every man: "Be advised: learn justice and do not despise the gods", and "Be assured that the
16.36 gods will remember right and wrong."[63] |

The third argument. The end is that which chiefly motivates the agent. Natural affections [*storgai phusikai*][64] motivate without respect to utility and pleasure. For instance, a father loves his children, but not for the sake of his own utility. Therefore, pleasure is not the end, but rather those very affections [*storgai*] and virtues without regard for pleasure. Moreover, the Epicureans argue with nature on this topic, for they erase the natural affections when they deny that a man by nature desires good for another, but [claim that] he only strives for his own utility and pleasure.

63 Virgil, *Aeneid* VI.620, I.543.

64 Melanchthon frequently employs the Greek term *storgai phusikai* to refer to the natural affections which bind humans to their offspring. Elsewhere, he defines the term as "natural benevolence" (CR 13.541). Below, he refers to the natural affections towards procreation and rearing of children, self-preservation, and self-defence against unjust violence.

Rightly, Aeneas was led by piety, not pleasure (as Virgil says of him), when he approached his father: "Piety prevailed over the harsh journey; it helps me see your face, etc."[65] Valla applies another line from Virgil | to the Epicurean teaching: "Patriotism and immense desire for praise prevailed."[66] He does not see that Virgil connected virtue and reward. For I do not deny that souls are motivated by rewards, but the principal end should be virtue. p. 25

The fourth argument. Heroic impulses, which produce the most excellent actions, motivate without respect to utility. Therefore, we do not undertake the actions of the most excellent virtues for the sake of our own pleasure or utility. Therefore, pleasure is not the end. The antecedent is obvious. For just as Ovid was driven to write his poem by the impulse of his genius rather than by rewards or any external utility, so were Alexander, Torquatus, Scipio, and Caesar all incited to courage not by popular praise or conveniences, but by guiding nature. Therefore, those very same impulses, not pleasure, are the end.

The fifth argument. That which abolishes many of the most beautiful virtues is not the chief end. Looking chiefly to our own utility is antithetical to many outstanding virtues. Therefore, our own utility is not the chief end. The minor premise may be confirmed with many examples, but the most illustrious are those of continence, justice, and friendship. If someone keeps himself from another man's wife solely for the sake of danger, as Epicurus wants, I ask whether, if the danger is taken away, is the immorality similarly removed? Likewise, I ask whether it is lawful to go back on a promise
if no danger will follow? | Likewise, does nature lead us towards helping p. 26
others, or lead us solely for the sake of our own advantage? | In adverse 16.37
circumstances, is it right to desert friends if there is no hope of gain? In all of these scenarios, a sane man's reason judges that he should do the right thing even if advantages and dangers are removed. Therefore, Epicurus's opinion should be rejected, especially by Christians. For Christ preaches so much of the cross, yet in the meantime we still know that the goods of the body may be rightly sought in their own place, provided that virtue remains above them.

65 Virgil, *Aeneid* VI.688. In this passage, Aeneas approaches his father Anchises in the Underworld.

66 Virgil, *Aeneid* VI.823. Valla cites this line in *De voluptate ac vero bono libri III* (Basel: Andreas Cartander, 1519), fol. 52ᵛ.

Are the Stoics Right to Contend That Nothing Is Good except Virtue?

This question is only controversial in its terminology. For the Stoics conceded that life, health, and wealth are all things that should be sought, but they did not attribute to them the name of "good", and they misinterpret the term "good". So then, it does not befit good men to sow "strife over words" [*logomachias*] for the purpose of confusing honest teachings. In philosophy, "good" [*bonum*] signifies something that particularly agrees with nature. Therefore, there are two types of goods. [The first is] natural good, that is, something that is conducive to the preservation of nature or is created for a good use, such as food, drink, health, wealth, and government. Thus, the term "good" includes some ambivalent things. The second meaning is moral good [*bonum morale*], which is in actions, agreeing with nature by the judgment of the mind. The name "good", understood in this way, merely means | "honourable" [*honestum*],[67] and virtue alone is such a good.

Good.

Natural good.

Moral good.

p. 27

In the scriptures, "good" is understood in three ways. First, it is that which God has created or ordained. All so-called "goods of nature" are of this sort. For all creatures are destined for some use and for the preservation of nature. Second, "good" signifies something indifferent [*adiaphoron*], that is, a concession by the law of God.[68] Good is understood in this way when Paul says, "It is good for a man to not eat meat" [Romans 14:21]. Here, good is contrasted with what is prohibited. Third, "good" signifies the actions of virtue which God commands, or the true worship of God, and indeed God's commandments, as the Prophet says: "This is good: to walk before God and to fear God."[69]

Three types of good in the scriptures

However, I do not want to spend too much time refuting the Stoics when both the sacred scriptures and common speech attribute the name "good" to things that are useful. And indeed, the Stoics themselves added a correc-

67 Here I have translated *honestum* as "honourable" to signal the distinction between the terms *bonum* and *honestum*. However, as Melanchthon says below, the terms *bonum morale* and *bonum honestum* are interchangeable and both refer to moral goods.

68 *Adiaphoron* (plural, *adiaphora*) literally means "something indifferent." In Stoic philosophy, *adiaphora* was a category that included external things like money and fame which were indifferent for virtue. In his theological works, Melanchthon famously used the term to describe points of Christian doctrine and praxis which were non-essential and open to debate among various confessional viewpoints. Melanchthon's concept of *adiaphora* would become highly controversial in the conflicts between Philippists and Gnesio-Lutherans following the 1548 Augsburg Interim.

69 cf. Micah 6:8.

tion to their own paradox, because they | decided to affirm the opinion that 16.38
Preferred things [*proēgmena*] useful things should be sought in their own place. Accordingly, they came up with another term, "*proēgmena*", that is, "preferred things."[70] Now, if you ask here why useful things should be preferred, you will still arrive back at the cause: because they agree with nature. And of course, the general definition of a "good" is that it is something which agrees with nature.

Therefore, one should retain the division of Aristotle, who includes under "goods" not only virtue, but also useful and pleasant things, although he
The honourable good [*bonum honestum*]. makes distinctions of degree. He calls that which should be sought for its own sake the "honourable good" [*bonum honestum*]. Virtue alone is the honourable good, | or moral good [*bonum morale*], as it is also called, and p. 28
this degree [of good] holds the highest place. Opposed to this is vice or wickedness, which is called "evil" in the genus of morals, or[71] evil of fault [*malum culpae*]. Next, a useful good [*bonum utile*] is a thing which agrees with nature for the preservation of the body, and which should be sought for the sake of something else, namely for the sake of usefulness. For instance, good health, life, wealth, etc. A pleasant good [*bonum suave*] is related to useful [good], for it signifies that which is sought because it provides enjoyable stimulation to the senses or the soul. These two [goods], namely the useful and the pleasant, are called "things indifferent" [*adiaphora*] in their relation to the genus of morals. Therefore, although they are not goods morally speaking, they are still good things by nature, created for some use that is worth seeking. Opposed to this is the evil of punishment [*malum poenae*], as it is commonly called, according to that verse: "I am God, who makes peace and creates evil" [Isaiah 45:7]. And "There shall be no evil in a city unless God creates it" [Amos 3:6].

This established distinction should be observed, because both in moral philosophy and in religion it is proper to establish degrees so that we would know which things should be sought and in what order. Just as Aristotle thought, we should not applaud those cruel opinions which imagine that useful things should not be sought, and there are certain others who "remove distinctions of things," as Cicero puts it.[72] But the order should be preserved, lest utility be preferred to virtue.

70 In Stoic philosophy, *proēgmena* were those things which were indifferent when compared with the ultimate human end of virtue, but were still preferred in the course of life. For example, beauty, health, and good reputation were all *proēgmena*.

71 1546: *sed*. 1540 correctly reads *seu*.

72 Cicero, *Verrine Orations* 2, II.2.50 (123).

What Is Virtue?

p. 29 Thus far, we have established that the end of man is virtue, | or the action of virtue, as Aristotle says.[73] Now it remains for us to speak about virtue. So then, philosophy has an exceedingly simple and plain definition: Virtue is a habit which inclines the will towards obeying right reason. For there
16.39 are two principal and immediate causes of virtue: | knowledge which governs and will which obeys. As Aristotle says, "Desire must pursue the same things that reason asserts,"[74] because there are certain notions [*notitiae*], divinely placed in the mind, which discern good and evil, and it is God's ordinance that the will obey these right notions. This obedience is called virtue, or the action of virtue. And therefore virtue is, in general, a certain obedience. Therefore, Plato wisely claims that virtue in general is the justice by which man's lower faculties obey reason, and in this way, he defines that universal justice or virtue in general to be concord among all the faculties within a man, that is, [concord] of the appetites towards reason, just as there is a pleasing harmony if the other notes, namely the *mesē* (which is the fifth), the *nētē* (which is the octave), and the double octave all correctly harmonize with the bass, that is, the lowest note. For just as the lowest note rules the other notes, so the mind governs the rest of the faculties.[75] Thus, Plato generally calls virtue that justice in which every part holds together in harmony, that is, the lower ones obey the higher one, as will be said again
p. 30 below concerning universal justice. |

What Are the Causes of Virtue?

The proximate efficient causes of virtue: the judgment of reason and an obedient will.

It is well-known that a habit arises from repeated actions. But one should inquire into the proximate and helping causes [*propinquae causae, et adiuvantes*] of honourable actions. The efficient proximate [causes] of honourable actions are the mind or judgment (commonly called the pronouncement of right reason) and the will obeying that judgment. For in order for there to be some certain structure to virtue, the will must be governed by the judgment of the mind. Moreover, that judgment is knowledge of the

73 cf. *NE* I.7.15 (1098a.16–17).

74 cf. *NE* VI.2.3 (1139a.25–26).

75 This discussion is found in book IV of Plato's *Republic*, which culminates with the definition of justice as harmony between the forces in a man and the analogy between the parts of a man and a musical scale in 443c–e.

law of nature and of the divine law and of all doctrine, which[76] has firm reasons derived from the law of nature and the divine law, or which is an explication of the law of nature and the divine law. Therefore, the Jurist said that "Justice is a constant and perpetual will which renders to each his due."[77] That is, it is a habit of will which is ruled either by natural principles or by laws which are firm and certain because they both are in concord with the laws of nature and have been passed by the magistrate's authority. Yet just as theoretical principles, | such as "The sum is greater than any of its 16.40 parts," are firm and perpetual, so are moral and practical principles also certain and confirmed, although they shine somewhat less brightly in the souls of men on account of the infirmity of the human race, which is easily led away from these principles, such as when idolaters fight with nature, or people | murder their aging parents, etc. p. 31

Three helping causes.

The other cause is the will, the freedom of which we will discuss later. But first, the three helping causes should be considered, namely doctrine [*doctrina*], natural impulse, and habituation or discipline, which includes household instruction and government. For just as these helping causes are needed in the arts, so [are they needed] in morals. Nobody learns music or writing without doctrine,[78] even if we naturally know certain principles. However, doctrine must arouse and illuminate these very natural notions. For we see this among the barbarians, who, because they are not taught, have covered up and nearly extinguished even the common judgment of nature. For example, the Scythians did not consider it wrong to slaughter their elderly parents, for without doctrine it was as if they had forgotten natural knowledge. And as in the other arts, in the same way there is need here for a richer and more developed doctrine, so that souls might more closely consider the precepts and more firmly assent to them. And when doctrine illuminates minds, then the will, captured by the beauty of virtue, more easily obeys. But I will speak only briefly about doctrine, since there is consensus that it is necessary.

Doctrine [*doctrina*]

Natural impulse.

The second helping cause is natural impulse. For just as the poets and other excellent craftsmen are aided by a peculiar impulse of nature (according to the line, "You will neither say nor do anything without Minerva's

76 This and the following relative pronoun "which" (*quae*) are ambiguous and may refer either to knowledge (*notitia*) or doctrine (*doctrina*).

77 Ulpian in D.1.1.10.pr.

78 While in English, "doctrine" has a largely religious and academic connotation, Melanchthon's term *doctrina* embraces the broader sense of education, teaching, or instruction.

assent"),[79] in the same way, outstanding virtue cannot be achieved without a peculiar inclination and impulse towards virtue, like Alexander or Caesar
p. 32 had towards courage and certain other virtues. | These are rightly called "natural impulses" and they are the gifts of God, and it is common to speak of the "heroic impulses", and for this reason, Cicero says: "There has never been a great man who did not have some divine inspiration."[80] The natural philosophers seek the cause of such inclinations in bodily constitution, which the stars somehow affect, but divine impulse still plays a role as well. Aristotle calls these inclinations "natural virtues" [*phusikas aretas*].[81]

However, Plato poses a weighty question: Since virtue is a unique force
16.41 of nature, may it be acquired through our practice or habituation?[82] | We should respond that whether the heroic impulses are present or absent, we can still acquire virtue through our own practice. In fact, one must apply doctrine and practice, which foster outstanding virtues in heroic natures and ordinary virtues in other ones. Thus, even those who do not have excellent impulses, provided they are not endowed with monstrous dispositions, may still be habituated to paint, sing, or write verses in a passable manner. In the same way, the actions of the virtues can also be accomplished to a moderate degree even without heroic impulses. For this reason, God wants all men to be compelled and ruled by laws, and hardly anyone is so monstrous that he has no natural affections [*storgai phusikai*], which are good inclinations towards many virtues and are commonly implanted in men.

The third helping cause is discipline, or habituation, or practice, for these
p. 33 all mean the same thing. So then, we return | to the example of the arts. Just as in learning the arts, practice and experience must be added to doctrine and nature, in the same way, in acquiring virtue, one needs not only doctrine and natural impulse, but also a certain long period of habituation, which produces and solidifies the habit. This principle is obvious, yet still it is surprising how lightly many people treat it, for they apply much less diligence to the formation of their character than craftsmen do to learning their arts. For this reason, in former times, the laws instituted various exercises for the youth, and God handed down ceremonies in his own law so that the people might be habituated through certain exercises. He also added punishments of every type, like a prison, so that there would be an opportunity for exercising the actions of all virtues.

---

79 Horace, *Ars Poetica*, line 385.

80 Cicero, *De Natura Deorum* II.66 (167).

81 cf. Aristotle, *NE* VI.13 (1144b.1–1145a.11).

82 cf. Plato, *Meno*, 70A.

Moreover, there are many extremely weighty sayings about discipline, which would take too long to recite here. Aristides, when asked how he had attained virtue, gracefully bound together the causes, saying: "The main cause is nature, and I diligently assisted it."[83]

Thus far, we have spoken of the philosophical virtues. But in regard to the Christian [virtues], causes should be added: the knowledge of the Gospel and the Holy Spirit encouraging and bolstering human strength. And whenever we will consider how great the weakness of human strength is, we will understand what is lacking from philosophy, and we will love Christian doctrine all the more for showing us the solution to this great weakness. | p. 34
But I will speak more fully about these | causes below, in the question about 16.42
free will.

The Matter in Which [the Virtues Exist][84]

The subject of virtue is the human soul.

The human soul is the subject in which the virtues exist. The matter that [the virtues] are about is called their object. There are distinct objects for distinct virtues.

The Formal Cause

The formal cause is the action itself.

The formal cause of actions is the action itself, that is, the impulse [*motus*] of the will which obeys right judgment. Some impulse of the heart also assists this movement [of the will], as can be observed in the case of terror and other passions, since the heart is the organ of the appetitive faculty, or the seat of the passions, as I will discuss below.[85] So then, when the most precise definitions are built up from formal causes, it follows that the definition which I provided above is the most suitable, namely that virtue is obedience in which the will obeys right reason.

The Final Cause

According to the philosophers, virtue itself is the end which should be sought for its own sake. But it is more accurate to add another end which the law of God shows: namely, God himself. One should seek virtue for God's

83 Aristides was an Athenian statesman and general during the Persian War. Herodotus describes him as "the best and most just man in Athens" (*The Histories* VIII.79).

84 i.e., the material cause.

85 Here and elsewhere, *affectus* is rendered in this translation as "passion." While the modern connotation of that word is largely negative, Melanchthon uses it in a neutral sense. The term encompasses negative emotions like fear and anger as well as more positive feelings such as joy or hope.

sake, that is, in order to render to God that obedience which is owed to him and to illustrate God's glory, that is, to invite others to the knowledge of God. Then there are less important ends, namely, the rewards of the virtues. Rewards are less important ends.
p. 35 For the laws bring murderers and thieves to punishment, | and they protect the just, and God likewise rewards upright deeds with bodily and spiritual rewards. One may seek these less important ends in their own place, so long as one does not abandon the chief end.

Is the Human Will Free?[86]

Now that we have discussed causes, the next step is to inquire into the freedom of the will. Is the human will free? That is, can one obey and reject the judgment of reason? It is well-known that the philosophers and theologians have often raised this question, and it has frequently stirred up massive tumults. For this reason, I will provide a more copious discussion on this topic.

First, then, I shall lay down a true and solid claim. Philosophy does not
16.43 speak of the affections [*de motibus*] | of the heart before God, nor of the interior, nor of the perfect obedience which the law of God requires. Instead, it speaks about the morals of civil life, that is, of a certain moderation of the passions towards men, and about external actions. Concerning these subjects, it should be determined that the human will is free insofar as it pertains to the morals of civil life. Put another way, the human will can in some way obey the judgment of reason and pursue or reject things offered to Human will is free insofar as it pertains to the morals of civil life.
p. 36 it in matters pertaining to those morals, and it can | command the external members to obey the judgment of reason. In this way, it can also somehow moderate the passions and can perform honourable external actions through its own power, without renewal. The sacred scriptures clearly teach and emphasize this doctrine. For they testify that there is a certain righteousness of the law, or of the flesh, or a human righteousness, which men achieve through the strength of their own nature, just as in Romans 9:[31], [where] Paul claims that the Israelites follow the law of righteousness. Without a doubt, he means here that they performed the external works of the law. Elsewhere he says the same thing: "The Gentiles naturally do those things which are of the law" [Romans 2:14]. Therefore, humans must have some certain choice and liberty by which they prescribe for themselves the

The sacred scriptures testify that men achieve the righteousness of the law through their own strength.

Choice, that is, *proairesis*.

86 1538: Sections entitled "Recite the Aristotelian Definition [of Virtue]" and "Why [Aristotle] Calls it a 'Disposition concerning Choice' [*habitum electivum*]" are inserted here before the section entitled "Is Human Will Free?"

duties of the law, for otherwise it would be the case that men could [only] do contrary actions.

The second argument. God commands that all men, even those who have not been reborn, be coerced with laws and discipline. All of this discipline and political ordination would be useless if man could not obey the laws in any way. Therefore, there must be a certain liberty, and for this reason Paul says "The law was laid down for the unrighteous" [1 Tim. 1:9], that is, to restrain them. And "The law is a tutor" [Galatians 2:24], that is, it teaches, coerces, and habituates men. And what would it mean to deny this liberty in external actions, other than to destroy universally every law in states, to allow infinite license for all types of wickedness, | and to dissolve the entire p. 37
society of the human race? Therefore, in order that discipline, good morals, and peace may be preserved and bolstered, it is necessary to teach men about this liberty, so that they know that they can obey the laws in their external manner of life, and [know] that it is God's will that they strive to obey with their entire souls.

Men can habituate themselves to arts; therefore, they have a certain choice.

The third argument. Experience in the arts attests that men can apply and habituate themselves to certain arts and to the various works of those arts. Therefore, it is clear that there is a certain choice and freedom. For otherwise, even the arts would have been revealed to the human race in vain | if men could not apply themselves to them in some way. These argu- 16.44
ments clearly and without doubt demonstrate that the human will has a certain freedom in external actions. And these things which we have said do not contradict Paul's teaching precisely because they add much clarity [to it].

The Stoics.

Nevertheless, not only did the Stoics universally deny freedom in human actions, but they also denied contingency in every motion and event. They contended that everything happens by necessity, and they called this necessity "Fate." Their position should be repudiated and rejected because it is harmful to morals, and it is contrary to many of those most solid arguments which we will recite below. The Stoics did not even defend the necessity of fate with arguments taken from nature or true foundations, | but with p. 38
logical sophistry, summoned from elsewhere and poorly stitched together, which I will recite in order to add clear solutions.

Stoic arguments concerning necessity.

The First Stoic Argument. Two contradictory things cannot be true at the same time. This is true: Cicero will be consul. Therefore, the opposite cannot be true. If [the opposite] cannot be true, it follows that the other statement is necessarily true, that Cicero will be consul.

Solution. I reject the minor premise. For this proposition that Cicero will be consul, insofar as it is a proposition about the future, is not determinately [*determinate*] true. For truth follows the existence of a thing, and just as a thing has existence, so is a proposition true. However, the future does not yet have existence. Therefore, a proposition concerning a contingent future is not yet true, but it is uncertain, because the thing does not yet exist. Therefore, because the proposition that "Cicero will be consul" is uncertain, it cannot yet be inferred that the opposite is impossible. Moreover, even if the minor premise is true by the necessity of the consequence,[87] that is, because it will turn out to be so, still the necessity of the consequence does not bring about necessity simply.

Cicero, in his book *On Fate*, responds to this argument [that everything happens by fate] in this way: he would rather deny that every proposition is either true or false. "I would rather take that hit," he says, "than claim that
16.45 everything happens because of fate."[88] But Cicero does not explain why |
p. 39 propositions[89] concerning | the contingent future are not determinately
true or false. But Aristotle does explain this, as he claims that truth follows the existence of a thing, and just as a thing has existence, so is the proposition true. However, the future does not yet have existence, and it is possible that it will not come to be.

The Second Argument. Connected causes [*causae connexae*] move out of necessity. All events happen by connected causes; therefore, all things happen by necessity.

The Stoics support the major premise, since in natural processes, there is no generation of crops unless the earth is prepared by the sky. The sky does not function unless it is moved, therefore it has a moving cause. On account of this similarity, [the Stoics] imagine that even the will is moved by other connected causes, namely by objects or natural inclinations. This is the second Stoic argument in sum.

Solution. I deny the major premise for this reason: because, although there is some connection among natural causes, nevertheless, no such connection links the will with external causes. For the will is not compelled by necessity, but it acts freely and contingently, and the freedom of the will is the cause of contingency in human actions. Moreover, even non-rational movements have contingency caused by the instability of elemental mat-

87 *necessitas consequentiae*. Muller, *DLGTT* p. 229: "not an absolute necessity … but a necessity brought about or conditioned by a previous condition or by a preceding contingent act or event so that the necessity itself arises out of the logic of the contingent circumstance necessarily being what it is when it is."

88 Cicero, *De Fato* X.21.

89 1546a incorrectly reads *propositionis*. 1540 and 1546b: *propositiones*.

ter, | such as we see in the variable movements of the wind and bodies in p. 40
the air. Moreover, natural philosophy is the usual way of explaining how the natural causes proceed, how they are initiated, or how the lower causes are supported by the higher ones. Even if celestial causes insert inclinations into men, they are still only partial causes, and the will is able to resist them. Thus, Cicero also rigorously disproved this argument of the Stoics concerning antecedent causes [*de causis antecedentibus*], and he denies that the will can be coerced by certain objects or inclinations, or as they put it, by antecedent causes.

These are the principal arguments of the Stoics. Now that they have been explained, similar ones can be evaluated easily. Cicero adds a third argument concerning divine determination, which the theologians somewhat clarified:

Divine determination is immutable, and necessarily true. All things hap-
pen through God, who determines them. | Therefore, all things happen by 16.46
immutable necessity.

Solution.

First, I respond to the minor premise. Divine determination is different in those things which particularly depend on [God's] will and in those things which principally arise from our own wills. In one way, God determines [*determinat*] the coming resurrection and similar things which he has decided that he himself will bring about. In another way, he foresees and
determines human sins, which he permits. | This foresight or determination p. 41
attaches absolutely no necessity to our will; for he foresees things because they will happen, and he determines the extent to which he will permit them. Now I respond to the major premise: Divine determination is immutable and true by necessity, specifically by necessity of the consequence, which does not mean necessity simply. God foresees the atrocities of Saul and he determines the extent to which he will permit them. This foresight and permission impose no necessity upon Saul's will, and likewise Saul is punished because he sinned. But Saul had still had the ability to avoid those crimes. Therefore, logically speaking, the necessity of the consequence does not, in itself, destroy contingency or freedom.

The Stoic position on necessity should be refuted especially because it is detrimental to morals. For instance, Zeno's young slave excused his own sin on the grounds that he had done wrong because he was compelled by his teacher's [concept of] fate.[90] And he obscures God's glory when he

90 cf. Diogenes Laertius, *Lives of Eminent Philosophers* VII.1.23.

makes God the author of sin. Moreover, Euripides clearly says: "If the gods do something wicked, they are not gods."[91]

Disputations of the theologians about Fate.

Now I proceed to the disputation of the theologians, some of whom wanted to deny entirely the freedom of the human will, although in various ways. One approach is that of Valla, who, in utterly Stoic manner, denies freedom on account of divine foreknowledge and determination. But this
p. 42 erases not only | the freedom of the will, but also contingency universally in every action, both natural and voluntary, good and evil. However, the Scriptures distinguish between good and evil actions. And there is an entirely different question regarding all actions in general, not just good actions:
16.47 namely whether | they can be brought about by human will. But I will only say briefly about this first approach that one should consider the will of God which is set down in the word, and one should not make judgments about God's mysterious governance apart from his word. Moreover, God's word testifies that God is not the cause of sin, nor does he will or ordain sin. Therefore, sin arises strictly from the free will of the Devil and of man. Therefore, let us conclude that there is some freedom and contingency, and that contingency and freedom are not erased because of foreknowledge or determination in general. For God foresees and permits sins, since they do happen.

Some verses concerning necessity.

But someone will object with some verses concerning necessity, like this one: "It was necessary for Christ to suffer" [cf. Luke 24:46]. Here, a distinction must first be made. For some events have been ordained by God, namely those which strictly and chiefly arise from God's will, such as the sending of Christ and the resurrection of the dead. Other events have not been ordained by God, that is, they do not chiefly arise from God's will. This
p. 43 category is different from the one above. Accordingly, sins certainly | do not arise from God's will, but from man's will, etc. Therefore, these verses which speak of the divine promises or ordinances, such as "It was necessary for Christ to suffer", have nothing to do with the second category.

Many other verses will be raised in objection. Ephesians 1:[11]: "God does all things according to the counsel of his will." This should not be universally applied to both categories, that is, to the good and evil actions of men, but it refers particularly to actions in the Church, that is, to the sanctification, protection, and glorification of the godly. For we can be sure that these things are motivated, governed, granted, and protected by God.

91 See Euripides, *Dramatic Fragments, Bellerophon*, 286b.7. Melanchthon likely knew this from Plutarch, *Moralia*, "On Stoic Self-Contradiction" (1049E). Melanchthon gives this quote in Latin and Greek, but I have translated it only once to avoid repetition.

Another verse. Proverbs 16:[1]: “A man prepares his heart, but God gov-
erns his counsels.” This saying and many similar ones refer to outcomes,
which should be distinguished from action of the will. For example, Pompey
decides that he wants to go to war, but God can prevent that outcome in
a variety of ways. Therefore, even when a decision or action of the will is
free, still the outcome, because it has many other causes besides our will,
is not in our power. This interpretation helps in prompting us to fear God,
for it warns us that we do indeed have choices, but that they do not come
to fruition unless God supports them. | Therefore, let us be careful not to p. 44
choose something contrary | to God’s will, just as we see that tyrants like 16.48
Pharaoh, Saul, and many others have made attempts against the godly in
vain.

Likewise: [Proverbs 16:4]: “God makes everything for himself, even the impious, etc.” Therefore, God is the cause even of the impious will.

I reject the conclusion, and the reason is, that although God creates nature, which the impious then abuse, God still is not the efficient cause of that impiety or sin. And nature should be distinguished from the movement of the will, which arises from the free will itself. Yet God still for the sake of his own glory tolerates the impious so that some of them might be converted and the punishment of others would display God’s judgment, as did [the punishment] of Pharaoh, Saul, and similar people.

Yet we should be humble when considering and discussing this entire question, because the human mind does not understand the ways of divine governance. But in regard to this question, we should hold opinions that are useful for morals, in agreement with scripture, and accepted by the judgment of good and godly men: namely, that there is divine foreknowledge and determination, but that the human will still has some contingency and liberty. For God is not the cause of sin.

Whether we can achieve perfect obedience.

I will also speak of a second way in which the freedom of the human
will is denied: that is, on account of the weakness of human faculties which
renders us unable | to obey truly the law of God, and likewise to achieve p. 45
perfect obedience. Paul chiefly argues in this way, and he explains what this
weakness of our faculties is, to what extent they can fulfil the works of the
law, and that they cannot achieve perfect obedience. Therefore, when we
argue about the freedom of the will, let us reflect upon ourselves, and in
the meantime let us put aside those arcane disputations about the ways of
divine governance.

Moreover, to this second approach, I respond in this way: that there is a certain freedom to perform honourable external actions. To put it another way, the human will can perform external actions of the law with-

out renewal. For this reason, scripture distinguishes the righteousness of the flesh from spiritual righteousness in order to show that man may perform those works without renewal. This is sufficient for moral philosophy [*Ethice*]. For philosophy speaks of the discipline or honourable external actions which God still requires. Nevertheless, this very freedom is often impeded when it is either overcome by the weakness of our nature or incited by the
16.49 power | of the Devil, who urges our souls towards wickedness.

Therefore, it is difficult to maintain even external discipline, and philosophy acknowledges this weakness, just as Seneca says in his tragedy:

> "So when the sailor propels the freighted boat
> Against the current, his labour goes to waste.
> p. 46 The vanquished ship is dragged away by the rushing flow |
> What reason demands, passion conquers and rules."[92]

Accordingly, on this point it will now be helpful to offer a comparison with Christian doctrine, which displays the causes of weakness and promises help. In this way, Christian doctrine itself becomes all the more delightful when it is also put to use on this subject. And here it becomes clear that moral doctrine [*doctrina Ethica*] is not complete unless it is joined with Christian doctrine, which commands one to acknowledge the blessings of Christ and seek the help of the Holy Spirit against our own weakness and against the Devil. And the promises of help are not in vain, provided that we make use of them, according to that verse: "The son of God came to destroy the works of the Devil" [1John 3:8].

So finally, at long last, this is the very thing which is called "moral" [*ēthikon*]: that is, tranquillity and moderation are produced when souls are illuminated by the true knowledge of God, which imparts true consolation, rules every impulse [*motus*] of the soul, and directs it to the glory of God. Just as Paul says, "Let the peace of God rule your hearts" [Colossians 3:15]. For by faith, in which we declare that God is favourable to us because of Christ, we are heard, aided, and consoled in every affliction, etc.

And because the passions of the godly are ruled by true fear of God and true faith, their impulses are more orderly. Accordingly, David is more morally good [*ēthikōteros*] than Augustus; he is less prideful in favourable conditions because he fears God, he has consolation in adverse circumstances,
p. 47 and he tolerates injustices | with a more even spirit. David's impulses are

---

92 Seneca, *Phaedra* I.181–184.

more agreeable and more active than those of Augustus, although Augustus was also morally good [*ēthikos*].

Concerning interior actions before God.

There is another question concerning interior actions before God, namely concerning the fear of God, faith, love of God, true patience, and similar spiritual actions which are characteristic of the godly. Concerning these, there is a particular question as to whether a man without the Holy Spirit can produce true fear of God, true faith, true love, etc. The | usual response 16.50
regarding these things is that these affections [*motus*] cannot be produced without the Holy Spirit. But there are three causes joined together: the word of God, the Holy Spirit, and human will. For it is useful to direct our minds to the word, because the Holy Spirit is efficacious through [the word] when we support ourselves with the word of God, but the Holy Spirit is not efficacious in those who resist. The will, in and of itself, can reject and even spurn the gifts of God, or on the contrary, with the help of the Holy Spirit, [the will] can resist its own weakness and assent to God's promise. Thus, it was written: "He will give the Holy Spirit to those who ask" [Luke 11:13], but it does not say "to those who resist" or "to those who scorn". On this point, the ancient writers said: "Grace leads the way and the will follows."

From all of this, it is sufficiently clear to what extent the will has some freedom, and to what extent it does not. Certainly, as has been said, there is some freedom pertaining to morals, which moral philosophy [*Ethica*] discusses, and which God also teaches. | However, it benefits the godly tre- p. 48
mendously to add the doctrine about the cause of human infirmity and about the help which Christ offers.

I have now addressed four topics in order: I refuted the opinions of the Stoics; I spoke about contingency in general, and then about freedom in external actions; finally, I addressed spiritual actions. This distinction has shed some light on this controversy.

What Is a Passion?

Thus far, what virtue is and what its causes are have been explained. Now, virtue should be compared with certain related subjects. So then, one related topic is the passions. For in some cases, the passions resist virtue, and in other cases they aid it.[93] And there are many reasons why it is beneficial to consider diligently the sources and nature of the passions. First, it is

93 The English term "passions" usually holds the connotation of negative impulses, but Melanchthon's term *affectus* embraces both positive and negative impulses.

necessary to maintain the distinction between passion and virtue. Second, because the absurd Stoic opinions about the passions are read and because many praise them on account of their novelty, it is helpful to remind the students what they should think about these Stoic opinions. For sometimes they are foolishly introduced into the church, where error produces many troubles.

So then, the term "passion" particularly refers to the appetites of the senses and of the will. Therefore, the beginning of this disputation is the
p. 49 division of the appetites. There are three types of appetites | in human nature. There is the appetite of the nutritive faculty, for instance, hunger
16.51 and thirst. | The physicians call this appetite "natural," and it arises principally from the nutritive faculty, even if, in the case of hunger, certain movements also contribute, such as when black bile stirs up hunger in the cavity of the stomach. Moreover, the organs of these appetites are all members ordered toward nutrition. There is nothing more to say about this first class [of appetites] in this question about the passions.

I. The natural appetite.

The second class is appetites of the senses, such as pain or delight in touching. Then there are the impulses [*motus*] of the heart: happiness, sadness, hope, fear, love, hate, anger, and pity.[94] The third class is the appetite of the will. But the heart also serves the will in stirring up impulses. Therefore, I conjoin the second and third classes in my definition. A passion, as it is properly called, is an impulse [*motus*] by which a sense or the will pursues or flees from something presented to it. In delight or pain in touching, the organ is a certain network of nerves, dispersed throughout all of the flesh under the first layer of skin, which is called the *corium*. But the organ of all the other passions not pertaining to touch is the heart, which in its own fibres [*villi*] either expands, as in happiness, or contracts as if retreating, as in sadness or fear. Therefore, just as the skin is affected by striking it, so is the heart stimulated by things which it encounters that are agreeable or disagreeable. And there are fibres in the heart which are
p. 50 proper to these impulses [*motus*]. | We can admire this indescribable variety of impulses in the heart, although we cannot fully see the causes of such impulses. Hence, therefore, one can in some way understand what a passion is.

II. The appetites of the senses and heart, and the impulses.

III. The appetite of the will. What is a passion?

---

94 As Melanchthon goes on to explain below, a *motus* refers to what, in modern English, would be called emotions (such as anger, hate, or happiness). In Melanchthon's understanding of human anatomy, these emotions are caused by specific impulses or movements of the heart. Thus the term *motus* contains both the more general meaning of "emotion" and the more technical sense of "movement" or "impulse".

Whether the passions are natural impulses or violent ones?

Galen asks whether [the passions] are natural impulses, or violent [*violenti*] ones. Speaking of the moderate [passions], he responds that these are natural impulses, that is, they have absolutely no external origin.[95] However, the immoderate [passions] corrupt nature like an unrestrained flow. But beyond the passions, there are two other impulses of the heart: the pulse of the arteries and the *palmos*, or heartbeat, which are entirely distinct from the passions. And a passion should not be understood to be a species of these two impulses, because it is a species distinct from them.

Should Stoic *Apatheia,*[96] Which Entirely Erases the Passions from Nature, Be Affirmed?[97]

Two types of passions. Some of them are good, like the affections [*storgai*].

By no means. For there are two types of passions. Some of them agree with reason, such as love for one's spouse and children, benevolence towards those who are well-deserving, pity | towards victims of calamity, and wrath 16.52
against those who cause harm. These passions are good and they are called "natural affections" [*storgai phusikai*]. They would have been present in human nature even if it had not been corrupted by original sin. And these passions are impulses towards virtue, and they produce virtues when | the p. 51
judgment of reason is added to strengthen them. For just as it is easier to spur on a horse which is already fast in itself, so is it easier for reason to direct the will which is aided and stimulated by a good passion. In this way, then, virtue is finally perfected at that point when will and passion equally obey reason. Thus, let it be known that not all passions are opposed to virtue, but that some of them are the cradles or supports of the virtues. Other passions are opposed to reason and the law of God, since they desire another person's goods. Such impulses are vicious. So then, later, I will discuss from

---

95 In the *Summary of Moral Philosophy*, Melanchthon makes several references to the anatomical theories of the ancient physician Galen, whose Greek works had been published in Venice in 1525. Melanchthon's first edition of his *Commentarius de anima* (1540) also relied on Galenic anatomy. In 1543, Andreas Vesalius' *De humani corporis fabrica* offered a new account of human anatomy based on direct empirical observation. Melanchthon eagerly read and annotated Vesalius' work and incorporated Vesalian anatomy in his 1552 revision entitled *Liber de anima*. Melanchthon's knowledge of Vesalian anatomy, however, postdated the 1540 revisions of the *Summary of Moral Philosophy*, and thus did not influence this work. For an overview, see Vivian Nutton, "Wittenberg Anatomy" in *Medicine and the Reformation*, ed. Cunningham and Grell (1993).

96 In Stoic philosophy, *apatheia* was a state of freedom from passions, and was understood as a chief component of the flourishing life.

97 1538: "Should Stoic *Apatheia*, Which Simply Rejects All Passions, Be Affirmed?"

where this disparity among the passions arises. But first, the Stoics must be refuted, and it must be proven that the passions should not be erased from human nature, and that they are not mere flights of fancy, but that they exist naturally in men.

This is the first argument. God did not create the organs of the passions in living creatures in vain. The organs of the passions naturally exist in men. Therefore, the passions also exist in nature, and they are things divinely created in human nature. The minor premise is clear from the nature of the nerves, which are organs of pleasure and pain. For the nerves were divinely created; therefore, their action is a natural thing and should not be erased from nature. The argument against Stoic *apatheia.*

Likewise, the impulses of the heart are natural, and they are ordered such that they are incited by the different motions of the fibres [*villi*], and such
p. 52 that the different humours serve different impulses. In wrath, the impulse | of the heart stirs up yellow bile. In sadness, the impulse of the heart stirs up from the spleen black bile which is poured out in sorrow and often causes abdominal pains. In fear, the blood rushes back to the heart. These impulses are established in nature. Therefore, the passions are also established in nature.

The second argument. The gifts which proceed directly from God are good things and should not be discarded. The heroic impulses are particularly gifts of God, and they proceed directly from God. Heroic wrath is like
16.53 this; for instance, when Skanderbeg was about to fight, | blood would spout from his lips,[98] and as Virgil says of Aeneas, "A great wrath rose up in him."[99] Therefore, the passions are not just flights of fancy, nor should they be entirely erased from nature.

The third argument. Divine law commands us to have passions, as [when it says] "Love the Lord your God" [Mark 12:30] and "Love your neighbour" [Mark 12:31]. And Paul lists "lack of natural affection" [*astorgia*] among the most odious vices [2 Timothy 3:3], that is, being unaffected by the favourable or adverse conditions of those close to you. Therefore, some passions are good and pleasing to God. For this reason, Stoic *apatheia* should be repudiated because it contradicts both nature and the word[100] of God. Therefore, even if the harsher beliefs of the Stoics occasionally garner praise, the wise

---

98 Gjergj Kastrioti (1405–1468), also known as "Skanderbeg", was an Albanian commander who led a rebellion against the Ottoman Empire.

99 Virgil, *Aeneid* XII.108.

100 1546b: *verdo*. Other editions correctly read *verbo*.

reader should still apply judgment and know to flee from absurd opinions
which disagree with nature and the word of God.

In actuality, the good passions are established in nature to be the spurs,
or, as Aristotle says, the aids, of virtue. But the evil passions, | that is, the p. 53
ones which depart from reason and the law of God, must be resisted. The
teachings of the sacred scriptures should be understood wisely, lest they
be applied to Stoic opinions. For although scripture demonstrates that all
passions in an ungodly man are vicious, still it intends that a distinction
be maintained, namely that only some [passions] are entirely vicious in
themselves and should be rejected. But the other passions, which are div-
inely implanted, have been polluted by that disease of corruption which
is in human nature. For instance, Alexander possessed many good pas-
sions and heroic virtues, but because he lacked the fear of God and faith,
these other gifts did not please God. He also added vices: he did not give
thanks to God or acknowledge God's presence, he relied on his own abilities,
he sought his own glory, and he rushed headlong into every wickedness.
But the good natural passions are praised in godly men because they also
possess the fear of God and faith by which it happens that other good
works become pleasing. Therefore, it is easy to respond to these objec-
tions.

Theological objections

The senses of the flesh are death. Likewise they are enmity towards God.
Therefore, all passions are vicious.

Response: I concede the conclusion. All [passions] are vicious. Some [are
vicious] in themselves [*per se*], others accidentally [*per accidens*] because
good [passions] are polluted in various ways and are not directed to the
end to which they are obligated, namely, that obedience be rendered to
God. | Finally, they are not pleasing to God without fear and faith. Let us 16.54
be content with this simple and plain solution, although another may be
added: Every passion of the fleshly nature is vicious before God without
faith and without the Holy Spirit, because the fleshly nature | either care- p. 54
lessly despises the wrath of God or rages and despairs in genuine terror
at God's judgment. But this solution is a bit obscure. For this reason, let
us use the prior one. This is how one should respond to the statement,
"Every thought of the human heart is prone to evil at all times. Therefore,
all passions are evil." Response: I concede the conclusion. Some [passions
are evil] in themselves; others accidentally. However, this is not consistent
with the Stoics, since the Stoics want to destroy all passions, good or evil. On
the contrary, the law of God demands good passions: fear of God, faithful-
ness, tenderness, love towards one's spouse and children, and other pious
impulses.

From where the great discord among the passions within man [originates].

Hence it is easy to understand that Stoic doctrine, even on this topic of the passions, diverges widely from Christian doctrine. But this great wonder captivates the philosophers: From where does the great discord among the passions within man originate? Other natures do not fight with themselves, but they obey those laws which are divinely imposed upon them. The sun follows its course in order. Beasts have impulses which agree with their own natural inclinations. It is only men who do not obey those laws which God placed within them. Christian doctrine alone explains the cause of this discord, illustrating that original sin [*morbum originis*], that is, the corruption of human nature, is the cause of this discord. For if human nature were not corrupted by inborn vice [*vitio originis*],[101] every passion would obey the law of God and the judgment of right reason. For humans were
p. 55 created for this obedience, | just as birds were created for flight and fish for swimming. But because human nature has been corrupted by inborn vice, it has lost a firm and clear knowledge of God as well as obedience and harmony of the faculties within itself. As a result, the human mind now, in itself, has doubts about God and lacks the fear of God, faith, etc., and there is disobedience among the lower faculties which produces endless inordinate desires which disobey the law of God. Yet in the meantime, some good passions still remain, and they operate concerning those matters subject
16.55 to our senses, namely, in matters concerning civic conduct. | Even if these [good passions] have been contaminated by the contagion of evil, still they are certain natural impulses and gifts of God, just like the true notions of those things which are subject to reason.

Christian doctrine illustrates this cause of the vicious passions, and it should be cherished all the more because philosophy, although it examines the weakness of nature, still does not root out its cause. Therefore, on this point, [philosophy] is aided by Christian doctrine, which both shows the cause of this sickness and presents the cure of which the Gospel preaches.

In the fifth book of Galen's *The Doctrines of Hippocrates and Plato*, there are some elegant verses, which he says are from Cleanthes, which describe the conflict of reason and the passions. For Reason says this to Passion:

> Reason: "Pray tell me, what is it that desire wants?"
> Passion: "That I would do everything that I want, for that is worthy of kings."

---

101 *vitium* has the meaning of both "vice", in the technical moral-philosophical sense, as well as the broader sense of "defect" or "imperfection".

Reason: "Explain this again to me more clearly."
Passion: "That whatever I desire would come to be."[102]

These verses | most clearly depict the inordinate and rashly errant impulses of the soul. Therefore, the weakness of nature must be acknowledged, so that reason might resist it and use its own strength, as well as the help of Christ, and shape and support good impulses. p. 56

What Does Aristotle Think about the Passions?[103]

Aristotle adds the judgment of the mind as a governor over the passions, which he says are necessary in nature, and he commands it to call them back to the mean.

Living things would not be able to pursue what is fitting or flee from what is contrary unless they possessed appetites and passions. Just as pain moves a beast to flee from excessive heat or cold, so Aristotle understands the passions to be necessary in nature, and he does not want them to be erased from human nature. Still, because he understands that they are disordered, dissimilar, and in conflict with each other, although he does not clearly perceive the cause of this discord, he merely adds a charioteer or helmsman, namely the judgment of reason, and commands that all [of the passions] be called back to the mean, lest either he erase the appetites | entirely from 16.56 human nature, or the passions themselves escape their bonds. Therefore, he says that wrath is the accomplice of courage, but that it should be deployed as a soldier, not as the commander. This is because he understands that these impulses are given to men to be useful in this way: to be either tools or goads towards virtue, provided that they are governed rightly. This position of Aristotle's is fitting for civic morals. For the laws also need this step to coerce the passions, since they do not punish the passions apart from | p. 57 actions; they only punish deeds, just as it is said: "No one is punished for a thought."[104] And Homer depicts Achilles in this way; when Achilles drew his sword in wrath against Agamemnon, Athena dragged him back by the hair so that he would not commit a crime worthy of punishment while overcome by rage.[105]

102 Galen, *The Doctrines of Hippocrates and Plato* V.6 in *Claudii Galeni Opera Omnia*, ed. Kühn, (1821–1833), vol. V, p. 476.

103 Before this section, the 1538 version includes a separate section entitled "From Whence Arises this Disparity of Passions in Human Nature". This section was revised and included under the previous heading in the second version.

104 Ulpian in D.48.19.18.

105 Homer, *Iliad*, I.188–214.

Moreover, the Christian doctrine concerning the passions is entirely clear. It commands the good passions to be ruled by the law of God and the divine order of things to be maintained, as it commands that a spouse, children, and friends be loved, but in such a way that God is more important. Further, it commands that the evil passions, namely those which dissent from the law of God, be resisted, because even the vicious passions cannot be entirely purged from the soul in this life. Yet obedience in those who believe in Christ and fight against the vicious passions is still pleasing to God, according to [Romans 8:13]: "If by the spirit you put to death the actions of the flesh, you will live, etc."

Recite[106] the Definition of Virtue Handed down by Aristotle[107]

"Virtue is a disposition concerning choice, consisting in a mean with respect to us, according to some principle, that is, as a wise man judges."[108] "Concerning choice" [*electivus*], that is, acting deliberately and willingly. For choice [*proairesis*] encompasses both knowledge or judgment of the mind and the choice of the free will. For Aristotle creates degrees of action, which, although they are similar in appearance, still differ in the things themselves.
p. 58 For example, Cato's harshness is similar to courage, although it is a long way |
from virtue. Lentulus, Scipio's successor, imitates Scipio's courage, although
16.57 the difference is enormous.[109] Therefore, Aristotle derives the distinction |
from causes, namely because in some cases, knowledge is incorrect, or judgment is lacking, or the will is not particularly present in the duty. Therefore, there are these degrees of actions: some are by nature [*phusei*]; some by belief [*doxa*]; some by wish [*boulēsei*]; and some by choice [*proairesei*].[110]

"Concerning choice"

Degrees of actions.

106 *Recita*: the verb is in imperative form, signaling that this work was a teaching document intended to guide students through various arguments about moral philosophy.

107 In the 1538 version, a version of this section appears before the heading entitled "Is Human Will Free?"

108 Melanchthon provides an approximate Latin translation of Aristotle's definition of virtue in *NE* II.6.15 (1106b.36–1107a.2). Melanchthon's translation reads "*Virtus est habitus electivus in mediocritate consistens, quo ad nos, ratione aliqua, ut sapiens iudicat.*"

109 After Scipio Africanus' successful campaign against Carthage in Spain, he returned to Rome in 205 BCE, leaving Lucius Cornelius Lentulus in command in Iberia.

110 This seems to be loosely based (with significant departures) upon Aristotle's discussion of *proairesis* in *NE* III.2. (1111b.4–1112a.17). Among other changes, Melanchthon interprets Aristotle's category of *boulēsis*, usually understood as "wish", as false pretence of virtue. He also collapses Aristotle's category of "desire" or "passion" (*epithumia* or *thumos*) into the single category of nature (*phusis*).

Nature [*phusis*]. *Phusis* means the inclination of nature apart from judgment, with this distinction, that some people are by nature aggressive, and others are sluggish. Cato is by nature obstinate and harsh.

Belief [*doxa*]. *Doxa* means belief, as when men assent to some opinion apart from correct judgment or when they are moved by false belief. For instance, Brutus had been tainted by Stoic teachings. He held up the example of Cato, and because he wanted to be similar to him, he strove to become harsher and less restrained.

Wish [*boulēsis*]. *Boulēsis* means pretence [*simulatio*].[111] For example, Thraso feigned courage, Domitian feigned clemency, and so on and so forth. These degrees differ from virtue because the complete causes of virtue are not united.

Choice [*proairesis*] So then, there is a fourth degree, choice [*proairesis*], when something is done with right judgment and willingly. For example, Fabius is courageous. He understands when he should retreat and when he should fight, and he does not flee from danger when it is necessary.[112] Moreover, knowledge of the divine command and of our vocation is relevant to right judgment. | p. 59 Additionally, there are two types of virtue: common and heroic. Heroic virtue is when great men are spurred to certain honourable actions by a special divine impulse. From this arises outstanding virtue beyond the common capacity of men. As such, there was heroic courage within Achilles, Alexander, Caesar, and Scipio, that is, [courage] which exceeded that which can exist in men without special divine impulse. Therefore, although choice produces common virtue, nevertheless, for that surpassing virtue which is called "heroic", one needs a special divine impulse, which aids choice. That is, [the divine impulse] renders the mind clearer in judgment and makes the will more lively, just like how in the arts, the heroic artist stands far above the middling artists, as in music Josquinus far surpassed the common musicians.[113]

---

111 The Greek term *boulēsis* is usually translated as "wish", but Melanchthon here identifies Aristotle's category of *boulēsis* with a sort of caricaturized, false version of virtuous action. For example, Thraso, whom he mentions here, was an obnoxious and bombastic character who appears in Terence's comedy *Eunuchus*. Melanchthon appears to mean that someone like Thraso projects a blustering pretence of courage, but does not possess actual courage.

112 Quintus Fabius Maximus Verrucosus, also known as Cunctator (the delayer) was a famous Roman general of the second Punic War who led the Roman response to Hannibal's invasion of Italy. Fabius famously waged a cautious war of attrition and avoided direct engagement.

113 The French-Flemish musician Josquin des Prez (ca. 1450–1521) was widely considered one of the greatest musical composers of the Renaissance.

16.58 And these people are blessed, even if they occasionally do something extraordinary, just as the Greeks say that Hercules shattered the oars of that ship, the Argo, while he was rowing, and for that reason he no longer applied himself to rowing. Pindar most sweetly says this about heroic virtue: "With God's prompting, the beginning is pleasing and the end sweet."[114] And such are the virtues of the saints, which the Holy Spirit stirs up, as [the virtues] of Abraham, David, Paul, and others. It is most useful to maintain these degrees of actions and virtues, | p. 60 for the similarity among actions often deceives the careless, as the harshness of nature misled Cato to be the instigator in sparking a civil war.[115] The imitation of Cato misled Brutus, the imitation of Sulla deceived Catiline, and the imitation of Caesar misled Antony. It often happens that weak character, outside of its own vocation and beyond its strength, does not correctly strive to emulate great men.

The virtues of the saints are heroic.

Why Does [Aristotle] Say "Consisting in a Mean with Respect to Us"?[116]

I respond: There are two types of mean. The first is according to the arithmetic proportion, namely where the terms are simply separated by the same interval, as in 1, 2, 3. These terms are all separated by one, and the second number exceeds the first simply by the same amount by which the third exceeds the second. This is perfect and immutable equality. Although this idea fits with commutative justice, as we will hear below, nevertheless, it does not fit the other virtues, as temperance does not demand the same measure of food for each person, but a hearty youth should eat more than a sick elderly man.

Arithmetic Mean

So then, there is another mean according to the geometric proportion, in which one does not ask whether there are equal intervals between the terms. Instead, there is a comparison of many things and numbers, and an equality of proportion is established, just as 4 and 2 | p. 61 have the same proportion as do 10 and 5. Here, the proportion is similar, but the intervals are not equal. And this proportionality is the mean of which Aristotle speaks here, the thing which he calls "a mean with respect to us," namely, [a mean] derived from the circumstances and comparison of them. And this fits with many virtues, as for instance in charitable giving, when | 16.59 a poor man will give a small amount, but a richer man will give more in accordance with his

Geometric Mean

114 Pindar, *Pythian Ode* X.10–11.

115 i.e., Cato the Younger.

116 This heading is absent in the 1538 version.

resources. In this way, [Aristotle] intends to establish a mean by comparing proportions.

The courage of Fabius is different from that of Marcellus. Fabius saw that his fresh recruits should not be thrown into battle against Hannibal's superior veteran troops, especially because the state was hard-pressed and exhausted. But a little later, since the state had more spirit and strength, Marcellus never[117] refused a fight, for it was also the case that Hannibal's troops were at that time weaker and the general himself was hated on account of his dishonesty and cruelty. Therefore, although both men were courageous, nevertheless, the one was closer to being fearful and the other closer to being rash, but both preserved the proportional mean, because just as Fabius' times called for delaying,[118] so did later circumstances demand aggression.

Innumerable examples can be gathered, but from the ones which I have recited, it is clear enough how the circumstances alter this mean. In the same way, doctors seek a mean, as for instance when, in accordance with proportions, they prescribe exercise to some bodies | and rest to others. p. 62
The jurists also frequently gather a mean from the circumstances, and they want [the circumstances] to be accounted for when they order the mean to be taken up broadly [*en platei*]. So then, let the students consider how praiseworthy Aristotle is, since he alone defined the virtues as means. For it is most useful in life for men to be habituated to moderating the impulses of their souls and confining them between certain boundaries, as if with a bridle.

It is a most sophisticated thought that the virtues are means. For the formal [cause] of a virtue is the moderation of its passion, as the action of courage is the very moderation of fear, that is, not succumbing to or being disturbed by anguish in such a way that, being overcome by anguish, we act contrary to nature or justice. Therefore, the learned praise this definition highly. Let the students be reminded of Isocrates' saying: "Because it is difficult to attain a mean, it is better to err on the side of less rather than more",[119] just as in the geometric proportion, the middle number is closer to the lower one than the higher one, as in [the sequence] 1, 3,
9. | 16.60

117 1546: *nunquam* (never); 1540: *nusquam* (nowhere).

118 1540 and 1546: *contationem*, i.e. *cunctationem*.

119 Isocrates, *To Nicocles* 33.

Was Plato's Saying That "Nobody Is Willingly Evil" Correct?[120]

I respond: Plato is absolutely not talking about external actions. He does p. 63 not deny the freedom of the will in | external actions, and he does not think that humans commit wicked deeds from necessity or that the passions cannot be restrained. Rather, he thinks that there is a certain astounding division within man, namely between judgment, or reason, and the passions, or weakness, which resists the judgment of the mind, and indeed [he thinks] that many men do have natures that are badly tempered, distorted, and difficult to control. Antony had this kind of innate intemperance, or Catiline this kind of innate cruelty. Therefore, Plato said: "Men are not willingly evil,"[121] that is, they have inclinations which both resist reason and are born within their bodies, and these [inclinations] can be controlled with difficulty, according to that saying: "Everyone follows the seeds of his own nature."[122] And in that disputation in the *Timaeus*, the main point of discussion is that distorted temperaments are the causes of many vices, and that those vicious inclinations in temperaments are confirmed by bad training and intemperance.[123]

Moreover, Plato certainly does not deny the freedom of the will, seeing that he commands those vicious natures to be reined in by laws, discipline, doctrine, and good training. Therefore, it is clear that Plato truly attributes freedom to the will in governing external actions, even if this weakness in men is not of external origin. And Galen cites this saying of Plato in his book entitled *That The Soul's Character Depends on Bodily Temperament*, where p. 64 he most brilliantly discusses the causes of actions.[124] | Therefore, this is the true meaning of Plato's statement. Accordingly, he should not be twisted to deny the freedom of the will.

---

120 1538: "Was Plato Right to Say that Men are Evil Unwillingly?"

121 Plato, *Timaeus* 86d–e, cf. *Protagoras* 345d–e.

122 Propertius, *Elegies* III.9.20.

123 See Plato, *Timaeus* 86B–87C.

124 Galen reproduces numerous quotes from this passage of the *Timaeus* in *The Soul's Traits Depend on Bodily Temperament* 789K–791K.

The Division of Virtues[125]

The virtues are governed by the judgment of the mind. Therefore, the vari-
ous species [of virtue] will have to be derived, as if from a cause, | from those 16.61
notions [*notitiae*] which govern them. For diverse causes beget diverse species. Moreover, those notions are principles or practical conclusions, that is, ideas which are naturally known, which are called the laws of nature, and which govern honourable actions towards God and towards men. No order could be established or imagined which would be more fitting than the Decalogue, which we should recognize as the sum of all laws. Therefore, it is easy to enumerate and distinguish [the virtues] according to the Decalogue. To the first table pertain the virtues by which we interact directly with God. But philosophy or natural reason cannot teach what is needed about this genus of virtue, because natural reason only knows some teachings of the law, and indeed it is entirely ignorant of the Gospel of the free forgiveness of sins. Therefore, [natural reason] cannot teach anything about faith or faithfulness towards God, and in the course of life, it is greatly beneficial to understand the weakness of human nature in this matter, so that we would learn these virtues elsewhere and exercise faith by the call of the Gospel in prayer and other pious practices.

So then, these are the true virtues | which Christian doctrine teaches, p. 65
which pertain to the first commandment: fear of God, faith, love of God, and obedience in divinely imposed afflictions. [Those which pertain] to the second [commandment]: prayer, thanksgiving, confession, preaching of the Gospel according to one's calling, keeping of vows. To the third [commandment]: the observation of ceremonies, reverence, and preservation of the ministry of the Gospel. Moreover, it has been said elsewhere how far natural reason or philosophy can go, namely, to command us to acknowledge that there is one God, the creator and ruler of nature, who is wise and just. Likewise, that God has endowed us with certain honourable notions, according to which reason commands us to obey God. Likewise, [reason] understands that atrocious deeds are divinely punished, it commands that oaths must be honoured, and recognises that there is need for certain ceremonies. Therefore, philosophy only provides a partial teaching about certain duties of reverence, but it teaches nothing of faith. I have covered these things very briefly in this way because the topic demands that the students be reminded

125 The appendix to this text contains a translation of Melanchthon's 1538 section entitled, "What is the Division of Virtues?" In the 1540 revisions, that section was replaced by the text presented here.

here about the distinction and series of virtues, and about what is lacking in philosophy.

Now I arrive at the second table. To the fourth commandment pertains universal justice, that is, universal obedience to the magistrates or the laws and piety towards parents, children, etc. To the fifth [pertain] particular justice, which warns us not to afflict injury upon another person's body, as well as gentleness and courage. To the sixth [pertain] chastity and temper-
p. 66 ance. | To the seventh [pertain] particular justice, which warns us not | to
16.62 steal another's property, as well as generosity. To the eighth [pertains] truthfulness, which safeguards trust in agreements and contracts and forbids mendacity in all speech and insidious dissembling in every action.

It is profitable to distribute the virtues in this way according to the Decalogue. For this enumeration is very simple, and the arrangement found in the Decalogue is the most fitting and it has learned demonstrations. The philosophers derive the laws of nature by considering man's particular causes [*causae*] and effects [*effectus*],[126] since the causes demonstrate that there is a God, that God is the creator of the human race, that God is just and punishes atrocious deeds, and that God should be obeyed as creator. These notions beget all human or natural reverence towards God, which the philosophers also call "religion". For they must admit that reverence towards God is the primary virtue, even if philosophy cannot instruct us as needed about these virtues by which we deal directly with God. Rather, as has been said above, the Gospel preaches about these virtues.

Moreover, the philosophers also derive universal justice from notions about God. For reason understands that this distinction between good and evil is divinely implanted in our minds and that God should be obeyed according to that [distinction]. Therefore, universal justice is obedience to
p. 67 God | according to all of these honourable notions.

Then, most of the laws which govern the remaining virtues are derived from the effects [*effectus*], since the effects demonstrate that we are born for procreation, for the preservation of our children, and for society. Hence come these laws: Children should be protected. Society should be preserved,

---

126 In Melanchthon's theory, knowledge of causes provides information about man's purpose and end. For example, recognising that God is the final cause of human existence leads a person to understand that he must worship and glorify God. The effects, which can also be translated as "operations" or "tendencies", refer to the observable characteristics of human behaviour, such as the propensity to procreate, protect children, and enter into society. Thus, investigation of causes and effects can provide knowledge both about man's origin and man's natural activities, which form the foundation of Melanchthon's theory of moral philosophy.

and any who try to dissolve common society should be repelled and destroyed. That is, force should be repelled with force. Certain virtues arise from these laws, namely piety towards one's children, from the law that children should be protected. And because the weaker should be ruled by the stronger, we understand that children should obey their parents. From another law about the preservation of society arises justice, which prohibits injustices, as well as the relatives of justice: gratitude and generosity. From the law about defence arises courage, which is the repulsion of injustice. And [courage] must be guided by justice.

It is most proper for man to seek truth and reject and flee from dishonesty. For society cannot be preserved without the truthfulness of contracts and legal decisions. Hence arises that virtue called "truthfulness". Likewise, | 16.63
the preservation of nature demands moderation in food, drink, and other pleasures, and from this arise temperance and continence. In this way, it is easy to understand that the division of virtues should be taken up from the laws of nature, which are notions divinely imprinted upon the soul, | and 16.64
they may be recognized and arranged by inspecting the causes and effects which are proper to man, as has been discussed. | For the causes show that p. 68
there is a God and that God should be obeyed. The effects show that we are born for procreation and for society.

[16.63] **Book II**

On Justice

In listing the virtues, religion should be the first thing discussed.[127] But the doctrine concerning the fear of God, faith, prayer, and the remaining Christian virtues cannot be treated sufficiently without expounding the whole doctrine of the distinction between Law and Gospel. Therefore, one should consult the apostolic writings about this genus of virtues. Nevertheless, the philosophers treat in large part the virtues of the second table, which govern external actions towards men in civil society. Among these, the first virtue is justice, and Aristotle rightly says that justice is "more wonderful than both the morning star and the evening star".[128] For justice governs the remaining
p. 69 virtues and is the fundamental bond of civil society. |

Is the Use of the Term ["Justice"] Straightforward?

Absolutely not. For in one sense, "justice" generally signifies obedience to all laws and encompasses all the virtues, as when we say, "Aristides was a just citizen." The sacred scriptures often speak in this way about the justice of law, where justice should be understood as obedience to all laws, as in [Psalm 119:121]: "I have done judgment and justice" and in Isaiah [56:1]: "Do justice, for your salvation is near," etc. For, as I shall say next, the primary virtue is obedience, which is called universal justice. For there can be no society unless it is held together by this bond. Aristo[tle?][129] illustrates this most elegantly: There were eight robbers who became accustomed to practicing their brigandage together. A disagreement arose among them, and four of them began[130] to disagree with the others about their booty. Later, after four of them were captured, another disagreement arose and two of them started a quarrel. Then two were captured, and only one was left. What was to happen then, unless his right hand quarrelled with his left?[131]

127 The second book contains no marginal headings.

128 Aristotle, *NE* V.1.15 (1129b.28–29).

129 It is unclear whether Melanchthon refers to Aristotle or Aristophanes here. On at least one other occasion (p. 99 of the 1546a/b *PME*), he refers to Aristotle by the abbreviation "*Aristo.*", which he uses here. The source of this anecdote is uncertain.

130 The 1540 and 1546 editions read *ceperunt* ("they seized"). As the editors of the CR point out, the sense of the sentence indicates that this should be *coeperunt* ("they began").

131 Presumably there was another step—in Melanchthon's recounting, the number of

A second sense. "Justice" means only that virtue which renders to each 16.64
his own in lawcourts and contracts.[132]

Third. In Paul's disputations, "justice" [*iusticia*] means the imputation of righteousness [*iusticia*] or divine acceptation [*acceptatio*], as when he says, "It was imputed to him as righteousness [*iusticia*]" [Romans 4:3].[133] The philosophers say nothing about this sense, but I bring it up to highlight the variety of senses [which that word has]. For this distinction sheds some
light on theological disputations. | For since Paul teaches that we are freely p. 70
reckoned to be righteous [*iustos*] because of Christ, it is necessary to understand "righteous" as "accepted", even if imperfect obedience accompanies that acceptation, as evangelical doctrine teaches more broadly.

How Many Species of Justice Are There?

Aristotle takes up his divisions of justice from Plato, and he attributes names to the species in order to distinguish and clearly explain those things which Plato discussed all mixed together. The first division is between universal and particular justice. Universal justice is obedience to every law, and it encompasses all of the virtues. Therefore, then, the name of justice in general can be applied to the entire chorus of virtues, because it renders the obedience owed either to the laws or to the magistrates. For in truth, the primary virtue is obedience towards God, if we want to speak as accurately as possible, or towards the magistrate, if we are speaking of civil matters.

In this way, then, Plato derives the force and nature of all the virtues from obedience, and he copiously describes this species, and makes it twofold. There is private justice in individual men, namely, the obedience of the inferior faculties to reason, and he calls this the primary virtue. But he could have defined this justice much more truthfully as obedience towards God.
However, Plato establishes an order among the human faculties, and he || p. 71
observes that there is one certain standard, namely, the judgment of reason. 16.65
And he rightly saw that the other forces within man should correspond to

---

robbers oddly goes from eight to four to one. Nevertheless, the point of the story is clear enough.

132 A reference to the famous Roman law maxim to "render to each his own" found in D.1.1.10.1 and Inst.1.1.3, emphasizing that this second sense is purely legal.

133 Part of this ambiguity is due to the fact that *iusticia*, as well as its Greek cognate *dikaiosunē*, can mean both "justice" in the narrower sense and "righteousness" in the broader sense of moral or spiritual rectitude. In the New Testament, Paul often uses the term *dikaiosunē* to refer to the "righteousness" of or before God. See also Romans 1:17, 3:21, 5:21.

this standard, and accordingly he added a comparison to musical chords. Just as the deepest and weightiest voice, the bass, is fixed and governs the others, so is the judgment of reason (namely, the law of nature) certain. Then, the middle voice [*mesē*] signifies the appetites of the heart, and when they are ruled by reason, there is harmony among the forces within a man. The *nētē* is the octave, which is the furthest away from reason, such as the appetites for pleasures in food and drink, which are less obedient to reason.[134] But these should also be ruled and restrained by reason.

Plato says that this harmony and agreement is primary justice, and the primary virtue. From this internal justice, as it were, the model can be applied to the society of the human race, and in the same way, obedience to the laws is called justice. That is to say, what is owed is rendered to the rulers. Besides, even though the name "obedience" is not listed among the names of the virtues, let us remember here that [obedience] is singularly important for justice, and that obedience is actually the primary virtue, precisely because it renders to God what is owed to him. Or, as Plato says, because by [obedience],[135] the inferior faculties harmonize with reason and obey it as a governor. Or, because [by obedience] we fulfil what the laws
p. 72 require. |

What Is Particular Justice?

Simonides' definition fits this well: "Justice is the virtue which renders to each his own."[136] For justice governs the actions which we should undertake towards others, and it governs them insofar as they are done towards others. There are only two species of this: distributive justice and commutative justice.[137] This distinction is derived most aptly from nature, and it can be understood correctly by examining human society as a whole. For in

134 Plato's analogy of a musical chord can be found in *Republic* 443d–e. Melanchthon here uses the Greek names for the notes in a chord.

135 1540: *quia*. 1546: *qua*. The latter reading better fits the syntax.

136 Plato, *Republic* 331e. Melanchthon provides the second half of the quote ("which renders to each his own") into Latin (*quae suum cuique tribuit*), which echoes D.1.1.10.1 and Inst.1.1.3.

137 Melanchthon's term is [*iusticia*] *commutativa*, corresponding to Aristotle's term *diorthōtikon* (see *NE* V.4.1 (1131b.25)). In English, this is frequently rendered as "commutative", "corrective", or "rectificatory" justice. I have rendered it "commutative justice" to preserve Melanchthon's own term. In the 1538 text, a different version of this section is included here with its own heading, which reads: "How Many Species of Particular Justice [Are There]?"

the entire society of life, there are only two types of interactions. Either
we "commute" or exchange things, or we arrange people in orders, as in
the establishment of governments, magistrates, and the various classes of
people in states, the army, or families.[138] | Here, there is no one who does 16.66
not understand that the entire society of life is governed and preserved by
these two parts.

So then, we exchange things through contracts, and since that exchange,
which is for our sustenance, carries on into infinity, total equality must
be preserved within it.[139] That is, equal should be rendered for equal. For
exchange cannot continue in perpetuity unless the exchanges are recipro-
cal, because if some people were to give without compensation, once their
resources were finally exhausted, they would die of starvation. Hence those
most honourable sayings: "Give something and take something" and "I give
with my hand, but I also take with it." And the laws too, whenever they deal
with contracts, | aim most diligently at this equality. p. 73

For this reason, Aristotle defined commutative justice as that which
exchanges things which are equal according to the arithmetic proportion,
that is, the proportion which simply produces an equal interval between
terms into infinity. For the arithmetic proportion is that in which three or
more numbers all have equal intervals without respect to proportion, as in
1, 2, 3, 4. Here, each number is always separated from the next by 1. There
are other examples of this type, as 3, 6, 9, 12, 15. Here, each number is always
separated from the next by 3. Aristotle applies this formula to commutative
justice, and it is easy to see the reasoning behind this application. For just
as every term here is separated simply from the next by an equal interval,
so there should be a simple equality between buyer and seller. The buyer's
value should be the same as the seller's value.

Now, from other passages of Aristotle and Plato, it is apparent that in this
way they mean equality of difference among the many. For instance, in the
fifth book of the *Politics*, Aristotle forbids the use of the arithmetic propor-
tion in electing magistrates.[140] That is to say, he forbids electing all persons
equally to any office whatsoever without discrimination and discernment.
That is what arithmetic equality is popularly imagined to be, as when people
say that all Christians should be allowed to make decisions in the Synod.
For those who think that way believe that | the learned and the ignorant p. 74
alike, without distinction, should be admitted to speak their opinions, but

138 This distinction is found in Aristotle, *NE* V.2.12–13 (1130b.30–1131a.9).

139 See Aristotle's discussion in *NE* V.5 (1132b.21–1134a.16).

140 Aristotle, *Politics* V.1.7–8 (1301b.29–1302a.8).

Plato, Isocrates, and Aristotle all disapprove of this type of equality in the election of magistrates. In contracts, however, this arithmetic equality is necessary, and the buyer's value and seller's value should be simply equal, just as there are equal intervals in the arithmetic proportion.

16.67 Further, commutative justice is useful not only in contracts, but in all of life, wherever things require evaluation or careful balancing, as in penalties, in which loss and gain are evaluated as well as crimes and punishments, and as in talionic punishment, which imposes the death penalty for murder and other comparable crimes like public force [*vis publica*] or violent robbery.[141] However, one should not think that there are no cases in which a judge or merchants should consider the geometric proportion. Indeed, it is applied in deliberation, in consideration of the circumstances, but before coming to trial or to the forum. Before there is a sale, the prices of the salient goods must be established. Before the judge punishes the thief, the law about the penalty for theft must be clear. But prior to the consideration of the circumstances, there is a simple evaluation of things in relation to each other, such as murder and capital punishment, [or] theft and restitution alongside some pecuniary penalty. After this, milder or harsher penalties are established in accordance with the diversity of circumstances, nations,
p. 75 and times. |

What Is Distributive Justice?

Distributive justice is the ordering of persons in all of life, both public and private, according to the geometric proportion. Specifically, it is by this that hierarchies of offices and persons are constituted, and by this that appropriate responsibilities are assigned to individual persons. For example, the highest function in the church is the exposition and determination of doctrine. Second is the administration of judgments, and third is the administration of ceremonies. The lower functions include management of incomes, buildings, and alms. As a result, suitable people should be sought for each category. For determining doctrine, a man should be chosen who surpasses others in doctrine, piety, and prudence, but such learning is not required for the other positions. In the administration of incomes, learning is not necessarily required, but it is sufficient that the person be a diligent steward. When this proportion is observed, the ordering is just

141 *Vis publica* was a category of outrageous and flagrant crime which included offenses such as attacking and looting houses with an armed band. See D.48.6.

and the Church is harmonious and healthy. But when the highest authority of determining dogma is handed to an ignorant and impious pontiff, who scorns the judgment of God and defends impious beliefs in order to build up his own tyranny, and when a learned and pious man, worthy of a higher position, is cast down to a lower role which he does not happen to deserve, then the entire harmony of the church is confounded. | 16.68

Thus, if Marius were to govern the domestic affairs of the republic but Catulus were sent to fight the Cimbri, the republic would be endangered at home and abroad.[142] For Marius was a successful warrior but a trouble-making populist at home. | Conversely, Catulus was well-suited for preserv- p. 76
ing the tranquillity of the city, but he was not equally successful in military matters. Thus, the prince will strongly prefer to give the office of chancellor to a wise man rather than to one who is ignorant, dull, or foolish. And in the same way, in the family, one should consider which tasks are best suited to which persons. Indeed, in all of private and public life we should observe degrees of responsibility and talent, and we should consider the merit, ability, and character of others so that we might appoint each to his own station and role. This justice is the foremost preserver of republics and of private custom.

For these reasons, Plato most wisely said that the best state of the republic is for it to be constituted by the geometric proportion, and indeed he adds that this proportion in the republic is a gift of God.[143] And even though [this proportion] infrequently applies to human affairs, whenever it does apply, it produces the greatest benefits. From this passage of Plato, Aristotle undertakes this most elegant analysis of the species of justice according to the arithmetic and geometric proportion, and this application is not difficult for the one who sees Plato's meaning: For in discerning what positions people should hold (not only in distributing penalties and rewards or in electing magistrates, but generally, publicly and privately, in every distinction), [Plato] always keeps a place for industry and virtue, just as Aristotle recounts the same distinction in the fifth book of the *Politics*.[144] | p. 77

142 Quintus Lutatius Catulus and Gaius Marius were the two consuls in 102 BCE during the Cimbrian War. Marius was made famous as a great general in the Jugurthine War, while Catulus was more famous as a poet, author, and patron of public works.

143 Although this attribution is vague, Melanchthon likely refers generally to Plato's plan for a republic ruled by philosopher-kings, the wisest men in the city, which Plato lays out in the *Republic*. In Melanchthon's framework, such a plan would align with the geometrical justice of assigning roles according to talent.

144 *Politics* V.7.14 (1309a.33–37).

Therefore, distributive justice is useful for distinguishing persons in all of life, public and private. And diligence is necessary in distinguishing persons in life and assigning each to his proper place. For the republic also needs people with different skills, and the practitioners of the various arts are divine gifts to human life. Therefore, none of them should be abandoned, for their industry is necessary for life, nor should the order be disturbed. That is, a farmer should not apply himself as a doctor, nor should an unlearned man apply himself as a preacher. Rather, let each man remain in his own place. This is what distributive justice and the geometric proportion teach. So then, this is the geometric proportion: when there are three or more terms, it is not the interval between the numbers that matters, but rather
16.69 the constant equality of proportion, as 6 and 3 have the | same relationship as 20 and 10. Just as Caesar was well-suited for war, so was Cicero suited to domestic government. Just as Peter and Paul were suited for speaking in the synod, so suited are those who truly surpass others in doctrine and piety, not in titles, just as Paul says [Romans 2:11]: "God does not show partiality to men."[145]

On the Definition of Justice among the Jurists[146]

"Justice is a constant and perpetual will which renders to each his own."[147] Plato says that this was Simonides' definition, although that properly refers
p. 78 to particular justice. | Nevertheless, the genus involved in this definition is will, by which is meant, according to the conventions of Latin, the "disposition" [*habitus*] or "action" of the will. Then the two differentiating properties [*differentiae*],[148] "constant" and "perpetual", follow it, meaning that the will is governed by certain knowledge which is either natural or in agreement with natural principles. For although the details and cases

145 In the context of this passage, Melanchthon's difficult mathematical analogy of arithmetic and geometric proportions can be more easily understood as the difference between a strict equality and an equality based on ability. Strict equality, or equality according to the arithmetic proportion, should be preserved in situations such as contracts, punishments for crimes, and purchases. Equality based on ability, or equality according to the geometric proportion, seeks to match higher talents with higher offices (i.e. good generals with military posts, good craftsmen with work in the skilled trades). Therefore, the proportion of talent and office is preserved, even if generals and craftsmen are not strictly and arithmetically equal.

146 1538: "Is it Right to Say that 'Justice is a Constant and Perpetual Will'?"

147 A quote, with slight emendation, from D.1.1.10.pr. See also Plato, *Republic* 331e.

148 i.e., the characteristics which differentiate species within a genus.

vary, the mind still contains certain notions [*notitiae*], that is, practical principles, or corresponding reasoning deduced from principles, from which one adjudicates what is just in a variety of cases and accounting for diverse circumstances. When the will obeys these, it acts justly.

The next part of the definition, "which renders to each his own right [*ius*],"[149] is a differentiating property describing the particular duty of this virtue, namely that justice should be exercised toward others insofar as there are outstanding duties owed to them. So then, this definition is clearest in commutative justice, as the buyer must pay the price to the seller, for otherwise, exchanges would not be sustainable. Likewise, in distributive justice, criminals must be punished for their crimes. Thus, the seller's right [*ius*] is rendered to him when he receives payment, and the thief's right [*ius*] is rendered to him when he is punished.

So then, this is the causal definition: the genus is will, meaning the disposition or action of the will. "Constant and perpetual" signifies the efficient cause, namely, that will or action is governed by certain knowledge, that is, by practical principles, | and by reasoning which is in agreement with p. 79
these principles. Those two words are not placed idly. For just as certainty is desired in the other arts, so in this doctrine of morals, one should inquire whether it arises from certain principles, that is, whether it is a firm ordination of God. | For an investigation into an art aims to determine this: 16.70
namely, whether the doctrine concerning [that art's] principles is certain, firm, and received from God. Therefore, these words "constant" and "perpetual" signify that this doctrine arises from certain principles. And if the definition is understood in this way, then it will be clear, firm, and full of erudition. It also embraces many disputations about the grounds of knowledge, about principles, and about arguments, which are good conclusions which arise from principles. Lastly, this is the final cause: "which renders to each his own right." In the same way, the other arts and virtues are recognized by their final causes, just as medicine is the art which protects and restores health to the human body.

The First Division of Right[150]

The term "right" [*ius*] often means the faculty of having, using, or doing something according to some law, either natural or positive. For example,

149 Melanchthon here inserts the term "right" [*ius*], which appears in D.1.1.10.pr but is absent in his definition above.

150 1538: "How Many Types of Right Are There?"

the owner of a house has a right [*ius*], that is, a faculty, of having the house according to positive law, that is to say, if he holds it by the edict of a praetor.[151] But there is another meaning, likewise in common use, of the word
p. 80 "*ius*": it signifies | the laws themselves, or the notions [*notitiae*]. According to this meaning, "*ius*" is divided into the law of nature [*ius naturae*] and positive law [*ius positivum*]. And this is the typical definition: The law of nature signifies natural notions about morals, that is, practical principles, as well as both the right conclusions and necessary consequences arising from those principles. The Decalogue, which is the epitome and sum of the laws of nature, illustrates what these notions are in the best and most fitting way. For this reason, students should devote themselves to their order and content. The philosophers discern them by investigating the causes and effects of man, as I have said above, since effect should be subordinated to cause. Man is created by God, therefore he should obey God. Likewise, human society should be protected; therefore, crimes that disturb society, such as murder, adultery, theft, and lying, should be prohibited. Such arguments are full of erudition, but because they are so lengthy, we should use the Decalogue as a summary.

The jurists recite certain headings,[152] but at times they distinguish between the law of nature [*ius naturae*] and the law of nations [*ius gentium*].[153] They call the good impulses [*storgai*] common to humans and the rest of the animals "the law of nature", such as the impulses towards procreation and rearing of children, towards self-preservation, and towards defence against unjust violence. But they call the natural notions the "law of nations", and they add examples like the division of private property,
16.71 contracts, and faithfulness in agreements. | In contrast, the philosophers have not used these distinct terms, and instead they refer to both concepts
p. 81 as the "law of nature", because | they understand law to be the notions, and they derive the law of nature from the mind and knowledge of God. For this

151 In Roman law, the rights of possession and ownership were often clarified and strengthened by official pronouncements of the praetors known as "possessory interdicts."

152 *capita*, the term for the various headings within Roman law.

153 Roman jurists made a distinction between the law of nature and the law of nations. The law of nature was that law which was common to humans and animals alike: a natural propensity to reproduce, raise children, and protect oneself from aggression (see D.1.1.1.3). The law of nations was that which law common to humans only (D.1.1.1.4), and included things such as private property, slavery, and contracts (Inst. 1.2.2). Melanchthon here is highlighting the disparate meanings of the "law of nature" in the different contexts of jurisprudence and moral philosophy.

reason, they do not discuss the passions of beasts. For all of those notions are like a footprint of God, impressed upon minds, which declares that there is a God and declares what the will of God is according to the law, that is, that God is wise, good, just, and that he punishes wrongdoing. For as we acknowledge that we have minds, and that God appears clearly in those minds, so we infer that God must be some type of mind. Likewise, when we see that there is a notion of order in our mind, as well as a distinction between good and evil, we infer that this nature does not exist by mere chance, and we infer that God discerns between just and unjust, good and evil.

Thus, because the philosophers derive the law of nature from the human mind and the knowledge of God, and because they speak solely of human actions, they do not have distinct names for the law of nature and law of nations. All true demonstrations in moral philosophy are properly the law of nature or law of nations. And because these demonstrations are, without doubt, divine ordinations established in nature, or notions of the divine ordination in nature, then the natural law [*ius naturale*] is rightly said to be the divine law [*ius divinum*]—just as Paul openly speaks of *dikaiōma theou*, the justice of God, in Romans 1:[32]. Therefore, that rule which says that "He who violates the law of nature sins mortally," is true.

Positive law is a pronouncement of the magistrate which adds some specifications to the law of nature according to | probable reason, not neces- p. 82
sary reason.[154] For example, the law of nature generally teaches that theft should be punished. Then, the magistrate adds a specification, namely the mode of punishment, and in so doing he follows probable reason. More spirited natures should be bound with stronger shackles. Germans cannot be coerced by light punishments. Therefore, one must use capital punishment. Natural reason commands parents to take some care of their children

154 Probable reason (*ratio probabilis*) was an important medieval and Renaissance concept. Because much of human life involves acting upon knowledge that is not absolutely verifiable, the category of "probable reason" was used to analyse propositions that were likely, but not certain, to be true. Melanchthon frequently appeals to this category of thinking, particularly in reference to legal judgments, where absolute certainty was almost always impossible. See, for example, Cicero's definition in *De Inventione* I.29.46: "That is probable which for the most part usually comes to pass, or which is a part of the ordinary beliefs of mankind, or which contains in itself some resemblance to these qualities, whether such resemblance be true or false." (H.M. Hubbell's translation in LCL 386). For probable reasoning more broadly in the late medieval and early modern world, see Rudolf Schuessler, *The Debate on Probable Opinions in the Scholastic Tradition* (Leiden, 2019), esp. pp. 1–99.

provided that the children demonstrate the piety which they owe. Therefore, parents should leave to them a fourth or a third of their estate, which was called the "*legitima*".[155] This was owed according to natural law, and, unless the children committed certain crimes, the parents could not disinherit them. These conclusions do not follow from necessity, but rather they follow from certain determinations drawn from common understanding. For just as doctors, on account of various circumstances in their treatments, use probable reason to intensify or moderate the form of their remedies, so
16.72 do lawmakers harden or soften the general | notions according to differing circumstances.

Therefore, positive law is properly a certain determination of the natural law, [applied] in a certain manner and on account of certain circumstances. This determination has some probable reason, as was said above about the penalty for theft. However, because circumstances vary, there is a certain dissimilarity among positive laws in diverse nations. Nevertheless, positive law must still be governed by some rule, namely, it should not disagree with
p. 83 natural law. | Demosthenes' definition of law fits with this description of positive law.[156] For his opening claim, that law is the gift of God, rightly advises that the standard for every law must be the notions which are divinely impressed in human nature. But what follows refers particularly to positive law, the decrees of the wise, and the common pact of the city. For here, Demosthenes means a notion explicated and interpreted by the wise and promulgated by the ordained authority.

Is the Law of Nature Always Immutable?

Just as the light in the eyes remains the same, provided that they are healthy, so the principles of the arts shine perpetually in sound minds. Moreover, it has been said that the law of nature [*ius naturae*] or laws of nature [*leges naturae*] are natural[157] notions. Concerning these, when it is asked whether the law of nature is immutable, the right response is that the entire harmo-

155 The *legitima portio*, or forced share, was the portion of the estate from which the decedent could not disinherit his children without legal cause.

156 See Demosthenes, *Against Aristogeiton I*, 16, which reads "The law is that which all men ought to obey for many reasons, but above all because every law is an invention and gift of the gods, a tenet of wise men, a corrective of errors voluntary and involuntary, and a general pact of the whole state, in accordance with which all men in that state ought to regulate their lives" (quoted, with slight alterations, from J.H. Vince's translation in LCL 299). This quote is cited in D.1.3.2.

157 1546a: *naturales*. 1546b: *naturles*.

nious collection of natural notions is immutable, just as the light in healthy eyes remains the same. However, there is a certain hierarchy among these notions, and the lower notions yield to the higher ones. For example: The law of nature commands that one return a deposit.[158] But if [the depositor] returns in a murderous rage to reclaim his sword, then that law is overridden by a higher one: Do not harm anyone who has harmed no one. Therefore, it is lawful not to return the sword.

Accordingly, the law of nature is immutable such that each of the notions should be preserved in its own place and in order. This explanation has been given to claim that one should examine the whole order of the laws, and that each law should always be kept in its own place. For even if it is indeed the law of nature to use things in common, nevertheless, because | this law p. 84
now exists in our depraved nature, it conflicts with a higher law: do not harm anyone who has harmed no one. So now, reason teaches that there should be distinctions of ownership because many people, incited by unjust rapacity in this depravity of nature, would harm others under the pretext of the law of common property. Therefore, since true and right reason as well as demonstration | illustrate the present need for ownership to be dis- 16.73
tinguished, we shall say that the distinctions of ownership come from the law of nature. That is, they are derived from natural reason.

Aristotle provides a somewhat denser distinction. Certain natural things are necessary such that, if they are changed (especially if the change were universal), a corruption of nature would follow. These things in particular are immutable, and they are indeed practical principles, or conclusions drawn from them by necessary consequence, such as "Do not harm anyone who has harmed no one"; "Parents should raise their children"; "Keep honourable agreements." For the dissolution and destruction of human nature would immediately follow if anyone were allowed to assault the property and bodies of others at his whim. But there are other natural things of an inferior degree, and if these are changed, corruption and severe depravity of nature do not immediately follow. For example, it is natural that we prefer to use the right hand over the left, but it is possible for a person to be left-handed without corrupting nature. Certain changes to this class of principles are tolerated because a change of this type neither corrupts nature nor strays far from true and strict reason. | For the laws cannot heal every p. 85
vice, so they ignore and tolerate certain smaller ones.

158 In Roman law, a *depositum* was a type of contract in which the depositor entrusted an item (the *depositum*) to a depositee for safekeeping. The depositor could return to claim his deposit at will. See D.16.3.

As such, because the ancient lawgivers could not completely prohibit usury, they took care to restrict it and to tolerate it in moderation even though it was contrary to nature. But moderate interest did not depart too far from nature, and this custom did not corrupt nature. The same goes for polygamy; although it is indeed contrary to nature, God still tolerated it in the people of Israel. But in these matters, one must judge wisely, and laws should not be made from [these] examples, nor should any example be approved without divine testimony. For because God is the sole creator of nature, the law of nature is likewise under his power alone. And this should also be added: Even though moral principles are firm just like the principles of natural philosophy (such as, "heavy things fall downward", etc.), nevertheless our assent to moral principles is weaker because of the corruption of nature. For because natures are not sufficiently obedient, this assent becomes weaker, the very notions are darker, and we easily assent to contrary fancies.

What Is the Difference between Strict Law and Equity [*Epieikeia*]?[159]

Strict law does not mean a perverse[160] interpretation of the law, as was the
16.74 case here: When one had agreed to a "truce of thirty days", | he ravaged the
enemy's fields at night. Or when the Roman legate, having made an agreement with Antiochus to leave him half of his navy, cut all the ships in half
p. 86 to deprive him of the whole fleet. | This kind of deception is not strict law,
but chicanery [*calumnia*]. So then, strict law is when the laws are followed harshly without exception, even if some circumstance allows for relief, as if a judge were to give the death penalty to a young thief who had erred by some accident of poverty, absent any notable atrocity or insolence. But even though there is a difference between chicanery and strict law, still, whenever the circumstances call for an exception, it is often difficult to tell

159 Melanchthon's terms here and throughout the rest of the passage are *summum ius* and *epieikeia*, two opposite terms in humanist jurisprudence. *Summum ius*, or "strict law", refers to a strict adherence to the letter of the law in all circumstances, and derives here from Cicero's axiom "*summum ius summa iniuria*" (*De officiis* I.10.33, loosely translated as "the strictest law is the height of injustice"). The Greek term *epieikeia*, or "equity" (see Aristotle, *NE* V.10 (1137a.31–1138a.3)), refers to the relaxation of harsh laws and the accommodation of written law to extenuating circumstances. For Melanchthon on *epieikeia*, see Kisch, *Melanchthons Rechts- und Soziallehre*, pp. 168–185.

160 *calumniosa*: relating to *calumnia*, or false accusations and legal chicanery more generally.

the difference. When Fulvius gave the death penalty to the Capuan senators, he was right to use strict law because they were enemies. Even though all of them were probably not equally responsible for the defection, all of them still did defect, and it was lawful to punish them all.[161] But when the elder Manlius punished his own son, it seems that those more dire circumstances should have called for an exception.[162] Thus in Milo's case too, the circumstances required the relaxation of punishment.[163] For even if Milo did not kill Clodius immediately [*in continenti*], Clodius had still started the fight, so that, moved by a justified grievance [*iusto dolore motus*],[164] it seems that Milo had hunted him out of his hiding place. But Milo had harsher judges who were urging the application of strict law for the particular reason that he had not killed Clodius immediately [*in continenti*].[165]

In contrast, equity [*epieikeia*] is the moderation of the law in some circumstance, especially in a case which the law does not principally treat. For example, when the law commands that a thief be hanged, it refers to | p. 87
an adult thief who committed his crime insolently. Sometimes, the law permits the relaxation of this penalty at the discretion of a wise judge in a case which the law does not principally discuss. For example, if someone, in poverty and misguided on account of his age, committed a petty theft without cruelty, the judge may relax the penalty. Therefore, one can understand where equity principally has a role, for it does not approve of crime or abolish the laws, | but it occasionally mitigates some circumstance, 16.75

161 Livy, *The History of Rome* 26.14–16.

162 Livy, *The History of Rome* 8.7. During Rome's war against the Latins, Titus Manlius Torquatus, a famous Roman general and consul, decreed that no soldier should leave his military post. In response to taunting from the Latins, Manlius' son bravely raced out and killed one of their Latin soldiers in a spectacular duel. Nevertheless, Manlius ordered his own son to be put to death as punishment for violating the consular decrees.

163 Melanchthon refers to the case which Cicero pled in the *Pro Milone*. Titus Annius Milo had killed Publius Clodius Pulcher in a conflict on the Appian Way. According to Milo's account, Clodius had set an ambush for him. Clodius was wounded in the skirmish and fled to a nearby inn, where Milo found him and had him killed. In *Pro Milone*, Cicero argued that Milo had killed Clodius in self-defence.

164 Melanchthon frequently uses the phrase *iustus dolor* (which I translate here as "justified grievance") several times in reference to homicides. The idea is that the killer (here, Milo) was justified in his action because he had suffered an overwhelmingly offensive injustice.

165 According to Roman law, a person could defend himself immediately (*in/ex continenti*), that is, during the moment of the initial attack. If the attacker fled or the violence ceased, pursuit and vengeance were not allowed. See D.43.16.3.9.

especially in cases which the law does not principally discuss. For no law can possibly account for every case and circumstance.

Therefore, equity is said to be the interpreter of the laws, and this mitigation is not without justification, but it follows some higher law. For when diverse laws which cannot all be obeyed equally come into conflict, the higher law is to be preferred. For example, if someone were to deposit his sword with you while in a good state of mind, but try to retrieve it later in a rage, the lower law commands you to return the sword, but the higher law forbids the wrathful person to do harm, namely, “Do harm to no one.” Therefore, it forbids you to return the sword. Equity is not being careless with the laws or slack in discipline, but it must be ruled by a certain reason, just as people say, “Dispensation is not dissolution.”[166] For exceptions which are contrary to the law of nature and the divine law should not be granted.

But these things will become clearer with a few examples. On the Sabbath, the Jews were forbidden to do daily and mundane tasks, lest such things impede the ministry of the word. That was the chief intention of
p. 88 this law. | Therefore, Christ did not violate the Sabbath when he healed the sick, nor did his disciples when they plucked the heads of grain, because these works did not impede the ministry of the word. This relaxation was a certain equity regarding the law of the Sabbath, even if the Jews, having a harsher understanding of the Sabbath rest, have distorted the law with false interpretation and excessive harshness such that now they even prohibit cooking any food, etc. But equity can be better seen in the case of the Maccabees, who fought on the Sabbath [1Maccabees 2:41]. For defence of the citizens was a necessary duty, and necessary moral duties should be preferred to ceremonial duties if both cannot be kept. And in this duty, the Maccabees preserved the intent of this law. For they did not do this in order to abolish the Sabbath by their examples, but to protect and defend the ministry of the word and the Sabbath.

So then, since the variety of cases and affairs is so vast that a single pronouncement cannot possibly account for all of them, yet circumstances occasionally demand some intensification or relaxation, this doctrine of equity must be considered diligently. Menander’s verse recommends this,
16.76 too: “The laws are most excellent, but those who regard them too strictly | become false accusers.” These are Menander’s words and they contain a most useful admonition if understood correctly, for experience shows that whatever is written most correctly in the scriptures, laws, agreements, cov-

166 1540 erroneously reads “*dissipatio non sit dissipatio*”.

enants, and contracts is often shockingly distorted. | For this reason, one should always seek the principal meaning of which the law speaks, and then when the circumstances fall outside of this, one should seek a dispensation. In the Pompeiian law on patricides, Emperor Hadrian commanded that a man who had killed his own son (because the son had committed adultery with his stepmother) should merely be exiled, even though private murder could have been punished more harshly according to strict law. But Hadrian considered the circumstances in his decision, namely, the father's justified grievance.[167] In Aulus Gellius XII.7, the Areopagites freed a Smyrnean woman who had fatally poisoned her husband and his son because they had murdered her son from a previous marriage.[168] In their sentence, the Areopagites decided that they would revisit the case after 100 years. In this way, they did not approve of a flagrant crime, but they also relaxed the penalty on account of the mother's justified grievance. p. 89

The fables even tell us of divine legal trials, and such examples are attributed to the gods to demonstrate that the relaxation of law is approved by divine authority in accordance with some probable reason. In *Against Aristocrates*, Demosthenes recites two trials held by the gods on the Areopagus.[169] In one, Mars was absolved after having killed Neptune's son Halirrhothius, because he had defiled Mars' daughter Alcippe. Then, Orestes was absolved of murdering his mother. In these cases, the judgment of the gods mitigated the punishment. For although those killers could have been punished more harshly according to strict law, nevertheless the judge made allowance for justified grievance. Learned men have attributed such trials to | divine authority in order to prove that exceptions may be rightly granted on account of certain circumstances. p. 90

But there are more examples in the Scriptures. David | ate the bread of the presence out of necessity [1 Samuel 21:4–6], but by this example he did not abolish the law. Instead, he showed that observing ceremonies is not the thing which justifies us before God, but rather that civic rites, which are to be kept in certain times and which allow for dispensation when necessary, yield to morality except in cases of offense. For cases of offense and scandal should be distinguished from simple observance, as in 2 Maccabees 7, where those godly men acted rightly when they chose to be killed rather than eat pork. For that was not a matter of simple observance, but rather a demand 16.77

167 This story is recounted in D.48.9.5.

168 The Areopagites were the members of an Athenian lawcourt which met on the Areopagus.

169 Demosthenes, *Against Aristocrates* 66.

to set an example of throwing away and destroying the law.[170] In cases like this, the ceremonies do not allow for dispensations.

Therefore, one should diligently inspect the causes of these examples. In 2 Chronicles 20, Hezekiah made outstanding use of equity, but outside of a case of scandal or confession.[171] When, during the Passover celebrations, many people had not previously purified themselves through the customary ceremonies, Hezekiah still commanded them to eat the Passover meal, but he prayed for them, since the ceremonies of purification had not been performed. For he understood that prayer and faith are the chief purification and better than the ceremonial one. Another example: Although Joshua mistakenly promised peace to the Gibeonites, whom he was supposed to kill, still he refused to go back on his oath. For he knew that it would cause
p. 91 a greater scandal to violate his oath | than to violate the other command to kill his enemies. He still preserved the intention of the law in some way, since the Gibeonites embraced religion and were pressed into slavery.[172]

There have always been quarrels in the church, such as the fight over the date of Easter and over similar *adiaphora* which do not have a clear mandate from God. And even if these matters are indeed free, still Paul took a moderate approach, such that the Jewish rites should be commonly practiced among the Jews, but not among the Gentiles, lest he seem impudent to some or superstitious to others [Galatians 2:11–21]. Finally, it should be added that the Gospel itself teaches a wonderful equity concerning divine law. For it teaches that even the fledgling and imperfect obedience of those who believe in Christ is pleasing to God. The greatness of God's mercy shines forth in this equity, and the godly are stirred up to a love of doing right when they ponder how great God's goodness is, that because of Christ the mediator, a meagre and weak obedience pleases God.

16.78 These examples show how | broadly applicable the doctrine of equity is to every part of life, but it is most useful in government, where many concessions to human weakness are necessary. Scipio forgave injuries caused by the

---

170 In this episode, Antiochus IV Epiphanes gave seven Jewish brothers and their mother the choice between renouncing God's law (by eating pork) or meeting a gruesome death. Melanchthon here intends to differentiate cases like this, where relaxation of religious observance would mean an outright rejection of God's law, from simpler cases where strict laws could be relaxed without broader scandal.

171 The correct citation is 2 Chronicles 30:15–20. By "confession" (*confessio*), Melanchthon refers to cases of confessing or denying one's faith under duress.

172 See Joshua 9, where Joshua granted peace unknowingly to his enemies the Gibeonites, who had sought a treaty while disguised as foreign travellers.

tribune for the sake of public tranquillity.[173] In contrast, Coriolanus brought war to the country by avenging injustice with strict law.[174] In Athens, after Thrasybulus' victory, the citizens who were unjustly driven out could have invoked strict law to reclaim their patrimony, which had been possessed by others, and even to kill those possessors. | However, Thrasybulus exer- p. 92
cised equity and enacted an amnesty, that is, the forgiveness of injustice, so that the conquered were spared and, for the sake of peace, possessions did not change hands lest another war arise.[175] This moderation benefited the city by bringing the Athenian civil war to an end. These and similar examples should be considered so that we may learn both to understand and to love equity, just as many precepts advise us to do. A certain Greek epistle contains some precepts about managing female slaves, saying that they should be like lute strings, which snap if they are too tight and sound flat if they are too loose. And Sophocles says that massive trees, because they cannot bend, are uprooted by a burst of rushing waters while those low and pliant shrubs which give way are not uprooted.[176] The Scriptures, too, encourage one towards this moderation when they say, "Be not overly righteous" [Ecclesiastes 7:16], and "Whoever wipes his nose too much draws blood" [Proverbs 30:33].

Should Matters Be Adjudicated according to Written Law or according to Equity?

There are two questions. The first is whether it is more acceptable to use written or established law in public affairs, or to allow the magistrates to judge things according to a natural equity which is determined without written law, just as many barbaric peoples who have no written or established laws do today. Aristotle treats this question fully | in the third book of p. 93
the *Politics* and pronounces that it is better to use written and established

---

173 According to Livy, Scipio Africanus was accused (potentially by Quintus Petilius, a tribune) of embezzlement. In order to avoid further harassment, Scipio retired to Liternum. See the *periocha* of book XXXVIII, in LCL 313, pp. 205–207.

174 Gnaeus Marcius Coriolanus was a successful Roman general in the war against the Volsci. During a grain shortage at Rome, Coriolanus argued that grain should be sold to the people at an ordinary price only if they restored the ancient rights of the Senate. Predictably, Coriolanus' harsh proposal was unpopular, and he was exiled from Rome. He fled to the Volsci and led their forces in attacking Rome. See Livy, *History of Rome* II.34–40.

175 See Xenophon, *Hellenika* II.4.18–43.

176 cf. Sophocles, *Antigone*, lines 710–714.

law, because uncertain opinions easily give rise to discord.[177] For where there is no written law, it can often happen that each judge sees things his
16.79 own way. And the powerful and the princes especially need laws | written by a weighty authority, for they are unwilling to yield to the private opinions of judges, but they will yield to the oracles of the laws.

Moreover, written law restrains the judges' passions. For this reason, Aristotle handed down this most memorable saying on the dignity of written law: "He who puts the law in charge hands authority to God and to the laws. But he who puts man in charge elevates a wild beast. For desire and wrath corrupt even the best men, but law is a mind without desire."[178] Let the students remember this saying so that they might have a greater love for written law. For even if tyrannical men chafe uncomfortably at the bonds of the law, still it must be established that it is better to use written laws, and that the ignorant should not be granted license to disparage the written law. For God even gave written laws to his own polity, and the Attic and Roman republics learned through experience that it is impossible to keep peace without written law. But at this point, [written law's] usefulness is now apparent, so I will add no further discussion about this first question.

The second question is whether, where written law exists, the judge should make pronouncements according to what is written or according
p. 94 to equity—that is, his private reason—and eschew the written law? | This question has given rise to many lengthy discussions about strictness and equity. But I set down a simple, plain, and true rule. As a rule, one should decide according to written law, especially in those cases which the law principally discusses. For obedience is owed to the written law just as to the magistrate. Therefore, one may not stray from the written law. Likewise, the judge's opinion has authority not because it is private reasoning, but because he is the voice of the law. Therefore, the judge should follow the law, not his private opinions, and equity does not conflict with written law. For in those cases which the law principally discusses, the legislators discerned by most serious deliberation that what they established was the most equitable solution. Therefore, in that law entitled "Concerning Trials", the Codex puts it rightly: "In all things, the rationale of justice and written equity was more pleasing than strict law."[179] This text prohibits straying from what is written and it advises that whatever is written is equity.

177 See the discussion in Aristotle, *Politics* III.11.1–9 (1287a.1–1287b.35).

178 cf. Aristotle, *Politics* III.11.4 (1287a.28–32).

179 C.3.1.8. Melanchthon adds the word "written" (*scriptae*), which is lacking in the Codex.

Now, someone will object: But Aristotle calls equity the "unwritten relaxation of the law". I respond: Aristotle generally | refers to equity as a relaxation 16.80 of the law, either written or unwritten. For just as nowadays there are many exceptions written in the very text of the laws and in the commentaries of the interpreters, so in Athens, the laws were relaxed, clarified, bent, or intensified by decrees which they called *psēphismata*.[180] | The same p. 95 thing occurs in every republic. The law says that he who kills a man should receive capital punishment. The text itself adds to this law an exception in the case of accidental homicide, and the doctors of law add further exceptions. Nevertheless, it is obvious that these written exceptions should be followed because they are laws, or they have the force of law. For the consensus of the doctors should be thought to have the force of law not only because it is supported by honest and weighty reason, but also because of the authority which has been granted to the professors.[181]

But it will be asked whether unwritten equity should be followed, just as the ignorant often contend. My response here is the same as above. As a rule, written law should be preferred, and one should not stray from it in a case which the law principally discusses. For what would be the point of writing laws if anyone were allowed to decide any case by his own private judgment, spurning the law? Such barbaric license is unworthy of well-mannered men. But sometimes, cases do arise which are not principally discussed by the law, and honest reason demands moderation on account of some outstanding circumstance. Here, even if there is no written equity, the judge should still make some exception. For example, the law about hanging a thief speaks principally of him who steals with wicked intent; it does not speak principally about the modest man who is driven to theft by hunger. | Therefore, the judge will punish this man more mildly. Such a case p. 96 has room for equity, which does not stray from what is written since what is written speaks principally of a different case. Thus, Milo should have been absolved because he did not start the fight, even if he was later excessive in his self-defence. For he did not kill Clodius immediately, but, nevertheless, Clodius had already mustered arms several times against that brave man,

180 Generally, a *psēphisma* was a decree passed by the Athenian Assembly (*ekklēsia*) which specified existing laws (*nomoi*). In many cases, these added provisions which made the laws more applicable to particular circumstances. Aristotle mentions the distinction between more general *nomoi* and more specific *psēphismata* in his discussion of equity in *NE* V.10.7 (1137b.27–29).

181 Here Melanchthon refers to the early modern German practice of *Aktenversendung*, in which judges would refer especially difficult legal cases to the law faculties of German universities.

and since Milo had just fought for his life, he had a most justified cause of grievance and wrath. Therefore, [Milo] had a highly probable excuse. So then, Aristotle teaches about the relaxation of the laws in this way, and he says that laws should be bent a little, like the Lesbian or lead ruler, to fit the
16.81 case.[182] | However, there is a limit to this, namely, [it should only be applied] where there is clear and probable reason. It was for this reason that the Emperor declared that the adjudication of the laws and equity should be referred back to himself in obscure matters.

When Does Ignorance Excuse an Error?

Human laws punish voluntary crimes but remit the penalty either in whole or in part for involuntary ones. And of these civil crimes it is said: "Transgression is not[183] transgression unless it is voluntary." For since human laws are passed in order to restrain men, they punish those things which are avoidable, that is, voluntary. Therefore, the causes of crimes, namely judgment
p. 97 and will, must be considered. Sometimes, | an error of judgment occurs, which is ignorance. Sometimes, the will is impeded by force.[184]

Ignorance should be discussed first. There are two types of ignorance: one of law, and one of fact, as that maxim states: "Ignorance of fact excuses, but not ignorance of the law." But this maxim needs further interpretation. For ignorance of fact does not always excuse [a person], and ignorance of the law must be carefully distinguished. Therefore, first, it should be known that no sane person, of the age at which he can exercise judgment, is excused by ignorance of the natural law. For this reason, Aristotle says that it is excusable if someone errs in the laws, that is, the positive law. But it is not excusable if someone errs in that law which he calls primary, that is, the natural law. In the same way, ignorance of the divine law is not an excuse.[185] For the moral law is also the law of nature, as discussed above. Then, concerning the Gospel, the strictest precept stands declared to the entire human race by the very voice of the Eternal Father, who says of Christ [Luke 9:35]: "This is my beloved son, listen to him." He commands all to

182 See Aristotle, *NE* V.10.7 (1137b.30–32), where he discusses the famous lead ruler of the Lesbians, which could be bent to measure irregularly shaped stones.

183 1546: *non esse* 1540: *non esset* ("would not be").

184 In attributing involuntary crimes to ignorance or compulsion, Melanchthon echoes Aristotle's position in *NE* III.1.2–3 (1109b.35–1110a.4).

185 The 1540 reading is to be preferred here: "*nec ignorantia iuris divini excusat*". Both 1546 editions erroneously read "*ignorantia iuris divini excusat*."

acknowledge Christ and accept his blessing. Thus, the Gospel of Christ was spread throughout all the earth. Therefore, ignorance of the Gospel excuses no one.

Moreover, the Holy Scriptures make a certain distinction between those who sin knowingly and those who err by ignorance. But still, the ignorant | 16.82
are not freed from punishment, for he who knows the will of the Lord but does not do it receives a harsher punishment, but he who does not know | p. 98
receives a milder punishment [cf. Luke 12:47,48]. Some excuse ignorance with the phrase "holy simplicity," but Christians should know that God's command is for them to recognize rightly the Gospel, which cannot be understood without great study, meditation, and conversation with learned men. And Peter commands Christians to be prepared to render an account to those who come seeking [cf. 1 Peter 3:15]. And Jerome says, "Christians commit two similar sins concerning doctrine: they deceive and they are deceived."[186]

Second. Wilful ignorance [*ignorantia affectata*] of positive law or of fact does not excuse. Wilful ignorance is [ignorance] of something concerning law or fact which everyone is responsible for knowing. Aristotle provides a beautiful description: "Ignorance which someone willingly brings on himself is not an excuse but a perversity."[187] The same goes for universal ignorance, that is, when we know nothing of those things which we ought to do. Then, he commands the judge to punish ignorance if a person is the cause of his own ignorance. Aristotle defines wilful ignorance in the following way. These are his[188] words: "For it is neither ignorance in choice (which is perversity) nor universal ignorance that make an act involuntary …"[189]

Therefore, ignorance of the law does not excuse the judge, because he is responsible for knowing of it on account of his office. Nor[190] does ignorance of the law pertaining to his case excuse a litigator, as Scaevola said: "It is shameful for a noble man approaching cases to be ignorant of the law with

186 cf. Jerome, Letter 56.8 (PL vol. 22, col. 584). "For a Christian, there is not much difference in the vices of deceiving or being deceived."

187 Melanchthon gives this quote in Latin. It is a paraphrase of *NE* III.1.15 (1110b.31–32), which he cites subsequently in Greek at the end of this paragraph.

188 "his" (*eius*) is absent in 1546a/b.

189 Melanchthon gives this quote from *NE* III.1.15 (1110b.31–32) in Greek. In this passage, Aristotle goes on to state that particular ignorance (i.e. ignorance of particular circumstances as opposed to wilful or universal ignorance) makes an act involuntary.

190 The 1540 reading ("*nec*") is to be preferred to the 1546 editions, which incorrectly read "*ac*".

p. 99 which he is engaged."[191] But exceptions | from this category are usually made for women and soldiers, in whom error of law is pardoned. Nor does lack of skill in an art excuse artisans like architects, doctors, or others, and indeed lack of skill makes them culpable, as Celsus says in the Digest under the title "Of the Actions [Arising] from Hire."[192]

Nor does ignorance in one's own action provide an excuse. For example, if someone wants to take back a sale because he did not know the value or worth of his own good when he sold it, in this case, it is of no use for this seller to claim ignorance, just as the text says: "Help the mistaken, not the stupid."[193]

Third. There is a certain probable ignorance of fact, either pertaining to oneself or to another, which serves as an excuse, namely if someone
16.83 does not know those things which | do not pertain to his own duty or those things which he should not necessarily investigate. For example, if someone, for some probable reason, does not know that his relative has died, and does not seek his inheritance, he does not forfeit his right. Such was the ignorance of those in Paul['s letters] who unknowingly ate food sacrificed to idols.[194] And many cases are cited, for it is out of human weakness that they do not know the laws, provided that trickery is lacking. For this reason, Euripides says in *Hippolytus*, "He who sins unknowingly is absolved of trickery and guilt."[195] And it was out of ignorance of fact that Jacob unknowingly married the sister of his betrothed. Accordingly, he was judged less harshly.[196] Nevertheless, even if the jurists discuss these things at greater length, they still derive their remaining points from these philosophical beginnings.

p. 100 Aristotle shrewdly distinguishes | wilful ignorance from probable ignorance. He says that they differ in that it is excusable that someone sins, unknowing, and that a sin is committed on account of ignorance, when ignorance alone is the cause of the error. But when it is not ignorance, but our own outstanding folly and cupidity which are the cause of the error, ignorance is no excuse, just as drunk people sin, not on account of ignorance, but being ignorant, and the cause of the ignorance is a bad will which,

---

191 A quotation, with errors, from D.1.2.2.43.

192 D.19.2.9.5.

193 A paraphrase of D.22.6.9.5.

194 See 1 Corinthians 10:25–27.

195 A Latin translation of Euripides, *Hippolytus* lines 1334–1335.

196 In Genesis 29, Laban deceitfully gave his daughter Leah to marry Jacob instead of her sister Rachel, whom Jacob loved.

moreover, has brought drunkenness upon itself.[197] For this reason, Aristotle says that the sin of a drunk man should be punished twice.[198]

What Are Said to Be Voluntary Crimes?

Voluntary actions are those in which both intention and free will are
employed. Involuntary actions are those [performed] either when intention
is not employed, or when the will is restrained by force or succumbs and sins
in an impossible situation. So then, involuntary and compulsory [actions]
should be understood to be the same thing, which, as Aristotle says, have
an external origin, like when a man is dashed against a rock by a storm.[199]
Thus, when we are driven by love, wrath, hate, fear, and similar passions, the
action is not said to be involuntary or compulsory. Further, regarding fear,
it is correct to say that coerced will is still will. Therefore, an oath sworn out
of fear must be kept. For even when beset by many abuses, the will retains
liberty | in choosing external actions, and it can prefer some external actions p. 101
to others, as in [the case of] jettison while sailing; one prefers to lose the
cargo rather than face a shipwreck.[200] In the same way, a man caught by
pirates prefers to promise money than to put his body in danger. Therefore,
Hercules' wife responded rightly to the tyrant who threatened to force her
into another marriage by saying "Whoever can be coerced | does not know 16.84
how to die." The liberty of the will remains in choosing external actions,
even when the passions resist.

Aristotle proposes three degrees of actions: voluntary, compulsory, and mixed.[201] He calls those actions "voluntary" which we choose after deliberation, willingly and without coercion and fear. For example, Verres willingly despoiled Sicily. "Compulsory [actions]" [*violenta*] are those such as sexual defilement performed entirely by force. Aristotle calls "mixed actions" those in which the will, in order to avoid some greater harm, moved by terror, chooses a lesser harm, such as someone who promises money to a pirate to prevent his body from being harmed. These mixed actions are technically voluntary, but they are still different from those which are chosen without any terror. For this reason, the laws apply some moderation in these cases, since they do not grant a legal action to those who seek to enforce promises secured through extortion.

---

197 For this distinction, see *NE* III.1.14 (1110b.24–27).

198 *NE* III.5.8 (1113b.31–32).

199 cf. *NE* III.1.3 (1110a.1–4).

200 See *NE* III.1.5 (1110a.8–11).

201 See *NE* III.1.1–12 (1109b.30–1110b.17).

Other degrees of crimes are enumerated as well, and it is useful to distinguish them: evil intent [*dolus*], gross negligence [*lata culpa*], minor negligence [*levis culpa*] and most minor negligence [*levissima culpa*], and then cases which happen by chance [*casus fortuitus*].[202] For just as true virtue exists when there is the application of both right judgment and the
p. 102 free will | obeying[203] right judgment, so the highest grade of crime is when
someone sins both intentionally and with a free will. The remaining cases are: Gross negligence, which is when someone sins by wilful ignorance or wilful negligence, as if someone, in keeping a deposit, does not even demonstrate the normal diligence that he would apply to his own possessions, or if someone is neglectful in his own responsibilities or fails to take care of things which are usually common knowledge or are usually done by the average person. So, gross negligence is akin to evil intent, because, as has been stated above, wilful negligence is malice, as Aristotle says. It is useful to remember that law, "What Nerva", set forth in the Digest under the title "On Deposits", for it exhorts us to diligence, and shows how negligence deserves the most serious blame. It reads: "What Nerva said, that 'evil intent deserves more blame', displeased Proculus, but it seems absolutely right to me. For even if someone is not as diligent as human nature would like, nevertheless, unless he demonstrates his characteristic level of care also in keeping a deposit, he is not free from offence. For a man acting in good faith will not show less diligence towards [deposits] than he would towards his own belongings."[204]

Minor negligence and most minor negligence are below this grade, for there is no will to do wrong, nor is there wilful negligence, and indeed there is even average diligence, which nevertheless fails somewhere in some
16.85 circumstance. Cases of chance truly | are excusable, as when someone, res-
p. 103 cuing a person who has fallen in a river, rips out the eye | of the man pulled
out of the river. In all of these cases, one must observe that these degrees arise either from an error of judgment or an impediment of the will. For those reasons, then, those actions in which intent and free will both cooperate should be called "voluntary".

---

202 Roman law assigned various degrees of fault for injuries. *Dolus malus* referred to wicked intent (see D.4.3.1). *Culpa*, in its various degrees of *lata culpa, levis culpa*, and *levissima culpa*, referred to negligence (see D.50.16.213).

203 1540: *obtemperans*. 1546: *obtemperant*. The former reading better fits the syntax of the sentence.

204 D.16.3.32.

Whether Princes Should Change Impious Worship When Bishops or Higher Lords Fail to Act or Forbid [Them from Acting][205]

This question is frequently raised in these times, and answering it correctly allows the pious to support churches with greater zeal. For it is absolutely morally right [*ēthikon*] to love and support churches, because this is the highest end established for all men: that they would devote themselves to illustrating and magnifying the glory of God. Yet many people contend that the duty of establishing churches has nothing to do with laymen, but pertains only to the bishops, because no one should meddle in another's calling, yet the offices of the bishops and of the political authority are distinct. They also throw out many other arguments which we will recite and refute clearly below. Others contend that the authority of the higher lord should be obeyed, because a higher lord has a greater right in the affairs of his inferior. But | casting aside these sophistical arguments, I give my own p. 104 answer: Princes and magistrates should eradicate impious worship and see to it that true doctrine is taught and godly worship is established in the churches. I will prove this position with a host of clear arguments.

All are commanded without distinction to believe and confess the Gospel, regardless of approval or opposition from the authority of the bishops or anyone else. For it is written [Romans 10:10:] "With the heart one believes unto justice, with the mouth one makes confession unto salvation." Similarly, [Matthew 10:33]: "Whoever will deny me before men, I will deny him before my heavenly Father ..." Likewise [Psalm 116:10]: "I believed; therefore

205 This section, one of the longest in the work, is reproduced (with minor variations of spelling and typographical errors) from a separate tract entitled *De officio Principum, quod mandatum Dei praecipiat eis tollere abusus Ecclesiasticos* (*On the Duty of Princes: That God's Mandate Commands Them to Abolish Ecclesiastical Abuses*). It appears in MWA I.387–410 and in German translation in MD II.199–225. This tract is absent from the 1538 and 1539 editions of the *PME* and makes its first appearance in the 1540 edition. It is also included in both 1546 editions. *De officio Principum* was printed as a separate tract several times, including six times in Latin: at Wittenberg in 1539 and 1540, at Augsburg and Basel in 1540, as part of Melanchthon's *Opera* in Basel in 1541, and again separately in Basel in 1549. There were also German translations printed at Nuremberg in 1539 (twice) and Strasburg and Wittenberg in 1540. See Keen, *A Checklist of Melanchthon Imprints*, pp. 38–39. Note the change in tone from the rest of the *PME*. This is Melanchthon at his most fiery and pugnacious, and the tone reflects the heightening political tensions as Germany headed towards outright confessional war in 1546. The CR (3.240–258/nr. 1520) incorrectly states that Melanchthon sent this tract to Elector John Frederick in 1537. For more on the content and context of this tract, see Estes, *Peace, Order*, pp. 135–177.

I have spoken." Also 1 Peter 2:[9]: "That you would declare the power of him who called you out of darkness." And [Psalm 102:22]: "In assembling kings and peoples together, that they might serve the Lord …" Also [Psalm 51:13]: "I will teach the wicked your ways." And [Psalm 145:11]: "That they shall declare the glory of your kingdom."

Indeed, confession means to show publicly that you do not assent to idol-
16.86 atry, and that you impart unto others that very same | kind of doctrine which you yourself embrace. Likewise, [confession means] destroying external blasphemy among all people over whom you rule. Just as a father should eradicate blasphemy in his own family, even more so should the prince do so in his own realm. For whoever does not share right doctrine, and likewise, whoever does not eliminate external blasphemy among those whom he rules—that person does not confess, but appears rather to agree with
p. 105 the blasphemers. Therefore, the prince should change impious worship | and should not be deterred by the judgments of the bishops or a higher lord, according to the verse [Acts 5:29]: "One must obey God rather than men." Also, [Galatians 1:8]: "If someone preaches another Gospel, let him be anathema!" [Matthew 10:37]: "Whoever loves his father and mother more than me is not worthy of me."

Therefore, this first argument is derived from the necessity of confession, which doubtless entails a command to share doctrine. This is simply necessary and it is a part of confession, just as Christ says [Matthew 5:16]: "Let your light shine, so that your Father may be glorified …" And Sergius the Proconsul did not only listen to Paul, but he wanted him to be heard in all of the province.[206] And the power does not confess if it does not share doctrine. Rather, it often happens that, in the very fact of not sharing, it allies with the enemies of doctrine. Nor indeed does that man[207] confess who allies with the enemies of the Gospel and is forced to support savagery.

The second argument: God specifically commands those who rule to obey the Gospel and allow it to be propagated. Psalm 2:[10–12]: "And now, O kings: understand and receive instruction, you who judge the earth. Serve the Lord in fear, exalt him with trembling, kiss the son, lest God at some time become angry." Psalm 33: "Open your gates O princes, and be lifted up, O gates of the earth, that the king of glory may come in."[208] For the Psalm addresses kings and governments, which it calls "gates of the earth" by the common metaphor. Psalm 101 [102:22]: "In assembling kings and people

206 See Acts 13:4–12.

207 1540 incorrectly reads *his*. 1546a/b: *is*.

208 Melanchthon erroneously cites this as Psalm 33. The correct citation is Psalm 24:7.

together, | that they might serve the Lord."[209] Psalm 148:[11,13]: "Kings of p. 106
the earth and all peoples ... Let them praise the name of the Lord!" Isaiah
49:[23]: "And kings will be your nurturers, and queens your nourishers", that
is, princes and republics should support and defend the ministry of the
Gospel and provide a living for its teachers. For God ordained states for
this | reason: so that the Gospel may be spread. All powers must obey these 16.87
commands, even if higher lords or the pontiffs oppose them.

The third argument is derived from the office of the magistrate. The
magistrate is the guardian of the first and second tables of the law insofar
as they pertain to external discipline. That is, he should prohibit exter-
nal crimes, punish the guilty, and set a good example. Moreover, it is clear
in the first and second commandments that idolatry and blasphemy are
prohibited. Therefore, the magistrate must destroy external idolatry and
blasphemy and ensure that pious doctrine and pious worship are promoted.
For even if the magistrate does not change hearts or have the ministry of
the spirit, he still has his own office of preserving external discipline, even
in those things which pertain to the first table. Therefore, Paul confirms the
major premise when he says [1 Timothy 1:9]: "The law was established for
the unjust, the impious, and the profane", that is, for coercing them. We are
not calling for a return to the polity of Moses, but the moral law is perpetual
and of | every age. There is a moral and natural mandate to prohibit and to p. 107
punish idolatry and blasphemies because they are prohibited in the first
and second commandments, which are moral [commandments], just as
all peoples have punished perjury, and doubtlessly, the magistrate would
have been supposed to punish profane men, or the godless [*atheous*], who
delight in Epicurean discourses about God and providence. Daniel 3:[29]
shows the illustrious example of the Gentile king Nebuchadnezzar, who
announced an edict forbidding anyone to speak blasphemy against the God
of Israel. Therefore, the law about killing blasphemers in Leviticus 24:[16]
pertains to the second commandment.

Constantine, Valentinian, and Theodosius certainly followed this reasoning. For they outlawed the worship of idols and assigned capital punishment for those who made sacrifices in public. And these laws still stand today in the Theodosian Codex.[210] He even commanded the destruction of the idolatrous temples, namely to prevent after [his reign] the reinstatement

---

209 When citing the Psalms, Melanchthon follows the numbering of the Vulgate. In order that readers may easily look up these verses, this translation follows the numbering of modern English-language Protestant Bibles such as the NRSV.

210 See, for example, *Codex Theodosianus* XVI.10.

longer exposition or other proofs, and it cannot be shaken in any way. For there is no doubt that the Church as well as its prominent members should remove defenders of impious worship from ecclesiastical offices, just as the Old and New Testaments frequently command. In this way, the prophets led the people away from the established pontiffs whenever the kings did not remove the pontiffs, and whenever [the prophets] happened to receive godly kings, they removed ungodly pontiffs and priests. And as I have said above, the church at Antioch removed its own bishop, Paul of Samosata.

The sixth argument [derives from the principle that] association with persecution is forbidden. There can be no middle ground here,[212] as some imagine. Instead, one must ally himself with the persecutors or with the true Church. This is especially true for princes and magistrates—they must either obey or oppose persecuting kings. There is no middle ground between these things. Therefore, whoever does not want to pollute himself
p. 112 by associating with persecution should openly join with the true Church. | Relevant here are many passages of Scripture which prohibit association with enemies of the truth. Psalm 35: "I hate the assembly of the wicked, and I will not sit with the ungodly. I will wash my hands among the innocent, and I will go around your altar, O Lord."[213] Psalm 138 [139:22]: "I have hated them with perfect hatred." 2 Chronicles 19:[2]: "You aid the ungodly [...] therefore you deserved wrath, etc." Proverbs 24:[11]: "Rescue those who are led to death, etc." Matthew 12:[30]: "Whoever is not with me is against me." And in [1 Kings 18:21],[214] Elijah says: "How long will you waver between two sides?" 1 John 3:[16]: "We know love by this: that he laid down his life for us, and we should lay down our lives for our brothers."

Therefore, all must confess openly, and all must defend the true Church. For many and grave are the sins of those who, although they believe rightly, still hide their own beliefs and do not destroy abuses according to their own duty. For by their example, they primarily reinforce impiety, discourage the weak who depend upon their decisions, and confirm the madness of
16.91 the adversaries. These sins | should not be taken lightly. Therefore, those people are wrong who make no changes and conduct themselves in the

212 Both 1546 editions erroneously read *"Non licet esse malum"*. The 1540 reading, which is to be preferred, reads *"Non licet esse medium"*. For Melanchthon's targets here, the princes and theologians who occupied the "middle ground", see James Estes, *Peace, Order*, pp. 138–152.

213 Melanchthon erroneously cites Psalm 35. The correct attribution is Psalm 26:5–6.

214 The 1540 and both 1546 editions erroneously read *"4 Regum"*

middle although there really is no middle ground. And all association and familiarity with persecutors displeases God, produces scandal, and invites punishment.

The seventh[215] [argument] is from natural law. The proper and chief end of human society is to make God known. | The magistrate is the guardian p. 113
of human society. Therefore, all the more should he be the guardian of this chief[216] end, for in every action, the proper end should be principally sought and protected, just as a doctor should chiefly seek and protect health in healing. Therefore, in the governance of society as well, the governor should principally seek the proper end of society. For this reason, magistrates are wrong to divorce government from the end, believing that they are merely guardians of peace and of the belly.[217] They have another, greater duty: namely the defence of the entire law, the first and second tables, insofar as it pertains to external discipline. And on account of this heavenly office, God shares his own name with them, saying, [Psalm 82:6]: "I said, you are gods," that is, they are divinely chosen to conserve true religion, to prohibit and abolish idolatry, to preserve justice,[218] marriages, and peace, and to prohibit wickedness, etc.

In Deuteronomy 17:[19], God makes the king guardian of the law and of religious doctrine. And in the book entitled Wisdom [1:1], the beginning offers this precept: "Love justice, you who judge the earth, seek God, etc." I have cited many similar verses above which advise princes about this highest duty. Nevertheless, after the sacrificers began to pass laws by their own whim, having left the assembly behind, and no one was allowed to dissent | p. 114
from the opinions and judgments of the pontiffs, a belief crept into the minds of many that the princes have nothing to do with the care of the church, but that they are entrusted only with the protection of bodies and property, that is, that they are merely guardians of the belly. But if only the belly is to be cared for, what is the difference between princes and herdsmen? But we should think something entirely different: that polities have been divinely established with admirable wisdom and goodness, not only | 16.92
for seeking and enjoying the goods of the belly, but instead, much more [were they established] to make God known in society, such that eternal goods would be sought.

---

215 The 1540 and both 1546 editions erroneously read "sixth."

216 1546b: *paecipui* (typographical error).

217 *ventris custodes*. In Melanchthon's writings, "the belly" represents subjects' bodily needs such as food, water, shelter, and protection.

218 1546b lacks this comma ("to preserve the justice of marriages and peace").

Moreover, one should not hold up the examples of the ungodly. Neither Alexander nor Augustus undertook anything beyond the care of the body, no matter how praiseworthy they were as princes. I agree that very many [princes] have looked after this one part alone. For few understand their chief office, and fewer still recognize true religion. Yet still, God has occasionally raised up a few great heroes to establish the doctrine of true piety, like Joseph in Egypt, Nebuchadnezzar and his son[219] in Babylon, then Darius the Mede, Cyrus the Persian, and Constantine in Rome, and among the people of Israel, David, Solomon, Jehoshaphat, Jehu, Hezekiah, and Josiah. And these rulers were certainly not cowardly, because they reformed religion and indeed, in this duty, their courage and magnanimity shone forth. For they could not have changed the customary religion without the
p. 115 greatest dangers and hatred of the princes. |

Constantine ordered the closure of idolatrous temples, prohibited pagan sacrifices, instituted public teaching of the Gospel, granted stipends to teachers, and ultimately changed a great part of the ancient form of the Roman Empire, even though some of his peers, other princes, and a great part of the empire had viciously hated the name of Christ up to that point. For that reason, his peers Maxentius and Licinius mounted great wars against him and even gathered the nobility and the powers of Italy, Greece, Pannonia, and Thrace to themselves. But since [Constantine] dared to endure such danger and stand fast for the glory of Christ, he provided a magnificent model of defending religion to brave and good princes.

Daniel preached to the Babylonian king, commanded him to repent, and promised him remission of sins.[220] He also added certain duties, namely to love justice and work for the good of those who are unjustly oppressed, that is, to defend the innocent and especially the churches against the madness and savagery of the wicked. God chiefly demands this duty from the highest princes.

But the kings and princes of this age, although they see cruelty exer-
16.93 cised unjustly against the godly and | recognize many corruptions in the church, still support savagery and defend impiety, contrary to their conscience, lest they bring any hatred or danger on themselves. For they fear
p. 116 the conspiracies of the popish faction. | And—this is most unworthy of a heroic type—they betray religion and justice out of fear, laziness, or even hope of certain advantages.

---

219 According to the book of Daniel, the son was Belshazzar, who honoured Daniel for his correct interpretation of the writing on the wall. See Daniel 5:29.

220 Likely a reference to Daniel 4:25–27.

When Cassander asked the Athenians to count Alexander among the gods and to worship him with certain sacrifices, many people cursed this impious adulation. But Demades persuaded [the Athenians] to do it, namely, so that war would not be waged against them, saying, "Be careful not to give away the earth while you prevent an injury to heaven."[221] In the same way, many people now prefer to commit injury to heaven rather than to undertake either toil or danger for the defence of truth. But these cowardly and impious princes are entirely unworthy of that heavenly name: "I said, you are gods" [Psalm 82:6]. For God shares his own name with princes because he has entrusted them with the defence of divine matters: namely the Gospel, justice, peace, and discipline.

The eighth [argument]. Woe to the man who is author or approver of a scandal.[222] [cf. Matthew 18:7, Luke 17:1]. Princes who do not correct abuses are authors and approvers of horrible scandals. Therefore, there is no doubt that God is most gravely wrathful towards them. Here, the magnitude of the scandals and their true sources should be diligently considered, for the defence of idolatry is an insult to God. For those princes who prevent the people from hearing the pure doctrine of the Gospel are chiefly guilty for the many thousands of souls who are seduced and perish. | The fury of p. 117
our adversaries, who are becoming even more tenacious and severe,[223] is strengthened by the examples of the princes. And their lusts are strengthened as well.

So then, accordingly, in chapter 34:[10] of Ezekiel, God says this about all rulers: "Behold, I myself am above all shepherds and will demand my flock back from their hands, and I will destroy them."[224] And Amos 6:[1,6]: "Woe to you chiefs, heads of the people [...] you suffer nothing over the grief of Joseph." Surely these divine threats will not be in vain. Therefore, it is best that all princes take | account of their own salvation and free themselves 16.94
from these great scandals. There is no way to refute this argument.

However, as to the fact that scandals are raised in objection to us (i.e., that some people abuse liberty, or other things): these do not happen by

221 cf. Valerius Maximus, *Memorable Doings and Sayings*, VII.2, ext.13.

222 *scandalum*. Beyond the general modern meaning of "scandal", this term refers to something which causes another to sin. A prince's defence of idolatry was a scandal in that it caused his subjects to sin through idolatrous worship. An alternative, but somewhat awkward, translation is "stumbling-block."

223 1540: *saeviores* ("more savage"). 1546a/b: *severiores*.

224 Instead of "I will destroy them", the Vulgate reads, "And I will remove them from tending my flock".

the fault of doctrine, or princes. If the teachers and princes rightly perform their own office, as Ezekiel says, they are without blame [cf. Ezekiel 33:9].[225]

But, on the other hand, the main cause of great crimes lies with those who rule. For the crime of idolatry is much more atrocious than the other errors of the common people. And all other scandals collected in a great heap are nowhere near as great a crime as these three pillars of the Antichrist's reign: the profanation of the Mass, celibacy, and the fabricated authority
p. 118 of the Roman bishop. The profanation of the Mass is plainly idolatrous. |
Throughout the ages, how many shameful episodes has celibacy produced? And now, for six hundred years, Roman domination has incited so many ungodly wars. It should be seen on every side, then, who the true authors of scandal are! Concerning all of these things, Christ preaches: "Woe to the man through whom scandal comes" [Luke 17:1]. So then, the princes are authors of scandals wherever they forbid the preaching of pious doctrine and defend idolatry, the wild desires of priests, and other crimes.

By this point, I have recounted eight serious, solid, and true arguments which affirm those godly men who correct the church, and which indeed should have moved some more moderate [princes] to perform their duty in this matter. We preach in vain to the blasphemers, but still, Christ's commands should be set before them so that they may understand that their raving is condemned. I will add one more argument to be considered by those of moderate disposition.

God commands that we pray for governments and ask for their protection. For this civic life, established in the most beautiful order, is a unique blessing of God, and his goodness and wisdom shine forth in it. And God wills governments to exist for the sake of the churches. Pious minds offer these causes to God in prayer, so that God would preserve governments specifically because they have been established by his wisdom, and likewise, because they help and defend the churches, and because they perform their
p. 119 own duties for Christ's glory. | How then can one ask that these governments,
which have this chief goal, would abolish the doctrine and name of Christ,
16.95 utterly | destroy the churches, and butcher the members of Christ? Can
minds really pray, "Lord God, preserve this kingdom, that your name would be disgraced, the knowledge of Christ be extinguished, and the pious be butchered"? This is a prayer for ungodly regimes, from which pious minds must earnestly and vehemently flee.

---

225 Melanchthon here offers a cursory defense of scandals among the evangelical cause, perhaps having in mind Catholic critiques of the "abuses of liberty" in the Peasants' War or certain antinomian strains of Protestant theology.

Therefore, if the princes themselves want to pray to God, let them ensure that their prayers are not like this one. Instead, they should bring legitimate causes before God, namely, "Because you preserve governments so that they may protect your churches and allow the Gospel to be preached, accordingly, I ask that you would preserve my reign." These are the pious prayers which God hears. For what is the life of a man who cannot truly call upon God, who knows that he lives without God, rejected by him? This is the height of all calamity and misery.

Therefore, let those who rule ensure that their office serves the glory of God and the churches rather than fighting[226] against Christ, so that they may call upon God and delight in the prayers of the godly. For God will navigate the dangers as he has promised, since it is certain that the true Church will be preserved. They should also recognize this so that they will be diligent in their corrections, rightly establishing and honouring the churches, taking care to set up stipends for ministers, and encouraging the study of letters | which the Church needs. For we see even in the time of the Apostles p. 120
that there were educational assemblies in the Churches, since John and then Polycarp had schools. [The rulers] should transfer the resources of the colleges and monasteries to these necessary functions, as I will discuss later. But first, I will disprove certain[227] arguments which some have set forth.

First. The magistrate's duty is to take care of the body; the government of the churches pertains to the soul. Therefore, the magistrate should not touch ecclesiastical matters.

I respond to the major premise. The definition is incomplete when it says that the magistrate's duty is to preserve the body, or peace, because the preservation of external discipline pertains to the magistrate, not only according to the second table, but according to the first table as well. This is the complete definition: The magistrate is the guardian of the law insofar as it pertains to external discipline, and he preserves this law with physical force. | Just as he prohibits adultery, so should he prohibit and punish Epi- 16.96
curean discourse as well as external idolatry and blasphemy. For there is no doubt that the second commandment pertains to the magistrate. This is the difference between herdsmen and magistrates: the former looks after the bellies of his flock, while the magistrate should chiefly serve the glory of God. And because of this lofty office, God shares his own name with the magistrates. | p. 121

226 1540: *belligeretur*. 1546: *belligerentur*.

227 1540 erroneously reads *quadam*. 1546a/b: *quaedam*.

Moreover, I say that the magistrate is the guardian of the law insofar as it pertains to external discipline in order to preserve the difference between the magistrate and the ministry of the Gospel. The ministry of the Gospel proclaims the Gospel through which the Holy Spirit is efficacious in those who believe, as 2 Corinthians 3:[6] says: "He made us ministers of a new covenant—not of the letter, but of the spirit." Meanwhile, however, the magistrate has his own external office, and in order to prevent scandals he prohibits external idolatry just as [he prohibits] adultery or murder. Paul clearly teaches this, saying, "The law is established for the unjust, the profane, and the enemies of God." [1 Timothy 1:9]. And Paul calls this the "legal"[228] use of the law, that is, when the magistrate, by external discipline, restrains crimes which violate the first and second tables.

Therefore, we do not intermingle offices, but the magistrate has his own function pertaining to external discipline, just as the law commands that blasphemers be punished. Leviticus 24:[14–16] and Deuteronomy 12:[3]: "Destroy idols, etc." The minister of the Gospel has a different function: to declare the doctrine of the Gospel by which the Holy Spirit is efficacious. In light of this, the magistrate should chiefly orient his own office to magnifying the glory of God and should ensure that his confession shines forth in his own office, since these are the principal ends of all honourable functions in
p. 122 this political society. When | the Donatists were repressed by the decrees of the emperors, many people unfairly blamed Augustine, contending that the ungodly should be refuted by teaching only. But Augustine rightly taught that, in such cases, the duty belongs to the magistrate.

The second argument. No one may usurp another's office. Bishops alone should establish the churches. Therefore, the magistrates may not seize another's office.

To the minor premise I have two responses. First, the magistrates have their own responsibility concerning external discipline and the appointment of pious teachers, as I have described. Therefore, they do not impede
16.97 the office of the teachers. Next, | the minor premise should be denied, because, when bishops are the enemies of true doctrine, they relinquish their right of governing the churches, and the rest of the Church is mandated to remove them from government and to install pious teachers, as Paul clearly commands [Galatians 1:8]: "If anyone teaches another Gospel,

---

228 *legitimum*. In the 1535 *Loci Communes*, Melanchthon refers to this use of the law as "*civile*" (CR 21.405). In the 1543 *Loci Communes*, he refers to this use as "*paedagogicus*" or "*politicus*" (CR 21.716–717). In both editions, Melanchthon cites 1 Timothy 1:9 as the prooftext for this use of the law.

let him be anathema!" This command pertains to each and every remaining member of the Church, and they should remove and condemn ungodly teachers as anathema. Because the office of the princes and magistrates should chiefly exalt the glory of God, and because the rest of the people regard highly the judgments of their leaders, [the princes and magistrates], as the most prominent members of external society, must support the true church, | remove ungodly teachers, and appoint godly ones by their own p. 123
authority.

It is properly in the magistrates' power to distribute funds to be used. However, there is no doubt that they sin when they impede the correction of the churches because they refuse to divert away from ungodly pastors certain[229] funds which were intended to support pious ministers of the Gospel. They say that no one should be deprived of his own possessions, as if the ecclesiastical resources were not granted on behalf of an office. Paul clearly says that Christ ordained that teachers of the Gospel should make their living from the Gospel [1Cor. 9:14]. Therefore, it is wicked for enemies of the Gospel to use funds which are needed to support pious ministers.

We know how many colleges of canons and monks there are, and how rich they are. In these [colleges], there are either no learned men, or if there are any, they direct their erudition towards destroying the truth and overthrowing the Church of Christ. Meanwhile, manifold idolatry is practiced [in the colleges] in the profanation of the Masses and in the invocation of the saints, and many live contaminated by lusts. The princes will refuse to take anything away from these bodies as long as they want to seem just and not impulsive, and [as long as they] do not want to search for suitable teachers. But the impiety of this crime is manifold. For they are not promoting true doctrine, they confirm idolatry and lusts, they defraud the true Church, and they allow thieves and robbers to devour the church's funds. Yet it properly pertains to the office of the magistrates | to ensure that the p. 124
true Church has its due, as I will explain later. | 16.98

The third argument. No change should be made prior to the recognition of the synod. These controversies have not yet been adjudicated in the synod. Therefore, it seems that the matter should be deferred.

Shrewd men principally use this argument to restrain the souls of the many, for rashness is inimical to good decisions. It seems that it is laudable to bide one's time in such matters, and it seems characteristic of a moderate

229 1540: *quidquam* ("any"). 1546a/b: *quiddam* ("certain").

soul to wait for legitimate decisions and refrain from suddenly embracing the opinions of the few and the ignoble.

This appearance of wisdom is used as a pretext either for a secret hatred of the truth or for cowardice. For some controversies have no ambiguity. The crimes are notorious: performing Masses on behalf of others; invoking the gods;[230] withholding the whole sacrament; the superstition of vows; and celibacy. And although in these matters, everyone who is not fully Epicurean or totally stupid does see the truth, still we are commanded to wait for recognition, as if the authority of the divine mandate hangs on the approval of the bishops, kings, or any men,[231] like when at Rome, Tiberius proposed to the Senate that Christ should be counted among the gods.[232] And those delayers most accurately imitate this example of Tiberius, not wanting to embrace the heavenly mandates before approval by the senate of cardinals
p. 125 and bishops, who | openly are, and want to remain, tyrants and Epicureans.

But I respond in order to each of these propositions. The major premise is denied, because controversies over the word of God are different than controversies over human affairs, where human authority prevails. For the highest judge of all is the divine voice. Even if the whole world stands against us, each of us should obey the word of God, which they confess is handed down from God, just as Elijah complained that he himself was the only one left. The kings were at odds with him, the pontiffs and priests cursed him, and the people deserted him. Therefore, although he saw that he was in the minority opinion [*homopsēphon*] and had no allies [*homospondon*], still he would not abandon his position.

Similarly, Peter acknowledged that there were diverse opinions about Christ among the people—he was considered to be a prophet, to be Elijah—but he separated his own message from these and affirmed that this Jesus
16.99 was the son of God and the saviour.[233] Therefore, Christ | says [Matthew 16:17]: "It was not flesh and blood which revealed this to you, but my father in heaven." So I ask, should Peter have waited on the judgment of pontiffs, princes, or the people? One should not even wait for the judgment of the true church, as long as the word of God is known, just as Paul began to teach before he visited the Apostles. And in fact, he was teaching about the abro-

230 *invocatio divorum*: literally, "invoking the gods", a pejorative reference to invocation of the saints.

231 The 1540 reading, "any men" (*ullorum hominum*), is to be preferred to the 1546 reading "those men" (*illorum hominum*).

232 See Tertullian, *Apologeticus* V.2.

233 Likely a reference to the events of Acts 3:11–4:31.

gation of the law more freely than the Apostles were. By no means should one wait for the recognition of the adversaries. | It is plain that the popes and their co-conspirators are not the Church, but enemies of the Gospel just like the Pharisees and the ancient tyrants Antiochus, Diocletian, and others. They hold prejudices and exercise remarkable cruelty against all who agree with us. I have talked with many of them who were pretending to act with moderation, yet almost all of them really just excuse old abuses with new sophistry instead of correcting them. The disputations of these times have sharpened talented men on both sides. Therefore, the enemies of the Gospel (at least those who are more learned) embellish their errors much more elegantly than they used to. We often see our own writings used to hurt us. Afterwards, they write their opinions in blood; they command us to be killed. p. 126

When cardinal Aleander had come to Austria, he broke open the scab of savagery there and many godly men were most cruelly murdered, to the papal legate's delight.[234] In these victims, they apparently wanted to make a sacrifice to themselves, like when at Troy the Greeks sacrificed to the ghost of Achilles by murdering Polyxena.[235] However, at that point, Aleander had just returned from the synod and had been present at a meeting of cardinals which seemed to offer hope of moderation. But it was merely a trick, "promising good yet pondering ill in their hearts," as Homer says.[236]

Therefore, one should not wait for the official recognition of the papal faction, but God's mandate pertains to each person: to | hear, learn, embrace, and confess the Gospel. Each person in his own calling should display the testimony of his confession.[237] The head of household should prohibit idolatry in his family. The magistrate should ensure that his subjects are taught p. 127

234 Cardinal Girolamo Aleandro (1480–1542) was the papal legate who in 1520 was dispatched to Germany and the Low Countries to enforce the bull *Exsurge Domine* which had excommunicated Luther. Throughout his career he was a staunch enemy of the evangelical movement and famous as a persecutor of Protestants. The reference to Austria is puzzling. The 1540 and both 1546 editions read "*in Austriam*", and the 1539 Nuremberg German translation of the *De officio* reads "*in Osterreych.*" This may be a mistaken reference to the famous episode in Brussels, where, in 1523, Aleandro had been involved in executing two Antwerp monks because they had converted to Protestantism.

235 According to legend, after the fall of Troy, the Greeks sacrificed Polyxena, the daughter of King Priam, at the tomb of Achilles. There were many versions of the story, but Euripides' *Hecuba* recounts it in detail.

236 *Odyssey* XVII.66.

237 1540: "of his confession" (*suae confessionis*). Both 1546 editions read "of his calling" (*suae vocationis*). The former reading is more coherent here.

rightly. And because the authority of heavenly doctrine does not depend[238]
16.100 upon human approval, | one should not wait for the decrees of men, just as the [three][239] Israelites in Babylon did not wait for the decrees of a kingdom (or parliament, as they now say) but they courageously opposed the impious edict of the king.

Moreover, it benefits the godly to seek not the judgments of their enemies, but the testimonies of the true Church, just as Christ wants us to be enriched and confirmed by mutual admonitions when he says to Peter [Luke 22:32]: "And when you have turned back, encourage your brothers." Certain proven writers contain symbols and testimonies which, if we compare them to the Gospel, will make it clear enough what the ancient and pure doctrine of the true and catholic Church of Christ is. Therefore, princes should not take counsel with tyrants, nor with pontiffs, nor with hypocrites, monks, or others, but with the voice of the Gospel itself, and with the proven writers. And they should not be ashamed of hearing those things which are now being taught by the godly and the learned. For one should listen to the Church of Christ, that is, the assembly of the pious, not of the enemies of the Gospel, and opinions should be compared with the
p. 128 word of God. |

There are certain men who, either by nature or by depraved habituation, are prone to quarrels and love sophistry. These men, although the truth has been made sufficiently clear, still do not acquiesce to it, but perpetually mock and jeer just like the Jews, who, no matter how many times they are proven wrong, still try to slip away. The Devil gets his name from this custom, because he defaces, destroys, and mocks the words of God with his appalling slander.[240] Indeed, all men must recoil from this diabolical custom, but [this is especially the case for] princes, among whom a love of sophistry is most wicked. After the conscience has been convicted by true and firm testimonies, one should not seek foolish justifications for bending the truth. And if someone seeks truth with godly devotion to exalt the glory of God, to look after his own salvation and that of others, then God supports his attempt and helps it along, just as he says [Matthew 7:8]: "The one who

238 1540 and 1546a read "depend upon" (*pendeat*). 1546b erroneously reads *pudeat.*

239 The 1546 editions of the *PME* read "as the Israelites" (*ut Israelitae*). The 1540 edition reads "*ut res Israelitae*". The 1540 reading was a corruption of the original tract's text. The 1539 Wittenberg edition of *De officio principum* reads "as the three Israelites" (*ut tres Israelitae*), a reference to Shadrach, Meshach, and Abednego (Daniel 3:1–30).

240 Melanchthon's term for the Devil is *diabolus* (from Greek *diabolos*), meaning a slanderer or trickster.

seeks finds." But of the others, the lovers of mockery and sophistry, it is said [Isaiah 6:9]: "Hear, O hearers, and do not understand". That punishment is the height of calamity.

The fourth argument. The lower [magistrate] only has so much right in his territory as the higher | lord grants to him. The higher lord prohibited 16.101 changes [in the lower's territory], just as in his own prefectures. Therefore, no change should be made without his will.

I respond to the major premise: This is clearly true of the resources and produce of the territory. The lower [lord] holds the revenues and benefits | p. 129 which the higher lord concedes to him. But this is not true of the confession of the Gospel or of any works commanded by God. Confession stands above and beyond all human hierarchies, and God demands confession equally from servants and children of households, private citizens, and magistrates, as Matthew 10:[37] claims: "Whoever loves his father or mother more than me is not worthy of me." In the household, even the servants should confess the Gospel, as Joseph led his master to the true knowledge of God.[241] Daniel's friends, although they were servants, nevertheless opposed the royal edict about the statue.

There are many examples in sacred history which illustrate that lower lords not only professed with their mouths the doctrine of the Gospel against the edicts of the kings and emperors, as is proper, but that they even destroyed idols with their own hands. In a certain town of Phrygia, the prefect Adauctus, in the time of Diocletian, destroyed all the idols and persuaded the entire multitude to accept the doctrine of Christ. As a result, the tyrant then ordered the town to be sacked and all the citizens slaughtered.

In the time of Julian, in the most famous sanctuary of that era, not far from Antioch, the son of the pagan priest struck the statue of Apollo and knocked it off its pedestal.

Young women have also declared the strength of their faith with a similar magnanimity. Irene, the daughter of the emperor Licinius, disregarding the harshness of her father, who absolutely hated the Christian name, | cast p. 130 down and shattered the household gods and other images in her father's house with singular courage.

But mainly, those examples of confession among princes should shine forth which strengthen the other [princes], as when, with a crowd watching, a nobleman in the city of Nicomedia shredded public missives pronounced by Diocletian against the Christian religion.

---

241 See Genesis 41:38–40.

While Valentinian, who afterwards became emperor, was a military trib-
16.102 une, he threw a punch at the pagan priest who was bearing the holy water |
in the presence of Emperor Julian. By such examples, these princes intended to encourage the rest of the pious[242] as well.

Therefore, since God demands the confession of the Gospel from everyone, great or small, from all orders and ranks of men, free or slave, then that false argument [about] how great a right the lower [lord] has should not be brought up here. Confession pertains equally to all ranks.

So, when a higher lord delegates an office, he cannot prohibit that part which is peculiar to the office, and pertains to its substance according to divine and natural law. Moreover, it is established that all political offices should be directed to the glory of God. Every magistrate, higher and lower, each in their own place, should obey the second command of the Decalogue. That is, they should prohibit and punish external blasphemies which
p. 131 bring insult to God. | Nor should one obey the higher lord if he refuses to
exercise this part of his office, for instance, if he approves and reinforces shameful desires.

At this point, the major premise of the argument has been sufficiently refuted. I will not discuss the minor premise; princes preside over their own affairs and have *dominium utile*,[243] and the first duty of their office is to prevent tyranny from being established. Nowadays, I am not sure if they even remember that they are free.

For there are many [princes] who do not confess the pure doctrine of the Gospel, even if they desire the correction of the church and reject cruelty. Nevertheless, they are passive spectators, allowing tyranny to grow without limit when they should be using their authority to call bishops and kings back to moderation and true knowledge. This is fitting for heroic servants, just as when Achilles said that he would obey the sons of Atreus if they ordered good things, but if they commanded wickedness, he would not obey.

---

242 1540: *pios*. Both 1546 editions incorrectly read *impios*.

243 In a feudal system of land tenure, ownership (*dominium*) was often divided. The distinctions between *dominium utile* and *dominium directum* were complex and fluid, but in general, the difference was as follows: The higher lord held *dominium directum*, or ultimate property rights, in a piece of land. *Dominium directum* allowed a lord to dispose of property and collect rents from it. Lower lords possessed only *dominium utile*, which entailed mostly rights concerning use. Melanchthon's point here seems to be that *dominium utile* still granted significant latitude to lesser lords in handling their own affairs. For these divisions of *dominium*, see Richard Tuck, *Natural Rights Theories: Their Origin and Development* (1979), pp. 15–20, 40–41.

But, as to the fact that they magnify the praise of obedience, [saying] that it is a great piety to obey the Church and a great honour to comply with governments, this fine-sounding speech is a pretext for the height of wickedness: the Epicurean contempt for religion. For they do not preach obedience with the right intention, but they either strive to bolster tyranny or seek an excuse for their impiety, or cowardice and inaction. The godly should remember the apostolic saying [Acts 5:29]: "One must obey God rather than men." Ecclesiastical obedience never means | a conspiracy p. 132
for the defence of idolatry, lusts, and Neronian cruelty. Since the pontiffs who | teach and defend impious things should be cursed as if anathema, 16.103
no ecclesiastical obedience is owed to them. Moreover, we ourselves extol obedience with every type of praise. The civil offices should be entrusted to legitimate magistrates, but this rule should always be observed: If they command something to be done contrary to the mandates of God, we should obey God rather than men.

The things which I have gathered in this disputation about the office of magistrates are true and firm, and they are eloquently and expressly handed down in the word of God. I have no doubt that they also agree with the ancient canons, rightly understood, and I hope that good men will be moved by this admonition.

So let all the godly pray and beseech with genuine tears that those princes who are reviving the churches would support and enliven the study of letters and of those arts which the Church of Christ needs, and that they would ensure that the poor scholars in the schools are sustained by public generosity, trained rightly, and ruled by serious discipline.

Our adversaries in Germany, with hate for the Gospel, work diligently to oppress and extinguish all study of letters to the greatest extent they can, for they partly understand that [letters] are the revealers of true doctrine. And plainly, they rule in such a way, as I recall some abbots saying, that they do not want their monks to be versed in letters | because it would not be p. 133
beneficial for them for any monk to be, or seem to be, more learned than the abbot. Certainly, this ignorance is highly vulnerable to tyranny. In this way, just as they create[244] a wasteland in the churches, just as they produce no learned and pious teachers, so do they strive to foster a Cyclopean barbarism in all civic dealings. If only our own side would strive to make the study of letters flourish, for the glory of Christ!

244 1540: *faciunt*. 1546: *faciant*. The translation above follows the 1540 reading, which is more coherent.

God ordained that there would be great gatherings in the tabernacle for no other reason than that they would be like schools, where older men would teach and train the others in letters, the divine law, the histories, music, and medicine. For at that time, the priests handled these arts, and thus Samuel was educated in this way and thus the prophets Elijah, Elisha, and John the Baptist had these educational gatherings. Christ also preserved this custom, and then the Apostles and their disciples followed suit. At Ephesus, John had solid and diligent students, and afterwards, [so did] Polycarp
16.104 at Smyrna. |

And these gatherings were beneficial for establishing the teachers by which and the faith by which the Gospel would be spread. Since this demanded great diligence, the colleges of canons were then established so that posterity would know from whom they had accepted doctrine. Thus, Athanasius studied under Dionysius of Alexandria and Alexander.[245] And
p. 134 Basil, recalling his own teachers, said | that his ears still resounded with their sayings and voices. But afterwards, in the colleges, wealth produced luxury, and then came political power [*Imperia*], which did even greater harm to studies. Therefore, as the Church was snuffed out among the canons, so did they lose possession of doctrine.

Therefore, all godly men, and especially those who rule, should take care to retain the ancient example so that letters may flourish wherever the true Church is. What is more absurd than rulers and princes, enemies of the Gospel, flattering themselves for defending the ancient form of the Church although they are really just fighting about food or other foolish rites! They are not doing this to call the colleges back to studies, a matter which chiefly pertained to the ancient form of the Church.

But I will speak about these things no more. Let us now consider how necessary and pious is the duty of enlivening studies. For without schools and without doctrine, the purity of the Gospel cannot be preserved. And it is of greatest importance to know by whom and by what faith the Gospel was spread. Moreover, ecclesiastical controversies cannot be explicated fully without great erudition.

So then, although a few wealthy men cultivate these ecclesiastical studies, it is necessary to establish honest stipends for the pastors of the churches, the teachers, and the students in the schools. The resources of the colleges

---

245 Dionysius (c. 200–c. 265) and Alexander (bishop 313–328) were bishops of Alexandria and were trained in that city's famous catechetical school. Dionysius died before Athanasius (c. 293–373) was born, but Alexander was Athanasius' direct predecessor and mentor.

and monasteries should be reallocated for this purpose, [resources] which are now unjustly tied up and devoured | by those who are ignorant, lazy, and ultimately enemies of the Gospel. p. 135

As to the fact that Christ, in his teaching about the Last Judgment, says that he is all around, hungry and thirsty [Matthew 25:35]: Now let the princes consider that he truly is hungry and thirsty all around them, lamenting the tyrants who kill the godly, [lamenting] the colleges and the other greedy people who devour the revenues necessary | for preserving doctrine, and 16.105 finally also [lamenting] those cowards who do not support studies, who do not look out for posterity.

Here, I beseech and exhort all who rule to recognize the hungry and thirsty Christ, to rescue him, and to take care of their own ministers, that is, the pastors and scholars. It is certainly just and pious to allocate the resources of colleges and monasteries for this purpose, just as it is clearly written [1 Cor. 9:14]: "In this way, the Lord ordained that those who preach the Gospel should live from the Gospel." Nor should one invoke here the authority of the kings who gave these resources to the colleges, for they gave to the church, not intending that pastors would starve to death, studies be extinguished, and these funds be devoured in the meantime by other lazy and ungodly men. For that reason, it pertains to the office of the princes to look after the churches from this source.[246]

May Private Citizens Kill Tyrants?[247]

I respond: First, if the tyrant is a private individual who is seizing power through sedition and has not [yet] | obtained[248] power, those who are on p. 136 the side of the legitimate magistrates may privately kill him just as if he were a robber, especially if he is caught in the act, that is, if he is setting something in motion, riling up the people, or assaulting others. Thus, any private individual could have lawfully killed Catiline after his sedition was set in motion, just as Fulvius killed his son who was brought back while

246 This is the end of the tract *De officio principum*. In the 1538 and 1539 editions, which lack that tract entirely, the section entitled "May Private Citizens Kill Tyrants" is directly preceded by the section entitled "What Are Said to Be Voluntary Crimes?"

247 From this heading until the one entitled "Truthfulness", the headings are identical in the 1538 and 1540/46 versions, and the text is largely identical as well. The 1538 version ends after the section entitled "Truthfulness", but the revised and expanded version contains additional sections.

248 1540/1546b: *potius*. In both editions, the catchword on the previous page correctly reads *potitus*, as does the text of 1546a.

fleeing.[249] And the laws allow a person to kill his father if he has conspired against the republic.

Second: If the tyrant is in the magistracy, and he afflicts his subjects with an atrocious and flagrant injustice,[250] then the subjects may defend themselves, especially immediately [*in continenti*], both in private danger and in affairs pertaining to the republic. For instance, according to a Swiss story, the magistrate commanded a citizen to bring forth his son and throw a dart at him. And the military tribune in the army of Gaius Marius was lawfully killed by a youth whom that tribune was about to assault. The laws in the Digest allow the killing of a consul caught in adultery.

And in similar cases, if some people make themselves enemies, they are
16.106 rightly excused, even if they are not | avenging flagrant injustices immediately. Thus, Harpagus summoned Cyrus against Astyages, who had served Harpagus' own son to him to eat.[251] And when the tyrant of Vicenza commanded a certain citizen to send his daughter to him and the citizen then
p. 137 refused, the tyrant sent his bodyguards, | who seized her by force, and he returned her in the morning defiled and hacked into pieces. The father, after deliberating with his friends, sent the mutilated corpse to the Venetian senate and promised them that he would betray the city. In this way, the tyrant was overthrown. And this citizen, amidst such an atrocious and flagrant injustice, was absolutely permitted by the law of nations to become the tyrant's enemy.

Third: if the injustice is not flagrant, the jurists rightly say that the injustice[252] of the magistrates should be tolerated in order to preserve the

249 See Sallust, *The War with Catiline* 39. According to this passage, the son of the senator Fulvius was one of many Romans who flocked to Catiline at the beginning of the conspiracy. Fulvius had his son brought back from the journey to join the plot and had him killed.

250 For Melanchthon, an "atrocious and flagrant injustice" [*atrox ac notoria iniuria*] meant a crime so outrageous that the natural law and civil law allowed citizens to defend themselves, even against God-ordained political authorities. In his tract *De licita defensione* (*On Lawful Defence*, ca. 1546), Melanchthon wrote that "It is just to repel a manifest and atrocious injustice [*manifestam et atrocem iniuriam*], for both the natural law and the laws of the magistrates allow for such defence." See CR 6.152.

251 Harpagus was a Median general who served under Astyages, the king of Media. After a dispute between the two men, Astyages punished Harpagus by killing his only son, cooking him, and serving the boy to Harpagus at a feast. As a result, Harpagus promised Cyrus that he and his army would defect against Astyages if Cyrus rose up against the Median king. After Cyrus won the battle, aided by this mutiny, he took over Astyages' empire. See Herodotus, *The Histories* I.117–130.

252 The 1538 and 1539 editions read "*iniusticiam*". The 1540 and 1546 editions incorrectly

authority of matters which have been settled. For private citizens should not dissolve the state of the republic or usurp political authority, according to that [verse] [Romans 13:2]: "Whoever resists the magistrate also resists the ordination of God." Therefore, Caesar was killed unjustly. For, leaving aside the cause of war, he still held the magistracy at that time, which was surely granted by the laws and the consensus of the people. Nor did he destroy the republic's laws or prior decisions, but, having made decisions with greatest equity, he established peace in the government. And he did not sack the city as other victors in civil wars had done, nor did he publicly afflict the citizens everywhere with flagrant and atrocious injustices, but rather, he even restored his enemies to their former dignity. Therefore, it was unjust to kill him. For as I said before, the magistrates should be forgiven for minor injustices, just as Jason of Pherae says that he who strives after justice at the highest level nevertheless allows many injustices in minor affairs, and these should be forgiven in the one who protects the sovereign government and preserves the form, judgments, and laws of the republic.[253] | And p. 138
on the same point, Euripides says, "You tolerate the follies of the powerful rulers."[254]

Did Constantine Justly Start a War against His Relative and Allied Colleague Licinius, Who Was Committing Savagery against Christians?

Just as kings and princes should defend innocent subjects against their equals with arms and lawful war in other cases, so they should also defend pious subjects who are thrust into danger because of true doctrine. It is
for this reason that the prophet Isaiah | calls kings "the nourishers of the 16.107
Church" [Isaiah 49:23], because they should protect the Church from injustices. And Paul says, "Political power is for the good who act rightly" [cf. Romans 13:3]. And when political power [*potestas*][255] is directed towards the defence of the godly and the propagation of the Gospel, it performs its own highest duty, which God chiefly requires, and it becomes the worship of God. And we see in the sacred histories that God has honoured with great

read "*iusticiam*". For Melanchthon's engagement with the Roman jurists on the question of defence, see Diethelm Böttcher, *Ungehorsam oder Widerstand*, pp. 82–98.

253 cf. Aristotle, *Art of Rhetoric* I.12.31 (1373a.25–27).

254 Euripides, *Phoenician Women* 393.

255 In this section, Melanchthon uses the broad term *potestas* specifically to refer to political authorities. As such, in this section, I have translated it as "political power".

rewards those hosts who protected the godly, just as God said to Abraham [Genesis 12:3]: "I will bless those who bless you ..." And Obadiah was praised for hiding the prophets in caves when the queen commanded them to be killed [1 Kings 18:1–15]. Therefore, whenever some political power may justly
p. 139 undertake the defence of other just causes, | it may do the same in defence of the godly who are endangered for the sake of doctrine.

So then, Constantine was right to defend the subjects in those provinces which he himself ruled. He was also right to protect the honourable exiles. In addition, it was permissible for him to aid those provinces of Licinius which were begging him for aid and defence without breaking the alliance of [their] treaty [*foederis societas*].[256] For in every treaty [*foedus*], an exception is made for a case of justified defence. Because treaties cannot bind [one] contrary to the law of nature, or [bind one] to commit an injustice, especially a flagrant one, against anybody, for this reason, the Thebans acted rightly when they defended their allies against the Spartans and restored the Athenian exiles who had been afflicted with flagrant injustices by the Thirty Tyrants, whom the Spartans were supporting.[257] In this same way, Constantine acted rightly when he defended those who had sought aid from him against his equal. For it is permissible to give aid to the unjustly oppressed just as if they are allies, especially if they request it, just as the laws teach that alliances[258] may be legitimately established.

I will now leave aside other arguments that another part of imperial power pertained to Constantine in some way.

Here, the students should consider how many common topics [*loci communes*][259] converge in this question, namely:

---

256 Constantine (r. 306–337) and Licinius (r. 308–324) were allies and co-emperors of Rome. They were also bound by a marriage alliance, as Licinius was married to Constantine's half-sister. After an uneasy truce, Constantine attacked Licinius and eventually defeated him in 324, becoming sole emperor of the Eastern and Western Roman Empire. According to Eusebius (*Ecclesiastical History* X.8–9 in modern editions), Constantine's war against Licinius was justified because of Licinius' tyrannical oppression of his subjects.

257 After Sparta defeated Athens in the Peloponnesian War, the Spartans installed an oligarchic regime known as the "Thirty Tyrants." Thrasybulus, leader of the Athenian resistance, fled to Thebes, from where he launched his counter-attack. See Xenophon, *Hellenika* II.4.1–2.

258 1540 correctly reads *societates*. Both 1546 editions read *societatis*.

259 Melanchthon frequently made use of "common topics" (*loci communes*) to break down a complex subject into its important parts. Approaching the common topics individually allowed for a methodical approach to even the most complicated bodies of knowledge. Moreover, division of this sort also provided space for discussing

Concerning the duty of political power.
Concerning the law of war.
Concerning the law of treaties.
Whether princes may take up arms for the sake of religion. | p. 140
To what extent [princes] can adjudicate religious matters.
To what extent subjects are allowed to defend themselves. | 16.108

Concerning the duty of political power and the law of war, there is no doubt that political power should defend the innocent in just cases, whether civil ones or those pertaining to religion.

Concerning treaties, there is likewise no doubt that all treaties allow for exceptions in the case of justified defence, especially against flagrant injustice.

Nor is there any doubt that Christian princes should repel wars, even when they are started by their equals for the sake of religion, as is clear from the above passages.

Then, the common law of wars should be considered: Are they enemies? Are they practicing continual piracy? When are reparations and punishment available in addition to self-defence? Accordingly, the Christian kings have just causes to wage war against the Turks, because they have invaded our lands, and in the Mohammedan law [*lex Mahometica*] they profess that they are our enemies and proclaim perpetual war against us. For the Mohammedan law commands the Turks to wage war on all nations, even if there is no cause except that of propagating their sect.

Finally, even if none of these causes are present, godly kings should still prohibit blasphemy, lest it spread within their realms. | p. 141

---

the central disputes and disagreements about a certain topic. Melanchthon's *PME* is largely organized according to common topics, but, most famously, this was the method he used in his major theological textbook, entitled *Loci communes theologici*, where he presented a systematic treatment of Christian theology divided into topics such as "On Original Sin", "On Grace and Justification", and "On Good Works". For more on this method, see Robert Kolb, "Melanchthonian Method as a Guide to Reading Confessions of Faith: The Index of the Book of Concord and Late Reformation Learning", *Church History* 72.3 (2003): 504–524.

Does Prescription Excuse Conscience?[260]

I respond: it does excuse, for since the law is a better master of our affairs than any private owner, and since [the law] is a divine ordination, it follows that those to whom the law has assigned a thing justly become [its] owners by divine ordination. For the law established that ownership is acquired by prescription, lest ownership be perpetually uncertain and there be unending lawsuits. Therefore, things gained by prescription are held in good conscience, especially if there is a good title and no objecting conscience—that is, [a conscience] which knows for certain who the owners are. Nor should one object that conscience is in doubt, for one should consider the authority of the laws instead of private causes and understand that the law is the master of things. However, if someone knows for certain who the owners are, even if the judge does not pronounce contrary to prescription, then the reason of conscience should still hold in this case, and the matter should be settled with the owner, for nothing should be done contrary to conscience.

Hence, another question can be adjudicated, namely that funds given
16.109 to the churches for certain | abuses, such as Masses for the dead and similar things, cannot be sought back.[261] First, since [these funds] are held by prescription, what violence, what pillaging, what wars would come about? Therefore, the force of prescription should be maintained most of all in this case for the sake of public peace.[262] Second: The law is a better master of

260 Prescription (and the closely related concept of usucaption) was a Roman law mechanism for acquiring property through possession over an extended period of time. According to D.41.3.3, the concept is defined as "the claim of ownership through continual possession of a time defined by law." If a person continually possessed a piece of property, believed in good faith that he was the true owner, and held some reasonable title to the property, then after a defined amount of time (variable according to the specific situation), prescription granted property rights to the possessor. See DuPlessis, *Borkowski's Textbook*, pp. 187–193. The common law analogies are adverse possession and "squatter's rights". Melanchthon's argument here is that prescription, as a mechanism of the civil law and therefore a divine ordination, should excuse the conscience in these grey areas where true ownership is uncertain. However, as he states at the end of the paragraph, trying to gain property through prescription when one knows that one's own claim is dubious would be a violation of conscience.

261 Here, Melanchthon argues that donors who have given money to the Church to endow "abuses" such as the Mass cannot ask for their money back now that these funds have been reallocated for evangelical purposes. That is, donations given for Masses for the dead, etc., now belong to the churches by prescription and cannot be refunded.

262 D.41.3.1 states that "[Prescription] was introduced for the public good, specifically so

our affairs than private men. So then, | it is established in the Digest, in the laws about legates, that even if customs change, money earmarked for public spectacles cannot be sought back, but must be diverted to other public uses.[263] In the same way, the goods of the Church which were previously allocated towards abuses now should be transferred to true uses, that is, to supporting ministers of the Gospel, to supporting students whose studies are intended to serve the Church, and likewise to assisting studies useful to the Church. p. 142

Is It a Mortal Sin to Violate Civil Laws, That Is, the Edicts of the Civil Magistrates?

Moral [*ēthikē*] virtue does not only mean publicly restraining one's deeds and ruling external actions; it also requires choice [*proairesis*] in the soul, that is, deliberation and reasoned intention. Then [it requires] moral character [*ēthos*], that is, a soul habituated to restrain impulses and apply a certain moderation to one's deliberations. These two things are truly required for virtues, and youths should be trained to understand the power and nature of both of them. Deliberation, that is, *proairesis*, should seek the causes and reasons of all actions and should understand which things call the unruly soul back to the path like a bridle and show it what should be done.

But "moral" [*ēthikon*] is the name for that habituation of the soul—the level-headedness, moderation and steadiness by which one can restrain himself | until a matter has been deliberated, at which point he may do, with a certain agreeableness, what is absolutely right. p. 143

Therefore, since it is necessary to understand the causes of honourable actions, it is not enough to know the laws. Nay, in order to produce moral [*ēthikē*] virtue, it is absolutely necessary to understand the authority of the laws and the extent to which it is necessary to obey them. And the honourable soul, bolstered by this doctrine, will contemplate the laws and will understand how far they must be obeyed. Therefore, this analysis of the authority of the laws is relevant for moral [*ēthikē*] virtue.

Therefore, I first respond: Violating civil laws or the edicts of civil magistrates is a | mortal sin, even outside of cases of scandal, because Paul clearly 16.110

---

that ownership of certain things would not be uncertain for a long or almost unending duration. Instead, the designated amount of time should be sufficient for owners to seek restoration of their own things." One of the key rationales behind prescription was that it could establish lasting settlements in longstanding property disputes.

263 See D.33.2.16.

says [Romans 13:5]: "One must obey not only because of wrath, but also
because of conscience." That is, we should not just fear the civil punish-
ment, but we should also be aware that our consciences become guilty if
we disobey. Now, those of good mind should consider how important this
bond of obedience and public tranquillity is, since God himself requires
that we obey the laws and the magistrates.

[God] also claims that he will be the avenger if we disobey. And indeed,
God does punish both in this life and in the life to come, just as the fourth
commandment speaks of punishments in this life [Exodus 20:12]: "If you
want to live long in the land, etc." For that commandment concerning obedi-
p. 144 ence orders us to obey | not only our parents, but all those to whom parents
surrender their own authority—that is, the magistrates. For this reason,
many other passages in the scriptures preach about penalties paid in this
life, as Proverbs 24:[21,22]: "Fear God and the king, and do not mingle with
traitors, for disaster comes to them suddenly." And Christ says [Matthew
26:52]: "Whoever takes up the sword will die by the sword." For "taking up
the sword" means taking up a sword not granted by the laws and the magis-
trates. In other words, [it means] being seditious and disobeying the present
magistrates. And not only the examples set forth in the sacred scriptures,
but also the history of all ages testifies that in general, murderers, thieves,
perjurers, unjust judges, traitors, and tyrants are divinely brought to punish-
ment in this life. I say these things so that we may know that God requires
this tutelage [*paidagōgia*] to coerce men by the fear of punishment.

And this fear cultivates reverence for the laws, and creates morality [*ēthi-
kon*] in souls since it throws a rein on desires, so to speak, and habituates to
obedience.

There is no doubt that there are many woeful cases of punishment for
this barbaric liberty, which many claim for themselves, not wanting to be
ruled by the authority of superiors. For the divine law, which says [Exodus
20:12] "Honor your father and mother, if you want to live long in the land",
p. 145 does not err. In addition, our souls contain an even greater fear, | when we
believe that the violation of the laws will result in eternal punishment after
this life, unless we come to our senses.

So then, one should wisely understand this teaching about the edicts
of the magistrates, and especially about those edicts which do not com-
mand anything contrary to the mandates of God. And one should consider
whether those who disobey do so out of petulance, or because of some
16.111 other | cause which provides an excuse. Gerson's distinction does not dis-
please me; he distinguishes among the laws and says that some were passed
for the sake of necessity, namely those which are necessary for the common

peace, such as [laws] about thievery, murder, marriage, division of inheritances, taxes, military matters, trials, and similar things.[264] He says that others were passed not so much for the sake of necessity as for the sake of decorum, as when it was established that a woman should not marry before she has mourned[265] her previous husband.

I find this distinction pleasing not only because reason produces diverse obligations, but more so because the will of the magistrate, which simply requires obedience in the prior matters, is clear. In the other, lighter matters, it does not require [obedience] in the same way. So then, one should consider the will of the legislator and to what extent he intends to create obligations. Yet even in these lighter matters, there should be no petulance or contempt for government, for that is a bad example. Instead, it is conducive to discipline and to the tranquillity of the republic to habituate souls such that they magnify the authority of the law even in small things. Then, | p. 146
let us recognize this too: that we do not live for ourselves, but for the republic.[266] Therefore, we should take care that we do not harm the community by our examples. Plato said the same thing most weightily in the fifth book of *The Laws*: the best and most outstanding citizen, the citizen who brings the most glory to the state, is not the one who wins great victories or triumphs, but the one who surpasses others in his diligence in obeying the laws.[267]

But here, it will be asked whether the same reasoning applies to ecclesiastical ceremonies, which have been established by human authority. I respond that, concerning these, this rule should be observed: It is a sin to violate these [ceremonies] in a case of scandal. But outside of a case of scandal, they may be violated without mortal sin. For it is necessary to preserve the doctrine that ceremonies of these sorts are things indifferent [*res indifferentes*] and not necessary for justice before God, just as the use of the toga or Greek cloak is indifferent. This rule of Paul's is useful both for public peace and for the tranquillity of consciences.[268] For it preserves

264 Melanchthon here refers to the Paris theologian Jean Gerson (1363–1429). The precise reference here is unclear, but Gerson discusses the topic of law at length in *De vita spirituali animae*. See Gerson, *Oeuvres Complètes*, ed. Mgr. Glorieux (1962), vol. III, pp. 113–202.

265 1540 incorrectly reads *duxerit*. 1546: *luxerit*. The 1546 reading is to be preferred, especially since it has the same meaning as the 1538 reading (p. 100, *eluxerit*).

266 cf. Cicero, *Philippics* I.15.38.

267 Plato, *Laws* 729d.

268 Melanchthon refers here to 1 Corinthians 8:1–13 and 10:23–33, where Paul discusses eating meat sacrificed to idols. Paul's main point in these passages is that a Christian's

16.112 ceremonies | and commands the prohibition of offenses, public tumults, and the public dissipation of rites. On top of that, it frees the conscience from many superstitious beliefs and horrible torments; for if good minds believe that the observation of such rites is necessary even outside of a case of scandal, that will be a harsh slavery.

Among such a multitude of rites, as many times as consciences often run
p. 147 up against fasting, reciting prayers, | observing holidays, or similar things, many things[269] arise, especially for those who are worried about how they can always keep these rites. Therefore, this rule contains useful equity [*epieikeia*] which prohibits public scandals, preserves customs which are useful for tranquillity, and privately liberates consciences from danger.

So then, having understood the causes of the laws and traditions, good-natured men will love them even more. For this reason, it is beneficial to keep this in mind: namely, that these ordinations have been instituted by the Church on behalf of public good order [*eutaxia*], and that the Church does not want to throw a noose over private consciences. So then, it is most moral [*ēthikon*] to love common tranquillity and order, because good people will love these customs most when [the customs] benefit peace and order, especially when [people] have been liberated from superstitious opinions and understand that they may neglect these rites without danger outside of a case of scandal.

But here, it is disputed whether the ecclesiastical ordinations and the civil laws of the magistrates bind one in different ways. I respond: They do bind in different ways, and, although one may seek arguments, it is nevertheless simplest to adjudicate this from the plain and clear sayings of scripture. Therefore, I will first recite these [sayings], and afterwards I will also add some arguments and interpretation, lest something absurd be taken from our position.

p. 148 Concerning obedience owed to the civil laws, | Paul says that "one must obey not only because of wrath, but also because of conscience" [Romans 13:5]. This command binds us even outsides of a case of scandal, since divine authority must be obeyed even outside of a case of scandal. But concerning ecclesiastical ceremonies, Paul says [Colossians 2:16]: "Let no one condemn you in food and drink and on the matter of festival days." Likewise, in Galatians [cf. 5:1]: "Stand in that liberty for which Christ has liberated you, and do not be subjected again to the yoke of slavery." And Christ says [Matthew

---

behaviour in regard to "things indifferent" should never become a scandal, that is, it should never cause another Christian to sin.

269 1546b: *multae*. The reading of 1546a (*multa*) is to be preferred.

15:11]: "Everything that goes in the mouth does not defile a person," and the Apostle pardons those who violate traditions. | 16.113

For, since this doctrine—that traditions about food and similar things are not [matters of] worship or justice, but things indifferent—must be present in the Church, for this reason, the Gospel accordingly teaches that consciences should not be burdened by an opinion about necessity. However, because this life cannot do without ordinations and ceremonies, this equity [*epieikeia*] was needed so that they would be observed without obscuring the doctrine of true worship and the blessing of Christ, and likewise without burdening the conscience with infinite torments, which would dismantle faith. Therefore, the Gospel intends for us to understand that these rites may be omitted outside of a case of scandal, but that they should be kept for the sake of good order [*eutaxia*] and for preventing scandals. This liberty, since it was established by the authority of the Gospel, cannot be erased by human authority. | p. 149

I have shown from the testimonies of scripture that the obligation [to civil laws and to ecclesiastical ceremonies] is not the same. This is the simplest response to this question, but let us add reason as well.

The first [argument] is derived from efficient causes, that is, from the right of political power [*potestas*], and Gerson follows this. The civil magistrate has, by divine authority, the right of establishing laws [*ius condendi leges*] which are upright and useful in those matters pertaining to the defence of bodily life and civil society, such as [laws] about trials, penalties for crimes, contracts, inheritance, and similar matters, just as Solomon says [Proverbs 8:15]: "Through me, kings reign and establish what is just."

But ecclesiastical power is limited in that it has a mandate about what it should teach and [a mandate] not to devise new worship or burden consciences with traditions and ceremonies. For Peter says [Acts 15:10]: "Why are you putting God to the test, placing a yoke, etc." And Paul [Colossians 2:20–21]: "Why are you making decrees? Do not touch, do not handle, etc." Hence, because each power has its own right, their laws likewise obligate in different ways.

The second argument [is derived] from the final causes of the laws. The civil laws are the bonds of common society. Therefore, charity is always harmed in a violation. Therefore, because each person should offer, like a contribution to a feast,[270] his obedience, his tribute, and his resources to the

270 1540 reads *symbolam*, although in the first line of p. 150 it reads *symbolum*. 1546a/b: *symbolum* here and below.

defence of the common tranquillity, when they do not do this, they cheat the rest, for they enjoy someone else's services and offer nothing of their
p. 150 16.114 own. It is like a man who brings | | no contribution to a banquet—he cheats the other guests.

Likewise, the example of violation harms and disturbs the common tranquillity. Therefore, in the civil laws, the rationale of charity and scandal is always valid. However, many ceremonies are private household observances, the violation of which does not harm others. Therefore, because here, charity is not endangered, and scandals do not occur, these laws have a different authority. For we have already said that these become necessary and cannot be violated without sin at the point when violation produces scandals, that is, when it harms the faith and morals of others, or rashly disturbs the peace of others.

So then, even if it is useful to weigh out these arguments and to understand the causes and classes of the laws, nevertheless, it is safer to judge simply by those sayings of Scripture which I have recited and laid out above. For arguments have many ambiguities, and they do not sufficiently fortify the conscience. And if one judges from arguments alone and not from the Scriptures, clever men will be able to seek and fabricate many intractable problems at every point. But here, let the young be warned, that although they must understand that these *adiaphora* are not the worship of God, still, in the meantime, they should learn that the case of scandal extends broadly and must be guarded against with particular care. For in the violation of traditions, two things are endangered: discipline and tranquillity, or harmony of the public state. Furthermore, we who occupy ourselves with the studies of doctrine and virtues must especially understand the magnitude
p. 151 and force of both of these things. |

For first, certain ordinations are necessary for the sake of discipline. For a crude age must be trained by ceremonies and rites, holidays, set readings, and public and household exercises. For this reason, Paul [Galatians 3:24] calls the law a "tutor" [*paedagogus*]. For these ceremonies are a certain tutelage [*paidagōgia*] necessary in childhood.

Moreover, even though the Gospel offers a certain loftier doctrine, still it does not intend to abolish discipline and tutelage, but it commands that men be coerced, ruled, and instructed by tutelage of this kind. I have spoken elsewhere about the usefulness of this tutelage. For God is efficacious in those who allow themselves to be instructed and do not recoil from his word. Therefore, the example of violation of traditions is harmful. Because
16.115 it is common that nature | hates the bonds of the laws, these examples are freely imitated, and from them comes a contempt for general instruction

and all laws. For with the rites abolished, there can be no tutelage, and neither a crude age nor an ignorant multitude can be instructed.

Moreover, when the young and ignorant cannot be educated, unending barbarity and unending desolation must necessarily follow. In truth, how great a crime is it—how great a danger[271]—to set examples from which | p. 152
that desolation could arise? Besides, how much evil is there in the other facet of a scandal, namely that it disturbs the tranquillity of the Church and the republic?

For in this bodily life, ceremonies are needed also for the sake of peace, or for the sake of good order [*eutaxia*], which is most beneficial for man. When this order is dissolved, unending confusion follows. Educators have no authority; there are no set times for instruction; there are no sure teachers and no certain form of doctrine. In such confusion, the ministry of the Gospel cannot be preserved and the Church cannot be instructed.

Finally, just as the order and harmony of public rites unites men and brings them together, so the confusion of the order disorients souls and produces great tumults and eternal wars.

Therefore, we should consider that, in the violation of traditions, an example can broadly and easily spread to others. Then, we should consider how evil such an example is. Therefore, lest we burden our consciences with dangers, and lest we harm others, we should also observe whichever public rites with greater care. It is tyrannical to pay more mind to that which pleases us than to that which benefits others. For we are not born for ourselves alone, but our life belongs to others, and especially to the Church, that is, to the glory of Christ, [and] to the conservation of the ministry and the preservation of the people's tutelage [*paidagōgia*]. The Church chiefly desires to look after these two things,[272] which are of the greatest importance. | In them, we display our obedience, care, and zeal for the Church, p. 153
for the sake of the common welfare and tranquillity. Plato says that a person should love his homeland [*patria*] more than his own mother, because one's homeland is something divine.[273] But our true homeland should be the Church, and it truly is divine, for it is the temple of God and the gather-

271 Both 1546 editions read *periculum* ("danger"). 1538, 1539, and 1540 have a much harsher reading: *parricidium* ("parricide").

272 The structure of the sentence seems to indicate that the "two things" refer to 1) "the glory of Christ" and 2) "the conservation of the ministry and the preservation of the people's tutelage".

273 cf. Plato, *Laws* 740a.

ing of the members of Christ. Therefore, we should love it and freely obey
16.116 it, and devote | everything to its benefit and tranquillity.

Paul [Galatians 4:9] calls traditions "empty rudiments" [*egena elementa*], which, even though they are empty, that is, paltry things, perishable, not eternal—they are neither worship nor justice—they are still rudiments, that is, ordinations which this bodily life cannot do without for the sake of discipline and good order [*eutaxia*]. Therefore, those ordinations should not be done away with, but we should consider Paul's counsel. For although he calls them "empty," he still also calls them "rudiments", and he removes the value of justice in such a way that he demonstrates that there are occasionally ordinations which have their own utility.[274] For discipline has great power and there is no sweeter harmony than good order in the republic. For this reason, these things are called "rudiments," that is, ordinations, which
p. 154 maintain that harmony. |

Was Boniface VIII Right When He Decreed That the Pope, by Divine Right, Possesses Both Swords, That Is, Both the Ultimate Ecclesiastical Power and the Ultimate Power, Mandate, or Right of Conferring the Kingdoms and Governments of the World?[275]

The question about the difference between ecclesiastical power and the civil magistrates is a useful one. For reverence towards both powers is strengthened within measured dispositions when, with the offices rightly defined and distinguished, it becomes clear how great the dignity of each of them is. Moreover, this reverence is primarily a virtue which is particularly moral [*ēthikē*] and worthy of a good man. Understanding the proper duty of each power is also profitable in many areas. For it is characteristic of tyrants to

274 That is, by calling these things "empty rudiments", Paul both downplays the value of total righteousness (i.e., *iusticia*) regarding these ceremonies, while also showing that certain ordinations can be useful at some times.

275 Medieval political theory posited a division between spiritual and secular authority which was symbolized by the metaphor of the two swords. The "spiritual sword" belonged to the Pope and granted him authority over religious dogma, church institutions, and ecclesiastical forms of authority such as excommunication and interdict. The "secular sword" belonged to temporal rulers and included the coercive power to fulfil secular duties such as punishing secular crimes, levying taxes, and waging war. In the famous 1302 bull *Unam sanctam*, Pope Boniface VIII had claimed that the Church possessed both swords, and that the Pope merely delegated the secular sword to temporal authorities. For an overview of the two swords theory, see J.A. Watt, "Spiritual and Temporal Powers" in *The Cambridge History of Medieval Political Thought, c. 350–c. 1450*, ed. J.H. Burns (2008): pp. 367–423.

confuse different offices, but each should "set his own Sparta in order".[276] And because there are various disputes about this difference, a careful explication will contain much insight and good fruit.

First, it must be recognized that both powers, ecclesiastical and civil, are the gift and ordination of God. Therefore, both of them should be held in high esteem and thanks should be given to God for such blessings. And certainly, the ecclesiastical power was ordained and established by a clear and explicit mandate when Christ sent the Apostles throughout the whole world in the last chapter of Matthew [28:19]: "Go out and teach all nations." And because the Church has always | existed from the beginning of the world, p. 155
God has always established the ecclesiastical power with a clear word by a promise, as when he gave the promise[277] and the rite to Abraham | and 16.117
commanded him to pass these down to his descendants.

Concerning civil power, Paul [Romans 13:1] most clearly affirms that it is an ordination which God truly established and conserves, just as Daniel [2:21] says: "God bestows and establishes kingdoms." And because governments are the work of God and his good creations, it follows that administration has been approved by God and is pleasing to him. But a question arises here: Was civil power originally established by the explicit word of God, or was it merely approved afterwards? I myself certainly believe that civil power was established by the explicit word of God when it was said to Noah [Genesis 9:6]: "Whoever sheds human blood shall have his own blood shed", and then it adds, "by men." Therefore, [this verse] means that order should be established such that murderers are punished by certain magistrates.

This is the fundamental law, and it embraces all the rest of the polity. But even if someone disagrees on this point, he will still concede that God truly is the author of governments, both because he revealed the law about political ordination through natural reason and [because he] instigated heroic minds to establish governments, just as the Psalmist refers to "the one who gives security to kings" [Psalm 144:10]. And in the law, | God approves the p. 156
ordination of punishments with clear testimonies, as in Leviticus 24.[278] There was less need for an explicit mandate about the law, because it is

276 *suam quisque Spartam ornare debet*. Part of an ancient proverb: "Sparta is your lot, set it in order". The idea is that each person should take care of the responsibility granted to him. The proverb is a fragment of Euripides (see LCL 506.210) and appears in Cicero, *Letters to Atticus* 83 (IV.6) as well as in Plutarch.

277 1540: *promissione*. 1546: *promissionem*. The latter reading is preferable.

278 In this chapter, God institutes punishments for blasphemy, murder, and other crimes.

known to reason. But the ecclesiastical power absolutely required an explicit mandate, because the Gospel is not naturally known to human reason. However, as I have just said, it seems more correct to me that civil power was established with explicit words in that passage where the words were spoken to Noah. Therefore, political power or governments, from the very beginning of the world, have been divine ordinations, even among the pagans.

I have spoken of the origin of both powers, and now I will add a distinction.

Civil power is an institution in which superiors, namely the magistrates, have a mandate to command honourable morals in the external manner of life, to coerce men, and to punish with physical force in order to prohibit unjust violence, to punish crimes, and to defend the public peace. Moreover, one should wisely consider that this definition attributes to the magistrates not only defence of the peace, but also a mandate to preserve
16.118 discipline | or to preserve honourable morals. For the end of peace should be to create leisure—not for chasing after pleasures, but for educating and
p. 157 instructing children, for teaching religion, and for developing good morals. | Paul teaches this most authoritatively when he commands us to pray for the powers so that we can lead tranquil lives in piety and honesty [1 Timothy 2:2]. That is, the end of governments should not merely be peace, but that discipline, honourable morals, and religion would be preserved in peace. Therefore, in order for us to rightly understand the office of the civil magistrate, we should contemplate that the magistrates are the defenders of the law, just as Cicero compares the magistrate and the law when he says, "The Magistrate is a living law."[279] And Aristotle: "The ruler is the guardian of the laws."[280] Therefore, the magistrate is not just the guardian of this or that commandment, but of the entire law, that is, of both tables, insofar as it pertains to external discipline.

But first, the power of the magistrates must be bounded by some limits here: namely, that he does not have the authority to command anything contrary to the law of nature, contrary to the commandments of God, or contrary to the laws of his own country. Therefore, the power of the magistrates is not limitless, but it is bounded by certain constraints. For the magistrate holds his appointment [*procuratio*] from another, namely from the man-

---

279 cf. Cicero, *On the Laws* III.1.2. Cicero refers to the magistrate as a *legem loquentem* ("a speaking law"), not a "living law".

280 Perhaps a paraphrased reference to *Politics* III.11.3 (1287a.21), where Aristotle refers to rulers as *nomophulakas* (guardians of the laws), or to *NE* V.6.6 (1134b.1–2), where he calls the ruler the *phulax tou dikaiou* (guardian of justice).

date of God. For this reason, he should not depart from God's mandates, just as the most magnificent king Jehoshaphat preached: "Do not exercise man's judgment, but God's; whatever you decide will return to you. Let the fear of God be upon you" [2 Chronicles 19:6–7]. So then, below, we will speak more broadly about other questions [concerning] how this power is limited by natural, divine, and positive laws.

Second, because the civil magistrate is also the guardian | of the first table insofar as it pertains to external discipline, the magistrate should prohibit and punish blasphemy, idolatry, and false teachings, and he should ensure that true and pious doctrine is propagated and defend those who teach what is correct. First of all, the second commandment of the Decalogue confirms this opinion. And all magistrates should themselves obey the second commandment of the Decalogue and be its guardians. The second commandment prohibits and punishes blasphemies and false dogmas. Therefore, all magistrates should prohibit and punish blasphemy. p. 158

The second argument is derived from the chief end of the magistrates. The chief end of human society is to enable some men to teach others about God, so that the knowledge of God may spread. | The magistrate is the chief guardian of society. Therefore, he should also be the guardian of that very end, namely that the knowledge of God be rightly propagated. The consequence is valid according to that maxim: "Whatever makes something to be a certain way, is that and to a greater degree".[281] The magistrate guards society for the sake of the knowledge of God; therefore, he should all the more guard the knowledge of God insofar as it pertains to his own office. This argument is very learned, for it advises about two things which are most worthy of consideration: namely, what is the chief cause whereby men were made for society, and further, that the magistrate should be devoted to that chief end, such that he preserves the knowledge of God in [his] lands. But if | we compare kings and princes to this image, we will find very few who look to this goal and strive to achieve it. 16.119 p. 159

Most have acted to the contrary with all their might, for they have polluted religion with every wickedness and tried to destroy it, as if they were

281 "*propter quod unumquodque tale, et illud magis tale.*" This common scholastic axiom is derived from Aristotle's *Metaphysics* II.1.6 (993b.26–27). In this context, the axiom shows that, if the magistrate's function of guarding society and the laws is subservient to the chief end of protecting the knowledge of God, then the magistrate should also more directly guard the knowledge of God, i.e., he should punish blasphemy and idolatry.

structuring their kingdoms to wage war with God just like the Titans in the myths.

The third argument is derived from examples. The holy kings of Judah abolished impious cults, and on account of that they were praised and honoured with great rewards, as God says [1 Samuel 2:30]: "I will glorify those who glorify me." And the law in Deuteronomy [17:18–19] commands that kings keep the book of the law in their hands and preserve the religion handed down by God.

Our own magistrates, according to their own calling, should also imitate these examples because they pertain to the Decalogue. Likewise, Nebuchadnezzar [cf. Daniel 3:29] and Darius [cf. Daniel 6:26–27] declared edicts: "Let no one speak blasphemy against the God of the Israelites." At this point, some raise many objections. First: Faith is in the mind. The magistrate cannot change minds. Therefore, the magistrate should not punish errors of the mind. I respond to the conclusion. He does not punish errors of the mind alone, but external profession and blasphemy. Because the magistrate should protect external order and tutelage [*paidagōgia*], he should not permit ignorant men to spread scandals by which others are deceived and rush
p. 160 into error. |

The second objection: The magistrate can only adjudicate those matters about which he has laws. The magistrate only has laws concerning secular affairs. Therefore, he cannot adjudicate religious controversies.

First, the minor premise should be rejected. For the magistrate has a law
16.120 to punish blasphemy, just as the laws of all nations punish perjury. But | because there is not always a consensus about which opinions are blasphemous or impious, for this reason, some other adjudication [*iudicium*] must come first, namely, an inquiry [*cognitio*] about doctrine.[282] However, these things pertain not only to the magistracy, but to the Church, that is, not only to the presbyters, but also to the laymen who are qualified to judge, just as Paul says [1 Corinthians 14:30]: "If a revelation is made to one sitting nearby, let the first person be silent." And Christ intends for the Church to have the ultimate decision when he says [Matthew 18:17]: "Tell it to the Church."

Constantine's example is applicable here. When he held a synod, he himself was present at the disputation, and afterwards, he signed on to the

---

282 Here, Melanchthon's terms *iudicium* and *cognitio*, besides their more general meanings, are also the terms for Roman legal procedures, stressing the procedural element of determining doctrine in the church as described below.

decision and declared in public letters that he had been an equal participant throughout the entire discussion of the controversy.[283] And Emperor Marcianus, who held the synod of Chalcedon, said that he would be present at the synod, after Constantine's example, so that, after the truth had been made clear, he could then ensure that the one true resolution was declared to the people and [he could] prohibit depraved opinions. And Pope Nicholas says in Distinction 96: "The causes of the faith are common, and they pertain not only to clerics, but to laymen as well."[284] | And Alexander II sum- p. 161
moned the provincial magistrates to deliberation in the synod about the degrees of consanguinity.[285] Finally, history illustrates that many princes and kings have been present at synods.

Indeed, no one denies that princes should be summoned to deliberation in synods. But some people call into question whether kings also have a vote [*suffragatio*], or, as they say, a decisive voice. But kings should not be denied this vote if synods really are adjudications of the Church, as I have said previously. For they themselves are members of the Church, and when the bishops err, the laymen have a mandate to dissent from them, according to that | verse [Matthew 7:15]: "Beware of false prophets." And [Galatians 16.121
1:8]: "If anyone gives you another Gospel, let him be anathema!" This mandate applies equally to all people,[286] [commanding] that they judge about doctrine, according to their own position, from the word of God. And Peter commands that everyone be "prepared to render an account of their faith, etc." [1 Peter 3:15].

Therefore, kings should impose their authority when there is a danger that bishops will pronounce incorrectly. And Augustine writes in Letter 166 that Constantine initially committed the cause of Caecilianus to the bishops twice, and afterwards he heard the case and settled it himself.[287] And he argues in many words that these adjudications of doctrine also concern godly princes. For in the Church, one should not establish that tyranny in which the laity must approve and applaud without discrimination everything that the bishops decree. Nor should the Church | be a democracy p. 162

283 A reference to the 325 Council of Nicaea, which Emperor Constantine called and personally attended.

284 cf. Gratian, Decretum Dist.96, c.4.

285 Pope Alexander II, r. 1061–1073.

286 1546a: *omnes*. 1546b: *omues*.

287 In the numbering of modern editions, this is Augustine's Letter 105, Augustine to the Donatists in 409/410. A translation of the letter can be found in *Augustine: Political Writings*, ed. E.M. Atkins and R.J. Dodaro, (2004), pp. 162–173.

[*dēmokratia*] in which everyone is promiscuously granted a license to shout and propose dogmas. Instead, it should be an aristocracy [*aristokratia*], an arrangement in which those who rule, the bishops and kings, share their decisions and select men who are qualified to judge.

From these things, it can be sufficiently understood that the inquiry concerning doctrine pertains to the Church, that is, to the presbyters and princes. But once a matter has been investigated and adjudicated, the princes then become the guardians of external discipline and executors of the synod's decision, meaning that they prohibit idolatrous worship, blasphemy, and impious dogma and they punish those who profess [such things].

Another argument. The magistrate is only the defender of the body. Dogma does not pertain to the body. Therefore, the prohibition of dogma does not pertain to the magistrate. Response: The major premise should be denied, and this is the reason. For although the protection of the body does indeed pertain to the office of the magistrate because it is part of the law, nevertheless, it is not the chief end of the magistrates. Rather, the preservation of the law insofar as it pertains to external discipline is the chief end of the magistrates. For the magistrate is just like the law itself. Moreover, the law does not only teach about the defence of the body or property, but it primarily teaches about the glory of God and about discipline, just as Paul says [1 Tim. 1:9]: "The law was given to restrain the unjust, the blasphemers." Therefore, the error of those who do not want the magistrates to look after
p. 163 dogma is born entirely from | the fanciful idea that the magistrate is like an Epicurean, only having a mandate to defend the body. But one can easily
16.122 judge that this fantasy is false | if one considers that the magistrate and the law are equal, and that the chief end of the magistrate is the protection of the law, etc.

Therefore, the magistrate, who wields the sword, should also prohibit heresies (that is, impious dogmas) and punish heretics (that is, authors of impious dogmas). But in obscure matters, the Church's inquiry should come first. And in this way, the magistrate properly serves the glory of God, and the worship of God becomes his function when he takes care to protect, propagate, and honour true doctrine and, conversely, prohibit impious dogma. For it is in this way that he performs his chief duty, which properly pertains to the glory of God, and which properly earns him that title with which the magistrates are decorated in Psalm [82:6] ("I said, you are gods"), namely, because they have a divinely established office and should bestow upon men the divine things: religion, justice, discipline, peace, etc. It is for this reason that Isaiah [49:23] calls the magistrates "nourishers of the

Church", since they should nourish and protect pious teachers and should not exercise savagery against Christians.

There are other questions about civil power, some of which we will treat in order. Namely, concerning the laws: that laws contrary to divine or natural law should not be | observed. Likewise, that the magistrate[288] may not judge p. 164
contrary to the laws of his own republic. But we shall discuss these questions a bit later. At this time, I return to ecclesiastical power, which is the divine mandate of teaching the Gospel, administering the sacraments, ordaining ministers of the Gospel, announcing remission of sins individually or corporately, and making judgments concerning dogma. Also, excommunicating, by word and without physical force, those who are caught up in clear transgressions. There are many parts of this definition, and they are usually explained more fully elsewhere. Therefore, here I will respond briefly to the constitution of Boniface: By divine right, neither the Apostles nor their successors hold the sword, that is, the right to coerce with physical force. Therefore, neither do they have any right to occupy or confer the kingdoms of this world.

Many testimonies can be gathered from the Gospel. Christ says [John 18:36]: "My kingdom is not of this world." Likewise [Luke 22:25–26]: "The kings of the nations lord over them [...] but not so with you." For he distinguishes two powers. He allows | the kings to rule, but he does not allow the 16.123
Apostles to rule, that is, to use physical force under the pretext of ministry. And Paul says [2 Corinthians 10:4]: "The weapons of our warfare are not of the flesh." But I would add one opinion of Chrysostom, who, in the second oration on the dignity of priests, clearly distinguishes secular magistrates from bishops.[289] | He grants to secular magistrates the right of coercing p. 165
by physical force, but denies that bishops have the power of coercing by physical force.

Moreover, bishops or pastors of the churches may hold property, wealth, or other donations just like other Christians, because these are political things which are conceded to Christians. Accordingly, bishops may hold the jurisdiction over certain goods which is granted to them. [This jurisdiction] is a civil matter which has nothing to do with the particular office of the bishop, just as Paul's trade of clothworking had nothing to do with the office of Apostle. Yet Paul was still able to be both an Apostle and a clothworker. But the bishops should be careful, lest these faculties distract them from the

288 1540 incorrectly reads *Magistratus*. 1546a/b: *magistratui*.

289 John Chrysostom, *Treatise Concerning the Christian Priesthood* II.3 (PG vol. 48, col. 634).

office of teaching and governing the Church, and of examining the doctrine of those over whom they preside.

The Emperor had commanded Ambrose to cede the sanctuary to the Arians, but Ambrose [did] not obey.[290] For he was not allowed to obey someone giving impious orders, and the Emperor should not have removed a lawful ordination from the Church or appointed an impious teacher in the Church. For Ambrose was legitimately ordained and was teaching correctly. Moreover, the legitimate ordination involved the calling or election which was made by the people or by those to whom the people had entrusted this matter, and it involved the approval of the other bishops.

Moreover, it pertains to the bishops to make judgments about doctrine and to call synods, just as the old arrangement was that each bishop would
p. 166 hold a synod of his churches twice | a year. The Apostles also held synods. When Paul of Samosata was spreading impious dogma, the neighbouring bishops convened at Antioch and condemned him in front of the gathered Antiochene church. But, as was said above, in controversies about doctrine, the bishops alone should not adjudicate, but qualified men from the whole body of the Church should be selected, because the ultimate judgment should belong to the whole Church, that is, not only to the bishops.
16.124 Therefore, for | this very reason, because the authority of the Church is superior, emperors and kings should call synods when the bishops do not perform their own duties, just as Constantine called some synods and even ordered that those who refused to attend the synod should be stripped of their episcopacy.

I have spoken of the distinction between the two powers. For it benefits the doctors of the churches that they remember not to usurp the duties of the power of the sword. Conversely, secular magistrates should learn to revere ecclesiastical power and refrain from intruding upon the duties of the ecclesiastical power, just as Peter [1 Peter 4:15] prohibits us from being "meddlers" [*allotrioepiskopoi*] that is, from rushing to interfere in others' duties. Therefore, it was with great piety that the emperor Valentinian said: "This is the sort of man who should be elected bishop: one to whom the emperor himself is not afraid to bow his head." And indeed, in election, [Valentinian] did not take away the Church's right, but he commanded them to
p. 167 choose, etc. |

And although we have distinguished between the powers, still one can observe that the civil power should serve the Church for the sake of dis-

290 Ambrose, bishop of Milan (ca. 339–397).

cipline, just as any head of household is the minister and executor of the Church in his own household. For we should all obey the ministry of the word, and accordingly, the magistrate is minister and executor of the Church in the republic. For [the magistrate] himself should also obey the ministry of the word, and venerate it as if it were divine, according to this saying: "Open your gates, O princes" [Psalm 24:7,9].

Was Naboth Right in Refusing to Cede His Vineyard When the King Asked for It, Even Though Kings Are Said to Be the Owners Even of Private Resources?

I respond: Naboth was rightly allowed to keep his own vineyard, and the king could not legally force a citizen to sell it.[291] The reason is that the laws of nature or nations should not be violated. | 16.125

The distinction of ownership, or property, is of the law of nations, or as the philosophers say, of the law of nature. Therefore, it is unjust to disrupt the distinctions of ownership and seize another's goods without just cause. Thus, the law of nature supports private property, as does divine law, when it says [Exodus 20:15]: "You shall not steal." For the Decalogue, as has been often said, is the explication of the natural law which reveals that the law of nature is a divine decree. Therefore, tyrants sin | against God when they p. 168 steal their citizens' fortunes.

Moreover, when free men lawfully surrender their liberty and come under slavery, they surrender ownership and property. Yet no one is a slave by nature, so therefore, since Naboth was free and the owner of his own possessions, he had a right to keep his own estate.

But here, a verse concerning the right of the king in [1] Samuel [8:11,14] is put forth in objection: "This is the king's right [...] to take away your fields, etc." Therefore, kings are the lords of private resources.

I respond: This passage does not abolish the law of nature, but it is speaking specifically about taxes. Just as kings should not seize resources from free-born men, so all the more should they refrain from seizing their liberty, except when they punish certain crimes.

And although subjects owe taxes to kings for the sake of administration, as Paul indeed teaches [Romans 13:6–7], nevertheless, being a subject is not slavery, but rather, liberty must continue to exist under governments [*in*

291 In 1Kings 21, King Ahab of Israel offered to pay Naboth for his vineyard. Naboth refused, and Ahab's wife Jezebel had Naboth killed.

imperiis], that is, such that each man should keep what is his, that no one should be punished except on account of crimes, and that upright citizens have the protection that they deserve.

This is a simple and true response: Kings have a right to take something from private resources, specifically for the sake of administration, for the common necessity, but not in order to become owners of all private
p. 169 resources on the pretext of government. |

However, it must be recognized that there are different forms of rule and varying degrees of liberty in various places. Yet God approves every form of government which agrees with reason and nature. Therefore, the law of nature should always prevail, lest distinctions of ownership be disturbed. Moreover, [political] power, however defined, should preserve and obey the laws of its own country. Wherever the laws themselves grant liberty to the citizens and distinguish ownership of things, there the kings sin when they seize private resources.

Moreover, the Israelites had a law—and indeed it was divinely given—which distinguished possessions and granted private property to citizens.
16.126 No king could have lawfully abolished this law. For this reason, Ahab sinned | when he seized another man's vineyard. And God, when he avenges this crime, declares that he will exact a similar punishment on other tyrants. We ourselves are free in this way, as evidenced by the possession of liberty, and the Roman laws grant liberty to citizens and divide up ownership. Therefore, princes sin when they seize the resources of private citizens or when they fleece their people with extreme demands. For the law of nature forbids them to seize what is not theirs, and they must obey the laws of their own countries. Thus, the law of Theodosius gives this most honourable teaching in the Codex: "Worthy of majesty is the voice of that ruler who declares that he, the prince, is bound by the laws. For our authority depends on the authority of the law, and in fact, it is a greater sovereignty for the prince to
p. 170 submit to the laws."[292] | And in the Institutes, a rescript of Severus[293] and Antoninus is cited: "Although we are released from the laws, still we live by the laws."[294]

A common saying is often tossed around: "Everything belongs to the emperor." Even Ambrose cites this.[295] And they tell the charming story of

---

292 C.1.14.4.

293 1540, 1546: *Veri.* 1538 correctly reads *Severi.*

294 Inst.2.17.8.

295 See Ambrose, Letter 20.19, written in 385 in response to the emperor's demand that Ambrose surrender the church to the Arians. In that letter, Ambrose mentions the say-

Henry of Luxembourg,[296] the emperor, who, during a journey in Italy, had inquired about who was the owner of a certain castle. A certain jurist[297] responded that it was the emperor's, even though someone else was the owner, because everything belongs to the emperor. At this point, when another jurist protested and denied that everything belongs to the emperor, it was agreed that the issue should be adjudicated at Bologna, and the winner would receive a horse as a prize for his victory. At Bologna, to the emperor's delight, it was pronounced in favour of the one who had claimed that everything belongs to the emperor. Here, certain witty men have remarked that "The winner got the ride, but the other had it right."[298]

Furthermore, when we speak specifically of ownership [*dominium*], that is, of ownership [*proprietas*] of things, it is not true that all things belong to the emperor. For the division of ownership, because it is of the law | of 16.127
nations, cannot be erased just because a higher power[299] is created. Yet just as they say that all things belong to the emperor, so we say that all things belong to the laws. That is, the emperor is the supreme judge and protector of men, and all things should be (so to speak) "yielded" to his judgment when there is a dispute over their ownership. So, in summary, he has the right of distributing things just like the law does. Therefore, just as the law does not erase, but | confirms ownership or property, neither p. 171
does royal power erase property. All of these things are judged from that source, because the division of ownership is valid by the law of nature and the divine law. Therefore, free men retain their property, even if kings have been established. For [kings] may not erase natural and divine laws.

This disputation is useful because it shows in what manner we own our possessions, and it teaches that this property pleases God, but on the other hand, that tyranny and immoderate plundering displease him. And for this reason, the laws [*iura*] preach liberty, because liberty is a status in which each person may keep what belongs to him and [in which] citizens cannot be forced to do anything contrary to the laws or morality. Therefore, even

---

ing that "everything belongs to the emperor", but rejects it, denying that the emperor has power over the things of God. An English translation can be found in NPNF series II, vol. 10, p. 425.

296 Henry, Count of Luxembourg, who was crowned Holy Roman Emperor Henry VII in 1312.

297 1540: *Iurisconsultus quidem*. 1546a/b: *Iureconsultus quidam*. This translation follows the 1546 reading.

298 *Victor habet equum, sed alter respondit aequum*. Literally, "The winner has the horse, but the other answered fairly."

299 i.e., the emperor.

the laws themselves [*iura ipsa*] say that philosophy favours liberty. For such a status is most in accordance with human nature. Therefore, in book six of the Codex, [in the section] on the Syllanian Senate Decree, it reads, "[...] most of all to the liberties with which philosophy always concerns itself [...]"[300]

Now, even if the civil law attributes no property to slaves, still the law of nature, that is, natural reason and divine law, command slaves to be left some sustenance, just as Ecclesiasticus [33:25] says: "Burdens, fodder, and the lash for donkeys; labour, sustenance, and discipline for the slave." Although this verse refers to slaves, nevertheless, if someone interprets it
p. 172 rightly, it generally depicts the best state of the republic. |

For the first and most harmful bane of the republic is the idleness of the common people; therefore, it first prescribes honest labour.[301]

Second, there is also need for discipline, namely, that crimes be severely punished such that morals and peace are preserved in the republic.

Third, it is also fair for the citizens to enjoy their own labours, and the conservation of resources is needed for the education of the children. And it commands that some sustenance also be left behind to be [used] for the
16.128 defence of the republic. |

Finally, it should also be added that Ambrose was right not to yield the sanctuary to the emperor who demanded it so that he could hand it over to the heretics, because secular power does not have a right to command [anything] contrary to the legitimate calling of the Church. Therefore, [Ambrose] said that he had no fear of that maxim which asserted that everything belongs to the emperor. For this was not a conflict about yielding a sanctuary, but about yielding a vocation. And the emperor does not have the right to disrupt a legitimate vocation.

On Contracts

Whether Charging Interest Contradicts the Law of Nature

[In a loan], usury is money over and above the amount of the principal which is charged purely in exchange for the service of borrowing. For when some amount is added to the principal whenever a borrower has brought
p. 173 about an efficacious cause of loss [*efficax causa damni*], | such an addition is not usurious or illicit.[302] But an addition to which we agree in exchange

300 C.6.35.11.2.

301 In the Vulgate, "labour" (*opus*) actually comes last in the list.

302 A party provided an "efficacious" (*efficax*) cause of loss if there was a direct link of

for the service of borrowing, and when the borrower has not provided an efficacious cause of some loss, is usurious and illicit.

The scholars collect arguments to show that charging interest is contrary to nature.

First. It is unjust to charge money when no commodity is exchanged, that is, when someone charges money in exchange for nothing. The usurer, although his principal is secure, charges interest not in exchange for some thing (because his principal is secure), but only in exchange for the service of borrowing. Therefore, it is unjust to charge interest [*usuras*].

Second. A thing which does not naturally bear fruit should not be exchanged as if it does bear fruit. For example, it is lawful to receive something in exchange for renting a field because [the field] naturally bears fruit, even though the field itself is not forfeited.

However, money is not a thing which naturally bears fruit. Therefore, something should not be charged in exchange for a measure of value [*pretium*], since the principal remains secure.

Third. A measure of value [*pretium*] should not be a commodity [*merx*]. Money [*pecunia*] is a measure of value. Therefore, money should not be a commodity. I confirm the major premise, because whenever a measure of value becomes a commodity, the one who charges interest always receives something beyond that measure of value. Thus, something is added in exchange for nothing, and there is inequality. In this way, a few usurers exhaust the resources of cities. For transactions cannot continue indefin-
itely where | there is no equality. And in this way, this profit becomes larger p. 174
because | many people are poor and frequently so hard-pressed that they 16.129
want to obtain ready cash, even at a loss. For this reason, usury grows easily and the resources of others are exhausted. Therefore, this statement, that a measure of value should not be a commodity, is true and entirely aligned with reason.

Aristotle recites this argument in the first [book] of the *Politics* and on account of it he determines that usury is contrary to nature. Here are Aristotle's words: "The profits of those who charge interest are rightly despised [...] because, while exchange value [*pretium*] should be a medium by which one acquires a commodity, usury does not acquire any commodity, but only

causation between the wrongdoer's action and the damage done. That is, if the cause of loss was efficacious, the damage could be legally attributed to the wrongdoer. This statement sets up Melanchthon's distinction between "usury" (*usura;* money charged purely for the service of borrowing) and "compensation" (*interesse*; additional charges to the borrower when the borrower causes a real loss to the lender).

raises the exchange value. It is from this that it gets the name '*tokos*' [...] because money is born from money, which is entirely contrary to nature".[303] These are Aristotle's words.

Therefore, because charging interest is contrary to nature, the ancient lawgivers also prohibited usury, and Christian doctrine forbids it. And Psalm [15:5]: "Who has not given his money for interest." And Christ says [Luke 6:34]: "Give a loan, expecting nothing in return." For when he says "a loan," he is not commanding one to give a donation, but he intends for the principal to be returned. He only forbids charging something beyond that principal. Therefore, let us keep the pious rule that it is illicit to charge interest, and let us learn that God disdains illicit profits, especially the sort which exhaust
p. 175 other peoples' resources through some illicit pretext. | Moreover, a person who has paid interest does not sin. For he does not inflict an injustice upon others; rather, he suffers an injustice. This rule needed to be proposed[304] in advance, for there will be more discussion of usury below. But someone will object:

"Certain laws of the ancients permit usury. Therefore, it is not in conflict with the law of nature." I deny the consequence, and this is the reason: Although [the laws] permit, they still do not approve. For the laws cannot heal every vice, and for this reason they mitigate and turn a blind eye to certain ones. And I have said above that there are degrees of those things belonging to nature [*naturalia*].[305] Some are simply immutable, and others are mutable to a certain extent, as Aristotle says of those who use their left hand more easily than their right. In these mutable matters, the laws turn a
16.130 blind eye to some error. See, then, how slightly this departs from nature. |

The ancient Roman laws, as Cato says, punished a usurer fourfold, and a thief only twofold.[306] In later times, the avarice of the wicked trumped

303 This quote is a Latin translation of *Politics* I.3.23 (1258b.2–8). Melanchthon omits several clauses in his quotation, which are signalled here with bracketed ellipses. The Greek term for usury is *tokos*, that is, "offspring."

304 1546b: *tenenda*. 1540 and 1546a read *tradenda*, which fits better in the context. Melanchthon here means that it is important to establish, early in the discourse against usury, that paying interest is not a sin. This was a particularly controversial claim because of the teachings of Jakob Strauss (see below), who had argued stringently against interest, claiming even that paying interest on a loan was sinful.

305 *Dixi supra gradus esse naturalium*. Melanchthon does not here specify whether the *naturalia* refer to natural precepts, natural laws, or natural notions, but in his discussion above (see pp. 119–121), he discusses degrees specifically among the natural notions.

306 See the opening paragraph of Marcus Cato's *On Agriculture*.

the laws, and usurers were so rapacious that they even forced debtors to surrender their bodies into slavery. Because of this, Rome was racked by great unrest. And in Athens, Solon legally prohibited any citizen from being taken into slavery on account of debt or usury. Later, the emperors regulated usury in the Codex and forbade the use of "hundredth" [*centesima*] interest rates, that is, interest which equals the principal after one hundred months.[307] That is, [in a loan of] one hundred *aurei*, one *aureus*[308] [accrues] each month. | "Hundredth" rates are even mentioned in distinction 47 of p. 176
the Decretum, where the Nicene synod prohibits usury.[309] So then, this is the "hundredth" rate of interest.

Whether That Commonly-Used Contract, in Which Some Revenue [*reditus*] Is Purchased with an Agreement to Sell It Back, Is Lawful or Usurious.[310]

If someone will contend that these questions do not pertain to moral philosophy [*ethica*], I would ask of him in the meantime that he allow us to treat them, even if only as [questions] summoned from elsewhere. For certain[311] forms of contracts are necessary if we want to declare what sort of equality should be established in commutative[312] justice. Moreover, this very thing is moral [*ēthikon*]: to recognize that contracts are honourable things and that they are God's ordinations which have been given to the human race not simply for the sake of protecting life, but given so that the contracts themselves would teach us to exercise the duties of the virtues and mutual

307 cf. C.4.32.26. The *centesima* was essentially a twelve percent simple (non-compounding) yearly interest rate.

308 A standard Roman gold coin.

309 *Decretum* Dist.47, c.2.

310 In sixteenth-century Germany, Christians were not permitted to lend at interest. However, canon lawyers and theologians had developed justifications for certain annuity (*census*) contracts which were technically sales, but resembled loans at interest. In many of these *census* contracts, the buyer paid for the right to receive revenues from a piece of land. In some cases, the buyer could sell the annuity back for the purchase price. Thus, the distinction between an interest-bearing loan and this purchase of an annuity and eventual resale became quite blurry. Melanchthon's position here is that such arrangements, since they are allowed by the God-ordained magistrate, are acceptable. For a discussion of Melanchthon's teaching on these types of contracts, see Paolo Astorri, *Lutheran Theology and Contract Law*, pp. 347–354 and "Early Modern Lutheran Theologians and the Redeemable *Census:* Towards a Reformulation of the Interest Prohibition." *Studia Historica: Historia Moderna* 44.1 (2022): 53–76.

311 1540: *certe* ("certainly"). 1546a/b: *certis* ("certain [forms of contracts]").

312 1546a: *commutativa*. 1546b: *conmutativa*.

love. These contracts are sacraments [*sacramenta*] which instruct us that we should care about the interest of others as well as our own interest, because it is impossible for contracts to endure perpetually if what they exchange is not equal. Thus, it was with contracts that God bound humans together and impressed upon them the images of virtue.

Second. This is also moral [*ēthikon*]: when we understand that certain forms [of contracts] are rejected by the laws. We should recognize that the
p. 177 law is a | better master [*domina*] of our affairs than we ourselves are. More-
16.131 over, when we say that law is | master, we mean that God, who is the author of law, is the master [*dominus*].[313]

The example of Leviticus 25:[23] is relevant here, where the Lord says, "The land is mine; you are my foreigners and tenants."[314] Nevertheless, even if the Mosaic polity does not apply to us, this example still teaches that we should use things in such a way that we acknowledge that God is the owner of things, and that we are, as it were, God's tenants, etc. Therefore, we should not use things according to our own desires against the will of the owner, that is, the law and God.

But I arrive at a question. Gerson and others have wisely pointed out that commonly-used contracts [*contractus usitatos*][315] should not be immediately judged to be usurious. For since contracts are necessary in this life, and since a great variety of things occurs, the rejection of commonly-used contracts both disturbs the conscience and incites major disturbances in the republic, as we saw when Strauss,[316] having categorically condemned

---

313 The Latin term *dominus* means "master" or "lord", but also specifically refers to an owner of property.

314 The term for "tenants" here is *coloni*, a class of Roman tenant farmers who cultivated land that they did not own.

315 By this term, Melanchthon refers not to a specific type of contract, but to a general class of widely used contracts, which he describes below, which shared certain elements with usurious contracts. The question here is whether these contracts are permissible or are, in fact, usurious.

316 Jacob Strauss was pastor of the church in Eisenach who, in 1523 published a pamphlet condemning usury as well as the various contracts which Melanchthon discusses below. Among Strauss's more explosive claims was the assertion that it was a sin to pay interest. The implication of this claim was that debtors should refuse to pay back usurious loans, which predictably caused great controversy. In October 1523, Luther gently admonished Strauss in a letter. Melanchthon visited Strauss in 1524 to discuss the matter, and the controversy subsided later that year. See Hans Wiersma, "Luther on Lending: A Pastoral Response Regarding the Subject of Usury." *Word & World* 30.2 (2010): 191–199. For a modern edition of Strauss' works, as well as interpretive essays on his life and work, see *Jakob Strauss und der reformatorische Wucherstreit*.

these contracts which we are discussing, stirred up unrest in Thuringia. For this reason, one must apply prudence in order to avoid rash declarations. But the nature of contracts should be investigated, and one must apply erudition and humanity in analysing them.

Certainly, immoderate usury should be condemned because it unjustly exhausts the resources of others. On the other hand, however, we should be careful not to be too rash or harsh in passing judgment on those contracts of which | the laws approve. Therefore, this useful rule should be p. 178
kept: Contracts which are approved by the laws and the authority of the magistrate, that is, by a good and wise judge or jurist, are permissible for a Christian man. For a Christian may make use of political ordinations. And these ordinations are valid not only on account of reason, but also on account of the magistrate's authority, which God approves. Therefore, the Christian should train his conscience to understand that these things are permissible because God approves of the laws and the magistrates and wants us to make use of political ordinations. And in contracts, let [the Christian] be content with that mean, with that equality, which the laws and magistrates establish. That is, the good and wise judge | does not require 16.132
an indivisible[317] point or mean. For the laws themselves teach that a mean should be taken up broadly [*en platei*], that is, with some latitude, and that it is impossible to establish indivisibly one model alone in such affairs.

So then, we must recognize that there are three forms of contract of resale [*contractus redemptionis*] which we are discussing. The first form is when a certain estate [*fundus*][318] is purchased with an agreement to sell it back. Similar to this is the second form, when a certain revenue is purchased in a certain estate. These two forms are true purchases. Therefore, these contracts are not usurious. For usury occurs in loans, not in purchases. It is not usury when the produce of a field, which I have | purchased at an p. 179
ordinary price, exceeds the sum of the purchase price on account of the length of use. Nor is it usury if I sell a purchased field back to the very person from whom I bought it. But there are many questions here.

First, does an agreement to sell something back again violate the nature of a purchase? Likewise, does the condition of resale make the buyer less of an owner because he may not transfer the thing, but it is in the seller's

---

Die soziale Dimension der Reformation und ihre Wirkungen, ed. Joachim Bauer and Michael Haspel (2018).

317 *indivisibile*, i.e., strict or rigid.

318 In legal Latin, and hence in the context of this discussion, *fundus* refers to any property consisting in land. It is translated here and below as "estate".

power to recall the thing back to himself?[319] For this reason, then, some contend that these contracts are merely usurious loans involving collateral, and simulated purchases, because the seller may repurchase the thing that was sold. But they do not judge rightly. For even if someone can occasionally abuse the pretext of this contract, nevertheless, the form of the contract still cannot be invalidated on that account, because it is a sale truly and in fact.

Therefore, I respond to the first question: The condition of resale does not violate the nature of a purchase. This is supported by the laws, such as Codex [4.54.2], in the section concerning agreements between buyer and seller. These are the words of the law: "If your parents have sold an estate by this law, such that either they themselves, or their heirs, at any time or within a fixed amount of time, may offer the price to the seller, and it be restored; and if you are prepared to satisfy the aforementioned condition, [but] the buyer's heir is not; then, in order for the faith of the contract to be kept, the action of introductory words [*actio praescriptis*
p. 180 *verbis*] or the action from sale [*actio ex vendito*] are granted to you."[320] |
16.133 And the text is clearer in | the Digest concerning contracts of purchase and sale: "Whoever has sold an estate under the condition that he himself shall then hold it under a lease for a certain fee, or if he sells it under the condition that [the buyer] does not sell it in parcels to anyone else[321] except to [the seller] himself, or if some similar agreement is made; [the seller] may bring an action from sale [*ex vendito agere*] to fulfil that which had been agreed upon."[322] These laws both approve of the contract and testify that it is a sale. For they call it a "sale", and they grant an action from sale. So then, it stands established by common rule that in civil affairs, one should follow the judgment of the laws, and that the Christian may make use of those laws and contracts which are approved by the laws.

---

319 In Roman law, property owners had the right to alienate their own property. The question is whether the condition of resale restricts that right by only allowing sale to the original owner.

320 The *actio praescriptis verbis* (D.19.5) and the *actio ex vendito*/*actio venditi* (Inst. 3.23.5) were Roman legal actions, granted as remedies against violations in certain types of contracts.

321 1540: *alii*. 1546: *aliis*. The 1546 reading is grammatically correct.

322 D.18.1.75. This and the preceding Codex citation show that Roman law granted legal remedies (actions) to sellers who sold under the specific conditions discussed in this passage. The presence of legal remedies proves that these were true sales that were sanctioned by law.

I respond to the second question: Even if the condition of resale circumscribes ownership [*dominium*], just like many other conditions, nevertheless, it does not violate the nature of ownership, and it does not impede the buyer from truly being an owner. For if the true owner of a house pledges that he will convey that house to nobody except for you, either by donation or by sale, in the meantime, he still remains the true owner, although he cannot convey the house to anyone else. The jurist teaches accordingly in Digest [45.1.135.3], where it says that a slave was given with the condition that he not be transferred to anyone else, but [the recipient] still became the true owner of that slave.

Thus far, we have cited the authority of the laws. However, in order that we might also have reasoning from the nature of contracts, | I will add p. 181
arguments. For just like the laws, contracts are valid because of two things, namely, authority and reason. In loan [*mutuum*] and pledge [*oppignoratio*],[323] the lender has a right to collect his money. In this contract,[324] the buyer does not have the right to a refund of the purchase price. Therefore, this contract is truly a purchase. For if the buyer has no right to a refund, then it must be that some ownership was transferred to him in return, such that the equality of exchange is preserved.[325] | 16.134

Another argument. A thing which is purchased becomes the buyer's, but a thing pledged as collateral does not become the pledgeholder's. In our case, the estate which is purchased becomes the buyer's. Therefore, it is a true purchase.

I have said enough about the first and second types of contracts, for they do not involve obscure controversies, nor is it difficult to understand that these are true purchases. For the substantial properties of sale are present: an agreement, a commodity, and a price. For the commodity is the estate, or the right of receiving certain revenues which are grounded in a certain estate. For just as it is lawful to buy a servitude, namely of *iter* or *actus*, in another person's field, so is it lawful to buy the right to receive certain

---

323 These were two types of loan contracts. *Mutuum* was a loan of fungible commodities (usually money). *Oppignoratio* (which Melanchthon uses here interchangeably with *pignus*) was a type of contract similar to pawn, in which the lender loaned money and kept a valuable item of the borrower's as collateral. See DuPlessis, *Borkowski's Textbook*, pp. 301–302, 306–308.

324 That is, contracts with the condition of resale, which are being discussed in this section.

325 That is, if the seller has paid money, he must have received an equivalent value in return (i.e. ownership rights).

revenues, provided that this right is established in a certain estate.[326] For I have already addressed this case. And because the right should exist in some body, just as *iter* or *actus* are lost whenever a field is lost, in the same way, the right which we have been discussing is also lost. And just as that
p. 182 servitude can be a commodity, so is that right in our case also a commodity. |

Of the Third Form of This Contract

The third form of this contract is when the revenue is not established in a certain estate, but in the entirety of another party's goods, such as when revenues which are established in the entirety of some republic's goods are sold.[327]

Furthermore, [determining] whether this contract is a purchase is a somewhat more obscure disputation. But many learned jurists approve this contract and believe that it is a purchase. For the substantial properties of a purchase are present: a commodity, a price, and an agreement. The commodity here is the right to collect revenue, and because this right must exist in some body, all of that republic's productive goods are the body. For such a right may be established in all of these at once, just as some servitude, namely *actus* or *iter*, may be established in someone else's field.

For what Innocent[328] wrote is a most wise and correct assertion: that in this contract, one should see to it that the revenue is established in the thing or pertains to the thing, not to the person of the seller. And Innocent

326 A servitude [*servitus*] was a right to use another person's property in a specific way (in common law, roughly equivalent to an easement). Praedial servitudes (that is, servitudes relating to land, in contrast to personal servitudes such as *usufructus*) were placed over property, not persons. *Iter* and *actus* were two of the most common praedial servitudes relating to land, and they essentially corresponded to the common law concept of "right of way." *Iter* allowed a person the right to traverse another's property on foot. *Actus* allowed a person the right to drive a vehicle or beast of burden on the property. See DuPlessis, *Borkowski's Textbook*, pp. 161–171. Melanchthon's point here is that the right to collect revenues was a right in another's property analogous to these common servitudes.

327 This is a reference to the type of contract known as the *widerkaufflicher Zins* ("the redeemable *census*"), in which the buyer purchased an annuity (usually 5% of purchase price) not in a specific piece of real estate, but in the seller's entire body of goods. The contract was generally used when the seller needed capital, and thus the similarities with a loan at interest were obvious. Such contracts were officially sanctioned by Charles V in 1530 and they were widespread in Germany.

328 Pope Innocent IV. See Innocent's discussion of this sort of contract in his commentary on *Decretals* 5.19.5 in *Commentaria Innocentii quarti pont. Maximi super libros quinque Decretalium*. (Frankfurt, 1570), fol. 517^{r-v}.

adds that such a contract is not usurious, because in it, there is both a commodity and a price, and it is lawful to sell such real rights. There is no other difficulty with this form [of contract], except that it is a bit more obscure to say that an entirety of goods counts as a body, than (as was said above)
that a certain estate in which certain revenues | are purchased | counts as a 16.135
body—as when, for instance, 20 measures are purchased in a certain field, p. 183
and so when the field is lost, the buyer simultaneously loses the right. But, having sufficiently treated this question, it can be well enough understood that an entirety of goods may be regarded as a certain body, provided that it is also proportionally burdened, and whoever receives the revenue also takes on proportional risk.[329] Therefore, reasons should be added:

First. Some certain part may be burdened with a servitude. Therefore, an entirety of goods may be burdened with a similar servitude, and no reason for a discrepancy is apparent.

Second. A republic may donate to someone some revenues from the entirety of its goods, and the recipient may sell these donated revenues. Therefore, the republic itself may also sell such revenues.

Third. Revenues established some time ago, like tithes, may be sold. Therefore, new revenues may also be established and sold, if the body is so productive that it can sustain the new burdens.

Fourth. In a sale, we have neither a right nor any period of time to seek a refund. For since the right over the sale price is completely transferred to the one who receives [the money], it must be the case that some right, just like a commodity, has been transferred in turn to the buyer, for otherwise there would be no equality. But in this case, the buyer does not have a right to seek a refund. Therefore, it is a true purchase. This argument is derived from the very nature of purchase. For it is a characteristic of purchase that
one does not have a right to seek a refund. | p. 184

But the matter will become clearer after treating some arguments which are raised in objection to this position. Therefore, we shall solve these [arguments] here.

Counter-argument: In Codex [4.22.3], "That which is done is worth more than that which is feignedly conceived", the law says: "When a sale is made as a pretext for a pledge [*pignus*], it is not what has been written, but what has been done, which is examined."[330] In the third case, it is simply a sale

329 That is, if a person buys revenues in a collection of goods, he also takes on risk for that entire collection of goods. If the value of the collection decreases, so does the value of his revenues.

330 This rescript was part of a series of imperial laws designed to limit "simulated con-

as a pretext for a pledge which occurs. That is, a loan with a pledge [*oppignoratio*] occurs, not a sale. Therefore, it is entirely a simulated contract.

I confirm the minor premise because those goods in which the sale is imagined are, in fact, merely a pledge, even if the term "sale" is added as a pretext. Furthermore, the evidence indicates that what has been pledged is all the goods. I respond to the minor premise: This argument is apparently valid on its face [*eurprosōpon*], and it seems to undermine our own opinion, even though it occasionally happens that men abuse the outward form of
16.136 this contract. | Yet still, one should consider the foundations of our opinion, which, if they are true and firm, should be preferred to this objection.

So then, these are the foundations: It is certain that a person may establish revenues, just as other servitudes, in his own goods. It is also certain that he may alter, give away, or sell this revenue; these things are clearer than the midday sun. Therefore, a true sale can exist in our case, and not just a loan with a pledge [*oppignoratio*]. For it is clear that such a contract
p. 185 is different from a loan. For in a loan, the lender has the right | to collect on his loan. But in our case, the buyer of the estate or revenue does not have the right to seek a refund.

Therefore, I respond to the argument. Since our contract here truly differs from a loan, and has the substantial properties of a sale, it is not a sale made as a pretext for a pledge. Moreover, the fact that the entirety of goods has been pledged does not even invalidate the sale. For a collateral pledge does not invalidate a sale, as many sayings of the jurists confirm.

Another contrary [argument]. A right should exist in a certain body, so that when the body is eliminated, the right is understood to be eliminated. In the third case, there is no certain body, and more precisely, even if those

---

tracts" in which one type of contract was completed under the guise of another. In general, these rescripts (C.4.22.1–5) stated that simulated contracts were to be treated according to their substance, not according to their simulated forms. Here, a "sale made as a pretext for a pledge" (*emptio pignoris causa facta*) means a contract that is disguised as a sale, while actually being in substance a pledge (*pignus*), a type of Roman contract in which one party borrowed money and left a pledge as collateral. See *Borkowski's Textbook*, pp. 306–308. Such an arrangement would be disguised as a sale to avoid restrictions on interest-bearing loans. The substance of the counterargument here, as it relates to this third type of commonly used contract, is this: If party A pays party B a sum for the rights to revenues in all of party B's goods, then it must be the case that party A is merely loaning money to party B, with the entirety of party B's goods and revenues held as collateral for the loan. Melanchthon recognizes the force of this objection, but ultimately rejects it below because the buyer cannot seek a refund in such an arrangement, confirming that this is indeed a sale.

goods suffer a great loss [in value], the payment is still exacted. Therefore, the whole affair is simulated.

I respond to the minor premise. There is a certain body in which that right is grounded, namely, the entirety of those goods, just like there is a certain field in which a servitude is established. But just as I lose *actus* or *iter* in a part of a field which has been lost through alluvion,[331] in the same way, if those goods suffer a significant loss, equality should be preserved such that the buyer should in turn remit something in proportion. On this opinion, Baldus says that he approves of this contract, provided that this equality is preserved.

Another contrary [argument]. The risks of sale fall to the buyer.[332] In this contract, the seller alone is burdened because the buyer exacts payment even if those goods | have suffered a loss or disappeared.[333] Therefore, this p. 186
is not a true sale. I respond to the minor premise: The risk falls to the buyer if those goods, in which we understand the right to be grounded, suffer a significant loss, just as *actus* or *iter* vanish if the field vanishes through alluvion.

Another contrary [argument]: Leviticus 25:[15–16] commands that the produce of landed property be calculated proportionally. | Therefore, we 16.137
should also calculate produce proportionally when we buy a estate with an agreement to re-sell it, and [we should] return the estates free of charge, etc.[334]

---

331 *Alluvio* (see D.41.1.7.1–5) covered a variety of ways in which rivers could alter the size of a piece of land. A river could change course, cause an accretion of soil which enlarged a piece of land, or even rip away a larger parcel of land, carry it downstream, and deposit it on another piece of property. Roman law addressed all of these possibilities.

332 A reference to D.18.6.8.pr: "It is necessary to know when a sale is completed, for then we will know who bears the risk. For once a sale is completed, the risk falls to the buyer." The principle is that, once a sale has been completed (i.e., the item and price were agreed upon, but the sold item has not yet been delivered), the buyer bears the loss if the item is damaged or destroyed prior to delivery. See *Borkowski's Textbook*, pp. 271–272.

333 1540: *perierint*. 1546a/b: *perierunt*.

334 Leviticus 25:15–16 reads, "When you buy from your neighbour, you shall pay only for the number of years since the Jubilee; the seller shall charge you only for the remaining crop-years. If the years are more, you shall increase the price, and if the years are fewer, you shall diminish the price; for it is a certain number of harvests that are being sold to you" (NRSV). The argument here is that, according to the reasoning in Leviticus, when a person purchases a piece of land, he is only purchasing the number of crops that will be produced before the next Jubilee, when the land will be returned to its original owners. Accordingly, once those crops are "used up", the land's value

I respond: The consequence should be rejected because the Mosaic polity has nothing to do with us. Moreover, this obligation to return land in the Jubilee was a particular ordination of that people, just like circumcision. Further, it would be disastrous to apply that [ordination] to our republics as if it were necessary, although among that people it had a rationale and [was a] model of humanity. For God did not want any family to be despoiled, but wanted each person to preserve their own land. In this way, at the same time, families were preserved and there was less room for avarice, and the rich could not buy up the land of others for themselves. Therefore, this ordination was a useful bond in that republic, but it does not bind us, just as we are no longer bound by the law of circumcision. Rather, we should obey our p. 187 own laws, which agree with reason and are approved by our magistrates. |

Whether, in a Loan, Something beyond the Principal May Be Sought by Reason of Compensation

I respond: That which is owed to someone, either because he suffered a loss or because he was prevented from making some profit, is called "compensation" [*interesse*].[335] Accordingly, there is a distinction between compensation which arises from losses incurred [*damnum emergens*] and compensation from lost profits [*lucrum cessans*].[336] Say, for example, that someone was supposed to pay me 20 *aurei* on the first of May, and he did not pay it, and on account of that delay I have suffered some loss—namely, because then I owed another person, and so when I did not pay him, he

should be understood to be depleted and it should be returned free of charge if there is an agreement to resell.

335 The Latin verb *interesse* literally means "to lie between" or "to be different." In this context, *interesse* does not refer to usurious interest (i.e., interest on a loan), but rather to compensation for damages incurred in a contract. That is, the "*interesse*", or "*id quod interest*" is that amount which lies between the original amount owed on a loan and the higher sum owed after the borrower causes damages. For example, if a borrower's default or delay caused the lender to suffer a loss, the borrower would still owe the principal plus compensation (the amount of the loss). Melanchthon carefully distinguishes this concept of compensation for a loss from the concept of usury, or charges for loaning money. To preserve this distinction, and to avoid the connotations of "interest" in modern English, I have translated "*interesse*" or "*id quod interest*" as "compensation". For this translation choice, see also Paolo Astorri, *Lutheran Theology and Contract Law*, pp. 346–347, 350–354.

336 These were both established legal categories in early modern contract law. "Losses incurred" [*damnum emergens*] refers to a real loss arising from some decrease in property value. "Lost profits" [*lucrum cessans*] refers to reasonably expected future profits that are now foregone because of another party's actions. cf. Astorri, *Lutheran Theology and Contract Law*, pp. 350–354.

incurs his own expenses and demands these expenses from me. This is compensation arising from a loss incurred by me [*damnum mihi emergens*].

And another distinction must be observed. One loss occurs before a delay, that is, before the agreed-upon date of payment. Another loss occurs after a delay, that is, after the debtor has not paid on the established date. Now, therefore, I respond: That compensation which is charged to the borrower when a loss is incurred following a delay is true and not simulated [compensation].[337] For instance, say that someone was supposed to pay me 20 *aurei* on the first of May, and because he did not pay this, then someone else to whom I owe money incurs some expenses and demands these expenses from me. Here, I suffer a loss because of the delay of that person who owed me. In such a case, it is decided that compensation beyond the amount of the principal is owed, and can be lawfully demanded, even if there was no | stipulation[338] about compensation. This is in agreement with written p. 188
law and natural | equity. For whoever creates an efficacious cause of loss 16.138
[*efficacem causam damni*] for another should compensate him. In this case, the delay beyond the established due date presents an efficacious cause of loss. Therefore, it is absolutely fair that compensation be paid. In this case, it can be clearly seen that the compensation which is ordinarily charged to the borrower (that is, what he owes, even if there was no stipulation), is true and not simulated. From here, it can be decided that, whenever, in a loan, compensation is put forward as a pretext, particularly [compensation] which would by no means be owed[339] without a stipulation, [that compensation] makes it that the borrowing itself is not free, but it is like a price for the loan and a straining after profits from lending.[340]

---

337 Here and below, Melanchthon draws a distinction between "true" [*verum*] compensation and "simulated" [*simulatum*] compensation. In this framework, true compensation derives from actual losses, while simulated compensation is Melanchthon's term for fictive losses which were used to justify usurious loans.

338 *Stipulatio* was a very broad category of Roman verbal contracts. In Roman money-lending, a *stipulatio* was generally part of the loan contract which established details such as interest rates or due dates. See *Borkowski's Textbook*, pp. 298–300.

339 1538, 1539, 1540 read *deberetur*. Both 1546 editions read *debetur*. The translation follows the first reading, in which the subjunctive verb highlights the unusual nature of this compensation which would not normally be owed without a stipulation.

340 Here Melanchthon arrives at the main objection to compensation: it could be abused to create essentially usurious loans. While, in justified cases of compensation, lenders could legitimately charge more than the principal on the loan as reparations for damages, it was often easy for predatory lenders to invent fictitious cases of compensation to disguise usurious lending.

Of profits lost [*lucrum cessans*] after a delay, that is, when the debtor has not paid on the due date, [the jurists] declare that compensation is owed in the exact same way that we have just discussed about losses incurred. But in this second case, they only allow this [compensation] to persons who are involved in business. For in business, lost profits are very close to incurred losses, as Panormitanus writes in his commentary on [Decretals 5.19.8].[341] However, the judge may also apply this model to other persons by probable reason.

But for losses incurred and profits lost prior to a delay in a loan, the laws certainly grant no legal action unless there was some stipulation that
p. 189 compensation would be paid. | Accordingly, this stipulation is now commonly used in lending, and it is often a pretext for usury. Therefore, it is asked whether one may stipulate even about compensation prior to a delay. I respond: It is lawful to stipulate even about compensation prior to a delay. The reason: It is lawful to stipulate about just compensation [*iustam compensationem*]. Paying compensation [*id quod interest*] is just compensation [*iusta compensatio*]. Therefore, it is lawful to stipulate about [*iustam compensationem*].[342] I affirm the minor premise because the laws clearly distinguish between usury and compensation. In usury, profits are generated from the service of lending, and that very service is directed toward profit. But when one seeks compensation, one alleges real, not simulated, losses which have arisen particularly from this loan.

16.139 Moreover, no one should create an efficacious | cause of loss for another person, and for this reason, it should be diligently considered that usury and compensation are distinguished most prudently in the gloss on Digest [17.2.60.pr] and Codex [4.32.15]. On that account, the doctors affirm the stipulation of compensation, provided that the compensation is real and not simulated. And in [Decretals 3.22.2], the Pope[343] declares that a *fideiussor* who has paid on behalf of others should recoup both the loan and

341 The Italian canonist Nicolò de Tudeschi (1386–1445), commonly known as Panormitanus, wrote an extensive commentary upon the *Decretals*. For his commentary on *Decretals* 5.19.8, see the later printed edition: *Nicolai Abbatis Panormitani commentaria ad quartum et quintum libros Decretalium* (Tours, 1577), fol. 126v.

342 This syllogism is circular. In Latin, it reads, *"Iustam compensationem licet stipulari, solvere id, quod interest, est iusta compensatio: Ergo licet eam* [i.e., *iustam compensationem*] *stipulari."* This is likely an error, and the conclusion should read *"Ergo licet id* [i.e., *id quod interest*]." The implication is that "*id quod interest*", the specific type of compensation discussed in this passage, is a narrower category of just compensation [*compensatio*].

343 Lucius III (r. 1181–1185).

the amount of compensation. This case is very similar to the case in our question. For the *fideiussor* himself meanwhile gives money, as if in a loan, to the person on whose behalf he is paying.[344] Therefore, the doctors use this example, and they think that this stipulation is lawful, and that such compensation | may be sought from a contract. Thus, Hostiensis[345] on p. 190
[Decretals 5.19.16] judges that compensation is owed even on profits lost before a delay, but he adds: provided that this is not a pretext for usury. For although Hostiensis allows for some fair compensation, he still established certain boundaries, such as [limiting it] to those whose wealth is principally[346] in money and commerce. In this case, because they cannot go without large sums of cash without suffering a loss, it is fair to render some compensation, and he approves[347] this stipulation up to this point.[348]

And this compensation should be[349] moderate, in accordance with the judgment of good men or at least of a good judge. For equality in civil affairs is not handled rigidly, but with a broad approach [*en platei*], that is, with latitude. For this reason, no single point or single model can be established, except that one stipulates the same amount that a good man, even without a stipulation, would think it should be by probable reason. Or, [one stipulates the same amount] as the loss [incurred], or the approximate amount that the profit would have been, which he was in the meantime denied. This is a probable formula. But when profit is sought after, and for that reason, an immoderate additional fee is sought, especially when the lender sustains no loss, and does not usually profit that same amount by another honourable accounting, then | that compensation degenerates into usury. 16.140

344 *Fideiussio* was a form of surety in which one party, the *fideiussor*, agreed to act as surety for a debt if the principal borrower failed to pay. This passage in the *Decretals* commands two clerics to repay their *fideiussor* both for the original loan as well as for the losses the *fideiussor* sustained by the clerics' failure to pay.

345 Henry of Segusio (1200–1271), also known as Hostiensis, was an Italian canonist. Melanchthon here references Hostiensis' famous commentary on the *Decretals*, the *Summa Aurea*. See *Henrici de Segusio Cardinalis Hostiensis Summa Aurea, ad vetustissimos codices summa fide diligentiaque nunc primum collata, atque ab innumeris erroribus, quibus scatebat hactenus, repurgata.* (Venice, 1574), cols. 1612–1637.

346 1540: *praecipua*. 1546a/b: *praecipuae*.

347 1540: *probant*. 1546a/b: *probat*. The latter reading is probably correct, as Hostiensis seems to be the subject here.

348 It seems that cases of losses incurred prior to a delay would mainly pertain to professional merchants who required large amounts of liquid cash. For such people, loaning money diminished their liquidity and came with significant risks.

349 1538, 1539, 1540: *sit*. The 1546 editions erroneously read *fit*.

Therefore, those crude Saxon usuries, or others, which suck princes and republics dry like leeches, should not be excused on the pretext of compensation. Let us recognize in the laws that "compensation" [*id quod interest*]
p. 191 is an honourable term | and one which is full of humanity and equity. This honourable term should not serve as an excuse for the shameful avarice of usurers.

Thus far, I have recited the opinion of Hostiensis, and although Panormitanus on [Decretals 5.19.19] pronounces about usury a bit more modestly, still he shares the same position, provided that simulated compensation does not serve as a pretext [for usury]. For these are his words: "Note that, in a loan contract, compensation may be sought for profits plausibly lost after a delay."[350] But as to whether that argument can be held from its foundation: It could perhaps be said that, when the lender is led by good intentions and does not lend fraudulently, for the sake of profit, then he is excused from sin, although the alternate opinion is safer. Therefore, if the compensation is not simulated, Panormitanus also concedes that it may be sought before the delay, and this argument is honourable enough, if the sources are considered. For, as has been said above, compensation and usury are extremely different. The laws themselves judge that compensatory interest is most fair and honourable, just as Baldus says [in his commentary] on [Codex 4.32.19] that a common and fair compensation appears in every contract.[351]

Therefore, I conclude that it is lawful to stipulate compensation in the amount of a loss incurred [*damnum emergens*] even before a delay, and this is not obscure at all. For it is not usury to pay true compensation, and
p. 192 this compensation would be owed according to the judgment | of a good man, even if a stipulation had not existed, for nobody should create an efficacious cause of loss for another. However, even though the reasoning about profits lost [*lucrum cessans*] before a delay is a little more unclear, nevertheless, if there is a probable[352] reason, it should also be conceded that one may stipulate compensation in the amount of profits lost before a delay.

---

350 See Panormitanus, *Commentaria*, fol. 131^{r}. The quote is in the left column, in section 14.

351 Baldus de Ubaldis (1327–1400) was one of the most famous jurists of the Middle Ages. His voluminous writings cover both canon and civil law. His discussion of C.4.32.19 can be found in this later printed edition: *Baldi Ubaldi Perusini iurisconsulti … in quartum et quintum Cod. Lib. Commentaria* (Venice, 1599), fols. 92^{r}–94^{v}.

352 1540 erroneously reads *probalis*.

But, as I have said, there is a probable principle, namely, if the case is such that a good man would judge that compensation is owed to another, even if there had been no | stipulation. And this compensation should be 16.141
moderate and fair.

I have said these things to advise the students to discern usury from the seeking of compensation. Therefore, all loans in which the lenders stipulate a certain amount of compensation before a delay should not be condemned without discrimination. For good men can use this honourable thing well. And in these affairs, one should also consider that it is sufficient to have reasoning that is probable and in agreement with the laws, since the mean, as I said above, has a certain latitude. But when probable reason cries out in opposition, then it is agreed that the service of lending is directed only towards profit, because in honest purchases, that money would not produce such profit. These profits plainly appear to be usurious. Moreover, usury is unjust on account of many causes, since equality is not preserved in it. For the usurer gets back his principal as well as usurious interest beyond the principal, for which he gives nothing in exchange. Likewise, it is easier | p. 193
to lend money in this way than to spend it in a purchase, and a great and certain profit accrues.

For usurers do not take on risk, and the [borrower] often profits nothing from that money. This inequality is the cause by which usury easily drains the resources of others. It was for this reason that Cato compared it to murder. For when someone asked him what was the best way to provide for one's estate, he gave an answer about agriculture. When the other person asked about usury, Cato responded, "What is that, murder?"[353]

We have added these things here so that we might remember that, even in this doctrine of contracts, we are advised not only about our own benefits, but about the duties of humanity and virtue, namely, so that we might learn to direct our actions to the benefit of others and toward the common society of men.

---

353 This story about Cato the Elder is found in Cicero, *De officiis*, II.25.89.

Is That Contract of Partnership Lawful, in Which One Partner Contributes Money and the Other Contributes Labor, and He Who Contributes Money Demands a Share of the Profit, with His Capital Secure?[354]

There are various species of partnership,[355] but many[356] things can be determined from this form which I have mentioned in the question above. So
16.142 then, the laws approve of this contract, | in which one partner contributes money and demands a share of the profit, with his capital secure [*salvo*
p. 194 *capitali*], while the other partner contributes the work.[357] |

For the text in the Institutes [in the section] "On Partnership" [Inst. 3.25.2] teaches this clearly, in these words: "For there is no doubt that a partnership may be formed such that one contributes money and the other does not, and still the profit is shared between them, since often, someone's work is as valuable as money." Moreover, it should be added that this contract is not invalidated even if one [partner] is promised a greater share of the profit. For one must understand this about profit, particularly if profit is what is left after costs are deducted: that if he who contributes the labour has applied as much diligence and faithfulness as he should have, and if after that, some profit remains, [then] the other partner may lawfully receive a greater share of the profit, along with his secure capital, according to the agreement. However, if the first partner has displayed as much diligence and faithfulness as he should have, but the venture nevertheless earns no profit, or even suffers a loss, then in this case, the partners should share the loss equally, for the one who contributed the money should not be the only one penalized.

354 The question here is whether a partner can contribute money to a joint venture while having his initial capital investment guaranteed [*salvus*]. As Melanchthon explains below, a partnership in which capital investment is guaranteed seems to be a loan, not a true partnership. Hence, this sort of partnership was another way in which people could simulate loans to get around prohibitions on usury.

355 A *societas* was a Roman law contract in which two or more parties agreed to associate in a common endeavour for mutual gain (usually in business ventures). A *societas* could take various forms. Partners might contribute money, labour, skill, or anything else of value. The contract would usually spell out the details of profit and risk sharing. See DuPlessis, *Borkowski's Textbook*, pp. 289–293.

356 1538, 1539, and 1540 read "*multa.*" Both 1546 editions read "*multae.*" The first reading is correct (i.e., "many things", not "many species.").

357 That is, provided that the venture produces a profit, the laws allow the financial investor to recoup his initial investment. As Melanchthon explains below, if the venture produces no profit or ends up at a loss, the losses should be shared by both partners.

But here, it is asked whether, in a partnership, it is lawful to agree that he who contributes the money should suffer no loss and should have his capital secure, even if the other [partner] earns no profit or even suffers a loss. This question has greatly vexed the doctors. It seems to me that this contract in which he is promised his capital in this way is actually a loan, not a partnership. For the sharing of losses is characteristic of the nature of partnership, and such a partnership in which one partner is unwilling to take on any risk
is clearly | prohibited by the law [Digest 17.2.29.2], where Cassius says that p. 195
it is a "lion's partnership" in which one partner only experiences profits and the other only experiences losses.

Nevertheless, I have already spoken of lending above. In a loan, the capital should be secure, but no agreement should be added that he who is unwilling to take on any risk will demand an equal or greater share of the profit as if on the pretext of partnership. For in this case, there is no partnership. Moreover, it has been said above how a loan may be joined by an agreement that something called "compensation" be paid, provided that it
is moderate and has a probable reason. | 16.143

Whether Priests Are Usuaries or Usufructuaries[358]

There is an ancient question: May priests own property? Then, what sort of right do they have over their own revenues? There have been great contentions among the jurists about this topic. Some claim that priests only have use [*usus*]; others argue that they also hold usufruct [*usufructus*] of ecclesiastical funds.

So then, use is a right by which the possessor may use things or fruits to sustain himself and his family in such a way that he does not acquire ownership of the remaining fruits. Therefore, he cannot sell them to others,

358 *Usus* and *usufructus* were two personal servitudes in Roman law. Personal servitudes were attached to a person and granted that person a right to enjoy some property in a defined way. D.7.8.2.pr gives this definition: "A man who is granted *usus* may use the property, but not take its fruits." As Melanchthon notes below, this was generally interpreted to allow a usuary to take enough produce to support himself and his family, but nothing more. *Usufructus* was a more expansive right which allowed the usufructuary to use the property and take all of its fruits. The usufructuary also had a duty to maintain the property, i.e. keep buildings in good repair, cultivate crops, maintain the size of a herd or flock, etc. For Melanchthon's purposes, the most important difference between *usus* and *usufructus* was that *usufruct* granted the right to take and enjoy all the fruits of an estate (including produce, income from slaves, or any income the usufructuary gained by renting out the estate), while *usus* only granted rights to take fruits necessary for subsistence. For more detail on these personal servitudes, see *Borkowski's Textbook*, pp. 165–169.

p. 196 or convey them to others in his will. | There are several common examples, such as when the use of some prefecture is granted to a person.

However, usufruct is the right by which one may use things or fruits in such a way that the possessor acquires ownership of the remaining fruits, but he does not have ownership of the estate itself.

Therefore, when priests sometimes sell the remaining fruits, or donate them to others, or transfer them to others in their wills, this raises questions about whether they may rightly do this, since ecclesiastical goods are alms. For in alms, use alone is established, specifically so that the remaining fruits would be left over for the needs of the poor. And there is a grave constitution in the Decretum [Ca.10.2.7] which forbids bishops and deacons from alienating the leftover fruits, specifically because they were intended to support the needy. Yet this question is easy to adjudicate if we first establish that pastors of the Church or ministers of the Gospel may hold property. For the fact that this is pious and permissible will be sufficiently proven by this argument.

It is pious and permissible for all Christians to make use of political ordinations as good creations of God. Purchase, sale, property, usufruct and similar ordinations are political ordinations. Therefore, these things are permissible for priests just as for all other Christians. Nor is it the case that the
p. 197 pastors of the churches should be excluded | just because it is written [cf. Mark 6:8, Matthew 10:9]: "They may hold no silver in their belts." For in this
16.144 verse, this saying should be judged | according to the whole doctrine of the Gospel, which allows and approves the use of political things. In fact, when Christ adds [Luke 10:7]: "The labourer deserves his wages," he attributes property to [pastors], for wages are a person's property. And this saying of Christ includes two things. It encourages the teachers with a promise,[359] so that they would know that God will look out for them, as if he were their guarantee,[360] even if the world refuses to take care of them. Likewise, it instructs the Church that it owes wages to the teachers.

Why, then, does he say [Matthew 10:9]: "Do not possess silver, gold, etc."? I respond: These words do not nullify the civil use of things, but they prohibit other goods from being principally sought or looked after in ministry. That is, they prohibit those who have been called from abandoning the ministry because of their poverty, and they also forbid the ministry from seeking power and wealth. In this way, Christ prohibits diffidence and ambition, as

359 1540 incorrectly reads *promissionis*. 1546a/b: *promissione*.

360 *quasi fide iubere*: that is, as if God promised to be the pastors' *fideiussor* and to pay any debts on their behalf.

if he were saying: "Do not think that you should not teach unless you are sufficiently guarded by an escort arrayed for kings and lavished with great wealth." Likewise: "Do not grasp power for yourself, and do not seize the wealth of the republic on the pretext of ministry."

In the synod of Basel, there were disputes with the Bohemians about whether priests could hold property.[361] But we ourselves should flee from superstitious opinions and | hold with both hands the thesis[362] that the p. 198
Gospel approves of political ordinations, and therefore it allows property to all Christians.

Now I come to the other question, concerning which I respond: ministers of the Gospel are absolutely usufructuaries. And in fact, I am speaking of teachers, students, and similar persons who are in some administration. This is because wages are the property of the person who earns them. The income of the ministers of the Gospel is a wage, just as Christ says. Likewise, Paul calls for stipends [1 Cor. 9:14, 1 Tim. 5:18]. Therefore, ministers of the Gospel, because their whole wage is their own, have ownership in the surplus fruits of their wages, and they can[363] give away the surplus fruits, sell them to others as they wish, etc. So then, as such, they are usufructuaries.

However, it is objected: Usufruct[364] cannot be established in alms, because alms | are given for necessity, that is, for use alone, not so that part 16.145
[of the alms] may be directed towards profit, for in this way, the rest of the poor people are cheated. But the revenues of the churches are alms. Therefore, a usufruct cannot be established in them. This argument is rejected by the denial of the major premise, because use is established in some alms, and usufruct is established in others. For sometimes, the Church gives alms as a stipend, as to ministers of the Gospel, both teachers and students, and at other times it gives alms freely as needed to the poor, | whose labour is not p. 199
employed. This is indeed a pious and helpful distinction because it warns the idle not to defraud the Church, but to be content with modest alms. On the other hand, it also teaches that it is a necessary and obligatory work to give an honest wage to teachers and students. Therefore, it is no small crime to refuse to contribute anything toward supporting the ministers of

---

361 The Council of Basel was convened from 1431–1449. Among other issues, it addressed the Hussite heresy, which had broken out in Bohemia. The "Bohemians" here refer to Hussites.

362 Both 1546 editions have misspelled the Greek term as "θέσην". The 1538 Strasbourg edition correctly reads "θέσιν".

363 1540: *possent*. 1546a/b: *possunt*. The translation follows the 1546 reading.

364 All editions read *nisi fructus* here, but the context suggests that the correct reading must be *usufructus*, and that *nisi fructus* is a typographical error.

the Gospel, or even to rip away the resources of the churches, which are not merely alms intended for idle people, but rather in large part are stipends set up for and owed to teachers and students for the necessary preservation of Church doctrine. Therefore, let men of moderate disposition here learn what they owe to ministers of the Gospel. Paul says [1 Tim. 5:17]: "Those who lead well are worthy of a double honour." That is, first they should receive honour, then an honest wage.

Hezekiah is praised because he diligently ensured that the people gave to the priests those portions which the law assigned to them. And the text of 2 Chronicles 31:[4] says, "[S]o that they could devote themselves to the law of God." Therefore, this demonstrates that this generosity pleases God precisely because it is necessary for preserving religious devotion. The prophets even harshly threatened the people because they did not pay the priests what the law assigns to them. As Haggai 1:[6–11] writes, the reason why the
p. 200 crops failed is that the people did not pay what they owed to the temple.[365] | And Malachi 3:[10]: "Bring the whole tithe ... and I will open to you the floodgates of heaven."

These testimonies teach how necessary a duty it is it is to give a wage to the ministers of the Church.[366] And so that we might display greater faith, we should be exhorted by these most grave threats and divine promises,
16.146 which both advise everyone that | each of us should support the ministers of the Church according to his own calling[367] and resources, and indeed forbid the seizure of the resources of the churches, which is certainly no small crime. First, this offends the glory of God, because when funds are lacking, the churches will also lack learned and qualified ministers. Then, those who are in ministry are defrauded as well, and so are their poor children, who are nearly starving to death.

Therefore, let us recognize that that which is given to ministers is a wage, because they have usufruct over their own income. And this discussion instructs us to pay more diligently to the ministers of the churches that which has been set aside for them. Further, let each person be aware that he should contribute something to the conservation of the churches and the ministry, just as Paul says to the Galatians [6:6]: "The student should share with the teacher of the Gospel." And Solomon [Proverbs 3:9,10]: "Honor God with your wealth, and your barns will be filled, etc." For he means
p. 201 contributions which are intended for the preservation of ministry. |

---

365 1540 incorrectly reads *debebant*. 1546a/b: *debebat*.

366 1540: *Ecclesiae*. 1546a: *ecclesia*. 1546b: *Ecclesia*.

367 1540, 1546b: *pro vocatione*. 1546a: *provocatione*.

Did Mars Lawfully Kill Neptune's Son because of His Defilement [*stuprum*][368] of Alcippe, Mars's Daughter?

The Greeks imagine that the gods performed two capital trials in the Areopagus. In one, they say that Neptune accused Mars, for Mars had killed Halirrhothius, Neptune's son, because of his defilement [*stuprum*] of [Mars's] daughter Alcippe.[369] However, Mars was acquitted in the trial of the gods. Here, there is a question about the penalty for defilement: Was Mars allowed to punish the defilement of his daughter by killing? Second, if this punishment was harsher [*atrocius*] than was just, does he have an excuse in that he was violently disturbed with fatherly grievance at the harm to his daughter? Therefore, this question contains two chief common topics [*loci communes*]: one about the penalty for defilement, and the other about when killing has an excuse.

Of the first topic: Natural reason judges that defilements should be punished severely. To illustrate this, the Greeks contrived this penalty for defilers, and they even made God the author of the punishment in order to warn that God is offended if such punishments are not carried out. | 16.147
Therefore, in states constituted by law, there have always been laws about defilement.

However, there is a difference between forcible defilement [*stuprum vi factum*] and non-forcible defilement [*stuprum sine violentia factum*]. Roman law punishes forcible defilement and abduction specifically with capital punishment. And in the *Lex Julia*, both categories are classified as "public violence" [*vis publica*], which is the most atrocious of crimes.[370] | p. 202

The Mosaic law [Deuteronomy 22:25] and the Attic laws also punished forcible defilement with capital punishment.

But non-forcible defilement is a different matter, and in the Mosaic law, it carried this penalty: marry and pay the dowry.

---

368 In Roman law, *stuprum* was a broad category of sexual immorality which comprised sexual union outside of marriage between free persons. It included intercourse with unmarried women as well as widows, but did not include adultery with married women (that was classified as *adulterium*). As Melanchthon discusses below, *stuprum* could be either violent (i.e., rape), or non-violent and consensual. Because the crime entailed social disgrace for both parties as well as sometimes physical harm (in violent cases), the term is translated here as "defilement."

369 For Halirrhothius, Alcippe, and the trial of Mars, see Pausanias, *Description of Greece* I.21.4 and I.28.5.

370 For the Roman law punishments for violation and abduction according to the *Lex Julia*, see Digest 48.6.3.2–5.

In Attic law, it carried a milder penalty: marry or pay the dowry.

The Mosaic law was concerned with the honour of virgins, and it had a higher penalty, for it forced [the offender] both to marry the woman and to pay the dowry, and it forbade him ever to divorce her [Exodus 22:16].

Roman law instituted a more serious punishment. Namely, it commanded lowlier persons to be arrested and banished, but it punished non-lowly persons by confiscation of half of their goods.[371] Therefore, the Roman law is the most honourable, because it punishes defilement more severely.

Now I will answer the question. If Halirrhothius forcibly raped Alcippe, and Mars caught him just as he was violently seizing the girl, then [Mars] killed the youth lawfully, either because Hallirhothius had used force, or because he was, so to speak, a kidnapper. Whoever is protecting his own family from public violence [*vis publica*] may kill the attacker immediately [*in continenti*] without punishment. In this way, Mars avenged the violence brought against his daughter. Therefore, he killed Halirrhothius lawfully.

Another argument. Violent defilement and abduction are equivalent because both are public violence [*vis publica*]. One may kill a kidnapper if he is caught in the act of abduction. Therefore, such a defiler who is caught
16.148 may also be killed just like a kidnapper. |
p. 203 This defence of Mars is appropriate and it is derived from | the strict law about the punishment for violent defilement, or the punishment for abduction. And Mars uses this defence in Libanius. For he says that the girl was violently defiled, and that he, as a father, was lawfully allowed to avenge the disgrace violently inflicted upon his daughter.

He adds an example in order to prove that this defence or vengeance is natural, because even beasts become enraged with grievance and wrath and they defend or avenge any assault against their offspring. But I think that the Greeks imagined this case of Alcippe to be one of non-forcible defilement, for the judgment about violence is fairly straightforward. But the case of Alcippe seems to have been contrived so that there would be an uncertain dispute in this example, namely, concerning non-forcible defilement, whether it should also be punished so harshly, and whether a father, furiously disturbed by justified grievance, has an excuse. This case contains learned disputations. Therefore, if we imagine that, in the case of Alcippe, the defilement was not-forcible, I ask whether Mars was legally allowed to kill the violator. I respond: The Roman laws on marriage allow the father to kill both his married daughter and the adulterer [whom she has an affair

371 See Inst. 4.18.4.

with]. Moreover, the Attic and Roman laws allow a husband to kill the adulterer, but not [to kill] the wife too.

Pausanias cites a law of Draco, and there is a speech of Lysias, in which someone who had killed an adulterer is defended, and an Attic law is cited in which it is explicitly | written: "The husband may kill an adulterer with p. 204
impunity."[372] And indeed, it even adds that a man who lies with another's concubine may be killed with impunity. But these laws are referring to marriage and adultery; however, the laws do not allow a man who defiles an unmarried virgin without violence to be killed. Therefore, Mars was not lawfully allowed to kill Halirrhothius, if his defilement was nonviolent. Nevertheless, because this killing is very different from the homicides which are punished by the law, this fable was conceived to encourage the application of equity [*epieikeia*] in judging, if probable reasons recommend that the punishment be remitted or relaxed on account of the particular circumstances. | 16.149

Halirrhothius committed the initial injury, which caused the father's great and justified grievance. Therefore, since the father avenged this assault not because of his own desire, but because he was furiously enraged, the judge does not sentence him according to the law which punishes savage homicides committed out of one's own desire, without probable cause. Because of this distinction, [the judge] remits and relaxes the punishment, especially because in similar cases, the wrath of a father or husband is openly pardoned, namely, in the punishment for adultery.

Moreover, [this story] teaches that the gods (that is, kings) declare by their own example that they are severely enraged by defilements and lusts. Accordingly, they more easily pardon the one who punishes more severely. | p. 205
For these reasons, Mars was justly pardoned.

Nevertheless, even though [Mars] progressed further than the law allows, still, because this deed is different from those homicides which the law punishes with the ultimate penalty, there was there a need for things to be decided differently in this case. Accordingly, this fable teaches about two things.

First, it teaches that defilement deserves a serious penalty. In order to confer more authority upon this example, [the fable] is imagined to be a trial of the gods, so that we might understand that God requires punishment for defilements.

---

372 In *Description of Greece* IX.36.8, Pausanias mentions that Draco passed a law stating that the city would condone private killing of an adulterer. For Lysias, see *On the Murder of Eratosthenes*.

Second, it advises about equity [*epieikeia*], namely that on account of probable reasons for homicide, the penalties should occasionally be remitted or relaxed. Thus, in the Codex [9.9.4.1] Gracchus says: "Both night and justified grievance mitigate his crime."[373]

And in a certain place, it happened that a man went abroad and entrusted the care of his wife to his brother. The brother, having become more familiar with his sister-in-law, had incestuous intercourse with her. When the [other] brother returned and found out about this, he killed his brother. The magistrate, having heard the case, determined that no penalty whatsoever should be levelled against the killer. For the brother's crime was so wicked that it overwhelmed the harshness of the punishment. And it seems that the magistrate was not acting rashly in using equity [*epieikeia*] to remit the
p. 206 killer's punishment. |

Should Marriages Performed without the Consent of the Parents Be Ratified?

The partnership of marriage is especially relevant to justice. For the partnership of marriage is contracted in such a way that the spouse exchanges the right over his or her own body, in a certain way, for the right over another's body. And since there is justice, equality must be preserved on both sides
16.150 such that the man is not a | tyrant over his wife, but that he considers her an equal and does not trample her as an inferior.

For instance, Eve was created from the rib, not from the head or feet, in order to signify equality, and this union is ratified by divine law and the law of nature. Nevertheless, it has been asked whether a marriage performed without the authority of the parents, or others who are in place of the parents, is valid. Here, I will first recite the old laws, which annul marriages performed without the authority of the parents. Then I will speak of more recent pontifical decrees which hold the contrary position. I am not asserting that I would allow private citizens to ignore the settled law, but we are investigating causes, and I am speaking of the judgment of the magistrates and how in this case the current law should be moderated.

So then, that the ancient laws annul marriages made without the authority of the parents is clear from the Institutes [1.10.pr.], where the text clearly

373 Both 1546 editions erroneously read "Both night and justified grievance reveal [*revelat*] his crime." The 1538, 1539, and 1540 editions read *relevat* [mitigate], which is a correct quotation of the Codex.

says: "While children still belong to their families, they must have the consent of their parents, | under whose power they live. For both natural and p. 207
civil reason illustrate that this should be the case, [that is], that the command of the parent should come first."[374] And in [Decretum Ca.30.5.1], Pope Evaristus says that the consent of the parents is required for legitimate marriage. And Ambrose, [commenting] on the story of Rebecca, requires the consent of the parents, and he says that this practice is indeed so[375] honourable and in agreement with nature that even the poets taught it.[376] He cites Euripides' *Andromache*, when Orestes asks to marry Hermione, and she responds, "This matter is up to the decision of my father." These are the verses:

> "My marriage will be my father's business,
> It is not for me to decide."[377]

To all of this is added confirmation from the Decalogue [Exodus 20:12]: "Honor your father and mother," that is, that children, because they must obey their parents, do not have the right to make contracts without their consent. And since they are under the power of their parents, making contracts [of marriage], so to speak, secretly abducts another person.[378] For
these | reasons, there is a sufficiently clear morality in the ancient law. 16.151

And Paul, [writing] to the Corinthians, tacitly attributed authority to parents when he says [cf. 1Cor. 7:38]: "He who marries, does right, etc.", meaning that children should be married with the authority of their parents.
Moreover, problems are collected here which | arise if marriages performed p. 208
without the authority of the parents are ratified. Children deceived by fraud and trickery often enter into unfit marriages. And even though a person fooled by fraud does not truly consent, nevertheless, he is not freed afterwards, even if he desires to be freed after considering the matter. Sometimes, they enter into a dishonourable marriage driven by blind impulse. Further,

374 Melanchthon slightly changes the wording of this excerpt.

375 1540 reads *adeo*. 1546: *ideo*. The former reading better fits the syntax of the sentence.

376 See Ambrose, *De Abraham* I.91 (PL vol. 14, col. 453).

377 Euripides, *Andromache* 987–988. Melanchthon gives this quotation in Greek and follows it with a Latin translation. To avoid repetition, I have only translated the Latin here.

378 That is, in secretly marrying a girl without her parents' consent, the husband would essentially be kidnapping the girl, since, as a married woman, she would cease to be a part of the father's household, but this would happen without any permission from her father.

it is painful for the parents when their own children despise their parental authority, or when [the parents] are insulted by those who secretly and insidiously abduct their children from them.

These and other similar things are mustered to confirm the ancient laws, which invalidate marriages performed without the authority of the parents.
16.152 But now, the papal court pronounces otherwise.[379] For | marriages performed without the consent of the parents are not annulled. Here, certain people dispute whether there are firm reasons why things are now decided in this way, or whether it would be more correct to follow and restore the old laws. At this point, I will prudently avoid this disputation, but perhaps in some other place I will treat it more fully.

I have weighed a number of disputations about justice so that this tender age[380] would be equipped for matters of this type and recognize that the sources of these disputations on law and morals lie in philosophy. However, there is more dispute over justice than over the other virtues. For this reason, I will add a brief sequential catalogue of the remaining virtues,
p. 209 and indeed it is helpful | to illustrate and amplify these by oration. But making it such that their greatness can be somewhat better seen does not require subtle disputation so much as rhetorical ornament. Therefore, I will recite the following virtues: truthfulness, beneficence, gratitude, and friendship.

Truthfulness

[16.151] In that case, then, truthfulness should come first. In Homer, Achilles says that he hates people who think one thing and say another just as much as he hates death.[381] And heroic dispositions are pretty well like this, [being] forthright and hostile to the trickery and sophistry of dishonesty. And the more excellent a certain nature is, the more it loves truthfulness. From this,

---

379 According to the canon law of the late medieval period, marriages without parental consent were generally allowed. However, many Protestant reformers, including Luther, Johannes Bugenhagen, and Johannes Brenz, argued that parental consent was necessary. Several German states also adopted this principle in their sixteenth-century reform of marriage laws. See John Witte, Jr., "The Reformation of Marriage Law in Martin Luther's Germany: Its Significance Then and Now", *Journal of Law and Religion* 4.2 (1986): 293–351, esp. 323–330 and Paolo Astorri, "The Redefinition of Clandestine Marriage by Sixteenth-Century Lutheran Theologians and Jurists", *Law and History Review* 41.1 (2023): 65–92.

380 i.e., those of tender age, or students.

381 Homer, *Iliad* IX.312–313.

it can be understood that truthfulness is most suitable for man. Moreover, this virtue is taught in the Decalogue, in the commandment [Exodus 20:16]: "You shall not give false testimony."

So then, first, we will define the term, for truthfulness here does not signify knowledge, but a habit of the will, namely a love of truth and simplicity in all words and deeds, in every manner of life, and a sharp hatred of deception, pretence, sophistry, trickery, deceit, and any other artifice of this type.

There are two efficient causes: One is the judgement of reason, which understands that God teaches us the love | of truth, and [understands] that p. 210
we were created to be satisfied with the truth in our examinations of things, to agree to what is true in our manner of life, to bear [truth] before us, and indeed especially not to deceive, out of zeal for harm, those whom one may not harm. The other cause is the will obeying this judgment of reason, and on account of that, loving truth and fleeing from tricks and lies. | 16.152

The matter in which [truthfulness] exists is the human will, but the matter that it is about is called its "object".

So then, there are three objects with which this virtue deals. The first is doctrine, or the arts. For there are certain dispositions which believe that the highest merit of cleverness is to be able to overturn every correct statement with trickery and deceit and to spread new and bizarre opinions. But let it be known that such sophistical natures are monstrous and distorted. Therefore, the love of simple truth is a lofty virtue in doctrine and the arts. The second object is agreements and contracts,[382] trials, and testimonies. The third object is the expression of the will towards others, that is, being honest, not devising plots, and honestly speaking what one thinks whenever necessary.

The form[383] is the definition itself, or the thing itself, namely a habit in the will, which is the love of true propositions and of truth in agreements and in morals.

The final cause: The virtues should be sought for their own sake, namely because they agree with nature. For this reason, virtue | itself is its own chief p. 211
end, just as the philosophers say about virtue. But it is also philosophical and pious to establish obedience to God as the chief end of the virtues. Therefore, the end of truthfulness should be that we obey God, | who com- 16.153
mands us to love truth. After this, there are many lesser ends, that is to say,

382 1540: *contracta*. 1546a/b: *contractus*.

383 i.e., the formal cause.

benefits [*utilitates*]. For nothing is more harmful than a lie. False doctrine corrupts religion, morals, and arts. No trials or contracts can exist if truth is destroyed.

These ends are rather obvious, and they clearly testify that truthfulness is necessary in life.

Things contrary [to truthfulness]: Aristotle, following his custom, locates truthfulness between two extremes: between ostentation, or simulation, and dissimulation. And to which species indeed can those vices contrary to
16.154 truthfulness refer? Namely, untrustworthiness or zeal for lying, | arrogance of the type which Thraso had in the comedy,[384] and hypocrisy in morals like that of impostors feigning religion or of treacherous friends. Likewise, being suspicious, unfaithful, and deceitfully distorting the words and deeds of others. Sophistry, or sycophancy, that is, zeal for deception and trickery in doctrine, arts, business, and trials. These are the principal diseases of the Church and republic.

Things that are allied to truthfulness: Love of doctrine and zeal for inquir-
p. 212 ing into good things. Simplicity properly means | truthfulness itself, that is, speaking and acting rightly, without deception, without sophistical meaning.[385]

Beneficence

[16.153] Beneficence [*beneficentia*], or generosity, is a close relative of justice, for it also consists in a certain sharing. Justice shares things which are owed, while beneficence shares things which are not owed, particularly according to civil law. And moreover, because the society of the human race also has need of some free sharing, there are many duties [*officia*] which are not owed according to the civil law, which we should still share with each other in some way according to the natural law. Of this type are all the duties of which others have need, which we can render without inconvenience, according to that rule: "Whatever does not harm you, and benefits another, should be generously provided." Such things include not withholding running water, giving directions to the lost, or providing counsel to one who seeks it. Whoever does not share such things should be most justly considered and called a hater of mankind [*misanthrōpos*].

384 In Terence's comedy *Eunuchus*, the character Thraso is a swaggering and boastful military officer. In Greek, *thrasos* means "insolence".

385 The first version of the PME (the 1538 and 1539 editions) ends here. The second version (1540 and afterward) adds the discussions of beneficence, gratitude, and friendship.

The second precept: There are certain things which should be shared even at some inconvenience to ourselves, for the common society of the human race demands that we be affected by unjust dangers to others, and that we repel them insofar as we are able, even at our own inconvenience. For this reason, the powerful should protect the weak against injustices and the rich should be generous to the poor. For men, as the Stoics | clearly say, p. 213
were born for the sake of men, and therefore we are bound by natural obligation to those who are involved in danger, even when we are not bound by a civil obligation. For man was created to protect and aid other men insofar as he is able. Hence, there is that law of nature: "Whatever you want men to do for you, do also for them", and the writings of the doctors contain innumerable teachings commanding these mutual duties, and in fact, they are most elegantly depicted in Greek verses: | 16.154

> "For man saves man, city saves city.
> The hand washes the hand, and the finger washes the finger."[386]

So then, there are two types of services [*beneficia*]: public and private. By far, the more excellent are the public services, namely of those who establish, or defend, or protect republics. The teachers too should be counted in this place, who aid everyone else by sharing doctrine. Nothing is greater than this type of service, for nothing in all of human life is better than truth and knowledge of religion and the other good arts. So then, in the first place, there should be generous sharing with the teachers, according to that proverb, "The courts of the muses are bounteous."

Other services are private, namely when labours and resources are shared privately. However, because private resources and labours cannot suffice for everything, there must be a certain limit on generosity. Therefore, first, let there be this limit: we should give generously | in such a way that we p. 214
still somewhat preserve our patrimonies and our estates. For preventing patrimonies from being dissolved is of benefit[387] to the republic, and for this reason, the laws brand spendthrifts with legal disgrace [*infamia*] and prodigals are banned from managing goods. Therefore, the end and limit of beneficence, | which the very authority of public law prescribes for us, 16.155
should be this: We should support others from the fruits of our patrimonies, but in such a way that we do not deplete our patrimonies.

386 Erasmus, *Adagia* I.1.33. (ASD vol. II.1, p. 148).

387 1540 incorrectly reads *expetit*. 1546a/b: *expedit*.

Solomon most elegantly prescribed this limit when he said [Proverbs 5:16,17]: "Let your fountains pour forth [...] and you shall remain their owner, and not others with you." For he means that the fountain should produce streams which others can also enjoy; that is, the fruits of one's estates should be shared with the poor. However, in the meantime, we should ensure that we do not give away those same estates through unchecked liberality. In this way, he most sweetly depicts the commands of many outstanding virtues. For he teaches the extent to which generosity should be exercised towards the poor, and [teaches] that this diligence in preserving patrimonies is also necessary for the republic and for us. This diligence is a virtue called frugality, the neighbour of generosity. One [virtue] shares the fruit of the patrimony; the other preserves the patrimony. Indeed, good men should cultivate both of these virtues, not only for the sake of the manner of civic
p. 215 life, but also for the sake of religion. |

But we will speak more of the other a little bit later.[388] Now, we will teach, in order, those towards whom one should give generously. We have often emphasized that the law of nature is divine, and therefore we should recognize that this order is established by nature and approved by God. So then, nature teaches that one should give preference to his parents, children, and accordingly then to his relatives, and then to his fellow-citizens, over strangers.

Paul also affirms this order when he writes to Timothy [1Tim. 5:8]: "If someone does not take care of his own, especially those in his own household, he has denied the faith and he is worse than a nonbeliever." And [Ephesians 5:29]: "No one hates his own flesh." And several times, he rails against those who lack natural affections [*astorgous*].[389] For the *astorgoi* are those who strip themselves of the natural affections towards parents and children, or relatives. Moreover, this species of beneficence which obtains among parents, children, and relatives is called "piety". Hence, there are even laws about the forced inheritance share [*legitima*] which is said to be owed to children by natural law, since affection [*philostorgia*] is of the natural law. And among foreigners, first place should be given to guests, and

388 "the other" [*altera*] appears to refer to frugality [*parsimonia*]. Melanchthon does not return to this topic in this work. This, along with the rather abrupt ending of the work, suggests that the final sections of the *Summary of Moral Philosophy* were still something of a work in progress, even in the revised and expanded version.

389 *astorgous*: Those who lack the *storgai*, or natural affections towards family which Melanchthon sees as a significant natural positive impulse in human nature. Paul uses the term *astorgoi* in Romans 1:31 and 2 Timothy 3:3.

there are many reasons for this. For first of all, because this life requires both travel abroad and reciprocal exchanges, it is necessary that we cultivate the mutual rights of hospitality. Therefore, by the law of nations, it has always been wicked [*nefas*] to violate guests. Moreover, natural society binds us
not only to a few of our own, but to the entire human race. Therefore, | we 16.156
should not abandon those who have been deserted and are appealing to
our faith for refuge. | This species of beneficence is called hospitality, and it p. 216
has excellent precepts both in the holy scriptures and in the other writings and customs of the milder nations. Thus, the law says in Moses [Leviticus 19:33–34]: "If a foreigner lives in your land, [...] do not mistreat him, [...] but love him as yourself, etc." And elsewhere [Hebrews 13:2]: "Do not forget to be hospitable, for through this, certain men were even worthy of showing hospitality to angels."

Furthermore, above all, it is fitting for Christians to cultivate this virtue with the utmost dedication. For the Church is like a guest and exile in this world, and for this reason we should lovingly treat guests as fellow-exiles, so that, seeing that we ourselves hope to obtain a tranquil reception by God's goodwill, in turn we should show hospitality to others, and God honours this virtue with the amplest rewards. In [1Kings 17:7–16], when the woman of Zarephath took Elijah in when food was extremely scarce, and, offering him food, she was about to use up all that was left of her oil and grain, God multiplied the oil and grain such that it would last for three years. Then, Elijah even restored his hostess's dead son to life [1Kings 17:17–23]. The son of Elisha's hostess also came back to life [2Kings 4:32–36], and Obadiah hid 50 prophets in caves in order to defend them against the savagery of the woman Jezebel[390] [1Kings 18:4]. And Christ says [Matthew 25:35]: "I was a stranger and you took me in." And [Matthew 10:42]: "Whoever gives even a
drink of water to one of the least of these will not lose his reward." | p. 217

There are many other sayings and examples of this type in the scriptures which exhort us to hospitality and especially to take in and protect those exiles who, through injustice, have been banished for their devotion to true religion. Therefore, one must hope that the princes, who protect the followers of the Gospel at their own peril, would perform this duty which pleases God, and [hope] that God will remunerate this beneficence with great rewards. One must also hope that God will in turn defend [the princes] amidst these perils which they undergo on account of this godly duty.

---

390 1546a/b: "of the woman Jezebel" [*mulieris Iezabel*]. 1540: "of the woman of Israel" [*mulieris Israhel*].

Moreover, the passages concerning this virtue which are found in the poets and historians are well-known to everyone. Then, it is easy to decide in what order one should be beneficent to foreigners, for their need should be brought into consideration. But this rule should be kept in every virtue:
16.157 Nothing which conflicts with justice is done rightly. | Therefore, that Periclean [saying] should be observed: "One should do favours for friends as far
16.158 as the altars,"[391] that is, so long as we do not violate justice. | Accordingly, beneficence should be moderated chiefly such that injury is done to no one, just as the sacred scriptures teach: "Stolen offerings do not please God."[392]

Gratitude

[16.157] Gratitude should respond in turn to beneficence. For this reason, the very
p. 218 order of the virtues demands that we now | discuss gratitude. For gratitude is the virtue by which we give thanks that is owed to those who deserve it through their benevolence of soul, their love, and their other duties. I say "owed" because, by natural obligation, we owe our thanks to those who deserve it, even if we do not always have a civil obligation. Accordingly, because thanks is owed in some way, gratitude is the neighbour of justice, or a certain species of it. Therefore, because every injustice is inimical to human society, the ungrateful should actually be considered enemies of human society, for without this mutual and gratuitous sharing of duties [*officia*], human society could not survive. For unless duties are mutual, kindness cannot continue to endure, and such inequality is unjust and inimical to nature because we are all born for mutual preservation. Therefore, the jurists rightly say that we are naturally bound to return like for like [*antidōron*], and although the laws grant no legal action against any ingratitude, they do still notably punish the ungrateful. For instance, they drag ungrateful freedmen back into slavery; they allow donations to be revoked on account of ingratitude; they allow ungrateful children to be disinherited; and they allow a fief to be taken away from an ungrateful vassal.

But it is characteristic of the well-developed soul to recognize that ingratitude displeases God, that it is divinely punished, according to Solomon's
p. 219 saying, Proverbs [17:13]: "If you return | evil for good, evil will not leave your house."[393] The fourth commandment also teaches about gratitude: "Honor
16.158 your father and mother, | so that you may live long in the land" [Exodus

391 See Plutarch, *Moralia*, "Sayings of Kings and Commanders", 186C.3.

392 Perhaps an incorrect citation of Hosea 6:6, Psalm 51:16, or Jeremiah 6:20.

393 1540: Proverbs 17. 1546a/b: Proverbs 14. The correct citation is Proverbs 17:13.

20:12]. It should be sufficient to have taught these things about the causes of gratitude and the punishment for ingratitude, for books are filled with every praise of this virtue. Indeed, God has even fashioned for us a likeness of it in animals, in which we see that there is a certain sense of kindness. For there is the famous story of the lion, and storks have undertaken to look after each other [*antipelargein*].[394] So then, it is shameful for men to be surpassed by beasts in the duties of virtue.

In what way should a person give thanks?

Gratitude of soul, like the other virtues, should be perpetual. And since we should embrace gratitude for the sake of virtue, virtue itself should awaken and show itself in small favours, and it should bring forth true goodwill and a keen desire to be well-deserving, not only for the sake of fruits, but for the sake of our duty and our humanity. But the question is about the way [of showing gratitude] in performing external duties. We establish this by a certain reciprocity, according to Hesiod's teaching that we should pay a person back "with the exact same measure, and better if you can."[395] For it is most humane that Hesiod commands one to surpass the given favour, if indeed you can. Nevertheless, there are many things which cannot be repaid
by external duties, where greater | benevolence of soul and greater devotion p. 220
should be rendered, as, for instance, to God, to parents, to teachers, to the Church, to country, and to those who are well-deserving in the republic.

Friendship

Friendship is properly a species of justice by which benevolence is mutually [16.157]
exchanged for benevolence, and a certain particular and generous sharing of duties is established. And let it be known that friendship is a virtue, so that we may learn to cultivate friendships for the sake of virtue. Next, it
should be established | that [friendship] is also justice, so that we might 16.158
devoutly show mutual faith and benevolence.

394 The story of the lion is found in Aulus Gellius, *Attic Nights* V.14. In this passage, a runaway slave named Androclus was condemned to fight a lion in the Circus Maximus. When the lion approached Androclus, it recognized him and began to lick him affectionately. Androclus claimed that, several years prior, when he had escaped from slavery, he had saved that same lion from an injury and lived with it in a cave for three years. Unbeknownst to Androclus, both he and the lion had been captured on the same day and were serendipitously reunited in the arena. In *Natural History* X.32, Pliny claims that storks return to their nests and take care of their parents.

395 Hesiod, *Works and Days*, line 350.

16.159 What are the Causes of Friendship?

The efficient cause is the inclination, or judgment of human nature, towards cultivating society. Even though this urges us towards all men in general, nevertheless it particularly invites us to love and embrace those whom we know and to whom we are connected through experience. For this reason, friendship cannot extend as broadly as that common society which we have with the whole human race. Next, because friendship is a certain justice, it particularly binds us to those who in turn love us.

The matter[396] is the object, namely, the person who is to be loved. But because nothing is sought unless it is good, some good must necessarily exist, as a cause, in that thing which we have reckoned to be worthy of love.
p. 221 Moreover, these things are goods: virtue, merit, | and familiarity produced either by nature, law, or experience. For nature joins us to God, then it binds together spouses, parents, and children. Law joins us with our homeland, that is, with the Church and the republic and our fellow-citizens. Common life experience joins us with our neighbours and with our companions in studies and in dangers. These genera embrace every species of person with whom friendships are established and with whom there should be a certain bond.

For, in order that we may speak of friendships by nature, Aristotle most humanely says that, among spouses, there should not only be love, but also friendship, that is, a certain justice by which spouses, for the sake of virtue and humanity rather than utility, love each other, because nature invites us to this society, and moreover, in order that a certain equality proper to justice be established, lest one spouse tyrannically oppress the other, but so that mutual obligation and benevolence make them like equals, and so that this equality produces the sharing of decisions, resources, and household management, etc.[397] Moreover, although friendship between equals is different than friendship between nonequals, nevertheless, as I shall say later, a certain equality must be established. Accordingly, there is no friendship between parents and children, unless the parents determine that they have obligations to the children in turn, and do not consider them in the place of slaves or beasts.

The second degree is [the friendship] of those who are bound together by
p. 222 law, and moreover, this union, which we should have | with our country, the Church, and the republic, should be preferred to all other friendships. For

---

396 i.e., the material cause.

397 See the discussion of friendship between husband and wife in *NE* VIII.12.7 (1162a.16–29).

as it is said so honourably in Sophocles, friends should not be made more important than one's country, but, provided that one's country is secure, one should make friends: | "[The city] is the thing which saves [us], and 16.160
while we sail her on a straight course, we make our friends."[398]

The last degree [is the friendship] of those connected by experience. For this reason, Terence says this about proximity: "Or being neighbours, which I think is nearly the same as being friends."[399] For similarity is the common object of friendship. For all of nature is such that similar things are easily joined and mixed with each other. Hence the old [saying] goes, "Like attracts like."[400] Therefore, when we consider, as if they were our very selves, those people or things which delight us by their similarity and embrace them, similarity brings about benevolence. Finally, in all things there should be a certain similarity; virtue cannot be truly cherished by a soul that abhors virtue, nor can a true and firm friendship exist between wills which completely disagree, even if they might occasionally in some case be united. Therefore, Homer said that there is no firm agreement between men and lions.[401] That is, there can be no lasting friendships between the meek and the powerful, between philosophers and tyrants, just as Horace says: "Wooing a powerful friend is pleasant to those who have not tried it."[402] And Plato most elegantly said that his friendship with Dionysius was not true friendship, but "trivial friendship" [*mikrophilia*]. And the old man in Plautus' | [*The Pot of* p. 223
Gold] says that he cannot rightly mate a donkey with a cow, and he adds, "I wouldn't have a stable stable anywhere if there were a divorce!"[403] Finally, since in friendship, a certain equality must be created, for it is a species of justice, it is necessary that the objects be similar to each other in some way. For this agreement of objects creates a similarity of wills.

The formal cause of friendship is that mutual benevolence among friends which is aroused by the efficient causes and objects which I have recounted. That benevolence, since it is mutual, is a certain true connection and union of souls by which friend embraces friend just as himself. | Two sayings arise 16.161
out of this: The friend is another self; and friendship is equality. Accordingly, although friendships exist among nonequals, nevertheless, that very bond

398 Sophocles, *Antigone*, lines 189–190. This quotation is given in Greek.

399 Terence, *The Self-Tormentor*, lines 56–57.

400 Plato, *Gorgias*, 510B. Melanchthon cites this in Greek, and then gives a Latin translation, which I have omitted to avoid redundancy.

401 Homer, *Iliad*, XXII.262.

402 Horace, *Epistles*, I.18.86.

403 Plautus, *The Pot of Gold*, line 233.

of friendship makes them of the same sort in some way, for friends should not be despised as inferiors, but embraced as equals who are worthy of our friendship, especially because that mutual benevolence is a certain justice. Therefore, it should be understood that equal is rendered for equal. This is a most humane saying and is extremely useful in life. For it nourishes friendships, or rather, a most honourable opinion of one's friends dissolves contempt, in the same way that, because God declares that he is our friend, he thinks highly of us and judges us to be somehow equal to himself and
p. 224 worthy of love. | And it is pious to attribute this faithfulness and goodness to God, namely because we are like another self to him, and the angels feel the same way towards[404] us. In the same way, since friendship should exist between spouses as if with equal benevolence, they should share their other duties, and parents should feel the same way towards their children and princes towards their citizens. For there is no friendship if [friends] are despised as nonequals who are unworthy of our benevolence, our company, or our duties. Finally, as has been said above about objects, "like attracts like." Even if there is some dissimilarity, nevertheless friendship should produce some similarity, such that it is the case that "like attracts like." For this particularly pertains to the nature of friendship and "formal reasoning", as it is called.[405]

The final cause of friendship is primarily the very honour of virtue, for friendship should be sought and cultivated for the sake of virtue, even if no utility comes from it. This is because the mind judges that men were created for this society and that it is a virtue worthy of man to cultivate these bonds of mutual benevolence. And many sufficiently clear judgments have been impressed upon human nature, and they testify that friendships should not be cultivated for the sake of utility alone, but for the sake of virtue. That is, it is on this account that nature teaches us these duties. For parents are moved to love their children not by utility, but by the judgment and inclination of nature, and indeed, the power of love stands out especially
p. 225 in | the misfortunes of children, since parents can take neither utility or pleasure from them. This passion is called "affection" [*philostorgia*], and it is
16.162 praised not only in the books of the philosophers,[406] but | also in the sacred scriptures. Romans 13.[407] Therefore, just as the judgment of nature leads us

404 1540 incorrectly reads *ergo*. 1546a/b: *erga*.

405 That is, reasoning according to formal causes, which he discusses in this paragraph.

406 1540: *in libris philosophorum*. 1546a/b: *libris philosophorum* ("by the books of the philosophers").

407 The 1540 and both 1546 editions read "Romans 13", but the correct citation is Romans 12:10, where Paul refers to *philostorgoi*.

to friendship in this species, so does nature prevail over the calculation of utility in the other [species], and to be sure, it is the judgment and preservation of nature rather than utility, because we are led to society by nature even if no utility follows, and the source of friendship is domestic union and necessity. This argument is a clear enough refutation of Epicurus, who commands us to do everything for our own sake or for our own utility, for the mind and the natural affections of parents cry out against this.

Any good man also has friendship with the republic, not only for the sake of private utility, but for the sake of virtue, to such a degree that he does not hesitate to give his life for the republic if necessary, and such that not only do the Christian scriptures teach this, but the very law of nature has declared in this way that God is angry with those who do not love and defend the republic. Moreover, the human mind understands this: that God must be obeyed, even if no utility follows from it. Accordingly, Plato says that one's homeland is a sort of deity, that is, that it should be worshiped, because God demands that all of his blessings which are included in the name "homeland" [*patria*] be defended. And they are truly divine things, namely, religions, laws, | the propagation of citizens, etc. These are the p. 226
words in the fifth book of *Laws*: "One must tend to his homeland more than a mother tends her children. In this, [the homeland] is their master."[408] But I will refrain from gathering more arguments, for we have refuted Epicurus in general above. And because friendship is a virtue, it is necessary to seek it, like the other virtues, for its own sake rather than for the sake of utility. It is easy for Christians to discern this; they know that these duties should be measured by the will of God rather than by their fruits.

What are the Effects [of Friendship]?

Although, as I have said, friendship should be chiefly sought for the sake of virtue, nevertheless, much utility comes from it. For what holds for the other virtues also holds here: morality produces utility, and hardly any virtue is more fruitful than friendship. Therefore, the old proverb says that "Friends are more necessary | than fire and water." Likewise, "Man protects 16.163
man and city protects city".[409] Thus, mutual benevolence should beget a sharing of duties and resources which should extend as broadly as the proverb teaches: "All things are common among friends."[410] However, since the

408 cf. Plato, *Laws* V (740a), which Melanchthon quotes loosely in Greek.

409 See Erasmus, *Adagia* II.2.75 (ASD vol. II.3, p. 190) and I.1.33 (ASD vol. II.1, p. 148).

410 Cicero, *De officiis*, I.16.51.

resources and opportunities of friends are not equal, this sharing should be generous, not done with gain in mind. That is, gratuitous favours are owed in friendship just as they are owed of spouses to each other or owed of parents
p. 227 to their children. Therefore, | stingily tallying up each individual favour is unworthy of friendship, and it is characteristic of a merchant, not a friend,[411]
16.164 that "I give something and I take something in return", as the poet says. | Nevertheless, the mutual will of a true friend shall not lack opportunities to render favours. So then, it should be the case that we do favours for our friends just as Pericles said: "as far as the altar"—that is, provided that we can do so without causing harm.

Things Opposed [to Friendship]

Friendship is a mean, just like the other virtues. Therefore, friendship struggles with vices on both sides: that is, with the simulation of extravagant benevolence, and with misanthropy. The simulation of extravagant benevolence is called "flattery", and the degree to which it is evil is taught by one saying of Bias, who, when he was asked what was the most harmful beast of all, responded: "Among the wild beasts, a tyrant, but among the tamed ones, a flatterer."

Appendix: Melanchthon's Alternate Division of Virtues in the 1538/1539 Editions

The following section of the *Summary of Moral Philosophy* was included at the end of Book I in the 1538 (pp. 50–59) and 1539 editions (pp. 50–60), but absent in those editions from 1540 to 1546. I include the page numbers from the first edition (1538 Strasbourg).

p. 50

What Is the Division of Virtues?

Just like the arts, the virtues are also differentiated by their objects and ends. For medicine is differentiated from music because medicine deals with healing sick bodies, while music deals with sounds. In the same way, when the species of virtue are differentiated, one must investigate their objects and ends, and this is generally done in the division of the habits. So then, we will recount how

411 1540: *mercatori ... amico*. 1546: *mercatoris ... amici*.

the philosophers divide the species of virtue below. But first, we shall distribute them according to the progression of the commandments of the Decalogue, since there is no more fitting method of the virtues than the Decalogue. Therefore, the species [of virtue] can be derived most fittingly and precisely from the order of the commandments of the Decalogue. For its order is not without art [*atechnōs*], but is derived from the order of objects, according to the manner that logic demands the habits be divided.

God is the highest and chief object of good actions. Therefore, the primary and chief virtues should be the ones which concern God. Therefore, the Decalogue most appropriately teaches first about this genus of virtues. Besides, even if philosophy or human reason does not sufficiently understand those virtues of the first table (namely perfect obedience, perfect love, etc.), they still understand human discipline, which produces some shadows of those virtues. For certain notions about God, however obscure, remain within men, and the law of nature has not been entirely erased from their souls. | For this reason, phil- p. 51
osophy retains the following concepts: that there is a God, that God is just, that he demands obedience, that he punishes wrongdoing. And indeed, experience itself reminds reason that great and atrocious crimes are divinely punished, such that this is attested not only by the ruin of murderers and tyrants, but also by those terrors of conscience which divinely exist in every wicked person. Therefore, even philosophy itself posits religion—that is, reverence before God—among the virtues. And the laws of all peoples have punished the open contempt of religion.

The first commandment teaches about worship in souls. Therefore, the first virtue, even among the Philosophers, is reverence of soul, that is, the fear of God—that we have determined that there is a God, that God should be obeyed, that wrongdoing is divinely punished.

The second commandment teaches about external worship, that is, about the use of the divine name. The related virtue is reverence in swearing oaths, the preservation of honourable opinions about God, avoiding blasphemy and Epicurean speech, and the invocation of God.

The third commandment teaches about ceremonies, and the third virtue is reverence towards ceremonies and diligence in keeping pious ceremonies. These virtues are necessary for discipline and tutelage [*paedagogia*]. Therefore, philosophy or reason understands and requires these things, and lawgivers have passed the most honourable laws about them. And indeed, since the magistrate should be the guardian of the entire law, | insofar as it pertains to external dis- p. 52
cipline, he should also embrace these things. For this reason, these were the words for swearing an Athenian oath: "I will fight for the sacred things both alone and with others." Moreover, the true virtues of the first table are the true

fear of God, true confidence in mercy, obedience, the explication of doctrine, invocation, thanksgiving, confession, and the keeping of ceremonies.

The second table contains the virtues which deal with human society. First is obedience towards superiors. For this civic society cannot be maintained unless there is a certain order among men in which some rule and others obey. Therefore, even among the philosophers, the chief virtue is universal justice, that is, obedience to the laws and to superiors. The species are piety towards parents and children and the justice of magistrates towards subjects, and of subjects towards magistrates.

The fifth commandment orders about protecting bodies. To this pertains particular justice, which prohibits injuries to bodies.

The sixth [commandment] is about marriage, forbidding[412] wandering and impure lusts. To this pertains continence.

The seventh [commandment] orders about particular justice, which prohibits injuries to a person's property. And in this way, it establishes distinctions of ownership and it teaches one to preserve justice in contracts.

The eighth [commandment] orders about truth. For it is well-established
p. 53 that | faithfulness in agreements as well as truthfulness in trials, contracts, and all dealings are most necessary for human society. For deceitful and treacherous men cannot even be tolerated in private dealings.

In this way, all the virtues can be included under the Decalogue, and truly, no more fitting or appropriate method can be devised. And if you contemplate the commandments of the Decalogue in order, you will see something like a certain vision of the most beautifully constituted state. And in this way, Aristotle says that there is one best polity—that is, the one which agrees with nature. Accordingly, you may rightly claim that this one vision of a state is the best, which is expressed in the Decalogue. For it first established religion, and then the magistrate. Next, it adds the law of the magistrate which prohibits injuries, and afterwards it consecrates marriage, then distinguishes ownership of things, and finally it establishes trials.

And the Decalogue plainly philosophizes as it distributes the species of the virtues according to their objects. For the philosophers divide species both by their objects and by their ends. For some of the virtues govern common society, while others govern individuals towards the conservation of nature and of morals. Moreover, the ends of the virtues are derived from the ends of human nature, from which the laws of nature are also gathered.[413] So then, the ends
p. 54 of man are the conservation of nature, | the conservation of civil society, and

412 1538 incorrectly reads *vetant*. The 1539 Strasbourg edition correctly reads *vetans*.

413 Here, the 1538 Strasbourg edition contains the sentence "Moreover, the ends of man are

the exercise of proper actions. Man was made for society; therefore, man needs the notions and virtues governing society. Therefore, it is the law of nature that some rule and others obey. From this arises the primary virtue, universal justice, which is obedience to the laws. Then, in society there is also a need for mutual exchange, which cannot continue indefinitely unless equality is preserved in some certain measure. From this arises particular justice. And in contracts, trials, and then in all interactions, constancy in agreements and words is necessary. From this arises truthfulness. Defence against unjust violence is also necessary for society. From this arises courage. Likewise, a certain free sharing of duties is necessary for society. For because men exist for the sake of men, they should fulfil all duties which they can perform for others without inconvenience, at the time necessary for them. From this arises generosity, to which corresponds gratitude. For nature cannot be preserved unless there are mutual favours. Orderly thinking, reverence towards virtue, and a devotion to pleasantness in the communication of speech and in every interaction are also suitable for man. From this arises refinement or courtesy.

Certain notions and virtues properly govern individual men and lead them towards conserving nature, for instance: modesty, temperance, | and similar p. 55 virtues which produce moderation amidst pains and pleasures such that nature may be preserved. And there is a notion [*noticia*] about God born within men: that justice pleases God, that he punishes injustice. For this reason, nature commands that we fear God and call upon him. From this comes the virtue by which we worship God, which is called religion or piety. In this way, the laws of nature or natural notions which produce and rule the virtues are derived from the ends of human nature. This is a fitting distribution of the virtues which leads us to those very sources or causes, placed in nature, of the virtues. And if someone were to compare this division with that which is derived from the Decalogue, he will notice that the steps of either division do not differ greatly from each other.

The laws of nature are most suitably defined in this way: they are notions, divinely impressed upon human minds and born with us. That is, [they are] certain judgments about morals which are a certain light of the mind, just as the eyes are endowed with their own light. The philosophers call these "practical principles" [*principia practica*], and they call the conclusions derived from them "common notions and conceptions" [*koinas ennoias kai prolēpseis*], because

---

the conservation of nature, from which the laws of nature are also gathered." [*Sunt autem fines hominis conservatio naturae, unde etiam leges naturae colliguntur*]. This is a typographical error which is noted in the *errata* of the 1538 edition. The translation reflects this correction.

they are perceived by nature, that is, informed by nature, and we assent to them, and there is no need to prove them. And it is worthwhile to consider that, just as the other arts (like Arithmetic or Geometry) are certain because they arise
p. 56 from these principles, so is the doctrine of morals likewise certain | because these most certain notions give rise to it. Therefore, one should also consider that humanity has a certain wondrous dignity because this divine wisdom—namely, the very law of God—shines in their souls. For the natural laws are the very laws of the Decalogue.

The first law. Man was chiefly created to know God, namely, [to know] that there is a God, that he is wise, good, and just, the creator and ruler of things, that he punishes the unjust in this civil manner of life. Likewise, [to know] that God must be obeyed and his judgment feared. These things are the very voices of conscience in every man, and they are the conclusions which arise from demonstration.

Man owes obedience to the sovereign creator, because we were created for his sake, that we ourselves would obey him and glorify him.

The sovereign creator is God.

Therefore, man owes obedience to God.

The other matters concerning divine affairs pertain to this law. The law [is] about oaths, and likewise about not violating ceremonies. Concerning oaths, this is the reasoning: The human mind should truly establish that God looks upon human affairs and avenges wrongdoing. In oaths, we affirm that God is the avenger, and we ask that he also punish us if we swear falsely. Therefore, we
p. 57 should truly affirm this, and punishments await the dishonest. |

Concerning ceremonies: Men should preserve the knowledge of God.

Ceremonies are the symbols [*signa*] of the knowledge of God.

Therefore, ceremonies should be observed.

These laws pertain to the first table.

The remaining laws follow.

Every nature whatsoever desires to preserve itself and its own species as far as possible. For this reason, humans, just like the rest of the animals, are endowed with the desire and drive towards procreation. The difference, however, is that humans also possess the judgment that promiscuous intercourse displeases God, and therefore he decided that marriages should be contracted by certain laws.

Fifth. Man was created for society, as procreation itself and the rearing of children attest. Moreover, the chief end why we were created for society is so that men may be educated in society, and specifically educated about God. Therefore, the conservation of society is necessary. From this arises the law: "Harm no one." From this law arises the virtue of justice.

Sixth. In society, men need rulers and protectors, and for this reason, some must rule while others obey. From this arises the law that the magistrate is necessary, and that magistrates must be obeyed. These laws pertain to the fourth commandment, and they produce virtue, obedience, or universal justice. | p. 58

Seventh. The defence of the human race is necessary, and in order for the species to be preserved, as if it were a body, the vicious members must be removed. Therefore, punishments for those who disturb society are necessary, and therefore wars are necessary. To this pertains the law, "One may repel force with force", namely in legitimate defence. Also pertaining to this are the words of the jurist, who says, "Wars, slavery, political authority, etc. are derived from the law of nations."[414] And from this law comes courage, which is the protectress of justice.

Eighth. In this nature, because the desires of men do not allow us to enjoy things equally if they are held in common, the distinction of ownership is necessary. This law pertains to the seventh [commandment]: "You shall not steal." And from this arises the species of justice which, regarding possessions, renders to each his due.

Ninth. Nevertheless, because people still have need of the resources and services of others, exchange should be facilitated according to reason, and in order for that exchange to be perpetual, equality in mutual exchange should be preserved. From this arises contracts and justice which preserves equality in contracts. Hence, Euripides most honourably said, "Equal right, always."

Tenth. Pacts and agreements must be kept. For neither contracts nor legal decisions nor treaties between peoples can exist unless faith is kept in agreements and in words. Moreover, truthfulness itself is entirely in agreement with nature. For man was created to investigate and understand things, and truthfulness is to understand things as | they are. Therefore, human nature was created p. 59 for truthfulness. From this law arises truthfulness, prudence, and similar virtues, and these pertain to the eighth commandment: "You shall not give false testimony."

Eleventh. Because nature seeks its own preservation, it judges that, in eating, one should flee from that intemperance which harms nature, according to that [saying] of Hippocrates, "All that is in excess is opposed to nature." From this arises the virtue of temperance.

---

414 For the first quote, see D.43.16.1.27. The second is a summary of the content in Inst. 1.2.2.

Twelfth. Man alone understands order. Therefore, he judges that there should be varying grades of persons, places, and times. Likewise, he understands that the moderation of the passions agrees with nature. For immoderate pleasures and immoderate pains destroy nature, or at least certainly impede actions. From this arises modesty, which produces the moderation of passions. Likewise, refinement, which assigns actions suitable for persons, places, and times.

These are the chief laws of nature. And more can be gathered, but if they are desired here, they will be recounted below in the definitions of the virtues. For all of moral philosophy truly and in fact is the explication of the law of nature. For it shows how the precepts of those actions for which human nature was particularly created are written in nature. And because this is the case, it is easy to judge how great the authority [of moral philosophy] should be. For the law of nature is truly the divine law, as has already been stated frequently.

CHAPTER 2

Commentaries on Some Books of Aristotle's *Politics*

1 Introduction

The 1530 *Commentaries on Some Books of Aristotle's Politics* constitutes a decisive step in Melanchthon's development of a natural law theory of politics. In this text, the reformer asserted that the impulses to form society and establish government are an integral part of human nature. In other words, following Aristotle, Melanchthon claimed that human beings are naturally political, an idea which allowed him to elevate politics as its own particular *ars* governed by human reason apart from revelation. In the *Commentaries*, Melanchthon provided a vision of civil society that is rooted in the natural human desire for community, mutual benefit, and mutual protection. Similarly, he argued that government is a natural institution that reflects the natural hierarchies of authority and submission which characterize all human organizations from the family to the state. In the *Commentaries*, Melanchthon affirmed society and government as beneficial institutions which are legitimized by the order of nature—and by extension, by divine law.

While the work's title labels it as a commentary, readers should not expect a line-by-line exegesis of Aristotle's text. Melanchthon does comment upon certain select passages drawn from the first three books, but his choices are strategic ones that provide a point of departure for expounding upon certain important topics of politics, such as the formation of society, the necessity of government, and the importance of preserving existing laws. As such, the *Commentaries* is essentially a brief textbook in which Melanchthon uses Aristotle's *Politics* as a framework for advancing his own views of political life and the state. The prefatory epistle similarly indicates that the book was intended, at least in part, for classroom instruction. The result is, as Mads Langballe Jensen has labelled the *Commentaries*, "The first work of systematic political philosophy written by any Evangelical reformer".[1]

1 Jensen, *A Humanist in Reformation Politics*, p. 53. Of course, this was not the first explicitly political work by a Protestant—Luther's *On Secular Authority* and writings on the Peasants' War, as well as radical sermons and tracts by Thomas Müntzer and others count as that—but it was the first attempt to work out a systematic "science of politics" by any Protestant.

 HTTPS://DOI.ORG/10.1163/9789004774742-005

Melanchthon drafted this work between September/October 1529 and May 1530, in response to a concrete political crisis.[2] In 1524–1525, The Holy Roman Empire had been wracked by a series of popular upheavals. In what is broadly known as the Peasants' War, peasants and disgruntled middle-class workers including artisans, miners, and craftsmen engaged in a series of uprisings in Swabia, Thuringia, Saxony, and neighbouring regions.[3] While economic and social concerns were at the heart of these uprisings, there was an undeniably religious element in many of them, and fiery radical preachers such as Thomas Müntzer fanned the flames of rebellion. By summer of 1525, German princely and imperial troops had quelled the uprisings, but not without great violence. Around 100,000 rebels are estimated to have been killed in the conflict.

The Peasants' War had seriously disturbed both Luther and Melanchthon. Luther wrote a number of works in the midst of the conflict; his 1525 tract, *Against the Robbing, Murderous Hordes of Peasants* encouraged German princes to quell the rebellions violently, although in later tracts, he softened his tone. Melanchthon, too, was appalled by the unrest. He was particularly concerned that evangelical theology and ideas of Christian freedom were being perverted to justify anarchy, rebellion, and political chaos. As he wrote in a 1525 letter to his friend and colleague Joachim Camerarius, "Müntzer bears before him a barbarity which surpasses that of the Scythians, and one cannot even express how dire is the threat which he poses to all who disapprove of sedition."[4] Aside from an extended discussion in his 1528 *scholia* on Colossians, Melanchthon would not produce a more extensive treatment of the relation between politics and the Gospel until 1530, when this commentary appeared.[5] As Melanchthon reveals in the dedicatory epistle to this work, the *Commentaries* on Aristotle's *Politics* was part of a larger project of turning towards the ancient Greek philosopher in 1529 and 1530.[6]

---

2 For the composition date of the work, see Kuropka, *Philipp Melanchthon: Wissenschaft und Gesellschaft*, p. 278.

3 For a classic treatment of the Peasants' War, see Peter Blickle, *The Revolution of 1525: The German Peasants' War from a New Perspective*. Translated by Thomas A. Brady, Jr. and H.C. Erik Midelfort (1981).

4 See CR 1.741 = MBW 399.

5 For this Colossians commentary, as well as for Melanchthon's political involvement up until 1528, see Timothy J. Wengert, "Philip Melanchthon and a Christian Politics" and James Estes, *Peace, Order*, pp. 68–79.

6 Melanchthon had published a commentary on the *Nicomachean Ethics* in 1529, entitled *In Ethica Aristotelis commentarius* (Wittenberg: Josef Klug). For Melanchthon's turn to Aristotle more broadly in the late 1520s and early 1530s, see Nicole Kuropka, *Philipp Melanchthon: Wissenschaft und Gesellschaft*, esp. pp. 23–31, 176–183, 239–244.

Melanchthon looked to Aristotle to find a natural, rational basis for politics and moral philosophy which could counter the religious fanaticism that, in the reformer's mind, had characterized the disturbances of 1524–1525.[7] This much is apparent from his numerous references to such theologians in the *Commentaries*. In this work, Melanchthon openly condemned the Eisenach preacher Jakob Strauss and the radical firebrand Thomas Müntzer. Both of those men, Melanchthon claimed, had "incited the mob to take up arms against the magistrates."[8] He also singled out the Memmingen pastor Christoph Schappeler, who was suspected to be one of the authors of the Twelve Articles, a document which expressed the political and economic demands of the Swabian peasants. Melanchthon even targeted his former colleague Andreas Bodenstein von Karlstadt, accusing him of attempting to overturn the existing laws and replace them with Mosaic law. That Melanchthon considered Karlstadt to be an important part of the uprisings is obvious from his letters at the time; for example, in a letter dated May 15, 1525, Melanchthon alleges that the "Müntzerites, the allies of Karlstadt, are ravaging Thuringia with the cruellest depredations."[9]

The disastrous effects of mixing politics and religious zealotry led Melanchthon to draw a strict division between the realm of the Gospel, which was ruled by faith, Scripture, and the Holy Spirit, and the realm of politics, which was ruled by nature and reason. It is for this reason that Melanchthon condemned even theologians such as John Wycliffe, Huldrych Zwingli, and Wolfgang Capito—who were not directly involved with the peasant uprisings—because "although they teach the Gospel, [they] interfere in other offices and pass laws about the division of inheritance, taxes, contracts, and punishments for the wicked."[10] In mixing the Gospel with politics, these figures had made the same mistake as the fanatical peasants. Melanchthon attributed the same mistake to the Catholic church, especially the popes, who "have usurped governments and arrogated to

7 Most modern scholars have viewed the *Commentarii* as an explicit refutation of the theology underlying the Peasants' Revolt. See Kisch, *Melanchthons Rechts- und Soziallehre*, pp. 91–97; Noah Dauber, "Deutsche Reformation: Philipp Melanchthon", in *Politischer Aristotelismus: Die Rezeption der Aristotelischen Politik von der Antike bis zum 19 Jahrhundert*, ed. Christoph Horn and Ada Neschke-Hentschke (2008), pp. 173–191; Deflers, *Lex und Ordo*, p. 199. Ralph Keen also highlights the opposition to the caesaropapism of the Holy Roman Empire. See *Divine and Human Authority*, p. 199. Quentin Skinner briefly discusses the "vocabulary" of popular magistracy in the *Commentaries*, referring to Melanchthon's brief aside about Spartan ephors and German electors limiting the king's power. *The Foundations of Modern Political Thought: Volume 2: The Age of Reformation*, p. 231.

8 See p. 266 below.

9 See CR 1.740 = MBW 400.

10 See p. 238 below.

themselves the right of bestowing kingdoms".[11] For Melanchthon, a theologian's attempt to govern in politics was a violation of his calling and a mixing of offices. Theologians playing at politics would end just as disastrously as if they tried to practice medicine.

However, the application of religious radicalism to politics was not the only target of this work. As Mads Langballe Jensen has recently shown, Melanchthon also intended the *Commentaries* as a refutation of Ockhamist political thought.[12] Melanchthon knew Ockham's thought indirectly via the thought of Gabriel Biel and Jean Gerson, which he learnt from his Tübingen teachers Wendelin Steinbach and Conrad Summenhart.[13] But Melanchthon also knew Ockham's thought more directly. He had read Ockham's *Dialogus* in 1529, although he complained that the work was "duller than I would have expected; there is plainly no solid doctrine in that entire genre."[14]

In Melanchthon's reading, Ockham had grounded political authority entirely on human consent. As Melanchthon argues in the *Commentaries*, Ockham understood political institutions to be entirely conventional, and thus not based in the stable foundations of divine institution or natural law. One possible implication of this was that if the people had established rulers by consent, they could depose rulers by consent.[15] Melanchthon judged this idea to be profoundly destabilizing. In the commentary, he writes: "Certain people claim—falsely—that only the consent of the people grants political authority [*imperium*], just as Ockham says. [This is false] because princes lawfully rule over even the unwilling, and they lawfully seize control of governments not only through election or votes and the consent of the people, but also through just wars and the eradication of bandits, through legitimate succession, etc."[16] The danger, then, was that a view of political authority grounded purely in human consent could lead to rebellion and chaos. In contrast, Melanchthon believed, the idea of government grounded in the natural order, and by extension in divine law, would secure the state against wild revolts.

11 See p. 238 below.

12 See Mads Langballe Jensen, "By Convention or by Nature: Melanchthon's Criticism of Late Medieval Ockhamist Political Thought in the *Commentarii in aliquot politicos libros Aristotelis*." *History of Political Thought* 35.1 (2014): 1–28.

13 See Jensen, "By Convention or by Nature", p. 10.

14 CR 1.1083 = MBW 807. See also Jensen, *A Humanist in Reformation Politics*, p. 63.

15 Ockham's actual position was more complex than this. For consent in Ockham's thought, see Arthur Stephen McGrade, *The Political Thought of William of Ockham: Personal and Institutional Principles* (1974), pp. 103–109.

16 See pp. 257–258 below.

In response to these twin dangers—spiritual anarchy and Ockhamist conventionalism—Melanchthon presents here a vision of politics that is rooted firmly in human nature. Melanchthon's establishment of politics on a natural, Aristotelian basis was a major development within early Reformation thought and a departure from Martin Luther's more strictly biblical approach to politics.[17] In tracts such as his 1523 *On Secular Authority: To What Extent it Should be Obeyed*, Luther had presented a view of government as a direct divine institution. Luther's early political thought was rooted in Romans 13: "Let every person be subject to the governing authorities, for there is no authority except from God, and those authorities that exist have been instituted by God." The result was that all rulers, good or bad, were divinely ordained and must be obeyed. God had ordained "the secular government, which resists the unchristian and the evil such that they must outwardly keep things peaceful and calm."[18] One possible implication of this was that the purposes of government were almost entirely defensive and punitive. If government was instituted to restrain and punish human sin after the Fall, it was largely a bulwark against wickedness, a negative divine institution to maintain order and punish wrongdoers, not a good and natural part of human life.

Certainly, Melanchthon too understood the magistrate to have a punitive and restrictive function; political authority was, among other things, the power "of coercing men to obedience with the sword, and of punishing those who do not obey the laws."[19] However, Melanchthon also understood the impulse towards society and politics to be a part of human nature. As he writes in this commentary, "Aristotle collects the reasons why man is led to society by nature—it is not merely for the sake of utility."[20] In that same passage, Melanchthon leans upon Cicero as well to show that the existence of language is proof that humans are social creatures, for language would be useless without society. But government also sprang from human nature: "Therefore, just as the causes which lead us to cultivate society are impressed upon nature, so we should be aware that there are causes impressed upon human nature which lead us to establish governments and obey the magistrates."[21]

---

17 As Jensen has argued, the 1529 *Nicomachean Ethics* commentary and the 1530 *Politics* commentary constitute the beginning of Melanchthon's turn towards natural law in his political thought. See pp. 53–96 of *A Humanist in Reformation Politics*.

18 Luther, WA 11.251. "das welltliche [Regiment], wilchs den unchristen und bösen weret, dass sie eusserlich müssen frid halten und still seyn ..."

19 See p. 257 below.

20 See p. 241 below.

21 See p. 242 below.

However, does he mean human nature generally, or human nature specifically after the Fall? In some cases, he appears to mean the former. The impulse towards marriage and towards forming society is an integral part of prelapsarian human nature, but the formation of government and the institution of private property seem to be consequences of fallen human nature. He points to language (a prelapsarian phenomenon) as proof of man's natural social nature, but in the very next lines, he cites a quote from Aristotle extolling the virtues of society as a protection from unjust violence. Melanchthon does something similar in his discussions of property. He claims, following Aristotle, that the division of property "agrees with nature." Immediately afterwards, he argues for private property from the premise that lazy and avaricious humans would take advantage of common property, implying that property is only necessary after the Fall.

Although Melanchthon does not fully solve this problem, he was aware of it. As he treats the arguments for common property, he recognizes that his opponents argue for common property based on "the uncorrupted nature of man, as it existed prior to original sin."[22] Melanchthon rejects this premise and asserts, "When we ourselves talk about the present state [of man], after original sin, we correctly claim that the division of property is of the natural law."[23] Moreover, in his rejection of Wycliffe at the end of the work, he claims that "[A]fter Adam's sin, the law began to be necessary for coercing the ungodly. By the same reason, the magistrate who executes the law also became necessary. Therefore, natural dominion can also be defined in this way: it is the natural law which ordains certain men to rule for the purpose of coercing the ungodly."[24]

As a result, Melanchthon's concept of "human nature" in this text is somewhat ambiguous. He can affirm that marriage and sociability are fundamental parts of human nature, while government and private property may only be natural to fallen man. Accordingly, it is unclear whether Melanchthon understands natural law to be immutable, or whether he posits two separate prelapsarian and postlapsarian natural laws. In later works like the *Summary of Moral Philosophy*, Melanchthon would work out this problem with a theory about the hierarchy of natural law precepts, in which lower principles of the natural law yield to higher principles, thus preserving the overall harmony and unity of the natural law.[25]

22 See p. 252 below.
23 See p. 252 below.
24 See p. 270 below.
25 See the section of the *Summary* entitled "Is the Law of Nature Always Immutable?" on pp. 119–121 above.

But while his later works would address this issue in more depth, Melanchthon provided no detailed solution to this problem in the *Commentaries*.

Despite these difficulties, in the *Commentaries*, Melanchthon offers a view of politics that was both divinely consecrated and essential to human nature. Such a view allowed him to assert the necessity of politics in the face of radical spiritualism like that which had motivated the Peasants' War. It also allowed him to argue, contrary to what he saw as the explosive implications of Ockhamist political thought, that politics was not merely a matter of convention. Rather, politics had both a natural and a divine basis. In making this point, the *Commentaries* was a decisive step in Melanchthon's political thought, and in the burgeoning political thought of the evangelical movement.

2 Printing History:

1530. *Commentarii in aliquot politicos libros Aristotelis Philip. Melanch.* (Wittenberg: Josef Klug). [Claus 1530.37 / VD16 M 2737 / USTC 623223]

1531. *In Aristotelis aliquot Libros Politicos Commentaria, Philippi Melanchthonis Commentaria.* (Hagenau: Johann Setzer). [Claus 1531.12 / VD16 M 2738]. This edition also included commentaries on the first two books of the *Nicomachean Ethics*.

1531. *In Aristotelis aliquot Libros Politicos, Philippi Melanchthonis commentaria.* (Paris: Christian Wechel). [Claus 1531.38 / USTC 138046]

1532. *Officia Ciceronis, multo quam antea castigatiora, cum Scholijs Phil. Melan. Quae possint esse vice prolixi commentarij. Nam plaerique loci quos hactenus nemo attigit, hic enarrantur. Item, in Aristotelis Ethica & Politica Commentarij doctissimi, eodem authore.* (Hagenau: Johann Setzer, February 1532). [Claus 1532.16 / VD 16 ZV 3457 / USTC 679329]

1535. *Commentarii in Primum, Secundum, Tertium, & Quintum Ethicorum Philippi Melanchthonis. Eiusdem in Aristotelis aliquot libros Politicos Commentaria.* (Strasbourg: Johann Albrecht, March 1535). [Claus 1535.54 / VD16 A 3417 / USTC 623392]

1536. *In Aristotelis aliquot libros politicos, Philippi Melanchthonis Commentaria.* (Paris: Christian Wechel). [Claus 1536.49 / USTC 185738]

1541. *Operum Philippi Melancthonis* [sic] *tomi quinque, quorum Catalogos sequentes paginae indicabunt* (Basel: Johann Herwagen, August 1541), Vol. IV.266–286. [Claus 1541.9, VD16 ZV 18396] See also VD16 M 2330 and VD16 ZV 10690.

1548. *Ethicorum Aristotelis primi, II, III, et V. librorum enarratio per Philippum Melanch. Accesserunt eiusdem Oratio de Aristotele. Collatio actionum forensium Atticarum, & Romanarum. In Politicos aliquot Aristotelis libros Commentaria.* (Lyon: Sébastien Gryphe). [Claus 1548.39 / USTC 150025]

3 Translator's Notes:

This translation is based upon the first edition of this text: *Commentarii in Aliquot Politicos Libros Aristotelis* (Wittenberg: Joseph Klug, 1530). An edited version of the text can also be found in CR 16.417–452. As noted below in footnote 68 (p. 248), the only 1530 edition of the text that this editor has been able to access is missing half of one folio. For this folio, the translation is based upon the surviving text of the 1530 Wittenberg edition, and the gaps are filled in with the texts of the CR, the 1531 Hagenau edition, and the 1535 Strasbourg edition.

This text contains several difficult Latin terms, which I have translated as follows:

Civitas: Although a more accurate translation might be "political community", I have decided upon "state" as a less awkward term. In the text below, Melanchthon defines a *civitas* as "a society of citizens established by law for mutual benefit and, most of all, for common defence." Melanchthon uses this term fairly synonymously with *respublica*, which I have translated simply as "republic" to retain the original Latin sense of the text.

Imperium: Most generally, the term refers to the general idea of government, that is, political power and its related institutions and prerogatives. In the context of this work, *imperium* generally signifies the divinely-established institutions which legitimately use force to maintain order among men on earth. Accordingly, I have generally translated the word as "government". In some cases, *imperium* refers specifically to the supreme political authority held by a ruler, as in the term "*summum imperium*", or as in the context of rulers receiving *imperium* from the Pope, from the people, or from God. When used in this sense, when the term refers more properly to authority than to governmental institutions, I have translated it as "political authority." In other cases, when the term refers to concrete historical instances of government, i.e., the four world monarchies, I have occasionally translated it as "empire", to keep with the sense of those passages. Whenever I have translated the term in one of these latter two specific senses, I have also inserted the Latin term in brackets.

Ordinatio: In this text, Melanchthon repeatedly refers to government as an *ordinatio Dei*. This term has a dual valence. *Ordinatio* refers to the general way that political institutions establish order and hierarchies of rulers and ruled within human society. At the same time, *ordinatio* carries the theological idea that these political institutions have been specifically ordained by God. To capture both of these meanings, I have chosen to translate this term as "ordination".

Politia: I have translated this as "constitution", in its material sense, that is, the specific organizational principles which govern a state. Melanchthon, according to standard conventions, also uses this word specifically to refer to Plato's *Republic*, which I have noted when necessary in footnotes.

4 Edition

PHILIP MELANCHTHON'S COMMENTARIES ON SOME BOOKS OF ARISTOTLE'S *POLITICS*

Prefatory Epistle sig. Aiir / CR 2.452/M 855

Philip Melanchthon to that most illustrious man of the knightly order, Ulrich Schilling, his fellow-father.[26]

Just as we have previously expounded upon some notable passages from some books of Aristotle's *Ethics*,[27] showing how the Gospel approves of philosophy about morals and how we can apply it to our common life, so have we now undertaken to explain some distinguished passages in the *Politics*. But since some may criticize my plan because, on this occasion, it seems that the students are presented with a mutilated author, whom it would be preferable to read in his entirety, I should first of all placate these [critics].

You are the most reliable witness that I originally intended to produce a full interpretation of the entire Aristotelian text. For I undertook this project at your urging when I saw that you were admirably inflamed with a zeal for learning true and genuine philosophy. Therefore, I began to read aloud[28] in Greek, since | 2.453
Aristotle can be better understood speaking Greek than Latin by those who are only moderately educated. For not only does the Latin translation lack clarity, but | in my judgment, it is almost a totally different thing.[29] For the new sig. Aiiv

26 Melanchthon here and below uses the term *compater* to refer to Ulrich Schilling von Cannstatt (1485–1452). Melanchthon uses the term in two senses. First, since Schilling was the godfather of Melanchthon's late son George, he uses the term in its specific meaning as the godparent of one's child, i.e. "fellow-father." The term also has a broader and more familiar sense of "companion" or "friend".

27 A reference to Melanchthon's 1529 commentary on Aristotle's *Nicomachean Ethics*, entitled *In Ethica Aristotelis commentarius Philipp. Melanchtho.* (Wittenberg: Josef Klug, 1529).

28 *praelegere*, that is, specifically to read aloud in a classroom setting for the purpose of instruction.

29 Melanchthon may be referring to the medieval Latin translation by William of Moerbeke, or the more recent 1437 Latin rendering by the Italian humanist Leonardo Bruni. As Jensen points out, Melanchthon likely worked from the Greek text of Aldus Manutius published

style of speech in the Latin tongue deceives the reader such that he cannot see that Aristotle is talking about things that are well-known and established in the daily course of life. And unless these disputations are compared to [daily life], they cannot be understood at all. For those who fantastically discuss these [disputations] as if they were written about some other world stray entirely off course. But because the students do not have Greek books, and since in the great laziness of youth, nobody would copy it,[30] it fell to me to change the established manner of interpretation.

Then, because the Latin books were considered to be entirely unreliable, we arrived at the decision that it would be most beneficial for me to select and explain some prominent passages so that the students would have the summary of Aristotle's disputations, presented in the popular style of speech, and accommodated to the common course of life and to our customs. In the meantime, I do not oppose them reading Aristotle in his entirety if they so desire, and if anyone does this, he will see that our commentary sheds light on many of his arguments.

And there is already an example of this interpretation, written about the *Ethics*, which someone says is shorter than the dignity of those books demands.[31] Certainly, nothing would be easier for me than to surpass those old interpreters—however verbose they are—not only in the size of their volumes, but also
sig. Aiij^r in the amount and variety of subjects. But in the schools, | one really must observe a certain moderation in such matters, lest those talents, destined for greater arts as they are, be detained too long in these texts which are provided solely to prepare the youths for the other chief disciplines which contain knowledge about governing the republic. Therefore, since I wrote this commentary to be useful, not to show off, it is only fair to pardon me especially because I tried amidst my concision to include those subjects which are great and useful for adjudicating many controversies of learned men.

I shall do the same thing for the *Politics*. For I will choose those passages which will be of the most use in the higher disciplines, and we shall open them up and explain them to the best of our ability. For these books present the elements or principles from which the laws in republics are taken up and derived.

---

in Venice in 1498 (see *A Humanist in Reformation Politics*, p. 57). Sachiko Kusukawa's *A Wittenberg University Library Catalogue of 1536* (1995) lists the 1498 Aldine Greek edition with annotations by Melanchthon. See p. 9.

30 Melanchthon means that the students, not possessing printed Greek copies of Aristotle, were too lazy and unwilling to make their own copies by hand.

31 Melanchthon's 1529 *Ethics* commentary was indeed brief, filling only seventy-five pages of a slim *octavo* volume.

And it benefits those who deal with the laws to recognize their sources and principles. And it is a certain part of humanity [*humanitas*] not to be ignorant of this doctrine, which demonstrates | the causes of all honourable and civic duties set out in nature. Indeed, I myself think that consideration of these most beautiful things can move and delight good men more than any other spectacle. 2.454

So then, I have decided, most agreeable fellow-father [*compater*], to dedicate this lucubration to you, since you inspired the work, so that I may in turn impress upon you this task: to defend against the unfair judgments of certain others this philosophy of ours, | which seems to me indeed more useful than those quarrels of the previous interpreters. But I leave the judgment of this matter to you, who, having now spent so many years among the most learned men in Italy and Germany, have dedicated so much of your attention to this genus of doctrine. And in my judgment, it redounds to your honour that you have considered it worthy to add, to the splendour of your lineage, the knowledge of those arts, which—since they are called "liberal"—should be cultivated first and foremost by noble men. For if any among the German knights actually learn letters, they love the other arts more than philosophy. And since you, setting a fresh example, have added philosophy to the other studies, I have always judged you to be worthy of high esteem. sig. Aiij^v

For this reason, initially, I slipped my way into your friendship with a singular focus, and later I even strengthened our relationship by a most holy bond when I invited you to be a witness at the baptism of my little son George. And since that act is filled with so much reverence that the sweetest title of "father" is shared among those who together baptize[32] the boys, it is easy to understand that we are bound together by the tightest bond. And I have no doubt that you, on account of your piety, would esteem highly this relationship, which would have certainly been more delightful to both of us if my little son had happened to live longer.[33] For he had already shown flashes of his personality, which gave us hope that he would be a delight to us, and this was one of many reasons | why, at his death, I was struck by incredible grief, which I have not yet been able to purge from my soul. In this way, I have a harsh enough reminder of your friendship, the memory of which has been most dearly soothing to me. I was sig. Aiiij^r

32 The 1530 text erroneously reads *iniciantur*. The errata at the end of the volume correct this to *iniciant*. In ecclesiastical contexts, the verb *inicio* (also spelled *initio*) often refers to baptism.

33 Melanchthon's son George died on August 15, 1529, about two months before his second birthday. On August 21, Melanchthon wrote to Caspar Aquila that "Nothing was ever dearer to me in my life than that boy." See MBW 813.

even moved by this private obligation to dedicate these books to you, so that
you may understand how dear you are to me, both because of your virtues and
most honourable studies, and because of this relationship of ours, which should
sig. Aiiij^{v} be reckoned to be so close because of the sharing of our fatherly title. Farewell. |

On Aristotle's *Politics*

[16.417] Politics is the art which contains certain general precepts about the ordering of a state [*civitas*]. Just as architecture is the art which delineates the forms of buildings, in the same way, politics describes the certain form of a state and discusses the division of property, marriage, magistrates, laws, the duties of the people, contracts, and punishments.

However, at the outset, it absolutely necessary to differentiate politics from
the Gospel, and to refute the opinion of those unskilled thinkers who imagine
that the Gospel is nothing other than a political doctrine according to which
states should be constituted. This error has violently shaken republics in more
than one age when fanatical men, having abolished some existing laws, try to
16.418 establish states according to the Gospel. But in our | own times, we see more
examples than we would wish showing why the reader must first be advised
here of the differences between political doctrine and Gospel [doctrine], and
sig. Av^{r} must be advised how | the Gospel approves of political doctrine.

Let us clarify this point with a comparison. Just as medicine is very different
from the Gospel, so is politics very different from the Gospel. And just as medi-
cine contains doctrine established by reason, so is politics established by reason,
and [politics] has no more to do with the Gospel than medicine does. But just
as it is preferable to have a godly doctor, so one also prefers the governor of the
republic to be godly. Nevertheless, those arts themselves have no relation to
the Gospel. For the Gospel reveals eternal justice which hearts receive through
faith. But in the meantime, it also commands adherence to the public laws and
16.419 constitutions of all the peoples among whom we live. |

In truth, politics is a doctrine about life's external actions: the possession of things, inheritance, contracts, and other similar matters. These things are not the same among all peoples. The Persians have their own laws, as do the Athenians and the Romans. So just as a Christian wears different clothing in one place, and counts days in a different way while in another, so may he adhere to the constitution [*politia*] of whatever place. Among the Persians, Ezra judges things according to the Persian laws, but in Jerusalem, he judges according to the Jewish laws. The centurion follows Jewish laws in Judea, but in Rome [he follows] the Roman laws [Luke 7:1–10]. Such things are no more relevant to the Gospel than are clothing or the counting of days.

Recognizing this distinction between the Gospel and politics is critical for preserving | tranquillity and fostering respect towards the magistrates. For those sig. Av[v] men should surely be judged to be seditious who, although they teach the Gospel, interfere in other offices and pass laws about the division of inheritance, taxes, contracts, and punishments for the wicked. For instance, in many places, preachers forbid the hanging of thieves, they pass laws about tithes, or they condemn contracts that are publicly accepted, etc. Wycliffe makes a great commotion and argues that tithes should not be paid to idle priests. Capito argues that princes should give back a portion of their annual taxes. Zwingli calls taxes "Harpies"; others make hunting public; the Anabaptists condemn legal trials, etc.[34] Beyond the mere fact that they are ungodly, these errors also undermine public tranquillity. Therefore, it is helpful to be well-fortified against this impiety, to maintain correctly the distinction between Gospel and politics, and to know that the Gospel pertains to the righteousness of the heart, not to the civil state. And indeed, [the Gospel] approves of all forms of republics, | provided that they 16.420 agree with reason, just as it approves of architecture or medicine which agree with reason.

There have been few writers in the church who have fully comprehended this distinction. Accordingly, Popes have usurped governments and arrogated to themselves the right of bestowing kingdoms. Therefore, we should carefully maintain that there is a great divide between the Gospel and politics, and that | sig. [Avi][r] all constitutions are approved by the Gospel, provided that they align with reason. And imagine how stupid it would be if some theologian wanted to practice medicine. Would everyone not ridicule him for practicing an art which he had not learned? In the same way, it is right to ridicule those preachers who want to govern cities, even though they have no experience in the republic. They abolish the old laws, even though they do not understand the reasons why they were passed. And having eliminated one law, they replace it with endless other ones. For that [saying] of Plato is true, that changing old laws is just like severing the head of a hydra.[35] And just as an entire building collapses when one single beam is removed, so changing just one law drags all the rest into ruin. And from this, endless turmoil must necessarily follow.

---

34 The references are to the English theologian John Wycliffe (ca. 1330–1384), the Zürich reformer Ulrich Zwingli (1484–1531), and the Strasbourg reformer Wolfgang Capito (1478–1541). Demands to make hunting public were found in the Twelve Articles, and legal trials were condemned in the Schleitheim confession. See the modern translations of those two texts in *The Radical Reformation*, ed. and trans. Michael G. Baylor (Cambridge, 1991), pp. 177, 235.

35 Plato, *Republic* 426e.

For this reason, all men who are great and skilled in ruling the republic cry out that all changes to the laws should be prohibited, no matter how onerous [this might be], for changing the republic always does more harm [than good]. This opinion is supported by many teachings of the greatest men, which we will cite elsewhere. But for now, we shall be content with the testimony of Duke Frederick of Saxony, who, if anyone, was the man most knowledgeable in the office [*toga*][36] of administering the republic, not only occupied in domestic administration, but also experienced in the greatest and most dangerous affairs of the entire German empire.[37] And his authority should hold great weight among us both by virtue of the singular divinity of the talent bestowed upon
sig. him, as well as because of | his extensive experience. Therefore, whenever he was
[Avi]^{v} presented with a case which seemed to bring about some change, he ferociously
opposed it, adding his reasoning with these words: "It makes a disturbance".[38]
16.421 By this phrase, | he meant that those who govern the republic should proceed
with the utmost caution, lest they sow any occasion or cause for disturbance. For once tumults have been incited, they take many years to die down.

Therefore, just as Socrates exiled the poets from his city in the beginning of his *Republic*,[39] we should not quite expel the theologians from the state, but we shall, nevertheless, remove them from the government of the republic lest they pass new laws, and we shall ask them to perform their own offices and to teach the pure Gospel concerning faith, the nature of eternal justice, repentance, and charity. This is the private doctrine of the godly, just like medicine is a private art. Meanwhile, let the kings and princes pass laws to restrain the ungodly and to promote peace through trials and punishments. In this way, Christ teaches: "The kings of the nations rule over them, but not so with you" [Matthew 20:25–26, Luke 22:25–26]. For he forbids private men to alter public laws and usurp governments under the pretext of the Gospel. They have the example of Christ, they have that of the Apostles who did not abolish the Roman laws, did not touch politics—they only spread the knowledge of God privately among the godly. But I will end here, since this topic has often been discussed elsewhere.[40]

---

36 Melanchthon here uses *toga* as a metonym for the office of governing the republic.

37 Frederick III (also known as Frederick the Wise), Prince-elector of Saxony from 1486–1525, a political ally to Luther and Melanchthon.

38 Melanchthon here quotes Frederick in German: *Es macht beuuegung*.

39 See Plato, *Republic* 398a–b; 595a–b.

40 Melanchthon treats this in the 1529 *In Ethica Aristotelis commentarius*. See fols. A3^{v}–A5^{v}.

That the Gospel Approves Political Ordinations sig. [Avii]r

The Gospel teaches spiritual and eternal justice, which belongs to the few. But in the meantime, the world needs another doctrine which functions like a prison for restraining the ungodly. Namely, [it needs] politics. So then, just as the Gospel approves the other arts necessary for life such as agriculture and architecture, so does it also approve those laws and political ordinations [*ordinationes*][41] that agree with reason. The theologian should explain this topic so that rulers and subjects alike would understand the dignity of the magistrates and the laws. In the first place, this will aid the magistrates' consciences, since they would know that they perform an office which was commissioned by God, | and they will 16.422
wait for and seek God's help. In addition, the subjects will obey with greater devotion as if [they were obeying] the vice-regents of God, because they will know that God established the magistrate and the political ordination for the benefit of life, just as he created the rest of the entire universe, this most brilliant sunlight, and the changing of the seasons, and just as he gave the fertility of the earth for nourishing living things.

In fact, we see God's presence more closely in the preservation of the republic than in nature itself. For amidst the Devil's great savagery, amongst such great human malice, republics could not exist | unless they were preserved by God. sig. [Avii]v
Now, God does protect governments, and the vengeance that the magistrate exercises is truly the work of God. Therefore, in the Psalm [82:6], God says: "I said, 'You are gods.'" Here, God plainly asserts that he has constituted the magistrates, for he says, "I said," that is, "I ordained" the magistrates. The fact that he calls them "gods" attests that they perform a divine office, and are vice-regents of God. Therefore, the political ordination is a good thing, just as Paul teaches in Romans 13.

These ideas should be inculcated in the souls of men, so that they would respect the existing laws and magistrates and reverently obey them. Moreover, [the question of] what the laws should be is no more relevant to the Gospel than is [the question of] which medicines should be given to those suffering from a fever.

Regarding these matters, the theologians act contrary to their own tranquillity when they deal with politics. For no thing in life has more or greater dangers than the administration of the republic. For this reason, even Demosthenes said

---

41 This term is translated as "ordination" to capture the capacious meaning of the term in Melanchthon's thought. In reference to government, the term has a dual valence here. It refers both to the ordering of the republic by political institutions, as well as the theological idea that these political institutions have been specifically ordained by God.

that if he could re-live his life, he would rather face certain death than approach the republic, even if he knew for sure that he would obtain the highest honours in doing so. In the midst of such dangers, God is present with those who are truly called, but he abandons those who, without a call, have usurped the republic through their own ambition, etc.

On the First Book of the *Politics*

sig. [Aviii]r / [16.421] Just as moral philosophy [*ethica*] discusses individual morals and collects the
16.422 causes of the virtues from nature, | in the same way, politics discusses civil society and the duties pertaining to society, and it deduces the causes of society from nature.

Therefore, the primary topic of this book concerns the causes of society.
16.423 Accordingly, the beginning of society is | the joining of male and female. This union produces the state, like a colony, from individual households.

Next, Aristotle collects the reasons why man is led to society by nature—it is not merely for the sake of utility. This topic is covered in almost the exact same words in Cicero's *On Duties*.[42] The argument is based on the fact that man was given speech, which is useless outside of society. [In Latin:] "For nature does nothing in vain". [In Greek:] "For, as we say, nor does nature make [things] in vain."[43] He also adds an encomium of civil society:

> "But the first organizer [of men] was responsible for the greatest good. For just as perfected man is the best of the animals, he is the worst of all when separated from law and justice. For injustice is most dangerous when it has weapons, and man is born having weapons for prudence and virtue, but he can use these for entirely the opposite purposes. Hence, apart from virtue, man is the most profane and savage [of animals], and the worst regarding sexual and gluttonous wantonness. But justice is political; for the process of justice [*dikē*] is the order of the political community."[44] |

sig. [Aviii]v

---

42 See Cicero, *De officiis*, I.7.22. Melanchthon also wrote a *prolegomena* and a *scholia* on *De officiis*. See CR 16.529–594 and 16.615–680.

43 A quote from *Politics* I.1.10 (1253a.9). Melanchthon gives this quote here in Latin and in Greek. The Latin translation is fairly loose. As the editors of the CR note, the Greek quotation contains a possible error: *oute* ("nor does nature make [things] in vain") instead of *ouden* ("nature makes nothing in vain"). The latter reading would make the Latin and Greek quotes match more closely.

44 *Politics* I.1.12. (1253a.30–38). Melanchthon provides this quote in Greek.

II

I have often advised that Aristotle's method should be closely observed, for there is no better creator of methods than Aristotle. Therefore, he is worth reading for this reason alone: so that we would take up from him examples of method, that is, of teaching a thing in the right order. So then, for instance, the other arts begin from certain common principles, which are known by nature. In the case of geometry: "The whole is greater than any of its parts." "[Two things] which are [each] equal to some third [thing] are also equal to each other."[45] In the same way, this art [of politics] also has its own principles, taken up from nature or from the end of man:

Man was created by nature for society.

The first society is the legitimate joining of male and female.

Now [Aristotle] adds other principles:

From that first society arises the household, in which there are parents, children, and slaves.

In a society of many people, it is necessary that some rule and others obey. | 16.424

And he gathers the causes of servitude [*servitus*] and government [*imperium*] from nature. For by nature, unwise and weaker things obey wiser and stronger things, because they need outside leadership, counsel, and defence. He offers an illustration of this from the parts of man.[46] In a man, some parts naturally serve while others naturally take charge and | rule. Similarly, in a multitude, by sig. B^r^
nature the wiser ones should rule and the unwise should obey.

Who would not delight in [Aristotle's] subtlety on this topic, when he so aptly gathers from the parts of man the sources and causes of government and servitude among men, and when, after he shows the causes of society, the first thing he does is speak of government in order to signify that no society can exist unless it is held together by government. Therefore, just as the causes which lead us to cultivate society are impressed upon nature, so we should be aware that there are causes impressed upon human nature which lead us to establish governments and obey the magistrates. And the philosopher's duty is to discern and explain such laws or common conceptions [*communes sentencias*] which are written in nature. The orators call the common conceptions of this sort "theses", because once they are established, many other things follow from them. Therefore, these theses in turn give birth to the civil laws, which are like hypotheses of these common conceptions: "Civil society should be cultivated"; or "Civil society cannot be preserved without government." From this, the laws

---

45 i.e., the transitive property: if a = c and b = c, then a = b. cf. Euclid, *The Elements*, in *Greek Mathematical Works: Volume I: Thales to Euclid*, trans. Ivor Thomas (LCL 335, p. 445).

46 See *Politics*, I.2.11 (1254b.2–9).

were passed about public force [*vis publica*][47] and about those who undermine the authority of the magistrate, etc.

Meanwhile, the students should remember that which I also said about the *Ethics*: that the law of nature truly is divine law.[48] Therefore, all conceptions
sig. B^{v} about civil society, those good and firm | conclusions gathered from nature, should be considered to be divine law and should be respected as such. The authority of these ideas should not be taken lightly. For just as the eyes are divinely endowed with a certain marvellous light for seeing, so does reason divinely have a certain light for judging those things which are necessary for bodily life. Now, this certainly does not mean that every philosopher's fantasy should be treated as an oracle, but one must apply discretion [to determine] which conceptions are affirmed from a certain cause, and which ones are uttered without demonstration. For the entire matter should be submitted to logic and demonstrations. And only those [conceptions] which hold together in demonstration
16.425 should be included among the laws of nature. | The Stoics and others mount many ridiculous arguments which are rightly repudiated because they do not have sufficiently firm causes. In the same way, in medicine or architecture many things are rejected despite the fact that, on the surface, they contain certain things that are similar to the truth. Nevertheless, when they are shaken and rattled, their faults become clear.

But I return to Aristotle so that I might explain this topic, which is more useful than any other in Book I. When he illustrates the analogy of government and servitude in the parts of man, he also discerns two species of government or dominion [*dominium*],[49] and it is easy to see that every species of government [*imperium*] and servitude [*servitus*] which the Jurisconsults enumerate have arisen from these, as if from springs.

sig. Bij^{r} The first species is called "despotic" government [*despotikon imperium*], | or you could call it a "masterly [*herile*] dominion."[50] This is how the soul controls the body, for the body is forced to obey the soul, which stirs and moves it, and

47 *Vis publica*, a category which covered severe and flagrant offenses against the public. The law covered a range of disparate offenses such as collecting unusual quantities of weapons, preventing a body from being buried, or gathering an armed band to expel a rightful possessor from his home. See D.48.6.

48 In the 1529 *In Ethica Aristotelis commentarius*, Melanchthon refers to "certain conceptions which are divinely written on the human soul, which we often call 'the laws of nature' …" See fol. A5^{r}.

49 See *Politics* I.2.21–22 (1255b.16–20). In Roman law, *dominium* usually refers specifically to property ownership, but Melanchthon uses it here as a synonym for *imperium*.

50 *herile dominium:* Referring to the absolute rights of the head of household. In early modern usage, the term commonly referred to despotic rule. See Richard Koebner, "Despot and

[the body] does not make particular motions without the soul, just as the slave is forced to obey the master and is entirely under another's power, or just as fettered beasts are forced to follow the one who leads them. The Greeks cleverly suppose that this is why "*despotēn*" [master] sounds like "*desmōtēn*", that is, one who puts another in bonds. From this species arises the harshest form of government, in which the lord, without any certain law, holds the power of life and death. The kings of the barbarians once held this sort of authority, and people now say that this is the form of government among the Turks, where the prince does everything according to his will, and the subjects, like beasts, are forced to obey whatever the tyrant commands.

The other species of government is called "kingly" [*basilikon*] or "political" [*politikon*] authority, that is, royal or civil rule. This is how the mind commands the appetite, with a certain law and for its own benefit. And it does not rashly force the appetite to obey. From this [species] arise legitimate governments in republics, which will be discussed below in the third book. And this species very clearly shows what government is: namely, to look out for another's benefit, and to govern and defend others. For the mind understands what is beneficial and what is harmful, it rules and coerces the appetite, and it strives to preserve the health of the whole body. From this example, | [Aristotle] takes up that oft-cited sig. Bij^v
saying [in Greek:] "That which is able, by virtue of intelligence, to think ahead, that one is naturally ruler and naturally master." [In Latin:] "That which excels in deliberation naturally rules the rest."[51] | 16.426

After [Aristotle] proposes these species of government and servitude, he teaches that they exist in the family. For he will later model the state after the image of the family, and for this reason, he first discusses economics at length. The head of household [*pater familias*] rules his slaves like a despot [*despotikōs*], and his children with a kingly lordship. But for his wife, a gentler government is more appropriate, [a government] which he calls "political" [*politikon*], a relative of kingly [government].[52]

Here, there is usually a discussion about why Aristotle says that some people are born slaves [*servi*], while the jurists teach that *servitus* [i.e., slavery] is contrary to nature and that all men are originally born free by natural law.[53] This

Despotism: Vicissitudes of a Political Term", *Journal of the Warburg and Courtauld Institutes* 14.3/4 (1951): 275–302.

51 Aristotle, *Politics* I.1.4 (1252a.31–32). Melanchthon gives here the quote in Greek and follows it with a more concise Latin translation.

52 Aristotle, *Politics* I.5.2 (1259a.39–1259b.1).

53 See Aristotle, *Politics*, I.2.7 (1254a.13–17) and *Digest* 1.5.4. The term *servitus* is a complex

should be explained in the following way: Aristotle is talking about the cause of what the jurists call "*servitus*", while the jurists are talking about the effect, that is, about a concrete form of *servitus*. For Aristotle, *servitus* means the weakness of character which makes it necessary for one to be ruled by another's deliberation. For the jurists, [*servitus*] means a certain arrangement by which the victor constrains the conquered.[54]

And indeed, Aristotle does argue against those who think that this *servitus* is contrary to nature. For he shows that there are causes, established in sig. Biij^r nature—namely weakness of character—| and since this is born within men, it is necessary that they be ruled by another's deliberation. If some people do not suffer themselves to be ruled, they should be suppressed and coerced by force so that the remaining multitude of the human race can be preserved, just as one must sometimes amputate a diseased limb from the body lest the whole body perish. Here, therefore, the more excellent [parts] suppress and constrain the weaker ones by force, because nature teaches us, having set out the parts of man in this way, that the more excellent ones should preside and rule.

But why is there a need for this subtle argumentation? The call to "Honor thy father and mother" [Exodus 20:12] subjects all men to servitude. Yet because that concept is written in nature, one should understand that the causes of servitude truly are established in nature. Therefore, Aristotle correctly rebukes those who, with an immoderate and unjust craving for freedom, find fault with that institution of servitude received from the law of nations. To use his words, they "declare it unconstitutional" [*graphontai paranomōn*].[55] But we may even more justly condemn the fanatics of our age who, under the pretext of the Gos-

---

one. Melanchthon's point in this passage is that there is a distinction between Aristotle's general category of *servitus* (servitude) and the Roman jurists' concrete institution of *servitus* (slavery). In Melanchthon's mind, Aristotle's *servitus* meant the general principle of subservience and subordination, whether in the family or the state. He understood Roman slavery to be a narrower subset of Aristotle's general category. Melanchthon's point here, which he directs against the "fanatics of our age" (i.e. those whom he saw as rebels in the Peasants' War), is that general distinctions of political authority and subservience are natural and necessary. For more on this point, see Jensen, *A Humanist in Reformation Politics*, pp. 78–81. For the relationship of this argument to sixteenth-century serfdom, see Noah Dauber, "Philipp Melanchthon: Deutsche Reformation", pp. 181–183.

54 In Roman law, slavery was generally understood as an alternative to being killed when a person was captured in war. See Inst. 1.3.4; D.1.5.4.2–3.

55 *Politics*, I.2.16 (1255a.8–9). That is, they bring a *graphē paranomōn*, the Athenian legal procedure for declaring a proposed law unconstitutional.

pel, have called the common people to the liberty cap,[56] that is, to freedom, and have claimed | that servitude is contrary to the Gospel. But because we 16.427
have frequently spoken about this matter elsewhere, at present it is sufficient to advise the reader that just as the Gospel does not abolish the command to "Honor thy father and mother", neither does it dissolve governments or servitude. Instead, by its own testimony, The Gospel confirms | and teaches that sig. Biij^v^
rulership and servitude must exist in the world to coerce ungodly and fleshly men. And the saints make use of these things just as [they make use of] the other good creations of God.

III

[Aristotle] has not yet finished discussing the household economy, but after he has enumerated [the parts of] the family, it is necessary to discuss conserving and cultivating it. Accordingly, he teaches that there are two means of acquiring wealth [*res familiaris*]:[57] One of these is natural, and the other is devised by artifice.[58]

Natural reason includes these species of acquiring wealth:[59]

Herding,

Farming,

Hunting—to which he joins depredation, which is itself honourable and aligned with nature provided that it is practiced in lawful wars. For the magistrate should wage war in order to repel brigandage [*latrocinia*].[60]

The fourth species is commerce, in which we sell our own domestic goods so that, having sold those which we have in surplus, we import others which we otherwise lack. He calls this "economic commerce" [*oeconomica mercatura*] and praises it, since it is necessary for life, and it was also necessary for men to use it before the invention of money, when by the exchange | of one's own sig. Biiij^r^
goods or services one could procure whatever one lacked. Moreover, there is the

56 The *pileus*, or "liberty cap", was the cap which Roman slaves received upon manumission.

57 *res familiaris*, that is, one's household wealth or patrimony.

58 See *Politics* I.3.6 (1256b.7–8), where Aristotle classifies herding, farming, and hunting as arts derived from nature.

59 See these categories in *Politics* I.3.4–5 (1256a.29–1256b.7). The last category, commerce, is discussed in I.3.10 (1256b.40–1257a.5).

60 Aristotle includes depredation and robbery as sub-categories of hunting. See *Politics* I.3.4 (1256a.35–36). According to Thucydides, piracy and predation did not yet have a stigma in archaic Greece (*History of the Peloponnesian War* I.5.1–2), so they may have been considered acceptable means of subsistence. Melanchthon here stretches the category of depredation to refer to the magistrate's just war against lawless brigands.

commerce, as they call it, "permitted commerce", in which[61] domestic goods are sold today even by respectable people for whom doing business is otherwise shameful.[62]

The means of acquiring wealth which has been devised by artifice also has its own skills and works, which still should be shared liberally. [For instance], there is a slave's hiring out of his labour.[63] Of this sort is the commerce which is called "transactional,"[64] when we buy [a good] in order to turn around and sell it for a higher price, or rather, when the purpose of this is profit rather than
16.428 use. Aristotle critiques this | because, although use should be the purpose of a purchase since nature teaches us to make contracts for the sake of use and for the sake of necessity, here it seems that there is another, more underhanded goal: namely, profit. Such unscrupulousness is repugnant because it does not seem properly related to necessity, and therefore it cheats those who were going to buy such a thing for the sake of use. And if there are other defects in this species of commerce, which belong to men rather than to the thing itself, there is no need to recite them here.

On Usury

Usury is also numbered among those species of acquiring wealth devised by
sig. Biiij^{v} artifice. Moreover, Aristotle critiques it and says that it is contrary to nature, | because money was not invented to beget more money, but to be a medium in the exchange of goods. But in usury, money begets more money, and therefore the Greeks called it '*tokon*' [offspring], from '*tiktō*' [to beget].[65] For usury is profit

61 1530 erroneously reads *qui*. The 1535 Strasbourg edition correctly reads *qua*.

62 Roman law placed restrictions on participation in commerce by the political elite. For example, the 3rd Century BCE *Lex Claudia* forbade senators from owning large shipping vessels. See Livy, *Ab urbe condita*, XXI.63.1–4, which claims that the *Lex Claudia* was introduced since "all commerce was seen as indecorous for senators". Although this may be the general Roman background, it is unclear what exactly Melanchthon is referencing here. The editors of the CR suggest that this is a reference to the feudal *ius regalium*, that is, the sale or transferal of royal privileges and prerogatives to other elites.

63 The Roman legal term here is "*operarum locatio*", which was a specific type of contract in which a labourer hired out his services. This sentence is somewhat awkward, but it appears that Melanchthon is here citing these contracts of hire as an example of acquiring wealth through a means devised by artifice.

64 Greek: *kapēlikē*. Aristotle contrasts this sort of trade, which aims at limitless enrichment through buying and reselling, with trade aimed at providing goods for household operations. See *Politics* I.3.17 (1257b.17–30) and I.3.23 (1258a.38–1258b.8).

65 *tokos* is the Greek word for "interest" as well as the generic word for "offspring", while *tiktō* is the Greek verb for "to beget" or "to produce." Interest is money begotten by money.

which is added to a loan,[66] or when one pays back something more than the principal on account of the loan. Here are Aristotle's words, for it is pleasing to quote them since they are often cited by learned men in this disputation about usury:

> [in Greek:] "Usury is most reasonably hated on account of the fact that wealth comes from money itself, and not from the thing for which money was created. For money was created for the sake of exchange, but interest increases money itself. [Interest/*tokos*] takes its name from this; for offspring [*tiktomena*] are similar to their parents, and interest [*tokos*] is money begotten from money. For this reason, of all forms of money-making, this one is the most contrary to nature."[67]

That is,

> [in Latin]: "Usury is rightly hated, because through it, money is acquired from money, although [money] was not established for this purpose. For [money] exists for the sake of exchange, but usury increases itself, and from this it takes the name of "interest" (*foenus*), because the offspring are similar to the parents, and in interest, money begets money. Therefore, this manner of acquiring money is most contrary to nature."

From[68] this argument of Aristotle's, learned men have collected many[69] other [arguments] by which they show that usury is contrary to nature: | [sig. Bv^{r}] 16.429

Regarding those things for which use means consumption, use cannot be separated from the thing itself, and there cannot be a separate charge in exchange for use [alone]. But in usury, the use is sold separately from the thing itself. Therefore, it is contrary to nature.

---

66 The word here is *mutuum*, a basic civil law contract for the loan of fungible goods such as money. In moral theology and canon law, *mutuum* was supposed to be a gratuitous loan; therefore, one major issue was whether charging interest violated the supposedly gratuitous nature of the loan. See, for example, Luke 6:35: *mutuum date, nihil inde sperantes* ("Lend and expect nothing in return"), reproduced in Decretals 5.19.10.

67 *Politics* I.3.23 (1258b.2–8). Melanchthon produces the quote in Greek, and follows it with a Latin translation.

68 In the only 1530 copy of this work available to this editor, this entire folio is torn in half vertically. The translation is drawn from the surviving text in the 1530 printed edition and supplemented by comparison to the 1531 Hagenau edition (sigs. G^{r-v}), the 1535 Strasbourg edition (sigs [p5^{v}-p6^{v}]) and the CR. Two minor discrepancies among these editions are noted in the following two footnotes.

69 1530, 1531 Hagenau, CR: *multas*. 1535 lacks this word.

Likewise, a commodity which does not naturally bear fruit should not be traded like a fruit-bearing commodity. But in usury, money, which is not naturally fruit-bearing, is exchanged, but something is still demanded [in return], as if from a fruit-bearing commodity. Therefore, usury is contrary to nature. For whoever hires out a field rightly harvests something, because the field naturally bears fruit.

Here, there has been a recent debate about whether Christians may make use of interest. We briefly respond that Christians are permitted to make use of contracts which the laws approve and judge to be honourable, just as Christians may use other political ordinations. Nevertheless,[70] although the ancient laws of the emperors permitted usury, they still did not approve of it or judge it to be honourable. For the laws do not approve of everything that they permit. For
[sig. Bv^{v}] the laws cannot eradicate every vice | from the republic, just as doctors cannot heal every bodily sickness, and there are even some diseases which they refuse to exacerbate with treatments. In the same way, the laws overlook and endure certain vices which, entrenched by longstanding custom, cannot be eliminated without great inconvenience. Therefore, the Christian shall not make use of usury, but he shall utilize the other legitimate contracts which the magistrate approves.

16.430 These days, many people enact ridiculous tragedies[71] | about the contracts which are in common use in our times. It is fitting for us to remember that judgment about contracts does not pertain to private men or teachers of the Gospel. The whole affair should be left to the magistrate. He should determine which contracts are to be approved, just as it is a doctor's job to decide which medicines should be given for a fever and which for pleurisy. Therefore, preachers should not be permitted to take up for themselves judgments about contracts, especially against the judgment of the public laws. For when the authority of these [laws] is undermined, massive disturbances in the republic are sure to follow. Rather, this is what pertains to the teacher of the Gospel: to warn that the public laws should be reverently cultivated, and that it is permitted to make use of all contracts which the law approves.

And indeed, the laws should not be interpreted inhumanely, but equitably [*epieikōs*],[72] such that there are concessions to the circumstances. In civil affairs,
sig. [Bvi]^{r} it is sufficient to use probable reason. One should not seek demonstrations |

---

70 In the 1530 text, this word is part of the missing section and is lost. The CR reads *aut*, but the 1531 Hagenau and 1535 editions read *autem*, which is more grammatically correct.

71 *miras tragoedias agunt*, a sarcastic phrase intended to mock these critics of contracts.

72 Equity (*epieikeia*), or the idea that strict law should be relaxed to accommodate the circumstances, was an important concept in sixteenth-century jurisprudence. Aristotle himself

or[73] absolutely exact reasoning in every case. Justice has a certain mean, but this should be taken up broadly [*en platei*], according to some probable reason. Nor should consciences be bound to one certain formula in such affairs; it is enough for them to obey public laws and magistrates. It is safe to follow the judgment [of the laws and magistrates] in civil affairs, provided that they do not stray too far from nature, but have some probable cause for their opinion.| sig. [Bvi]v / [16.429]

The Second Book of the *Politics*

The second book is entirely historical, for [Aristotle] lists various constitutions, and first he critiques the *Republic*[74] of Plato, who wanted everything to be common property—even wives and children.[75] For this is Socrates' idea of the republic in Plato. Aristotle collects several arguments by which he shows that Plato's theory is contrary to human nature and can in no way be proven. In truth, even from the very start, I have thought that the reader should be reminded that the legitimate division of property and the institution of marriage are the ordination of God, which cannot be changed by any human plan, just as human effort is incapable of altering the changing of the seasons, summer, winter, night, day, the course of the sun and the movement of the other stars. | Ignorant men 16.430
who think that constitutions exist apart from God's designs, shocked by the present defects that exist in republics, seek other forms of establishing polities, thinking that | these could be applied to another state by human design. They sig.
should banish this error immediately from their minds and recognize that a [Bvii]r
legitimate constitution and division of property are the work of God. If someone persuades himself of this, he will easily understand that the existing state should be preserved and cannot be changed.

Therefore, Aristotle correctly thinks that the division of property agrees with nature. This is what the jurists most eruditely say: that [the division of property] is of the law of nations or the natural law. But Plato's republic is totally contrary to nature. In the first place, it is quite simple to demonstrate the validity of marriage. For just as reason naturally | judges murder to be wrong, it 16.431

gives a treatment of the idea in *NE* V.10 (1137a.31–1138a.3). Melanchthon also addresses the concept at length in the *Summary of Moral Philosophy*.

73 At this point, the translation resumes directly from the intact 1530 edition.

74 The term here, *Politia*, refers to a constitution generally, but is also the Latin name for Plato's *Republic*.

75 See *Politics* II.1.2–18 (1261a.2–1262b.36). For Plato's theory of common property and common families, see *Republic* Book V.

also judges promiscuous sex to be wrong. Reason also dictates that marriages must be settled. For otherwise, one's progeny would be uncertain,[76] and the rearing and nourishing [of children] would freeze. Likewise, if one's progeny were uncertain, then it would be the case that no distinction of blood would be preserved in sexual intercourse, which is contrary to nature. "A man will leave his father and mother and cling to his wife, etc." [Gen. 2:24].

The proof concerning common property is also quite simple. There is a discrepancy between the causes of acquiring goods and the causes of preserving them in common; therefore, goods cannot be held in common. The antecedent is clear because whenever lazy men realize that they are taking part in some common endeavour, they will not put forth any effort. Likewise, men who are
sig. [Bvii]v desirous of glory or power | would still seize a greater share and prevent weaker people from using or enjoying many things. And massive disturbances would follow from this. Therefore, because desires of every type are born within us, the division of property is necessary. Aristotle marshals these arguments and much further evidence against Plato's theory.[77]

But I do not know what error makes it such that many people applaud Plato's theory everywhere, however inhumane [it might be]. I suspect that certain theologians, captivated by novelty, as often happens, have become excessively infatuated with his theory. But those who teach that common property belongs to the divine law are plainly wrong. And even more erroneous are those who teach that the Gospel commands things to be held in common, and this error still stubbornly persists in the minds of the foolish, so much so that even in the Decretum, in the eighth distinction, someone wrote an epigraph reading: "By divine law, all things are common to all people."[78] Moreover, as long as this idea holds sway, fanatical men will surely appear, contending through their superstitions that property must be held in common, and from this, it is necessary that great disturbances in the republic will follow. Rather, divine law and the Gospel command us to preserve the political ordinations and the legitimate division of property under them, just as the commandment teaches: "Thou shalt not steal" [Exodus 20:15]. See also Romans 13.

sig. [Bviij]r Plenty has been said about this topic elsewhere, and here | I only wanted to touch upon it briefly to warn my readers. Therefore, let us state more directly
16.432 that | the division of property is part of the divine or evangelical law, and these voices claiming that common property is part of the divine or evangelical laws should never be accepted because they bear the seeds of catastrophic turmoil.

76 That is, the paternity of children would be uncertain.

77 For the argument about laziness and over-consumption, see *Politics* II.2.2 (1263a.8–15).

78 Decretum, Dist.8, c.1.

And indeed, the text in the eighth distinction of the Decretum, although it has a poorly written epigraph, still clearly shows that God is the author of the legitimate division of property. For it reads: "God distributed human rights [*iura humana*] to the human race through the emperors and rulers of the age."[79]

But they defend their claim that all property is common by natural law in this way: that this refers to the uncorrupted nature of man, as it existed prior to original sin.[80] When we ourselves talk about the present state [of man], after original sin, we correctly claim that the division of property is of the natural law. And I do not think that one can find, among the ancient jurists, the claim that all things are common by the natural law. For they speak of the present state of nature, in which they see that the division of property is necessary. Therefore, they say, "According to natural reason, a thing which has no prior owner is granted to the one who occupies it."[81] This maxim teaches that, according to natural reason, one obtains ownership or property by occupation, and that this is in accordance with natural reason. Moreover, natural reason is the law of nature. I have said these things in order to advise my reader, lest he be deceived by those voices | which commend the Platonic community of goods, sig.
which occasionally garner flattery from the ignorant on account of their novelty [Bviij]^{v}
and create an opportunity for great and pernicious errors. | 16.433

No virtue adorns the recognition of Christ more than the fervent cultivation of political ordinations and magistrates. Therefore, those voices which disturb the public tranquillity should be kept far away from the Gospel.[82] If someone shouts that common property is part of divine law, counter him with this commandment: "You shall not steal" [Exodus 20:15]. For this commandment teaches that each person has his own property. If someone contends that common property is part of evangelical law, counter him with Paul, who calls the legitimate ordinations of the republic "ordinations of God". Romans 13:[1]. If someone argues that common property is of natural law, counter him with the judgment of reason—that human vices make common property impossible.

---

79 Decretum, Dist. 8, c.1.

80 Some medieval and early modern jurists drew distinctions between the natural law (the *ius naturae/lex naturalis*, which supposedly applied to men before the Fall) and the law of nations (the *ius gentium*, which was supposedly a concession to human nature after the Fall and included institutions such as slavery, war, and property). Melanchthon seems to reject these distinctions and posit a singular natural law which applies to men after the Fall.

81 This is a citation of Inst.2.1.12.; cf. D.41.1.3.pr. In Roman law, property without a previous owner could be acquired by the first possessor through *occupatio*.

82 i.e., they should not be allowed to minister or preach.

For the lazy would hope to be supported by the labour of others, contrary to the law of nature, which was confirmed with these words: "By the sweat of your brow will you eat your bread" [Genesis 3:19].

II

Aristotle goes on to reproduce the laws of many states which are generally familiar to readers of history. Ultimately, he argues that changing the laws is
sig. C^{r} dangerous.[83] And although he will talk about this subject elsewhere, it is still | worthwhile to recall certain quotes on this topic. These are his words: "It is clear that some mistakes of the lawgivers and the rulers should be overlooked; for changing [the laws] will not help as much as habitually distrusting the rulers will hurt."[84] For he thinks that the accepted laws should not be changed, even if they contain something detrimental. And the consensus among all men who are wise and skilled in governing republics is that, in general, changing the laws is dangerous. For this reason, Ulpian says: "When establishing new innovations, the benefit must be evident, etc."[85] And Demosthenes writes that the Locrians had
16.434 a law stating that if | someone was going to pass a new law, he would first have to explain it to the people with his neck in a noose.[86] If the law was unpopular, the noose would be tightened immediately to strangle the author of the new law. And Herodotus says that those who condemn their ancestral laws and customs are insane, because we naturally love our own country's institutions such that, if every person had the opportunity to choose the best laws, each man would still select those of his own country.[87] And the sacred scriptures rebuke those who change the laws. Ecclesiastes 10:[8]: "A snake will bite the one who tears down a hedge." For that passage speaks in many words about the magistrate who changes the form of the republic, which is compared to a hedge. And just as serpents infiltrate a garden when the hedge is torn down, so it says that such a magistrate will provide the wicked an opportunity against the republic. But
sig. C^{v} in my | judgment, nothing is more effective at dissuading people from plans to alter the established laws, than for us to recognize that the legitimate state of the republic is an ordination of God, and that it should be honoured for God's sake, as a sacred thing, even if it is imperfect.

But here one might ask, "To what extent should defects in the laws be tolerated?" In the *Ethics*, Aristotle teaches this: Laws should align with the natural

---

83 He refers here to *Politics* II.5.10–14 (1268b.22–1269a.28).

84 Melanchthon quotes this passage, *Politics* II.5.13 (1269a.16–18), in Greek.

85 D.1.4.2.

86 See Demosthenes, *Against Timocrates* 139.

87 See Herodotus, *The Histories* III.38.

judgment of human reason. Accordingly, if they totally diverge from the judgment of nature and destroy nature, they must be changed. But if they only slightly depart from nature, they should be tolerated. For just as a left-handed person cannot be forced to become right-handed without considerable inconvenience, so the laws should not be changed if they only diverge slightly from nature, because this will not occur without serious disturbances. And as a doctor does not stimulate all of the bad humours at once in an ailing body, so one must overlook certain defects in the republic. I spent a bit more time on this topic because it is a great and necessary insight to know that one must overlook and tolerate certain defects in the laws.| sig. Cij^r / [16.433]

Third Book of the *Politics*

I have often said elsewhere that Aristotle is the greatest creator of method, and for this reason, in these books, one should consider how some precepts derive from other ones in order. Just as the other arts | have their beginnings in very 16.434
common principles, so in this book, Aristotle also begins from common conceptions which are derived from the nature of man or from the end of man. Accordingly, he treated these principles in the first book: | By nature, man was 16.435
created for society. The first society is marriage.

Next, he adds those things which are necessary for preserving domestic society and which are part of the household. From this arises another principle, namely that dominion [*dominium*] and servitude [*servitus*] are necessary for the continuation of society. And that nature demands that some rule and others serve. Here he quite keenly recognizes that the origins of government and servitude are set down for us in nature. | From here, the state is created when many sig. Cij^v
households or families join together by a certain compact [*certo foedere*].

The second book treated the thesis about the division of property. The art [of politics] gradually grows from these principles. For now, in the third book, he begins to define the state [*civitas*] and the citizens, and he recounts the various forms of government in the states. So then, I repeat [what was said] above, that it can be seen how very profitable it is to observe method, so that we may understand the origins and the progressions, or the sources and the ordering of those things which are treated in the art.

Further, in the same way that we treated those extraordinary topics above, so shall we select here those things which are most useful for this common life. And the wise student should closely consider what use there can be in these disputations. Some things are useful for public affairs, like what we said above about usury. Other things, like what we said in opposition to Platonic common property, help adjudicate the controversies about civic matters which occasionally arise among the theologians. Moreover, in this entire course of study, one should observe how those things that we learn in each individual art can also be applied to those highest arts, which are critically necessary for ruling the republic, or for private life.

sig. Ciij^r A state [*civitas*] is a society of citizens established by law | for the sake of mutual benefit and, most of all, for the sake of defence.[88]

The citizens [*cives*] are those who, in this same society, may attain the office of the magistrate or of judging.[89] The end of every citizen is the public interest [*publica utilitas*], or, to speak more clearly, the tranquillity and security of public affairs.[90] In the same way, although there are different jobs aboard a ship, the
16.436 goal of every sailor is the safety of his vessel. |

A constitution [*politia*] is the lawful ordering of the state according to which some rule and others obey. Constitutions can be either just or corrupt. There are three just species of constitutions.[91]

Kingship is monarchy, or the rule of a single man who governs the republic according to the common interest. When this becomes corrupted, it is called tyranny, in which the monarch conducts government according to his own interest. Further species of kingship will be treated below.

Aristocracy is the rule of a small group of the best men who govern the republic for the public interest. Such is the state of the city of Nuremberg.[92] When aristocracy is corrupted, it becomes oligarchy, in which the few govern the state according to the interest of the powerful. Such was the Roman state in the time of Sulla, or the current state of the republic of Erfurt.[93]

---

88 Compare with *Politics* III.4.3 (1278b.23–25), where Aristotle claims that "the good life then is the chief aim of society ... but they also come together and maintain the political partnership for the sake of life merely." (H. Rackham's translation in the LCL). See also III.5.13 (1280b.29–35). The element of the good life is absent in Melanchthon's definition here.

89 That is, the citizens are those who can attain the office of magistrate or exercise jurisdictional functions, as Aristotle states in *Politics* III.1.4 (1275a.22–23) and III.1.8 (1275b.17–21).

90 cf. *Politics* III.2.2 (1276b.27–31).

91 For the three types of constitutions, see *Politics* III.5.1–4 (1279a.22–1279b.10).

92 In the sixteenth century, the free imperial city of Nuremberg was ruled by a city council made up of wealthy patrician families.

93 Lucius Cornelius Sulla (138–79 BCE) was an ancient Roman dictator who instituted reforms that elevated the power of the Senate. Erfurt, a prominent city in Thuringia, was led by a series of city councils which were largely occupied by wealthy citizens. In 1509, tensions between patricians and the middle and lower classes led to a revolt and the establishment of a new city constitution. The following two decades saw continuous struggles to reform the class makeup of the city's government. See R.W. Scribner, "Civic Unity and the Reformation in Erfurt", *Past & Present* 66 (1975): 29–60.

The third species is when ultimate authority [*summum imperium*] is in the hands of the people. When this becomes corrupted, Aristotle calls it | 'democ- sig. Ciij^v
racy' [*dēmokratia*], in which the mob directs its own authority towards increasing the power of the poor citizens against the elites. The masses dreamt of such a state during the Peasant's Revolt, and the Swiss state is not far from it.

At this point, a question arises: Which species of constitution is best? Without a doubt, monarchy or kingship is the best state, as Homer teaches: "A multitude of lords is no good thing; let there be one lord."[94] The Persian princes decided the same thing in the third book of Herodotus.[95]

Recent interpreters of this passage argue over whether one man should be the monarch of the entire world. Certain people proclaim that the Roman pontiff is a monarch, and they think that Christ delegated to him power not only to teach the Gospel, but also to establish and transfer the kingdoms of the world. They cite many testimonies from Gratian to support this position.[96] And it seems to me that those who think this way are entirely deceived by this argument: that just as they see kings anointed by the priests in the law, for this reason, they judge that kings receive political authority [*imperium*][97] from priests, and accordingly they reason that kings must now receive political authority from the
Pope. And since the Gospel does not | only concern one nation, but all nations, 16.437
they accordingly think that the Pope has also received the power of establishing governments among all nations. Therefore, they assign to him the power of forcing kings into alignment with his will as well as many other things which
there is no | room to list here. On this pretext, the Roman pontiffs have often sig. Ciiij^r
tried to rip away political authority from emperors, and to cast other kings out of their reigns, and for a long while now it has been commonly understood to be heresy if someone denies that both swords (for this is how they speak) pertain to the Pope.[98]

---

94 Homer, *Iliad* II.204.

95 Herodotus, *Histories* III.82.

96 Gratian was a Bolognese monk who in ca. 1139 compiled the *Concordia discordantium canonum*, a major collection of medieval canon law later known as the Decretum (see footnotes 78, 79 above). It was integrated as the first part of the *Corpus iuris canonici*.

97 In this paragraph, the term *imperium* refers specifically to the power and authority of political rulers, as contrasted with the power of spiritual leaders like the Pope. Accordingly, the broader term "government", with its institutional connotations, does not quite fit here, and *imperium* is rendered here as "political authority".

98 For example, Pope Boniface VIII (r. 1294–1303) proclaimed in the 1302 papal bull *Unam sanctam* that the Pope held ultimate authority in both secular and spiritual affairs, symbolized by the "secular" and "spiritual" swords.

But this opinion is entirely at odds with the Gospel, for Christ says, "My kingdom is not of this world" [John 18:36]. Also: "The kings of the nations rule over them, but it is not so with you" [Matthew 20:25–26, Luke 22:25–26]. One could cite endless other things which prove that the kingdom of Christ is not a civil kingdom, but an eternal one. Christ rules through the Holy Spirit in such a way that he justifies, enlivens, and governs the hearts of the saints. But in the meantime, he does not abolish the external ordination which God instituted to coerce the ungodly and preserve tranquillity among men. But we have spoken of this distinction elsewhere. For government should be distinguished carefully from the power of the bishop. The office of the bishop is to teach the Gospel, to remit sins, to warn the ungodly of God's judgment, just as Christ says, "Go and preach the Gospel, etc." [Mark 16:15]. This power does not pass laws about civil affairs or possession of goods, and it does not bear the sword to coerce men to obedience. It only teaches consciences about the will of God, shares the Gospel, soothes frightened minds, and warns the ungodly. In sum, it teaches about repentance and remission of sins.

sig. Ciiijv In contrast, government [*imperium*] is the power | of establishing laws for prohibiting outward injustices, of coercing men to obedience with the sword, and of punishing those who do not obey the laws. This definition is taken from Paul in Romans 3: The power wields the sword for the peace of the good.[99] So then, just as marriage is an ordination of God, even though marriage and the Gospel are separate things, so is government an ordination of God although it is a different thing than the Gospel. And if someone requires a clear testimony, government was established in those words spoken to Noah: "Whoever sheds the blood of man, by man shall his blood be shed" [Genesis 9:6]. For in this pas-
16.438 sage, God ordains a man who | exacts punishments; therefore, God establishes the magistrate.

Moreover, the natural judgment of reason is that there must be some who rule. Further, as we have often said, natural law or the natural judgment of reason is divine law. Government was also established in this commandment: "Honor thy father and mother" [Exodus 20:12]. For this commands obedience to superiors. Certain people claim—falsely—that only the consent of the people grants political authority [*imperium*], just as Ockham says.[100] [This is false][101]

---

99 The correct citation is Romans 13:3–4.

100 For Melanchthon's criticism of Ockham in this text, see Jensen, "By Convention or by Nature".

101 The editors of the CR treat the following sentence as a quotation from Ockham, but this cannot be the case, since the meaning of that sentence (especially the repeated *etiam*) refutes the idea that government is established from the consent of the people. Rather,

because princes lawfully rule over even the unwilling, and they lawfully seize control of governments not only through election or votes and the consent of the people, but also through just wars and the eradication of bandits, through legitimate succession, etc.

Moreover, certain people have argued that the Roman emperor is the mon-
arch of the entire world, using | citations from the Gospel: "A decree went out sig. Cv^{r}
from Caesar Augustus, etc." [Luke 2:1], and "Give to Caesar what is Caesar's" [Mark 12:17, Matthew 22:21]. But these words command Caesar's subjects at that time to obey him; they do not order the entire world to obey one Roman prince in all places. On the contrary, in other passages, scripture attests that the Romans, who then ruled a vast part of the world, would not always keep that same empire [*imperium*].[102] Therefore, accordingly, we should not think that either the Roman Pontiff or Caesar must be the monarch of the entire world. Rather, individual kings rule among their own peoples, just as there have always been separate kingdoms in the world. Moreover, there was a sequence of four empires [*imperia*], which the histories call "monarchies", not because they ruled
everywhere | or held a universal right of governance, but because they ruled a 16.439
vast area.[103] For God intended, through that occasion, to open the world to the Gospel and join together many kingdoms so that the Gospel could more easily spread to many people.

After Daniel was carried off to Chaldea, the knowledge of God was spread widely among the Assyrians and Persians. Similarly, in Roman times, the entire world lay open and it was safe for the Apostles to travel so that they could teach everywhere. And other cases could be gathered too. Perhaps God intended to demonstrate, in this changing of kingdoms, that he establishes kingdoms, and that they cannot be maintained by human power—or he intended to illus-
trate, when he ripped away | kingdoms from the most powerful nations, that sig. Cv^{v}
he punishes the unjust, etc. Moreover, the fact that scripture alone predicted the successions of empires in order marvellously magnifies the authority of Christian doctrine. And since things played out in exactly that way, it stands established that scripture was handed down by God, and that God is the author of empires. Therefore, let us always remember to venerate and honour diligently

---

the particle *nam* here introduces the reason why Ockham and certain others make their claims falsely (*falso*).

102 In this paragraph and the next, *imperium*/*imperia* refer to specific instances of government in world history. In this context, the term "empire" is the most appropriate English translation.

103 The idea of the four world monarchies can be found in Daniel 2:31–45 and 7:1–28. In Lutheran historiography, the four monarchies became the ordering scheme of world history. For Melanchthon's commentary on this in *Carion's Chronicle*, see CR XII.718–720.

the present governments [*imperia*] on account of God, who ordained the magistrate so that he might share the glory of his own name with them when he says, "I said, you are gods" [Psalm 82:6]. For he attests that magistrates have been established by his own authority and that they function in the place of God among men.

Of the Various Species of Kings

Properly speaking, a king is the ultimate power [*summa potestas*] over whom no higher magistrate judges. Moreover, there have been various species of kings in the world, because men, on account of the diverse customs of kings, in some cases have granted [kings] unrestricted power, and in other cases they have reckoned that [their power] should be restrained and moderated. The first species of kingship is that which existed in the heroic age, when kings ruled without established laws but for the benefit of the people. The head of household exercises this sort of domestic rule over his children.[104] This type [of kingship] is full of humanity, but it is rare amidst this great dearth of good princes. Further-
sig. [Cvi]r more, in its lesser forms, it degenerates into tyranny. | For "Tyrant" is the proper name for one who takes control of things by himself, rules without written laws, coerces the unwilling by force, and directs government to his own benefit. He demands not just favourable things, but also many things that are contrary to the interest of the subjects.

16.440 For these reasons, certain bonds have been devised which are thrown around such power. Laws have been imposed upon kings so that they would govern the republic according to written law. Therefore, there is a second species of kingship: ultimate authority [*summum imperium*], but circumscribed by fixed law. Certain nations have even added guardians for the kings who have the right to keep [the kings] in line. For instance, the Spartans added ephors who were permitted to arrest the king, as Thucydides writes.[105] Kings of this sort are not entirely autocratic [*autokratores*] or unaccountable [*anupeuthunoi*], that is, they do not possess ultimate power such that no one may overrule them or oppose their actions.

In our times, kingdoms are usually like this, for they have laws and they have guardians. Germany has the electors and France has certain princes in the parliament who are like the kings' ephors, although in some places they are more powerful, and in some places they are less so. For it is not safe to oppose the desires of kings, and accordingly, they easily break through these bonds. [Kings]

---

104 The Roman *paterfamilias*, or head of household, held virtually total legal control over the members of his family, including, at least in early Roman law, power over life and death.

105 Thucydides, *History of the Peloponnesian War* I.131.

allow themselves to be partly coerced only by religion, and thus this mixture of princes and bishops is highly advantageous, for the bishops are appointed, just like ephors, for tempering the force of royal power. And perhaps the clay mixed with iron in Daniel's statue [Daniel 2:33] | signifies this mixture of bishops and sig. [Cvi]^{v}
princes in every kingdom.

Here, some weighty questions are treated: Is it permitted for private men to kill tyrants? Or is it permitted to use force to repel violence which a ruler has committed contrary to his own laws? For it seems that the subject is bound to obey him insofar as he rules according to the laws. The Christian response to this question is quite simple. For the Gospel prohibits all private vengeance, and Christ says "Whoever takes up the sword will die by the sword" [Matthew 26:52]. Therefore, a Christian may not kill a ruler, no matter how tyrannical he is. Moreover, the subject is not only bound to his ruler because of that agreement, which, having been made between him and the ruler, binds the ruler to a certain justice; rather, [the subject] is also compelled to submit because of God's command, which orders him to honour magistrates, even evil ones, and forbids private men from using force against the magistrate. This is the safest course for a Christian to follow.[106]

Some call this into doubt and argue that a private person may use force to resist unjust violence committed by the magistrate. But these people think, according to human custom, | that whenever disobedience is permitted, resist- 16.441
ing violence is likewise permitted. But we should recognize that there is a vast difference between these things according to the Gospel, which forbids obedience if the magistrate orders one to commit a sin, yet still prohibits[107] private vengeance. | Therefore, Daniel, the Prophets, and the Apostles did not resist sig. [Cvii]^{r}
unjust violence, although at times they disobeyed rulers.

Another question can be asked about this topic: Which species of kingship does God approve? Keep in mind that there are various disputes about this matter among the theologians. Some think that subjects everywhere are truly slaves, and have nothing of their own. On the other hand, others argue that this harsh servitude is at odds with the Gospel. And on this impious pretext, five

---

106 Notably, Melanchthon would depart from this position later, as conflict between Protestants and the Catholic Emperor Charles V became inevitable. Melanchthon's mature resistance theory appears in Book II of the *Summary of Moral Philosophy*, as well as in a letter (likely written sometime in 1546) entitled "On Lawful Resistance" (CR 6.150–155) and in his 1547 revisions of Justus Menius' work *Von der Notwehr Unterricht* (Instruction On Self-Defence). For a modern critical edition of the latter text, see Schneider, ed., *Politischer Widerstand als protestantische Option*.

107 The word *prohibet* is missing in the text of the 1530 edition, a mistake which is corrected in the *errata* on sig. [Dvii]^{r}.

years ago [i.e., in 1525], they stirred up the mob to retake their liberty with arms by overthrowing the princes. An impious and seditious booklet was circulating, and it contained the argument that Christians should have an exemption from burdens and immunity from tributes. This booklet was said to have been
16.442 written by a certain Schappeler, who at that time was | a preacher in the city of Memmingen.[108]

This latter opinion, besides the fact that it is contrary to the Gospel, is even more pernicious than the first, which some people claim to be more bitter and inhumane. Therefore, the latter [opinion] should be entirely rejected, but the first argument, which I recall having been discussed by the Paris theologian John Mair, demands some consideration.[109] So then, this is what one should think: First, God approves all legitimate constitutions; that is, as Paul says, those which are a terror to evil works and bestow honour upon good work [Romans
sig. [Cvii]v 13:3–4], or which follow the judgment of reason and the | law of nature, and command good things and prohibit and punish evil.

Such a constitution is the ordination of God, no matter the nation to which it belongs, even if the form of government might be gentler in some places and harsher in others. For just as one uses severer remedies to cure diseases in some regions, and lighter remedies in others, more savage natures require harsher government. This fact produces various forms of governments. In some places, subjects truly are slaves. In other places, the power of kings is limited by the laws, and a certain liberty is granted to the people. This is the case in Germany, because the princes follow Roman law, and for that reason all subjects everywhere are not, properly speaking, slaves. Nevertheless, God approves of both forms, and in either place, he wants princes to follow the accepted law.

In the histories of the kings, when Samuel defines the right of kingship, he approves the harshest form of government, and labels it with this title: "The

108 This is a reference to the Twelve Articles, which expressed the demands of the Swabian Peasants during the Peasants' War of 1525. Among other demands, the document called for an end to various types of tithes and taxes, as well as relaxations of compulsory labour demanded of the peasants. Christoph Schappeler (1472–1551), a reformer at Memmingen, was widely considered to be the author of the Twelve Articles. For a modern translation of this text, see *The Radical Reformation*, ed. Michael G. Baylor, pp. 231–238.

109 John Mair (1467–1550) Scottish theologian and philosopher who taught in Paris. Melanchthon likely refers to Mair's Ockhamist idea that political rule was founded in popular consent. The implication of this position was that all political rule was over free people (i.e., not over enslaved people). As a result, a free people could depose a tyrannical ruler. Melanchthon does not mean that Mair subscribed to this "first argument" that all subjects are merely slaves; indeed, Mair rejected it. But Mair does discuss these ideas in his 1518 *In Matthaeum ad literam expositio* and his 1519 commentary on Lombard's *Sentences*. For further discussion of this point, see Jensen, "By Convention or by Nature."

right of Kings" [1 Samuel 8:11]. For the Holy Spirit means that legitimate government, however harsh it might be, is nevertheless approved by God. And Joseph | 16.443 subjected all of Egypt to the harshest servitude. Therefore, there should be no doubt that even the bitterest form of government is approved by God, provided that it does not command anything evil. However, one should not conclude that servitude must be similar among all peoples. In those places where royal power is limited by laws which allow subjects to own property and enjoy certain other benefits of liberty, there princes sin when, contrary to their own laws, | they sig. confiscate private resources from their subjects as if they were slaves. Ahab, [Cviii]r king of the Israelites, unjustly tried to confiscate Naboth's vineyard [1 Kings 21:1–16]. For although God approved a harsh form of government, as Samuel's words illustrate, he still moderated royal power by law among that people. For the law had granted private possessions to individuals, and it intended for families to retain their own patrimonies. Similarly, in our own case, those persons may hold property who are permitted to do so by the laws of government by which our affairs are adjudicated. Princes may not rashly change this state of the republic, and it would be violence to take away the possession of liberty from those who have held it thus far by the blessing of the law.

Moreover, even where there is true slavery [*vera est servitus*], still the lords may not seize everything. For the law of nature and the holy scriptures command that whatever suffices to feed a family should be left to slaves. For as it is written in Ecclesiasticus [33:25]: "Fodder, a switch, and a load for a donkey; bread, discipline and work for the slave." And the civil laws intend for slaves to keep *peculium*, and [these laws] are generally favourable to liberty.[110]

But liberty has certain boundaries within which it should operate. For both the law of nature and the divine law impose many burdens on the free: pay taxes, obey the magistrate, use one's resources and bodies to protect common society when necessary, and certain other things defined by law. Therefore, let us embrace liberty in such a way that, in the meantime, we still remember that God and nature itself compel us to obey | the magistrates and support civil sig. society with our resources and our lives. [Cviii]v

On Laws

The last part of the third book contains a discussion about whether it is better to govern a republic by the will of a good prince, without written | laws, or [to 16.444

110 In Roman law, because slaves were property, they could not own property outright. However, masters could allow slaves to hold property, such as money, a farm, or a shop, to provide for themselves and their families. This property was known as *peculium*. See D.15.1.

govern] by written and certain law.[111] Even in our own age, this question is often treated by unlearned men who, although they make legal decisions, they do so grudgingly, because they are forced, like children, to follow what the jurists have previously said, and they do not dare make their own determinations. This reign of the jurists galls ambitious men, whose madness is supported by those who are learned but engaged in another kind of doctrine. They argue that every single case cannot be comprehended by the laws, and since most things should be decided by the decision of a good man, they think that, having abolished the laws, all things should be referred to the prudence and equity of the judge. They also look at the state of trials and the courts, where the lawyerly arts make cases drag on indefinitely. This would not be the case if the judge had a strong authority unimpeded by laws.

Aristotle considers several arguments of this sort, but he ultimately determines that it is safer to judge matters according to certain laws and written
sig. Dr right.[112] This is because | the judge is rarely prudent enough to see, without laws, what is the most fair and most useful to the republic, or just enough that the laws are not needed to restrain his power. For some appearance of right often deceives the average man, whereas if he were guided by the laws, he would judge better. Sometimes, he indulges a soul which is impeded by partiality or hatred because he is not held by the bonds of the law. For license makes even good men into worse ones. Therefore, there is a need for these bonds, which, even if tyrants occasionally break them, are still beneficial for guiding and restraining the average person. For something is excellent if it is helpful in most cases, even if things sometimes turn out differently. For example, we practice medicine because it can usually heal the sick, even though it cannot cure every disease. On this point, how often would good men disagree among themselves in judging if they had no prescribed and certain model? Moreover, it is easy for massive upheavals to arise in the republic from such dissensions, and in order to prevent this, one should proceed with the utmost diligence.

But suppose that the men who judge are endowed with the utmost prudence and integrity, men who can never be deceived or make mistakes, who cannot be affected or moved by partiality or hatred—even then, certain justice and written laws would still contribute to tranquillity! For relentless litigators still
sig. Dv would not submit, would not yield to the judge unless | the law were certain. They always impugn either the good faith or the diligence of the judge unless
16.445 they understand what necessary cause the judge had for his decision. | There-

111 Aristotle poses a version of this question in *Politics* III.10.3 (1286a.7–9).

112 *Politics* III.11.3 (1287a.18–22).

fore, written law fortifies the magistrate against the quibbling of those litigators who, when they have become familiar with the law, see that the judge does not rule in error or according to his own private feeling, but that he follows a prescription which he is not permitted to change. And they understand that they must tolerate this law, which has been devised not for special interest or private benefit, but for preserving society and peace among citizens.

Accordingly, I believe that the laws were originally established because, previously, things were adjudicated by the decision of the magistrates. For the common people always complain about the magistrates, and for this reason, proposing settled laws seemed to be the surest way of appeasing the mob. For once these laws were accepted, it was not permitted to impugn their authority. Moreover, there were visible causes behind things that had been decided, and these freed the judge from the suspicion of favouritism, hatred, or error. If a decision was harsh, it was attributed to the law—but it was not permitted to be angry at the law, for [the law] had pleased everyone, since it was previously accepted and approved by the very person who now thought it too severe. However, why is there need for disputation? Every expert agrees that justice must be decided according to written laws. And they have innumerable reasons for this position, but there is no need to recount all of them here. | It is most fitting sig. Dij^{r}
for those who are not yet engaged in the republic to follow their authority.

No one is permitted to judge concerning the other arts except for the artists and those who are skilled in them. But concerning the manner of governing the republic, which is doubtless the most difficult of the arts by far, plainly unqualified men are the ones who judge. Not only is this absolutely disgraceful, but it is also extremely dangerous, since the tranquillity of the republic cannot be maintained once the authority of the laws is undermined. Therefore, this impudence was to be punished with public penalties. Meanwhile, let us keep Aristotle's opinion about this inscribed and engraved upon our souls, so that we may know that written law should be not only retained, but also devotedly cultivated. It is beneficial to plant such sayings in the minds of the young so that they would become accustomed to love the laws and to hold them in high esteem, and this indeed offers a great contribution towards developing good men.

These are Aristotle's words [in Greek]: "Therefore, on the one hand, he who orders the law to rule seems to order | God and the laws to rule.[113] But on the 16.446

113 Here, modern editions of Aristotle read "he who proposes that the law should rule seems to suggest that *God and reason alone* [*ton theon kai ton noun monous*] should rule." Melanchthon's Greek text reads "*God and the laws*" [*ton theon kai tous nomous*]. The full quote is from *Politics*, III.xi.4 (1287a.28–32).

other hand, he who orders man [to rule] adds a wild animal too. For desire is like [a wild animal], and passion twists even the best men when they rule. Therefore, the law is a mind without desire."

sig. Dij[v] That is, [In Latin]: "Those who want the law to rule the state | seem to want God and the laws to rule. But those who want man to rule place a beast in charge. For desire is something like [a beast], and the passion of the magistrate depraves men, no matter how good they are. Therefore, the law is mind without desire."

On this topic, nothing can be said that is more weighty or elegant than this saying from Aristotle. For when he says that if the law rules, God rules, he means that the law is a certain sure and firm conception, divinely written in nature, or, to speak more clearly, [it is] the voice of God which distinguishes just from unjust. For just as the philosophers believe that there is some mind which preserves this entire universe, so they think that certain notions, which are born with man and are the foundations of the arts, have been divinely placed in human nature. And in this, the philosophers are not mistaken.

Now, even if other nations have, on occasion, justly complained about their own laws, certainly at this time it is absolutely improper for Germans to complain when we use Roman law, which is full of humanity and equity, which was written by men most skilled in the government of the republic, which led this nation, formerly the height of barbarism, to a gentler and more humane life.[114] For it may be truly said that whatever humanity there is in the private morals of our people, whatever civic duties there are in the republic, were taken
sig. Diij[r] from the Roman laws, | under the instruction of which our people have gradually burned away that ancient barbarity. For what part of civic life is there which those laws do not address with the most humane and honourable precepts?

Although the Jewish laws were handed down by God, they still fit that people much better than they could fit us. For they were not passed in order to be imposed on other peoples. The constitution of Lycurgus had many disadvantages and defects. Solon's laws were more civil, but the Roman ones corrected
16.447 many things in them concerning marriage and other matters. | Therefore, the

114 In the sixteenth century, the Holy Roman Empire was undergoing a process of legal reform in which the *ius commune* became widespread across the universities and the *Reichskammergericht* (Imperial Chamber Court). In many cases, this learned jurisprudence replaced the use of the customary German laws (such as the *Sachsenspiegel*). While this legal reform was highly controversial, Melanchthon admired Roman law as an expression of natural reason and considered it to be a great civilizing force in Germany. See James Q. Whitman, *The Legacy of Roman Law in the German Romantic Era: Historical Vision and Legal Change* (1990), pp. 3–40.

laws of no city, of no people, surpass the Roman [laws], which order about all civic duties, trials, and contracts such that they are understood never to depart from nature, never to depart from reason.

In fact, in my judgment, even if the Roman laws were not used in court, they should still be read in schools for forming and sharpening judgment about civil affairs. Therefore, one should by no means tolerate the arrogance of those who, lacking this doctrine, trust themselves to see clearly the power of equity or draft more suitable laws. Oh, to be sure, any old theologian who has never participated in the republic and never practiced in court understands what form of trial is most useful for the republic, or what is fair in contracts or in the division of inheritance better than Papinian or Ulpian, both of whom spent their lives not only in these studies and in court, but also in | government sig. Diij^v
administration and in the most serious deliberations about the entirety of the republic![115]

However, I know of many men who, although they should be teaching in the churches, nevertheless burst into the forum and court and, scorning Roman law, they try to pass new laws. And in doing so, they employ neither skill, nor talent, nor any civil doctrine, but only pure impudence joined with extreme stupidity and impiety. They admire themselves as gods, and in comparison to themselves, they despise every Solon, Papinian, or Pontanus.[116] They do not know or even desire to know the ancient doctrine of civil affairs, but they thrust their own fancies upon men and demand that these be regarded as oracles. Theologians of this type "know well neither justice nor law", as Homer says of the Cyclopes, and they do not establish Christ's kingdom, but their own.[117] | A few years ago, 16.448
we saw the examples of Müntzer and Strauss, who incited the mob to take up arms against the magistrates.[118] Nowadays, preachers are doing the same thing

115 Papinian and Ulpian were two of the most prominent ancient Roman lawyers. Their pronouncements appear repeatedly in the Digest and other foundational texts of Roman law.

116 Pontanus is the latinized name of Gregor Brück, one of the most prominent jurists and legal advisors in the German Reformation movement. Melanchthon gave an oration on Brück's life in CR 12.350–360. Melanchthon wrote the dedicatory epistle to the *Summary of Moral Philosophy* to Brück's son Christian.

117 Homer, *Odyssey*, IX.215, which Melanchthon cites in Greek.

118 Thomas Müntzer (1490–1525) was a radical preacher and leader of the peasants in the 1525 Peasants' War. In 1523, the preacher Jakob Strauss (ca. 1480–ca. 1534) caused a controversy in Eisenach when he published a pamphlet claiming that charging or paying interest was a sin. This was an explosive claim, as it forbade debtors from paying interest on their debts. Luther wrote several letters rebuking Strauss, and Melanchthon visited him in Eisenach in 1524 to attempt to resolve the controversy. See Hans Wiersma, "Luther on Lending".

in certain great states. They have formed conspiracies to stir up violence against the lawful magistrates, so that, having cast down the Emperor, they might lay claim to liberty.[119] They would rather throw everything into chaos than lose their own kingdom.

But some excuse this on the grounds of piety, denying that a Christian should use the laws of the Gentiles. Accordingly, they either try to pass new laws or call us back to the Mosaic laws like Karlstadt, who vehemently argued that the
sig. Diiij^r Mosaic laws should be taken up after having eradicated the Roman laws.[120] | But let us remember that the present laws should be kept and revered. For just as the Gospel commands obedience to the present [political] power, so does it command obedience to the present laws. And it approves of their laws,[121] since the law is the voice of the magistrate. And in Romans 13, he is called "the ordination of God".[122] For without laws, without trials, without civil institutions, there is no ordination in governments. Yet Paul says that the magistrate is a certain ordination.

But he who knows the nature of Christian liberty will easily understand that it is not necessary to recall the Mosaic laws back into the courts. For the Gospel does not bind us to the rites or polity of Moses, as Acts 15 clearly attests, when [the Apostles] prohibit imposing the Mosaic law on the Gentiles. And they argue from the name of "Gentiles", for it was predicted that the Gentiles would believe in Christ, not that they should be forced to accept the Mosaic polity. For otherwise, they would cease to be Gentiles.

But some object:

---

119 Jensen (*A Humanist in Reformation Politics*, pp. 93–94) sees this as a reference to the negotiations, in 1529 and 1530, among Saxony, Hesse, and the imperial free cities such as Strasbourg about the creation of a Protestant defence league. In 1529, Strasbourg and Philip of Hesse had gone so far as to make an alliance with the Swiss Zwinglian cities. At this point, Melanchthon still opposed armed resistance to Emperor Charles V, so he viewed such a league as dangerous to the larger political order.

120 Andreas Bodenstein von Karlstadt (1486–1541) was a colleague of Luther and Melanchthon at Wittenberg who later came to adopt more radical proposals such as the iconoclastic removal of images and a more simplified order of worship. In 1523, he left Wittenberg and became pastor of the church of Orlamünde. Melanchthon saw Karlstadt's vision of Christianity as an attempt to reinstate the Mosaic laws. For example, in the 1522 tract, *On the Removal of Images*, Karlstadt vehemently argued that having images in churches was contrary to the commandment in Exodus 20:4: "You shall not make for yourself an idol."

121 Presumably, the laws of the Gentiles.

122 *Et Roma xiii vocatur ordinatio Dei*. There is no explicit subject in this sentence, but, considering the context of the following sentence, it is most likely that *magistratus* is the subject here.

"Everything which does not come from faith is sin" [Romans 14:23].
The magistrate who adjudicates according to Roman law cannot be certain whether his decision pleases God, because he does not have the word of God.
Therefore, he should seek the laws established by God. | 16.449

One should respond that the minor premise is simply false. For the magistrate who judges according to Roman law can have faith and be certain that his decision pleases God. For he has the | word of God in Romans 13 and elsewhere, sig. Diiij^v in which God approves the magistrate and the civil ordinations. This general testimony is sufficient for strengthening the conscience, just as scripture generally approves other external bodily functions, such as eating, farming, and building. And since these things are subject to reason, there is no need to teach each individual art in scripture. Scripture reveals God's will to us, but it does not teach us architecture, medicine, or similar arts which can be derived from reason.

The Magistrate Can Still Rule, Even If He Is Ungodly

Wycliffe, who argued that those who do not have the Holy Spirit relinquish their dominion [*dominium*], stirred up ridiculous tragedies in a certain place, and he gathered many sophistic arguments to prove his dogma.[123] We will recite some testimonies from scripture which demonstrate that even the ungodly may hold political authority [*imperia*]. For Christ says, "Give to Caesar what is Caesar's" [Mark 12:17, Matthew 22:21]. Yet it is obvious that at that time, Caesar was ungodly. And Paul calls the magistrate "the minister of God" [Romans 13:4, 6], and he was writing this to those at Rome, where he knew that the magistrates were ungodly. Peter commands obedience even to wicked magistrates [1 Peter 2:13–17]. Christ says, "The kings of the nations rule over them" [Matthew 20:25,

123 Melanchthon refers to the English theologian John Wycliffe (c. 1330–1384). In this section, Melanchthon attacks Wycliffe's argument that only the righteous (i.e., Christians) could legitimately hold political authority. Melanchthon does not appear to cite directly from a specific text of Wycliffe's. Rather, he seems to engage with a summary of the arguments presented in Wycliffe's work, *De civili dominio*. This text is available in the modern edited version of R.L. Poole: *Iohannis Wycliffe, Tractatus de civili dominio*, 4 vols. (London, 1885–1904). For the arguments treated here, see esp. Book I, chapter 1 (Poole vol. I, pp. 1–8), chapter 5 (I.37–39), and chapter 19 (I.136–137). In 1530, Wycliffe's *Tractatus* had not yet been printed. His *Trialogus* was printed at Worms in 1525, but that work contained mostly theological content and very little about politics. For this print, see British Museum, *Short-Title Catalogue of Books Printed in the German Speaking Countries* (1962), p. 913. It is possible that Melanchthon may have known of Wycliffe's political ideas through Thomas Netter's fifteenth-century *Doctrinale antiquitatum fidei catholicae ecclesiae contra Wiclevistas et Hussitas libri VI*, which was printed in Paris in 1521.

sig. Dv^{r} Luke 22:25], and there | he openly attributes the praise and title of lordship to the kings as they were in that age. And Daniel clearly tells Nebuchadnezzar that God gave the kingdom to him [Daniel 2:37]. And the Psalm refers to the magistrates as "gods" [Psalm 82:6], even though it frequently rebukes and criticizes them. Such verses should encourage the hearts of the godly, contrary to fanatical opinions, to tolerate and honour even evil magistrates, not because of the magistrate's private morals, but on account of God's ordination.[124] For God's very institution and mandate should be contemplated and revered, even
16.450 if [the magistrate's] private morals contain some vice. |

Moreover, Christians must remember that God appoints evil and pernicious magistrates over us because of the sins of the people. Therefore, we should blame our sins, not the magistrates, if there is something troublesome in government. Accordingly, that which Euripides said, that "One must bear the follies of the rulers,"[125] is most fitting for Christians to observe, for they know that governments are the ordination of God, and they have the most weighty commandments not to disturb this ordination, but to honour it religiously and obey it with their entire will.

However, as a mental exercise, we shall recite some of Wycliffe's particularly thorny arguments, which show that their author was certainly not of sincere or sound mind. Here is his argument:

> sig. Dv^{v} Civil dominion [*dominium civile*] is founded in natural [dominion]. |
> Natural dominion [*naturale dominium*] is to be righteous [*iustum*].[126]
> Therefore, civil dominion is to be righteous.

He proves the minor premise on the grounds that Adam received dominion in Paradise, while he had original righteousness [*cum originali iusticia*].

Response: the minor premise is false, because natural dominion does not mean being righteous, nor is it necessary that righteousness, especially private [righteousness], be joined with dominion. For although Adam was righteous when he received dominion, still, when he lost his original righteousness, since he did not die, he did not lose his dominion just as he did not lose reason. For

124 1530: *ordinationem. Dei Functio ...* The 1531 Hagenau and 1535 editions read *ordinationem Dei. Functio ...* The capitalization of *Functio* in the 1530 edition, as well as the correction in the later editions, indicate that the latter reading is correct.

125 Euripides, *Phoenician Women*, line 393.

126 The term here is *iustum*, which can be translated either "righteous" or "just". In the theological context in which Melanchthon uses it here, "righteous" is the more appropriate English rendering, although the concept of justice still remains.

natural dominion is nothing but the judgment of reason, deciding how and in what order we can use natural things advantageously and for protecting life.

If someone scoffs at this solution, a stronger argument is also available. Civil dominion is founded in God's ordination. God's ordination was instituted after Adam's sin. Therefore, civil dominion may fall to wicked men. Moreover, those things that are taken from divine law and the scriptures are always firmer than those taken from reason. For this reason, the present argument can easily overturn Wycliffe's reasoning. So then, the minor premise[127] is clear, for the reason that it is God's ordinance that some people rule and others obey. This was established in the commandment, "Honor thy father and mother" [Exodus 20:12] or
in the words spoken to Noah: "Whoever sheds | the blood of man, | by man shall 16.451
his blood be shed" [Genesis 9:6] or when Adam was granted authority over his sig.
family. [Dvi]^{r}

Indeed, after Adam's sin, the law began to be necessary for coercing the ungodly. By the same reason, the magistrate who executes the law also became necessary. Therefore, natural dominion can also be defined in this way: it is the natural law which ordains certain men to rule for the purpose of coercing the ungodly. For it is clear that Adam, after his sin, retained natural knowledge [*noticiam naturalem*] of the law just as he retained reason. Moreover, civil dominion is the execution of natural dominion. For in order to ensure the orderly government of the republic, it is necessary to bestow the magistracy upon certain persons and to exclude the rest from governing. This is called civil dominion, and it is a certain effect [*effectus*] of natural dominion.

Truly, what confusion there would be in the republic, not to mention in families, if magistrates and parents abdicated their dominion whenever they offended God! There would never be any peace in the family or the state. For
seditious men would have new pretexts every day | for tearing government away 16.452
from the rulers and refusing to pay their debts, since they would argue that anyone who calls in his debts cannot be a ruler. For it is easy to find sins to condemn in others. Wycliffe also argues in this way:

> Whatever the ungodly do, they do unjustly [*iniuste*].
> Consequently, they even hold property and political authority [*imperia*] unjustly. | sig.
> Therefore, they are not truly lords [*domini*].[128] [Dvi]^{v}

127 i.e., the minor premise of Melanchthon's own syllogism in the previous sentences: "God's ordination was instituted after Adam's sin."

128 In early modern jurisprudence, the term *dominus* can refer to a person who is the owner

Response: it does not follow that they are not truly lords. It only follows that they abuse their dominion, since they do not join it with faith towards God. But this abuse does not contradict the nature of dominion. It is as if someone were to argue the following:

> Whatever the ungodly do, they do unjustly.
> Consequently, they even eat unjustly.
> Therefore, they do not truly eat.

Here, it becomes manifestly clear that the conclusion does not follow [*anakolouthon esse*]. Possessing unjustly, just as eating unjustly, means possessing or eating without faith before God. It does not mean that possession itself is evil, or that food is evil.

But it shames me to recount such far-fetched and ridiculous sophistry. Nevertheless, it is still sometimes beneficial in disputations like these to show these examples to the youths for the purpose of sharpening their judgment, so that they may see what kinds of dreams deceive fanatical minds when they have departed, even momentarily, from the truth.[129]

---

of a thing (i.e. one who has property rights, or *dominium*), or to a person who has political authority.

129 Several editions of this commentary, including the 1531 Hagenau edition and the edition in the 1541 Basel *Opera omnia*, include Melanchthon's commentary on the fifth book of Aristotle's *Nicomachean Ethics* at the end of the *Politics* commentary. Book V of the *Ethics* addresses justice.

CHAPTER 3

The *Prefaces* and *Occasio* to Hesiod's *Works and Days*

1 Introduction

Of all the texts in this volume, the *Prefaces* to Hesiod provide the most approachable introduction to Melanchthon's concept of natural law. In the first *Preface*, Melanchthon presents readers with the question: Why should Christians read the pagan poet Hesiod? In answer, Melanchthon lucidly explains his understanding of the relationship between natural law and moral philosophy. In his view, Hesiod, just like the other wise sages of antiquity, was an authoritative source in moral philosophy because he drew his teachings from nature. The eternal standard of the natural law, apparent to all rational men in all times and places, determined the content of Hesiod's thought. Hesiod was a valuable author for Christians because God spoke through the poet by the inborn knowledge of the natural law.

It is for this reason that Melanchthon could so boldly claim that "those things which the learned pagans have derived from common sense and the judgment of nature and have passed on in their writings are no less divine commandments than those things which appear on the stone tablets of Moses."[1] As he goes on to say, natural moral laws are, in Paul's words, "written on human hearts" (Romans 2:15), and therefore the moral teachings of the virtuous pagans are no less divine than God's explicit words. The implication is that pagan thought is a valid source of moral and political insight. "The Christian scriptures teach us in one way about matters of religion", he writes, "but when it comes to the manner of civic life, Christ intended for us to obey the common precepts of nature."[2]

Melanchthon was careful to emphasize that Hesiod was not an authority on matters of religion and salvation. In the second *Preface*, he asserts that *Works and Days* contains teachings "profitable for your manner of life and for judging the common duties of humanity—for I am not speaking of religion here."[3]

---

1 See p. 280 below.

2 See p. 281 below.

3 See p. 285 below.

HTTPS://DOI.ORG/10.1163/9789004774742-006

He concedes that Hesiod's works contribute "nothing towards transforming the mind and imbuing it with religion" (that was the task of the Holy Spirit).[4] However, Hesiod could help students develop certain religious capacities, since studying the poet trained students in the language of the New Testament, cultivated eloquence for preaching and teaching, and sharpened students' natural talents for leadership in church and society.

In the *Summary of Moral Philosophy*, Melanchthon had categorized the poet's works as a "*paraeneticus libellus*", or a "booklet of moral instruction" which, much like the Ten Commandments, presented moral philosophy in a simple and digestible format. The poet's simplicity and gravity set him above the other philosophers and made him especially appealing to the educator of young students. Hesiod offered students the core of morality without engaging in distracting sophistry. The second *Preface*, addressed to Melanchthon's students, underscores this last point, presenting Hesiod as a foundational source behind the works of later jurists and philosophers. Hesiod's mastery of poetic language lucidly illustrated moral concepts, making his moral teachings "a brilliant portrait for viewing, illustrated with vivid hues".[5]

Melanchthon also valued Hesiod because the poet, perhaps more than any other classical writer, brilliantly illustrated the connection between moral and natural philosophy.[6] In Melanchthon's mind, truths about morality and about natural phenomena were both part of God's design for nature. Both human reason and the wonder of the natural world were testaments to God the Creator and pointed human beings towards God. In the first *Preface*, Melanchthon wrote that "Every most honourable and serious teaching about all duties should be placed before our eyes, and we should compare every part of our lives to them, just as sailors direct their course according to the North Star."[7]

These *Prefaces* and the *occasio* (a brief introduction to Hesiod's text) are masterpieces of Renaissance brevity and style. They show Melanchthon at his most compelling, arguing for natural law, the importance of education, and

4 See p. 288 below.
5 See p. 285 below.
6 Modern scholarship has noted the strong connection between Melanchthon's moral philosophy and his natural philosophy. For the best work on this subject, see Sachiko Kusukawa, *The Transformation of Natural Philosophy*, esp. pp. 67–74. For Melanchthon's attempt to integrate disparate fields of human knowledge, see Sandra Bihlmaier, *Ars et Methodus: Philipp Melanchthon's Humanist Concept of Philosophy* (2018). For Melanchthon's relationship to contemporary natural philosophy, see Günter Frank and Stefan Rhein, *Melanchthon und die Naturwissenschaften seiner Zeit* (1998).
7 See p. 280 below.

the virtues of classical literature. It is unsurprising that these essays became mainstays in German editions of Hesiod for over a century, and they are an excellent starting point for Melanchthon's theory of natural law.

2 Printing History

As the following bibliography shows, Melanchthon's *Prefaces* and *occasio* became classic introductions to Hesiod's works and were included in numerous editions, translations, and commentaries on the Greek poet. These brief pieces were printed separately over thirty times and were included in editions stretching well into the seventeenth century. Because Claus' list is extremely reliable, I have drawn from his work to list the specific contents (i.e., whether each edition contains the first *Preface*, second *Preface*, and/or *occasio*).

1527. *Praefatio in Hesiodum.* (Wittenberg: Josef Klug). [Claus 1527.44 / VD 16 M 4008 / USTC 686172]. According to Claus, this contains the first *Preface* only.

1532. *ΗΣΙΟΔΟΥ ΤΟΥ ΑΣΚΡΑΙΟΥ ΕΡΓΑ ΚΑΙ ΗΜΕΡΑΙ. Una cum praefatione ac luculentissimis enarrationibus Philippi Melanchthonis* (Hagenau: Heirs of Johann Setzer). [Claus 1532.20 / VD16 H 2710 / USTC 662421] First *Preface* and *occasio* (*occasio* appears for the first time in this edition).

1533. *ΗΣΙΟΔΟΥ ΤΟΥ ΑΣΚΡΑΙΟΥ ΕΡΓΑ ΚΑΙ ΗΜΕΡΑΙ. Una cum praefatione ac luculentissimis enarrationibus Philippi Melanchthonis.* (Paris: Antoine Augereau). [Claus 1533.36 / USTC 181446]. First *Preface* and *occasio.*

1534. *ΗΣΙΟΔΟΥ ΤΟΥ ΑΣΚΡΑΙΟΥ ΕΡΓΑ ΚΑΙ ΗΜΕΡΑΙ. Hesiodi opera et dies. Una cum duabus praefationibus, ac luculentissimis Enarrationibus Phil. Melanch. iam recens conscriptis.* (Hagenau: Heirs of Johann Setzer, February 1534). [Claus 1534(1535).10.1 / VD16 H 2694 / USTC 662412]. Both *Prefaces* (second *Preface* appears for the first time in this edition) and *occasio.*

1534 or 1535. *ΗΣΙΟΔΟΥ ΤΟΥ ΑΣΚΡΑΙΟΥ ΕΡΓΑ ΚΑΙ ΗΜΕΡΑΙ. Hesiodi opera et dies. Una cum duabus praefationibus, ac luculentissimis enarrationibus Phil. Melanch. iam recens conscriptis.* (Hagenau: Heirs of Johann Setzer, February 1534/February 1535). [Claus (1534)1535.10.2]. / VD16 H 2695 / USTC 662411]. Both *Prefaces* and *occasio.* Title page reads MDXXXV; sig [L8]^{r} reads MDXXXIIII.

1534. *Compendium grammaticae Graecae Iacobi Ceporini, diligenter recognitum. Hesiodi Georgicon, ab eodem. Ceporino brevi scholio adornatum, ubi obiter et Graecorum carminum ratio declaratur. Philippi Melanchthonis in Hesiodum praefatio, ac luculentissimae enarrationes, nunc recens adiecta. Epigrammata quaedam lepida ab innumeris quibus scatebant mendis vindicata.* (Köln: Johann Gymnich). [Claus 1534.13 / VD16 W 2686 / USTC 623747]. First *Preface* and *occasio.*

1541. *ΗΣΙΟΔΟΥ ΤΟΥ ΑΣΚΡΑΙΟΥ ΕΡΓΛ* [sic] *ΚΑΙ ΗΜΕΡΑΙ. Hesiodi opera et dies una cum duabus praefationibus ac luculentissimis enarrationibus Phil. Melanch. iam recens conscriptis.* (Frankfurt: Peter Braubach, February 1541). [Claus 1541.22 / VD16 H 2699 / USTC 662414]. Both *Prefaces* and *occasio.*

1541. *Compendium grammaticae Graecae Iacobo Ceporino autore. Adiecimus Hesiodi georgicon, doctissimo eiusdem Ceporini enarratum scholio. Ad haec Philippi Melanchthonis praefationem, ac luculentissimas in Hesiodum enarrationes. Permultis quidem non sine sudore, quae multorum hactenus fefellere diligentiam, integritati verae restitutis.* (Köln: Johann Gymnich). [Claus 1541.34 / VD16 ZV 21721 / USTC 623744]. First *Preface* and *occasio.*

1543. *In Hesiodi libros de opere et die, enarrationes Phil. Melanch. Una cum elegantissima authoris praefatione.* (Paris: Jacques Bogard). [Claus 1543.65.1 / USTC 116820(?)]. First *Preface* and *occasio.*

1543. *In Hesiodi libros de opere et die, enarrationes Phil. Melanch.* (Paris: Jacques Bogard). [Claus 1543.65.2 / USTC 116820]. First *Preface* and *occasio.* According to Claus, this title lacks the phrase "*Una cum elegantissima authoris praefatione.*" The USTC entry seems to include this and the previous printing under the same entry.

1545. *Compendium grammaticae Graecae Iacobo Ceporino autore. Adiecimus Hesiodi georgicon, doctissimo eiusdem Ceporini enarratum scholio. Ad haec Philippi Melanchthonis praefationem, ac luculentissimas in Hesiodum enarrationes. Permultis quidem non sine sudore, quae multorum hactenus fefellere diligentiam, integritati verae restitutis.* (Köln: Martin Gymnich). [Claus 1545.27 / VD16 W 2689 / USTC 623781]. First *Preface* and *occasio.*

1546. *ΗΣΙΟΔΟΥ ΤΟΥ ΑΣΚΡΑΙΟΥ ΕΡΓΑ ΚΑΙ ΗΜΕΡΑΙ. Hesiodi opera et dies una cum duabus praefationibus ac luculentissimis Enarrationibus Phil. Melanch. iam recens conscriptis.* (Frankfurt: Peter Braubach). [Claus 1546.23 / VD16 ZV 7840 / USTC 662413]. Both *Prefaces* and *occasio.*

1549. *ΗΣΙΟΔΟΥ ΤΟΥ ΑΣΚΑΙΟΥ* [sic] *ΕΡΓΑ ΚΑΙ ΗΜΕΡΑΙ. Hesiodi opera et dies. Una cum duabus praefationibus ac luculentissimis enarrationibus Phil. Melanth. iam recens conscriptis.* (Frankfurt: Peter Braubach). [Claus 1549.11 / VD16 H 2702 / USTC 662410]. Both *Prefaces* and *occasio.*

1549. *ΗΣΙΟΔΟΥ ΤΟΥ ΑΣΚΑΙΟΥ* [sic] *ΕΡΓΑ ΚΑΙ ΗΜΕΡΑΙ. Hesiodi opera et dies. Una cum duabus praefationibus ac luculentissima versione carminis Hesiodici, per Georgium Rotallerum.* (Frankfurt: Peter Braubach). [Claus 1549.12 / VD16 ZV 7841 / USTC 662409]. Both *Prefaces* and *occasio.*

1550. *Hesiodi Ascraei opera, quae quidem extant, omnia Graece, cum interpretatione Latina eregione, ut conferri a Graecae linguae studiosis citra negocium possint. Adiectis iisdem Latino carmine elegantiss. versis, & Genealogiae deorum a Pylade Brixiano descriptae Libris V. Accessit nunc demum Herculis Scutum, doctiss. carmine a Ioanne Ramo conversum. Rerum et verborum in iisdem memorabilium index.* (Basel: Johannes Oporinus). [Claus 1550.12 / VD16 H 2682 / USTC 662389]. Second *Preface* only.

1553. *ΗΣΙΟΔΟΥ ΤΟΥ ΑΣΚΡΑΙΟΥ ΕΡΓΑ ΚΑΙ ΗΜΕΡΑΙ. Hesiodi opera et dies una cum duabus praefationibus ac luculentissimis enarrationibus Phil. Melanth. iam recens conscriptis.* (Frankfurt: Peter Braubach). [Claus 1553.18 / VD16 H 2704 / USTC 662415]. Both *Prefaces* and *occasio.*

1557. *ΗΣΙΟΔΟΥ ΕΡΓΑ ΚΑΙ ΗΜΕΡΑΙ.Hesiodi opera et dies. Una cum duabus praefationibus, ac luculentis enarrationibus Phil. Melanth. profuturis etiam ad intelligenda Hesiodi praecepta.* (Frankfurt: Peter Braubach). [Claus 1557.15 / VD16 H 2705 / USTC 662418]. Both *Prefaces* and *occasio.*

1559. *ΗΣΙΟΔΟΥ ΤΟΥ ΑΣΚΡΑΙΟΥ ΕΡΓΑ ΚΑΙ ΗΜΕΡΑΙ. Hesiodi opera et dies. Una cum duabus praefationibus ac luculentissimis enarrationibus Phil. Melanth. iam recens conscriptis.* (Frankfurt: Peter Braubach). [Claus 1559.15 / VD16 ZV 19108 / USTC 662422]. Both *Prefaces* and *occasio.*

1560. *Hesiodi Ascraei opera, quae quidem extant, omnia Graece, cum interpretatione Latina eregione, ut conferri a Graecae linguae studiosis citra negocium possint. Adiectis iisdem Latino carmine elegantiss. versis, & Genealogiae deorum a Pylade Brixiano descriptae Libris V. Accessit nunc demum Herculis Scutum, doctiss. carmine a Ioanne Ramo conversum. Rerum et verborum in iisdem memorabilium index.* (Basel: Johannes Oporinus). [Claus 1560.11 / VD16 ZV 25379 / USTC 662391] Second *Preface* only.

1561 or 1562. *Hesiodi Ascraei poema inscriptum ΕΡΓΑ ΚΑΙ ΗΜΕΡΑΙ, id est, Opera & Dies. Accedunt in idem brevia scholia Iacobi Ceporini, per Ioannem Frisium Tigurinum denuo aucta: in quibus dictiones & sententiae quaedam obscuriores, atque obiter Graecorum carminum ratio declarantur. Enarrationes item luculentissimae una cum Praefatione Philippi Melanchthonis. Adiecta est etiam recens Latina interpretatio Ioannis Frisij, qua verbum verbo quam proprijssime redditur.* [Zurich: Christoph Froschauer]. Date on title page is M.D.LXII., date on last page is December M.D.LXI. [VD16 H 2715 / USTC 662379]. First *Preface* only.

1564. *ΗΣΙΟΔΟΥ ΤΟΥ ΑΣΚΡΑΙΟΥ ΕΡΓΑ ΚΑΙ ΗΜΕΡΑΙ. Hesiodi opera et dies. Una cum duabus praefationibus ac luculentissimis enarrationibus Philip. Melanth. profuturis etiam ad intelligenda Hesiodi praecepta.* (Leipzig: Hans Rambau). [VD16 H 2706 / USTC 662419]. Both *Prefaces* and *occasio.*

1564. *Hesiodi Ascraei opera, quae quidem extant, omnia Graece, cum interpretatione Latina eregione, ut conferri a Graecae linguae studiosis citra negocium possint. Adiectis iisdem Latino carmine elegantiss. versis, & Genealogiae deorum a Pylade Brixiano descriptae Libris V. Accessit nunc demum Herculis Scutum, doctiss. carmine a Ioanne Ramo conversum. Rerum et verborum in iisdem mem-*

orabilium index. (Basel: Johannes Oporinus). [VD16 H 2683 / USTC 662390]. Second *Preface* only.

1564. *Hesiodi Ascraei opera, quae quidem extant, omnia Graece, cum interpretatione Latina eregione, ut conferri a Graecae linguae studiosis citra negocium possint. Adiectis iisdem Latino carmine elegantiss. versis, & Genealogiae deorum a Pylade Brixiano descriptae Libris V. Accessit nunc demum Herculis Scutum, doctiss. carmine a Ioanne Ramo conversum. Rerum et verborum in iisdem memorabilium index.* (Basel: Johannes Oporinus). [VD16 H 2684 / USTC 662392]. Second *Preface* only.

1564. *Hesiodi Ascraei opera, quae quidem extant, omnia Graece, cum interpretatione Latina eregione, ut conferri a Graecae linguae studiosis citra negocium possint. Adiectis iisdem Latino carmine elegantiss. versis, & genealogiae deorum a Pylade Brixiano descriptae libris V. Accessit nunc demum Herculis Scutum, doctiss. carmine a Ioanne Ramo conversum. Rerum et verborum in iisdem memorabilium index.* (Basel: Paul Queck). [VD16 H 2685 / USTC 662383]. Second *Preface* only.

1566. *ΗΣΙΟΔΟΥ ΤΟΥ ΑΣΚΡΑΙΟΥ ΕΡΓΑ ΚΑΙ ΗΜΕΡΑΙ. Hesiodi opera et dies. Una cum duabus praefationibus ac luculentis enarrationibus Philippi Melanchthonis, profuturis etiam ad intelligenda Hesiodi praecepta.* (Leipzig: Hans Rambau). [VD16 ZV 26908 / USTC 662420]. Both *Prefaces* and *occasio*.

1570. *ΗΣΙΟΔΟΥ ΤΟΥ ΑΣΚΡΑΙΟΥ ΕΡΓΑ ΚΑΙ ΗΜΕΡΑΙ. Hesiodi Ascraei opera et dies. Una cum duabus praefationibus ac luculentis enarrationibus Philippi Melanchthonis, profuturis etiam ad intelligenda Hesiodi praecepta.* (Mühlhausen: Georg Hantzsch). [VD16 ZV 23275 / USTC 662423]. Both *Prefaces* and *occasio*.

1576. *ΗΣΙΟΔΟΥ ΤΟΥ ΑΣΚΡΑΙΟΥ ΕΡΓΑ ΚΑΙ ΗΜΕΡΑΙ. Hesiodi Ascraei opera et dies. Una cum duabus praefationibus ac luculentis enarrationibus Philippi Melanchthonis, profuturis etiam ad intelligenda Hesiodi praecepta.* (Leipzig: Hans Rambau). [VD16 H 2707 / USTC 662425]. Both *Prefaces* and *occasio*.

1581. *ΗΣΙΟΔΟΥ ΤΟΥ ΑΣΚΡΑΙΟΥ ΕΡΓΑ ΚΑΙ ΗΜΕΡΑΙ. Hesiodi Ascraei opera et dies. Una cum duabus praefationibus ac luculentis enarrationibus Philippi Melanchthonis, pro futuris etiam ad intelligenda Hesiodi praecepta.* (Leipzig: Georg Deffner). [VD16 ZV 28170]. Both *Prefaces* and *occasio*.

1591. *ΗΣΙΟΔΟΥ ΤΟΥ ΑΣΚΡΑΙΟΥ ΕΡΓΑ ΚΑΙ ΗΜΕΡΑΙ. Hesiodi Ascraei opera et dies. Una cum duabus praefationibus ac luculentis enarrationibus Philippi Melanchthonis, profuturis etiam ad intelligenda Hesiodi praecepta.* (Leipzig: Abraham Lamberg). [VD16 H 2708 / USTC 662416]. Both *Prefaces* and *occasio*.

1601. *Poemata Hesiodi Ascraei, quae extant omnia, cum interpretatione Latina emendatiore. Accesserunt enarrationes Dn. Philippi Melanchthonis in ἔργα καὶ ἡμέρας. Et analysis eiusdem poematis XXIII. Tabulis comprehensa a M. Erasmo Schmidt, Graecae linguae Professore Witeb.* (Wittenberg: Lorenz Seuberlich, Samuel Selfisch). [VD17 23:285002Z / USTC 2135554]. Second *Preface* only.

1603. *Hesiodi Ascraei opera, quae quidem extant, omnia Graece, cum interpretatione Latina eregione, ut conferri a Graecae linguae studiosis citra negocium possint. Adiectis iisdem Latino carmine elegantiss. versis, et Genealogiae Deorum a Pylade Brixiano descriptae libris V. Accessit nuper Herculis Scutum, doctiss. carmine a Ioanne Ramo conversum. Item, rerum et verborum in iisdem memorabilium index.* (Leipzig: Abraham Lamberg). [VD17 3:301142Q / USTC 2136809]. Second *Preface* only.

1612. *ΗΣΙΟΔΟΥ ΣΩΖΟΜΕΝΑ, Hesiodi Ascraei quae exstant omnia, cum interpretatione Latina emendatiore. Accesserunt enarrationes Dn. Philippi Melanchthonis in ἔργα καὶ ἡμέρας et Analysis eiusdem Poematis ac Theogoniae, XXXVI tabulis comprehensa, opera M. Erasmi Schmidt Graeci Professoris Witeb.* (Wittenberg: Lorenz Seuberlich, Samuel Selfisch). [VD17 23:295200Y / USTC 2016065]. Second *Preface* only.

1615. *Hesiodi Ascraei opera, quae quidem extant: omnia Graece, cum interpretatione Latina eregione, ut conferri a Graecae linguae studiosis citra negocium possint. Adiectis iisdem Latino carmine elegantiss. versis, et Genealogiae Deorum a Pylade Brixiano descriptae libris V. Accessit nuper Herculis Scutum, doctiss. carmine a Ioanne Ramo conversum. Rerum et verborum in iisdem memorabilium index.* (Leipzig: Abraham Lamberg). [VD17 3:308915S / USTC 2042872]. Second *Preface* only.

1623. *ΗΣΙΟΔΟΥ ΣΩΖΟΜΕΝΑ, Hesiodi Ascraei quae exstant omnia, cum interpretatione Latina emendatiore. Accesserunt enarrationes Dn. Philippi Melanchthonis in ἔργα καὶ ἡμέρας. Et Analysis eiusdem Poematis ac Theogoniae, XXXVI tabulis comprehensa, opera M. Erasmi Schmidt, Graec: & Math: Profess: Witeb.* (Wittenberg: August Boreck, Samuel Selfisch). [VD17 1:087942D / USTC 2110609]. Second *Preface* only.

The 1623 work above was also reprinted in 1662 (Wittenberg: Johann Selfisch; Jena: Georg Sengenwald) [VD17 75:712462L / USTC 2712240] and 1672 (Leipzig: Fuhrmann and Wittigau) [VD17 547:717256V / USTC 2622523]. If these are reprints of the 1623 work, Melanchthon's second *Preface* should appear in them, but this editor has not been able to confirm this.

Melanchthon's *Prefaces to Hesiod* also appeared in several collections of his prefaces and orations. See the following entries in Claus: 1544.74, 1546.98, 1555.83, 1558.63, 1559.55.

3 A Note on the Text:

Included here are three of Melanchthon's prefatory works on Hesiod. The first text is Melanchthon's *First Preface to Hesiod*, which begins "*Cum de enarrando*

Hesiodo deliberarem". I translate here the second half of this *Preface*, which addresses moral philosophy. The first half addresses themes of literature and rhetoric.

Claus [1527.44] states that this *Preface* first appeared in Melanchthon's 1527 *Praefatio ad Hesiodum* (Wittenberg: Josef Klug), and that there are only two extant copies. Without access to this text, I base the translation here on the much more widely available 1532 edition entitled *ΗΣΙΟΔΟΥ ΤΟΥ ΑΣΚΡΑΙΟΥ ΕΡΓΑ ΚΑΙ ΗΜΕΡΑΙ, una cum praefatione ac luculentissimis enarrationibus Philippi Melanchthonis* (Hagenau: Heirs of Johann Setzer, 1532). The entire *First Preface* can be found in sigs. aii^r–b[vi]^r of the 1532 edition as well as in CR 18.167–183. The translation begins on the bottom of sig. b^v: "*Hesiodi autem prior libellus totus ἠθικός est* ...", which can be found on CR 18.178.

The second text is the entire *Second Preface* (beginning "*Quod in Plautina fabula histrio praefatur*"), which first appears in sigs. B3^v–[B6]^v of the 1534 edition entitled *ΗΣΙΟΔΟΥ ΤΟΥ ΑΣΚΡΑΙΟΥ ΕΡΓΑ ΚΑΙ ΗΜΕΡΑΙ; Hesiodi opera et dies, una cum duabus praefationibus, ac luculentissimis Enarrationibus Phil. Melanch. iam recens conscriptis*. (Hagenau: Heirs of Johann Setzer, 1534). This translation is based on that edition. The text is also found in CR 18.184–190.

The third text is Melanchthon's *occasio*, essentially a brief summary of Hesiod's work, which first appeared in the 1532 Setzer edition at sigs. d[viii]^r–d[viii]^v. The translation is based on this 1532 edition. The *occasio* can also be found in CR 18.189–192.

4 Edition

The First Preface (1532)

N.B.: This translation includes only the second half of this Preface, *which addresses moral philosophy. The first half treats themes of literature and rhetoric.*

sig. b^v / CR 18.178 **Philip Melanchthon's Preface to Hesiod**|

[...] So then, the first book of Hesiod is entirely moral [*ēthikos*], while the second offers teachings about | agriculture and encompasses the rising and setting of the stars and many other subjects which are useful for understanding nature.[8] For this reason, search for moral precepts in the first book, since it is

sig. bii^r

8 Melanchthon's edition in 1532 divided the *Works and Days* into two books. The second book begins on line 383 in modern editions.

impossible to lead an upright life unless, admonished and habituated by certain laws and teachings, we learn to discern good from evil and try to embrace those things which are proper and flee from what is not. Every most honourable and serious teaching about all duties should be placed before our eyes, and we should compare every part of our lives to them, just as sailors direct their course according to the North Star.

However, because certain people do not sufficiently value Hesiod's teachings because the man was a pagan and seems to have taught things foreign and contrary to our religion, this common error must be corrected. However, while that discussion is too long to be fully developed here, I have nevertheless decided that it will be worthwhile for me to explain the force and authority of the precepts of Hesiod and many other wise and learned men. For when they had observed that these precepts are proposed to us by nature, they displayed what they had
discovered and recounted it in their writings, in order to instruct | those who, 18.179
on account of the weakness of their talents or their young age, or | even because sig. bii^{v}
they were depraved by habituation in so many bad examples, could not see those things themselves.

Accordingly, we have asserted that those things which the learned pagans have derived from common sense and the judgment of nature and have passed on in their writings are no less divine commandments than those things which appear on the stone tablets of Moses. For it is generally accepted that certain laws about morals are divinely engraved upon the human mind, such as these: "No one should be harmed;" "Parents should be honoured;" "Thanks should be given to those who deserve it;" "The magistrates should be obeyed;" "Those who are entrusted to our care should be nurtured and protected;" "Promises should be kept."

Although certain wise men displayed these discovered [laws] to the ignorant, why should we not also call them "divine laws" and obey them just like the divine voice? For the heavenly Father himself did not intend for us to privilege those laws which he wrote in stone over those which he had impressed in the very perception of our souls—those which, as Paul says, "He had written on human hearts" [Romans 2:15]. All men agree about these [laws] such that there is no barbarism so wild, no men so hopelessly evil, that they would not agree
and confess that the | things which those judgments prescribe are correct and sig. biii^{r}
who, when they disobey, do not still reproach and condemn their own sin, and fear the existence of some divinity to whom they will pay the penalty for their deed even if no mortals ever discover it.

No nation is so monstrous that it does not silently hate and disdain the wicked, the cruel, and the ungrateful, and approve of those things which bind the human race together in society. For those who slaughter their guests, mur-

der their aging parents, or honour no faithfulness in marriage—such people,
if they are admonished, are compelled by nature to admit that they are doing
18.180 something unworthy of humanity. | And for those who are troubled by their
own crimes, such torment and terror vex their minds that it seems to be some
divine force which compels them to be ashamed at their acknowledged sin, and
fills them with fear of impending punishment.

Therefore, the human soul contains certain laws about morals which both
govern private life and teach one to establish and maintain the republic, exer-
cise judgments, and protect human society. And just as we confess that we are
sig. biii[v] created and preserved by God, so we should not doubt that | we have obtained
the following things in this life from heaven: these laws of life, and those little
sparks which show us what is good and warn us that the divine always reigns
and watches over all of man's designs and deeds, and is wont to punish his
sins.

In one passage, Paul calls ideas of this sort "the truth of God" [Romans 1:25] because he wanted to signify that these opinions were not handed down by our ancestors through some error, nor did they suddenly creep up on us or become lodged in our souls. Rather, they are so fixed in our minds that no force can remove or uproot them. When I weigh the authority of these laws and consider how religiously God demands that they be followed, I am deeply moved, and I am even more captivated by the ones who write them down, since I recognize that it was not without some mind, or, as [Hesiod] says, without "divinity"[9] that they gave to us these commandments for living.

Therefore, those who do not understand from whence so many good com-
mandments and weighty judgments proceed do not actually understand the
teachings of these authors. The Christian scriptures teach us in one way about
matters of religion, but when it comes to the manner of civic life, Christ intended
for us to obey the common precepts of nature. And indeed, the manner of civic
sig. biiii[r] life is not irrelevant to the Christian. | For that reason, if learned and skilled men
have advised certain things about this subject, they should not be overlooked. So
then, Hesiod's simplicity and gravity in teaching is such that I myself would set
the commentaries of no other philosopher above him. [The philosophers] often
miss the truth amidst their bickering while they strive to dissect everything
18.181 and quarrel odiously. | For, not to mention other things, many of the philoso-
phers remove God from the government of affairs and deny that he cares about

9 *numen divum*, i.e., not specifically the Christian God, but the general sense of divinity which pagans like Hesiod acknowledged.

the affairs of mortals. Nor do they observe that nature itself testifies to us that there is some mind which governs these human affairs, protects the good, and punishes the wicked.

Therefore, Hesiod is better, for in his teachings about justice he assigns the most severe penalties to the wicked and promises rewards to the good. I am reminded of a passage in Lucian, who, in his usual humorous manner, demands from Hesiod, why, although he promised to write about "*tat' eonta kai ta essomena*"—"both present and future"—he nevertheless made no predictions and left behind no prophecies about things to come.[10] But I assert that even those whom they call "soothsayers" [*Chaldaei*], who foretell the winner in games of chance or dice or even predict the weather, | are not prophets in sig.
comparison to Hesiod, who predicts the outcomes and consequences of men's b.iiii^{v}
decisions. This divination is derived from the most certain causes, and is most worthy of a good man. We have seen many other men use it, such as Plato, speaking about Dionysius, when he predicted the disastrous fall of the Tyrant.[11] No other type of prediction is more useful in life than this one, and if Nero, Domitian, and many others had placed their faith in it rather than in the vain promises of fortune tellers, they would not have fallen into such calamities.[12] So indeed, when we listen to Hesiod recount the punishments which await the wicked, let us consider that it is a divine voice, not merely a human one, which frightens us away from evil | and invites us to cultivate virtue. 18.182

I have spoken of the argument of the first book. The second book treats the rising and setting of the stars and many natural [*phusika*] subjects. And because the schools usually teach certain technical treatises about the nature of things, such as *The Commentary on the Sphere*,[13] or Aristotle's *Meteorology* or *On the Heavens*, it seems to me that Hesiod should be given a place here too, since he commented with remarkable care on the changing of the seasons, the rising of the stars, and the duration of days. | And it seems that he is among sig. bv^{r}
the best of the Greeks in his treatment of astronomy; both Aristotle and Pliny

---

10 cf. Lucian, *A Conversation with Hesiod* 1.

11 See Plato's critique of Dionysius I of Syracuse in his *Letter VII* (309a–352a). In this letter, Plato recounts several visits to Syracuse and his failed attempts to reform the tyrant Dionysius by teaching him philosophy.

12 For these emperors' reliance on divination, see Suetonius, *The Twelve Caesars*, "Nero" 40.2–3 and "Domitian", 14–16.

13 Johannes de Sacrobosco's *De Sphaera Mundi* (c. 1230), a foundational medieval and early modern text on astronomy. Melanchthon wrote a preface to this work. See *Liber Iohannis de Sacro Busto, de Sphaera. Addita est praefatio in eundem librum Philippi Melanchthonis ad Simonem Gryneum*. (Wittenberg: Joseph Klug, 1531). This work, alongside Melanchthon's preface, was reprinted well into the seventeenth century.

saw him as an author to be taken seriously on that subject, and they cite his testimony many times.[14] Moreover, he has an extensive understanding of all parts of nature, especially concerning the motions of the heavens and the stars. I do not think that Plato spoke unfairly when he said that those who have no interest in this art are not men, but swine.[15] For there has never been a sane man, who, even if he reckoned that the other arts were devised by human effort, upon seeing the great spectacle of astronomy, would think that anyone other than God could have designed and invented it. Therefore, even Manilius, the pagan writer, denies that it could have been the case that we understand things set so far beyond us unless they were divinely illustrated in the souls of men. For he says:

> "Who of mere human heart would have attempted so great a thing,
> Desiring to be seen as a god while the gods themselves disapproved?"[16]

For he perceived that there was some similarity with the divine and that know-
ledge of those things could be obtained. Moreover, it is not agreeable at this time
sig. bv^{v} to enumerate the benefits of this art, for they are | nearly infinite, and certain
ones are placed before our eyes such that even the ignorant can recognize them.

Therefore, because Hesiod contains precepts about the weightiest matters,
18.183 and is conducive to forming morals, | establishing a right manner of life, and
understanding natural phenomena, who could deny that he is most worthy of reading? Indeed, I myself think that he should be re-read often and memorized word-for-word. For is it not true that the eyes never get their fill of gazing upon excellent paintings, but the longer they linger on them, the more their admiration and desire to look at them grows? For is there anyone who, every time he enters our church, does not pause at those panels which either Dürer or our Lucas placed there?[17] Does the same thing not happen in pondering a magnificent poem? And indeed, I would fear to say nothing of that trunk and tree,[18] which merited the reading of an excellent and splendid song or two. In

---

14 See, for example, Aristotle, *Physics* IV.1 [208b.30–34] and Pliny, *Natural History* XVIII.56 (201); XVIII.57 (213).

15 cf. Plato, *Republic* 535e. In this passage, Plato compares those who have no desire for learning to pigs. He does not specifically mention astronomy.

16 Manilius, *Astronomica* I.28–29.

17 Albrecht Dürer (1471–1528) and Lucas Cranach the Elder (1472–1553). Dürer's 1504 painting *Adoration of the Magi* adorned the Wittenberg Castle church, and Cranach created a series of works for the church throughout the first half of the sixteenth century. Although Cranach would later produce the magnificent Wittenberg Altarpiece, that work did not yet exist when Melanchthon wrote this preface.

18 *truncum ac caudicem*, probably a reference to the cross within the Wittenberg church.

this way, it is just like in Virgil, when an eager and exultant Aeneas sees a shield sent down from heaven and carefully considers the meaning hidden in it. And indeed, when not only the detail of the work, | but also its visions of the future stirred him and held his attention, then, sig. [bvi]r

> "Unable to get his fill, he rolled his gaze over each of them,
> Marvelling, he turns them over and over in his hands and arms."[19]

In the same way, you should never get your fill or become weary of reading Hesiod. Rather, fasten your eyes closely upon him, examine every passage with the utmost diligence, and make yourself so familiar with his teachings that, whenever you deliberate about some matter, his most honourable precepts come to your mind. Adopt and borrow liberally from him in your speech, too. Indeed, insofar as we are able with our mean talent and learning, we will make every effort to ensure that no one regrets devoting his time to our commentaries on this poet.[20]

The Second Preface (1534)

|Philip Melanchthon, Another Preface to Hesiod sig. B3v / CR 18.184

In of one of Plautus' tales, the actor says as a preface that he "is coming to ask for a just and easy thing."[21] I myself can give the same preface much more justly on this topic, since, unlike Plautus, I am bringing to the stage not some ridiculous adultery,[22] but the weightiest precepts of life as well as certain topics about the nature of things and the rising and setting of the stars. For I have decided to expound upon Hesiod's *Works and Days*, and I urge you to devote yourself to learning this poem with the utmost care and diligence. Although I suspect that you largely understand how in doing this, I am not demanding anything detrimental, or beneath you, or foreign to your office, nevertheless, I will explain the rationale behind my decision.

---

19 This episode occurs in Virgil, *Aeneid*, VIII.608 ff. The latter lines are a direct quotation of *Aeneid* VIII.618–619. The poem refers to multiple objects—the arms, armour, and shield which Venus brought to Aeneas—but Melanchthon here focuses only on the shield.

20 The 1532 edition of *Works and Days* also included Melanchthon's commentary on the poem. For a critical edition of this commentary, see CR 18.191–264.

21 A paraphrase of Plautus, *Amphitryon*, line 33.

22 Plautus' *Amphitryon* recounts how Jupiter deceived and seduced Amphitryon's wife, Alcmene. Hercules was supposedly the son of Jupiter and Alcmene.

I have always taken care to set those authors before you who simultaneously cultivate knowledge of things and are highly beneficial for developing richness of speech. For these two elements are closely connected, and, as Horace says, "they have a friendly union",[23] such that each one stands and relies on the support of the other. For no one can speak well unless his heart is instructed by knowledge of the best things, and our knowledge is lame if we cannot employ
sig. B4r the light of oration. And just as | sailors chart their every course by the fixed stars, so in our studies, everything should be directed towards acquiring right knowledge of morals and nature as well as a certain moderate capacity to judge and explain weighty matters. Indeed, Hesiod is useful for both of these things, even though Quintilian considered him to be an author of rustic poetry.[24]

The entire first part of the work is moral [*ēthikē*]. It contains laws about life and morals which will be profitable for your manner of life and for judging the common duties of humanity—for I am not speaking of religion here. But if we think that we should study the commentaries of the jurists or the disputations
18.185 of the philosophers, so that in civic affairs we can better | understand what is fair or unfair, and if we think that we should gather representations of justice, equity, and other virtues from their writings, then it may help to seek those same things from this poet, from whom those very jurists and philosophers copiously borrowed. And there is a certain pleasure in drinking from the springs, if you can, for as Ovid says,

> "Although water fetched for you tastes sweet,
> It is finer to drink from the spring itself.
> To pluck the fruit from a lowered bough is better
> Than to take it from a fancy platter."[25]

For the other writers who offered precepts and laws about morals, because their speech is rude and paltry, could not set the full form and power of virtue before
sig. B4v our eyes. But Hesiod displays a certain brilliant portrait | for viewing, illustrated with vivid hues unspoiled by any added pigment, just like the colour in Apelles' paintings.[26]

---

23 cf. Horace, *Ars Poetica*, line 411.

24 See Quintilian, *The Orator's Education*, V.11.19.

25 Ovid, *Epistolae ex Ponto*, III.5.17–20.

26 A famous painter from the time of Alexander the Great. See Pliny the Elder, *Natural History*, 35.36.79–97. As footnote 87 in the CR explains, this line about Apelles appeared in many different forms in the various editions of this text. The 1534 edition reads *planeque talem qualis Appelles color, in tabulis spectandum exhibet*. The reading that makes the most

Further, just as architects hold enclosed in their minds certain forms of buildings which they imitate in construction; and as in the painter's mind, there resides a certain excellent image of beauty, and, setting it in his mind and envisioning it, [the painter] guides his art and his hands towards recreating it; in the same way, we should engrave a certain image of virtue upon our soul, which we should contemplate and apply in our deliberations. And this will be the case as often as we shall make judgments about the morals and duties of men, if we diligently consider the precepts of the best authors and gather from them a sure reckoning of all our duties. | And just as they say that Zeuxis, when he 18.186 had decided to paint a portrait of Helen for the citizens of Croton, selected five women from among all the virgins of that city so that he could paint Helen according to their model,[27] in the same way, we should take from the choicest authors a certain account of virtue which rules and governs all our deliberations.

So then, it seems to me first and foremost that Hesiod is useful for this task, because he indisputably holds first place among the aphoristic writers. For he does not provide bare precepts, but he dwells in some passages on the praise of virtue, in others on the eradication of vices. And he gravely and reverently teaches that which is most dutiful in frightening the souls of men away from wickedness: that the good will receive divine rewards for their good deeds, and the evil will pay the penalty for their crimes. | For that most prudent man recog- sig. B5^{r} nizes that we are led by nature to conclude that these mortal affairs are governed by a certain divinity, and that God is the avenger of injustice and advocate of the good. In this way, Hesiod is a much more serious teacher of morals than any of the philosophers, who, having tried to destroy heaven like the giants in the fables, remove God from the administration of things and loosen human souls from religion. Diogenes used to say that Harpalus, who was considered a successful con man in those times, "gave a testimony against the gods", since he lived for so long and with such good fortune.[28] But how much more of a philosopher is Hesiod, since he teaches that the gods are near to men and see our wicked deeds?

I urge you to cherish this poem and familiarize yourself with it, since it is indeed divine, or at least it may be divine, according to the argument that Hesiod

---

grammatical sense is that adopted by the CR: *planeque talem, qualem Apellis color in tabulis spectandam exhibet.*

27 Supposedly, Zeuxis had selected five of the most beautiful virgins from Croton, and compiled the best of their features into a composite model on which he based his painting of Helen.

28 This sentence is a quote from Cicero, *De Natura Deorum* III.34 (83). Harpalus was a Macedonian aristocrat who, while serving under Alexander the Great, repeatedly embezzled large amounts of public funds.

the shepherd is said to have received reeds from the Muses and to have sung
these precepts by their inspiration.[29] Cicero tells us that boys used to memorize
18.187 Hesiod just like our youths are taught certain prayers. And the Greeks | esteemed
him so highly that they preserved at Helicon a copy of the poem engraved in
lead.[30]

So much for the first part of Hesiod's song. The second part is mostly about
nature [*phusikē*]: it concerns the nature of the earth and its fruits, the wea-
ther, and the motion of the stars. Knowledge of these things is most noble
and delightful. For since nature was created and fashioned for humanity's sake
and for our use, it is disgraceful to refuse to contemplate the beautiful design
of that whole edifice, especially because that inquiry is so greatly beneficial
sig. B5v for | preserving good health and directing many other parts of life. Who is so
iron-hearted that, when he sits in the theatre as the games are taking place,
he is not even once seized by the desire to watch? And seeing that no spec-
tacles or games can offer the viewer more pleasure or benefit than the variety
of nature, it seems to me that those who neglect to turn their mind or their gaze
to the contemplation of nature are more properly called "living corpses" than
men.

Finally, Hesiod is very helpful for learning to speak well, for he carefully selects words which, when used opportunely, confer dignity on speech and add the weight of knowledge. How much weight do you think he adds to his oration by his nearly tragic exaggeration when he calls kings "Bribe-eaters"?[31] How charming a creation is "Right by might?"[32] There are six hundred more figures of this type which are not worth listing here, lest they lose some of their charm when torn off from the whole oration like a limb from a body.

And what shall we say of the whole structure of the oration, and of the style of his sentences? Fabius esteemed these things so highly that he awarded Hesiod first place among writers of the intermediate style.[33] Virgil, the prince of the

29 See Hesiod, *Theogony*, lines 22–34. In line 30, the Muses give to Hesiod a staff (*skēptron*), while Melanchthon's term here is *calamos*, which can mean rods, pipes, or pens made of reeds.

30 See Pausanias, *Description of Greece*, IX.31.4.

31 See *Works and Days*, lines 221 and 264. The Greek term, which Melanchthon cites in the text, is *dōrophagous*.

Works and Days, line 189. The Greek term is *cheirodikai*—loosely, "those who assert their … by their hands."

…fers to Quintilian, *The Orator's Education*, X.1.52. According to Quintilian, the … style" of oratory was used to charm and delight the audience. See *The Ora-* …10.58–65.

Latin poets, and Ovid incorporated the choicest passages [of his] into their own works, and they judged[34] that this would add significant embellishment to their own poems. And without doubt, [Hesiod] will render our own speech richer and more eloquent. And one will not waste his time if he takes those things which we have excerpted from [Hesiod] and compares them to the Greek original, for in so doing, | the particularities of each language will be more firmly understood, 18.188
and | the style of each word and sentence will be seen more clearly when one sig. [B6]r
focuses on them.[35] It will also be profitable for you to set forth some particularly flowery passage into Latin verse by your own prowess, and it is difficult to express how much this exercise sharpens one's judgment, and how much it contributes towards cultivating richness of speech and acquiring the knowledge for explaining obscure matters—but we will advise about these things in our commentary.

Someone may ask: What benefit does this entire method of learning offer to piety? I would immediately respond that it benefits nothing towards transforming the mind and imbuing[36] it with religion, for the heavenly spirit accomplishes that through sacred language [*per sacrum sermonem*]. But Greek literature is necessary for understanding the language of the holy scriptures, and then, in order for us to make more accurate judgments about language, and to be able to interpret and explain religious dogma whenever the public benefit demands it, natural talent must be trained and cultivated broadly with every discipline. For just as ferns suddenly spring up in abandoned fields, so our talents, unless they are purified with elegant literature, have their intellectual power choked out and killed as if by hostile weeds, such that they cannot explain or make sense of obscure matters and bring them into the open[37] light.

Eloquence is a certain great virtue, and, as [Euripides] said in the tragedy, "the master of affairs,"[38] by which we can speak of obscure matters clearly and in good order, and no one can acquire it without wide training and great experience in those arts which are included in the name "humanities". This is the reason why I believe that these arts will profit even the study of religion, about which | sig. [B6]v

34 1534 erroneously reads *iudicavitque*. Later editions, such as the 1546 Frankfurt (Braubach) edition, read *iudicarintque*.

35 Melanchthon here refers to his "*Enarrationes*", the commentary which he included at the end of the various Hesiod editions. In the commentary, Melanchthon excerpts difficult phrases and glosses them with Latin translations and explanations.

36 1534 incorrectly reads *imbuendaque*. The correct reading, which is followed in many later editions, is *imbuendamque*. See CR 18.188, fn. 1.

37 1534 erroneously reads *apertum*. The correct reading is *apertam*.

38 Euripides, *Hecuba*, line 816.

I will not speak any longer here, lest I seem[39] to offer "twice-cooked cabbage" [*dis krambēn*],[40] as they say, since I have taken up this matter elsewhere.

So then, I exhort you as strongly as I can, just as I said at the beginning, to
18.189 decide for yourself what fruit is proper for you seek from your studies, and | to embark upon that course of studies which will render the greatest benefit to you personally as well as to the republic. "Is there something you are shooting at," says Persius, "At which you aim your bow? Or are you randomly chasing ravens with shards of brick and mud, unconcerned by where your feet take you, living moment to moment?"[41] And in this way, many people, after they have consumed a good part of their life in study, still do not seem to me to have considered what they are doing, or why they are toiling, or what harvest they should expect from their studies. But truly, is it not simple insanity that, although they have studied for so long, they can provide no firmer judgments about religion or
18.190 other things than a common person can, and whenever | the Republic demands their voice or their counsel, they are more silent than the fishes? But in truth, just as the traveller's first task is to choose his destination, so in your studies, before anything else, you should deliberate about the fruit of your studies, and then you should embark on a direct route for accomplishing the matter. In this way, we should read and become acquainted with every writer in order to have some certain things at hand about religion and nature, which we can produce as often as the course of life demands. And you should cultivate richness of speech, by which you will be able to speak your mind clearly whenever some controversy arises. Understand that this is the established goal of your studies to which you should direct every deliberation of your soul.

The Occasio

sig. [d viii]r / CR 18.189 The Poet's Occasion for Writing, and the Argument of the Books|

Since, when interpreting an author, one should first observe the writer's intent and the argument of the work, let us also examine Hesiod's purpose in writing this poem. Indeed, it is clear that Hesiod composed this poem for his own people, among whom he lived, specifically to prescribe for them a certain method for

39 1534: *videat*. The correct reading, *videar*, is found in the 1546 edition.

40 The original Greek proverb, which Melanchthon alludes to here, is *dis krambē thanatos*: "Twice-cooked cabbage is death." It was perhaps an allusion to the smell of re-heated cabbage, and a warning against redundancy. Equivalent to the modern English saying, "I don't chew my cabbage twice". See Erasmus, *Adagia* I.5.38 (ASD II.1, pp. 512–514).

41 Persius, *Satires*, III.60–62.

right living and, so to speak, laws for a more civil and more honourable life. For in the first book, he exhorts [the reader] to cultivate justice and teaches precepts which are useful and necessary for leading an excellent life. Then in the second book, he gives an account of agriculture and urges [his readers] towards hard work. For idleness often | begets many ills, and it is hardly possible for the 18.190
idle to keep themselves from wrongdoing. Accordingly, Hesiod reckoned that he should teach precepts not only about justice, but about hard work as well. And indeed, in that place[42] he also includes the most beautiful description of the seasons and the span of virtually an entire year. | He added many natural sig. [d viii]v
and astronomical subjects too: the weather, the rising and setting of the stars, and other things absolutely worth knowing, all of which Virgil indeed imitated in his *Georgics*.[43] | Moreover, all of this is taught not just for us to recognize and 18.191
observe the proper seasons for tilling and planting, but also because many civic duties depend on a fixed outline of the year and the seasons. Indeed, it seems that Hesiod received his occasion for writing this work from the injustices of his brother Perses, who had defrauded [Hesiod] in the division of his inheritance.[44] Therefore, he uses the character of Perses to exhort everyone to justice and equity.[45] | 18.192

Moreover, the poet Hesiod was a priest of the temple of the Muses at Helicon, a mountain in Boeotia. He lived in the village of Ascra, nestled right at the foot of that mountain. Further, Pausanias wrote that in his own times, there was nothing left of Ascra except a single tower, and he says that he had seen the *Works* of Hesiod carved in lead at Helicon.[46] In addition, Hesiod lived one hundred years after Homer, as the Suda says, and Cicero does not disagree that Hesiod came later [than Homer].[47]

The entire work, especially the first book, is hortatory [*parainetikon*] and moral. And the Greeks traditionally memorized this poet just as our youths

42 i.e., the second book.

43 The 1534 edition inserts here "And for this reason, I think that those who diligently compare Hesiod's teachings here to passages of Virgil will be doing something well worth his while."

44 See *Works and Days*, lines 27–44.

45 Several times in the *Works and Days*, Hesiod addresses his brother Perses to urge his readers to fairness and justice. See, for example, lines 10, 27–45, 274–292. This translation of the *occasio* is based on the 1532 Setzer edition, but in later editions, Melanchthon inserts here the Greek text of lines 274–276 and 248–250. See CR 18.191, n. 13.

46 Pausanias, *Description of Greece*, IX.31.4. The *Works* (*opera*) is a reference to Hesiod's *Works and Days*.

47 For various positions on the temporal relationship between Homer and Hesiod in the *Suda*, including the idea that Hesiod lived a century after Homer (an idea attributed to Porphyry), see *Suidae Lexicon*, ed. Bekker (Berlin: 1854), p. 484. Cicero believed that Homer had lived many generations before Hesiod. See *De Senectute* XV.54.

memorize certain prayers. Therefore, both on account of the knowledge of language, as well as on account of the civil precepts which are eminently useful and necessary for establishing an excellent life, it is right for the serious young student to love this poet above all, and to read and memorize him with the utmost diligence.

CHAPTER 4

The Preface to Xenophon's Collected Works

1 Introduction

In this *Preface* to Xenophon's works, Melanchthon presents a powerful case for the study of history. Unlike the other texts in this volume, this *Preface* does not touch upon the universal, transhistorical values of the natural law. It is concerned with the uses of history for navigating the complexities of moral life. Nevertheless, the *Preface* is included here because of its obvious ethical and political content, and because it provides an alternative perspective on Melanchthon's thought to that of the other texts. The major purpose of this volume is to demonstrate that the natural law was central to Melanchthon's moral and political thought, but this text shows that Melanchthon's approach to the morality of leadership and everyday life was not limited to legal and philosophical categories. His humanist moral vision placed a high value also on the wisdom needed to navigate the vicissitudes and particularities of political life, and such wisdom was to be acquired through the study of history.

As the works in this volume show, Melanchthon's approach to classical texts was supple and many-faceted. He drew upon philosophers like Aristotle and Cicero to work out a theory of natural morality. He looked to Hesiod as a teacher of natural moral precepts and natural philosophy. In the *Comparison*, he even read ancient oratory as a historical source for classical Athenian law. In the *Preface* to Xenophon, Melanchthon shows that classical literature could also be valuable in shaping character, providing ethical models, and above all, helping a person navigate the tempestuous winds of fortune.

The *Preface* opens with a critical question: If fortune seems to rule our lives, then what is the purpose of wisdom? The relationship between fortune and human agency had occupied much of Renaissance philosophy. One of the most famous answers was that of Niccolò Machiavelli, that "[F]ortune is a woman, and if you want to control her, it is necessary to treat her roughly."[1] In contrast to this aggressive view, Melanchthon provides a different metaphor: Fortune is like an unruly wind which a sailor must navigate. In his framework, it is not the ruler's forceful *virtú* that bends fortune to his will. Instead, the individual's

1 Machiavelli, *The Prince*, ed. Quentin Skinner and Russel Price (1988), chapter 25, p. 87.

 | HTTPS://DOI.ORG/10.1163/9789004774742-007

doctrina, his intellectual and moral formation, allows him to steer his life in the face of the contrary and unpredictable winds of fortune.

Throughout the *Preface*, Melanchthon posits the manifold benefits of studying history. Most obviously, history provides both positive and negative ethical examples. Xenophon himself holds up the brilliant example of King Cyrus as well as the disastrous model of Alcibiades. History also admonishes us about the danger of immoderate ambition, arrogance, and desire, as the tale of King David illustrates. More broadly, history facilitates self-reflection on human origins, a key trait which distinguishes humans from beasts. Ancient historians like Xenophon and Herodotus also provide insights into the pagan nations such as the Assyrians and Persians who appear in the Old Testament histories. With this point, we see Melanchthon already beginning to integrate sacred and secular history, a project which later Protestant historians like Johann Sleidan and David Chytraeus, among others, would continue throughout the sixteenth century.[2] In addition, Melanchthon praises Xenophon as a model of eloquence for aspiring orators and writers.

Finally, Melanchthon draws particular attention to Xenophon's theme of moderation in times of civic strife. Of particular importance here is the example of the Athenian amnesty, recounted in the second book of Xenophon's *Hellenika*, which picks up from the end of Thucydides' *History of the Peloponnesian War*. As Xenophon relates, after Sparta defeated Athens, the Spartans established an oligarchic government there which became known as the "Thirty Tyrants". The Thirty essentially served as tyrannical Spartan puppets until they were overthrown by the Athenian exile Thrasybulus, who re-established democracy in Athens in 403 BCE. The city was still bitterly divided between those who favoured democracy and those who favoured oligarchy, however. To make a way forward for Athenian civic peace, Thrasybulus granted a general amnesty that pardoned all but the most extreme oligarchists.[3]

When Melanchthon appeals to the amnesty towards the end of the *Preface*, the reader begins to get the sense that this work is both an ode to history as well as a bit of political manoeuvring.[4] While this volume has stressed Melanchthon's status as a philosopher, his conciliatory personality and widespread reputation as a brilliant thinker also made him one of the Reformation's most prominent

---

Lutheran universal history, see Mark Lotito, *The Reformation of Historical Thought* (2019) …-Tov, *Lutheran Humanists and Greek Antiquity*, pp. 35–82.

…unted in Xenophon, *Hellenika*, II.2.21–II.4.43.

…ent, see Batson, "Philip Melanchthon's Humanist Politics: Greek Scholarship …ssional Crisis", *Reformation & Renaissance Review* 24.1 (2022): 23–43, esp.

diplomats. The *Preface* to Xenophon highlights how Melanchthon could use his scholarly works to weigh in on matters of international diplomacy.

The parallel between Xenophon's depiction of Athenian civil strife and the religious conflicts within Germany was obvious. But this was in fact more directly a context for the *Preface*, for it was addressed to a sympathetic French ambassador and confidant of King Francis I, Guillaume du Bellay (1491–1543), who had been one of the chief diplomats tasked with building French connections with the German Protestant princes. From France's perspective, while the German princes offered an appealing ally against Francis' rival Charles V, the strategic benefits of an alliance with the Schmalkaldic League sat uneasily with widespread French opposition to Protestantism.

In the early and mid-1530s, Francis managed to navigate these tensions and offer his support to the German Protestants. In May 1534, du Bellay had travelled to Zürich, where he presented a plan for an ecumenical cooperation and political alignment between Protestants and French Catholics. In response to an invitation from du Bellay, Melanchthon quickly sent the king a highly ecumenical list of doctrinal articles (the *Consilium ad Gallos*) in which the reformer sought to highlight areas of agreement between Catholicism and evangelical theology.[5] In June 1535, Francis invited Melanchthon to Paris for a conference on doctrinal matters. Du Bellay followed up by personally encouraging Melanchthon to attend, but the visit fell through, not least because more hardline Lutheran reformers criticized Melanchthon's supposed compromises on core doctrinal matters.[6] After the abortive mission to France, and in the aftermath of the October 1534 Affair of the Placards, French mistrust of Protestantism skyrocketed, and by 1538, Francis I had swung back towards normalizing relations with Charles V, a situation reflected by the 1538 Truce of Nice.[7] In the summer of 1540, the status of Protestants in France would worsen considerably when the Edict of Fontainebleau codified persecution of French Huguenots. Thus, in early January 1540, when Melanchthon wrote this letter, he wrote as an embattled yet experienced intermediary between Francis I and the French Protestants, at a time when relations between the two sides were extremely precarious.

Although relations worsened as the year progressed, Melanchthon remained intent upon cultivating connections with France. In late 1540, Melanchthon

5 See Irene Dingel, "Melanchthon's Paraphrases of the Augsburg Confession".

6 For the negotiations between Du Bellay and Melanchthon, see V.-L. Bourrilly, *Guillaume du Bellay, seigneur de Langey, 1491–1542* (1905), pp. 173–213 and B.H. Pershing, "The Proposed Mission of Melanchthon to France", *Church History* 3.1 (1934): 41–59.

7 See D.L. Potter, "Foreign Policy in the Age of the Reformation: French Involvement in th Schmalkaldic War, 1544–1547", *The Historical Journal* 20.3 (1977): 525–544, esp. pp. 526

attended a convention at Worms to debate the Augsburg Confession with Charles V's representatives. The negotiations stalled, and on December 7, Melanchthon wrote to du Bellay, urging him to apply his considerable diplomatic skills to the meeting. In this letter, Melanchthon explicitly referenced the Xenophon *Preface* and wrote to du Bellay, "What I asked you there [in the *Preface*] publicly, I now ask again: that for the sake of learning, for the health of the Church, for the safety of so many nations, I urge you to be an advocate [to the king], lest the controversies of the Church be decided by ungodly arms, instead of, as befits great kings, being resolved by moderate counsels."[8]

In addition to its praise of history and its diplomatic aim, Melanchthon's *Preface* also introduced a triumphal achievement of classical scholarship in northern Europe. The *Preface* appeared in the first complete edition of Xenophon's Greek works, a three-volume edition published by Peter Braubach in Schwäbisch Hall in 1540.[9] Melanchthon did not edit this work, but the fact that he wrote the *Preface* for such a monumental work of philology is a testament to his great stature as the preeminent scholar of antiquity in sixteenth-century Germany.

2 Printing History

1540. *ΞΕΝΟΦΩΝΤΟΣ ΑΠΑΝΤΑ Xenophontis opera omnia, in tres partes distincta, quarum quaeque suos libros ostendet. Τὸ πρῶτον μέρος τάδε παρέχει. Ξενοφῶντος βίος ἐκ τῶν Λαερτίου. Κύρου παιδείας Βιβλία ή. Αναβάσεως Βιβλία ζ'. / Vita Xenophontis ex Laertio. Cyri Paediae lib. VIII. Cyri Anabaseos, i. ascensus in Persidem lib. VII.* (Schwäbisch Hall: Peter Braubach). [Claus 1540.79 / VD16 X 2 / USTC 707512]

1540. *ΞΕΝΟΦΩΝΤΟΣ ΑΠΑΝΤΑ. Hoc est, Xenophontis opera omnia, in tres partes distincta* ... (Schwäbisch Hall: Peter Braubach). [VD16 ZV 23091 / USTC 707484]

1545. Ξενοφῶντος ἅπαντα. *Xenophontis oratoris et historici, propter synceram et melle dulciorem Attici sermonis gratiam, veterum omnium iudicio longe clarissimi, opera, quae quidem graece extant, omnia, duobus tomis distincta, ac nunc primum a Seb. Castalione a mendis quamplurimis repurgata, & quam fieri potuit accuratissime recognita. His accessit graecus rerum gestarum Index perquam copiosus.* (Basel: Michael Isengrin, ca. 1545) [Claus 1545.11 / VD16 X 3]

1545. *ΞΕΝΟΦΩΝΤΟΣ ΑΠΑΝΤΑ. Hoc est, Xenophontis opera omnia, in tres partes distincta, quarum quaeque suos libros ostendet. Τὸ πρῶτον μέρος τάδε παρέχει.*

8 See CR 3.1191 = MBW 2575.

9 See CTC vol. VII, p. 82.

Ξενοφῶντος βίος ἐκ τῶν Λαερτίου. Κύρου παιδείας Βιβλία ή. Αναβάσεως Βιβλία ζ'. Hoc est, Vita Xenophontis ex Laertio. Cyri Paediae libri VIII. Cyri Anabaseos, id est, ascensus in Persidem libri VII. (Frankfurt: Peter Braubach) [Claus 1545.18]

Melanchthon's *Preface* to Xenophon was also reprinted in several collections of his orations and prefaces. See the following entries in Claus: 1541.81, 1544.74, 1544.98, 1555.83, 1558.63, 1559.55.

3 A Note on the Text

This translation is based upon USTC 707512; *ΧΕΝΟΦΩΝΤΟΣ ΑΠΑΝΤΑ: Xenophontis opera omnia, in tres partes distincta, quarum quaeque suos libros ostendet.* (Schwäbisch Hall: Peter Braubach, 1540), sigs. [1]^{v}–[5]^{r}. It is also found in CR 3.1113–1117 / MBW 2341. The text has been previously translated into German in MD III.218–224.

4 Edition

The Preface to Xenophon's Collected Works

sig. 1^{v} / CR 3.1113 / MBW 2341

Philip Melanchthon to the most illustrious du Bellay, Seigneur de Langey, counsellor to the magnificent King of France.

"Fortune, not wisdom, is the ruler of life", as someone said in a tragedy.[10] Although great and distinguished men as well as the common people are wont to applaud this proverb, it nevertheless stands in need of correction. We see that life is full of great mistakes, and even outstanding men are held back by terrible fortune and empires are shaken by fatal tumults, such that there seems to be little place for wisdom. And if we call to mind the best and wisest rulers of cities and empires, we will find many whose well-considered plans, it seems, had the most woeful ends.

In this volume, Xenophon describes the sequential destruction of three of the most prosperous cities when war had first broken out under the direction of Pericles, who "thundering" eloquently, (as they say in the comedies), threw Greece into chaos.[11] Accordingly, | Athens fell first. Next, the victorious state of sig. 2^{r}

10 Melanchthon's Latin is a citation of Cicero's *Tusculan Disputations* V.9 (25), which was in turn a citation of Theophrastus. The saying reflects a common theme in ancient tragedy, that fortune can ruin even the best laid-plans.

11 The three cities are Athens, Sparta, and Thebes. Pericles was the leader of Athens at the

Sparta fell into a similar calamity, even though it was led by King Agesilaus, who outstripped all other kings of his age in virtue and the magnitude of his deeds. Soon thereafter, Thebes also began to decline. Not long afterwards, Macedon pressed all of Greece into slavery while Demosthenes sounded a call to arms.[12] And how great was Cicero's mistake in committing command of the army and the whole republic to a youth who could not yet even rule himself?[13] Therefore, because the power of the fates or fortune is great, as men say, it is customary to ask: what good are the precepts of wisdom handed down in literature and
3.1114 history? | For if life cannot be ruled by the counsels of the wise, then why is doctrine recommended?[14]

I think that there are many men who govern lofty affairs who do not direct their plans according to any certain rule or doctrine. Instead, they set sail for wherever the wind blows and surrender themselves to fortune. But a man deserves more than this rash and blind manner of living. For even if that proposed rudder[15] is not always able to steer one's life, it is still gift of God, who intended for men to be habituated and governed through doctrine, and this gift is not useless or worthy of scorn. For not even medicine always cures a disease, but rather, as they say, "sometimes the sickness overcomes the skilful art."[16]

There is a great weakness in human nature. On account of that fact, it happens that men do not always obey doctrine. Many lack diligence, and [diligence] is
sig. 2v also overpowered in the absence of | fear and knowledge of God. And either God punishes the impiety of men, or that spirit, burning with hatred of God, runs rampant in some men, and just as that spirit is the author of human calamities,

beginning of the Peloponnesian War between Athens and Sparta. Xenophon's *Hellenika* picks up where Thucydides' *History of the Peloponnesian War* left off, covering the aftermath of Athens' defeat as well as the subsequent rise and fall of Sparta and Thebes. The reference to Pericles "thundering" is in Quintilian, *The Orator's Education* II.16.19, which is in turn a reference to Aristophanes, *Acharnians*, lines 530–531.

12 Demosthenes was the central figure in Athenian politics for about thirty years beginning around 354 BCE. He was the chief of the "hawkish" Athenian faction and he sought an aggressive Athenian response to growing Macedonian imperialism under Philip II and his son Alexander. See especially Demosthenes' *Olynthiacs* and *Philippics* for these anti-Macedonian speeches.

13 A reference to Cicero's support for the young Octavian.

14 For Melanchthon, the term *doctrina* encompasses a broad concept of education that shaped the student's mind and soul and prepared him for life and leadership. In this *Preface*, Melanchthon uses the term specifically to refer to education and training through the reading of ancient historical texts. To maintain consistency with the other texts in this volume, the term is translated here as "doctrine," although "education", "instruction", or even "training" all convey a similar idea.

15 i.e., doctrine.

16 Ovid, *Ex Ponto* I.3.18.

so he never ceases to inflict his own savagery upon the human race. Because this is the case, we should acknowledge our weakness, seek the true remedy, guide our minds with doctrine, and stir up diligence, which often prevails, but especially so when it is accompanied by the knowledge of God.

Therefore, the knowledge of history is highly beneficial in life because it holds forth contrary examples. By some [of these examples], it demonstrates how doctrine benefited many men, such as David, Cyrus, and Scipio. On the other hand, it shows others whose plans ended in failure, who were cast down from favourable circumstances and who ruined both themselves[17] and their republics: Pompey, Caesar, and Xenophon's subjects here, Alcibiades and Agesilaus. These examples warn us about our own weakness. For what Hippocrates says—that in disease, it is a bad sign if the mind grows sick[18]—is the most wretched thing in all of life: not to understand or acknowledge the sickness by which men, driven by some desire, rush to their ruin. Either by faith in their own strength or by some other error, they are swept beyond the limits until they crash.

Therefore, not only should we seek precepts about conducting affairs from history, which advises us about all sorts of different cases, but also Adrastia,[19] which appears everywhere in history, should admonish us about our weakness and exhort us to moderation. Otherwise, puffed up by pride and self-confidence, | we will undertake unjust | or unnecessary endeavours, we 3.1115
will strive against God's will, and we will relax our diligence like David did.[20] sig. 3r
This wisdom is great and necessary for all men, and most of all for those who govern human affairs. Moreover, even for average men, the history of all times carries great value for strengthening one's judgment and, so to speak, reining in immoderate impulses. Indeed, I have decided not to enumerate here the many other benefits [of history], which are much richer and fuller than words can adequately explain.

How shadowy would life be if God had not decided to preserve the histories about the origins of things: the birth and spread of true religion, the rise of superstitions, the succession of empires and their growth and decline? The histories of such things were not divinely preserved and passed down without the singular counsel of God, and the wise readily understand their utility. For if this lineage remained unknown, we could no more reflect back on the origins of things than can beasts.

---

17 *et se*. CR erroneously reads *etsi*.

18 cf. Hippocrates, *Aphorisms* II.6, II.33.

19 This Greek term means "the Inevitable," and it was a title of the Greek goddess Nemesis. The idea is that history gives examples of inevitable punishment for evil deeds.

20 The reference is probably to David's adultery with Bathsheba in 2 Samuel 11.

Further, in order to grasp the successions of empires, one needs not only the sacred histories, but also the records of the other nations. Therefore, I often think that it was by divine influence that there are brilliant Greek writers who survive, and who begin their history right at the point where the prophets left off, so that they speak like a witness about the older writers. Herodotus and
sig. 3^v Xenophon confirm that the Chaldeans | and Assyrians, and then the Medians, were the first people to have ruled vast kingdoms. These empires are described in scripture. Next came the Persians, from whom the Greeks begin their history. Moreover, knowing the succession of empires helps one understand scripture and contemplate the spread of true religion. Indeed, the description of the Babylonian captivity in Xenophon fits neatly with the account of Daniel. Truly, it even seems to me that Gobryas, whose son was killed by the Babylonian tyrant, was a part of Daniel's circle.[21] And the succession of monarchies found in the seventh chapter of Daniel is necessary for explaining the times.[22] Therefore, those who love true religion should not ignore these records.

Nor should the other benefits [of history] be neglected. Xenophon's history is complex, and it can instruct the reader with a certain variety of examples. In *The Education of Cyrus*,[23] he depicts a prince who, almost from the cradle, is so
3.1116 outstanding in all virtues—justice, magnanimity, prudence, temperance, | moderation, and integrity—that goodness and gentleness always shine throughout the land as Hesperus[24] shines among the stars. Therefore, because Scipio, who read these books even in camp among the trumpet-calls and clanging of arms, modelled himself entirely after this portrait[25]—although he undertook things that were most challenging, and most useful to his country—[Scipio's] victories, no matter how glorious, still did not even earn him as much true praise as did that moderation of soul by which he avoided doing anything to his fellow citi-

21 Gobryas features prominently in Xenophon's *Cyropedia*. The account of his son's death is found in *Cyropedia*, IV.6.1–11. Melanchthon may be identifying "Darius the Mede", mentioned in Daniel 5:31 and 9:1, as Gobryas, or he may be identifying Gobryas with another character in Daniel. See also Melanchthon's commentary on Daniel 5 in CR 13.852.

22 The succession of empires found in Daniel 7 provided the foundational organizing scheme for the Lutheran conception of history. Melanchthon's own historical work explained world history in terms of this scheme, as did the histories of his followers Johann Sleidan and David Chytraeus. See Melanchthon on the four world monarchies in the preface to *Carion's Chronicle* (CR 12.718–720).

23 Also known as the *Cyropedia*.

24 Hesperus is the evening star, or Venus, which is the brightest star in the twilight sky.

25 Scipio Africanus the Younger (184/5–129 BCE). For Scipio's emulation of Cyrus, see Cicero, *Letters to Quintus* I.1.23.

zens out of arrogance or to his enemies out of cruelty—a spirit which inspired rivals and glorified [him], as Cyrus himself glorified Cyaxares.[26] | sig. 4ʳ

And indeed, if only, following Scipio's example, the princes of this age would also read this history and rouse themselves to imitate it, such that Xenophon's saying could be made manifest: "Good rulers are no different from good fathers."[27] What astonishing examples of civic disturbances and acts are there in the history of the Greek cities! I will not mention them all, but every wall should have depicted the story of Theramenes, who, because he ensured at great risk to himself that the Athenian state would not be entirely destroyed, and afterwards strove to soften the savagery of his colleagues, was cruelly killed by Critias and his associates.[28] His death advises not only of the dangers which await moderate men in the midst of civil strife, but also advises us to bolster our souls such that we do not allow ourselves to be dissuaded from right belief by any terrors or punishments. Clearly, the republic often finds itself in times which call for a similar moderation and seriousness, and the value of such things is apparent in some verses about Palamedes, recited in the Athenian theatre after the murder of Socrates. In these verses, when the poet announced that Palamedes had been the greatest of the Greeks and the nightingale of the Muses, a benefit to the republic, he meant that the chief threat to tyrants is those who stand out in virtue and erudition. So then, here are those verses:

> "You have killed, you have killed the noblest of the Greeks,
> The nightingale of the Muses, who hurt no one."[29]

---

26 Cyrus' uncle Cyaxares is a major character in the *Cyropedia*. This may be a reference to *Cyropedia* VIII.5.17–20, where Cyrus honours his uncle with a palace in Babylon and a host of other gifts.

27 A paraphrase of *Cyropedia* VIII.1.1.

28 Theramenes was an Athenian leader and one of the Thirty Tyrants who were installed after Athens' defeat in the Peloponnesian War. Critias and his faction sought to impose a narrow oligarchy in Athens, but Theramenes wanted to preserve a broader democratic constitution. Theramenes also spoke out against many of the executions that took place during this time. See Xenophon, *Hellenika*, II.3.15–56.

29 This line is preserved in Euripides, *Fragments*, "Palamedes", 588. According to some accounts, during the Trojan War, Odysseus accused Palamedes of treason and planted evidence of his "crime", after which the Greeks stoned him to death. As such, Palamedes stood as a symbol of dubious state executions, and thus Athenian playwrights like Euripides used the figure of Palamedes to comment upon Socrates' death. Melanchthon likely borrowed this parallel between Palamedes and Socrates in Euripides from the ancient *argumentum* to Isocrates' *Busiris*, which appeared in the 1513 Aldine Greek edition of Isocrates. According to Kusukawa, *A Wittenberg University Library Catalogue*, p. 10, Melanchthon borrowed and annotated that book in 1536.

sig. 4v What a sweet example [Xenophon] recites—and an example most necessary in these times—when he narrates that the Athenians were granted an amnesty for their injustices when Thrasybulus regained control of the republic.[30] If only the relaxation of harsh laws would now bring about such a peace in the Church! For how barbaric is it to prefer to bring about destruction and desolation in the
3.1117 Church than to relax a few openly tyrannical laws? | This volume contains many such episodes which can teach the reader much about the republic, especially in these times.

Moreover, young men should also read this author diligently because of his eloquence. For indeed, the ancients admired the purity and elegance of Xenophon's speech so much that they called him "The Attic Bee."[31] And as Quintilian says: "And not to mention Xenophon's effortless charm, which no amount of striving can imitate, such that the Graces themselves seem to have fashioned his speech."[32] And let the studious reader attend not only to the sweetness of his style, but also the counsel and prudence which he applies in his speeches, which are as much more serious than Herodotus' speeches as they are sweeter than Thucydides', in which many sentences are so forced and wordy that even the attentive reader can hardly follow them.[33] For this reason, reading Xenophon will be very pleasing to the student of eloquence. Therefore, I rejoice that he has been printed again in Germany and will be back in the hands of serious students.[34]

sig. [5]r So then, since this | letter was to serve as a preface, according to custom, I wanted this author to appear particularly under the auspices of your name, illustrious Langey,[35] since I did not doubt that you above all others, occupied as

---

30 This is a reference to the Athenian Amnesty of 403 BCE. According to Xenophon, this was an oath of reconciliation which was sworn by the oligarchic and democratic factions after the Thirty Tyrants were overthrown. Intended to prevent a further cycle of retribution and bloodshed, the Amnesty became the foundation of future Athenian democracy. See *Hellenika* II.4.43.

31 See *Suidae Lexicon*, ed. Bekker, p. 752.

32 Quoted from Quintilian, *The Orator's Education*, X.1.82.

33 Melanchthon had also translated many of Thucydides' speeches. See CR XVII.1019–1112. They were published posthumously in 1562 by Caspar Peucer.

34 According to CTC vol. VII, pp. 81–82, this 1540 edition was the first complete edition of the Greek text of Xenophon. However, as Melanchthon implies, Xenophon had been printed in Germany (and elsewhere) previously. In 1520 at Hagenau, Melanchthon's mentor and relative Johannes Reuchlin had published the Greek text of the *Hiero, Agesilaeus*, and *Apologia Socratis*. Reuchlin's edition constituted the *editio princeps* of the latter two works, illustrating that, by the 1520s, German scholars had begun to make significant contributions to Greek scholarship.

35 Du Bellay's aristocratic title was "Seigneur de Langey".

you are in governing the republic with highly laudable prudence, diligence, and justice, would delight in reading this author, and would, so to speak, deliberate with him often about the weightiest matters. I even hoped that some, seeing you and admiring how greatly your erudition adorns you and how useful it is in your affairs, would more readily read these things, and, inspired by your example, would make an effort to instruct themselves with these letters as they approach the Republic. For without such instruction, what else are those who participate in government other than (as they are called in the theatre) "silent faces"?[36] Therefore, be assured that I have written to you fondly, and I will harvest great fruit from my counsel here if, when you confer about the republic with the powers that be, you exhort them to imitate the clemency of Cyrus or the amnesty decreed by Thrasybulus instead of following the savagery of those sycophants who everywhere inflame the wrath of the princes against us.

Farewell. 1540.[37]

36 *kōpha prosōpa*, a theatre term for those actors who were on stage but did not speak. Melanchthon uses the parallel to highlight the lack of wisdom and reason of uneducated rulers. See also Erasmus, *Adagia* I.10.78 (ASD vol. II.2.478).

37 The MBW dates this letter to sometime before January 4, 1540. See MBW 2341.

CHAPTER 5

A Comparison of the Chief Attic and Roman Legal Actions

1 Introduction

The *Comparison of the Chief Attic and Roman Legal Actions* is one of Melanchthon's most remarkable writings. On the surface, it seems to be an obscure historical work occupied with the minutiae of ancient legal systems. Upon deeper examination, the work is noteworthy for two main reasons. First, the *Comparison* was a foundational work in the Renaissance study of Athenian legal history. Second, by illustrating how the ancient Athenian and Roman laws agreed with the Ten Commandments (and thus natural law), the work concretely illustrates how Melanchthon envisioned the outworking of natural law in ancient history.

The *Comparison* was a highly original historical accomplishment. Scholars have not recognized the significance of the work until very recently, but the *Comparison* was the first comprehensive attempt by any European scholar to reconstruct the laws of ancient Athens.[1] Unlike Roman law, which had survived antiquity in the massive Justinianic compilations of the *Corpus iuris civilis*, Athenian law had not been preserved in any organized way. There were no textbooks of Athenian law, and, before the discovery and publication of Aristotle's treatise, *The Constitution of the Athenians*, in the late nineteenth century, there were very few ancient descriptions of the Attic legal system. In a Renaissance intellectual milieu that was obsessed with recovering ancient culture, Athenian law was a dark spot on the map. Previous Renaissance scholars such as Guillaume Budé and Annius of Viterbo had drawn shallow comparisons between Greek and Roman political and legal institutions.[2] Others had begun to study

---

1 As far as I am aware, the only extended discussion of the *Comparison* is Batson, "Sinai and the Areopagus". Much of the discussion below is drawn from that article, and I thank the editors for allowing me to reproduce it here. Other brief mentions of the work can be found in Noah Dauber, *State and Commonwealth: The Theory of the State in Early Modern England, 1549–1640* (2016), pp. 48–50 and Bauer, "Melanchthons Naturrechtslehre", pp. 76–77.

2 For Annius of Viterbo, see Anthony Grafton, "Annius of Viterbo as a Student of the Jews: The Sources of His Information" in Walter Stephens, Earle A. Havens, and Janet E. Gomez, eds., *Literary Forgery in Early Modern Europe, 1450–1800* (2018), pp. 147–169, esp. 163–164. For Budé's parallels between the Areopagus, Roman Senate, and French Parliament, see his *Annotationes*

 | HTTPS://DOI.ORG/10.1163/9789004774742-008

ancient Athenian society in some detail as well; in 1541, the French orientalist Guillaume Postel had published a work on Athenian political offices entitled *De magistratibus Atheniensium*.[3] But before Melanchthon's work, knowledge about the content and procedure of the Athenian legal system was virtually non-existent.

The main reason for this was that recovering Athenian law, unlike recovering Roman law, was a project with no clear starting point. The legal humanists of the sixteenth century, who brought their classical learning to bear in the historical study of Roman law, faced a monumental but relatively straightforward task. They began with a Justinianic compilation such as the *Digest* or the *Codex* and used their humanistic learning and classical erudition to edit and correct the text.[4] For example, one of the first and most important tasks of jurists such as Guillaume Budé (1467–1540) was to detect the ways in which Justinian's editors and medieval commentators had corrupted the original Roman text. Having discovered and purged such errors, legal humanists such as Budé sought to restore the Roman laws to their ancient meaning.[5] Work of this sort abounded, but Roman lawyers had a critical advantage in that they possessed four imposing volumes of Justinianic laws as a clear point of departure for studying their subject.

In contrast, the remnants of Athenian law were scattered across the literature of the ancient world. For this reason, Melanchthon, who by 1546 had taught, translated, or commented upon virtually every extant Greek author, was the perfect candidate for this task. Melanchthon marshalled his encyclopaedic knowledge of antiquity to draw bits and pieces from various ancient authors and use these fragments to assemble an overall picture of the Attic legal actions.

Melanchthon drew upon a variety of sources to complete this project. He turned to historians and geographers like Pausanias, Plutarch, and Xenophon for their anecdotes about Greek legal customs. Melanchthon also occasionally looked to Athenian dramatists such as Aristophanes and Aeschylus, whose plays

---

Gulielmi Budaei Parisiensis, Secretarii Regii, in quatuor et viginti Pandectarum libros (Paris, 1536 [original 1508]). See fols. XL^{r}–LVI^{v}.

3 Guillaume Postel, *De magistratibus Atheniensium* (Paris, 1541).

4 For the classic study of Renaissance legal humanism, see Donald Kelley, *The Foundations of Modern Historical Scholarship: Language, Law, and History in the French Renaissance* (1970). For more recent perspectives, see Douglas Osler, "The Myth of European Legal History", *Rechtshistorisches Journal* 16 (1997): 393–410; Zachary Sayre Schiffman, *The Birth of The Past* (2011), pp. 137–200, Paul J. DuPlessis and John W. Cairns, eds., *Reassessing Legal Humanism and its Claims: Petere Fontes?* (2016), and Susan Longfield Karr, *Jus Gentium in Humanist Jurisprudence: On Justice and Right* (2022).

5 See Kelley, *The Foundations of Modern Historical Scholarship*, pp. 66–76.

often offered details about legal processes. The most important source by far, however, was the Greek orators: Aeschines, Lysias, and above all, Demosthenes. Most surviving Athenian orations were actually courtroom speeches, and as such they contain a wealth of information about legal procedure, courtroom protocols, and specific types of prosecutions. In some cases, the orators even cited particular laws. Melanchthon drew upon all of these sources to reconstruct the chief Attic legal actions.

One of the remarkable features of Melanchthon's approach to studying Athenian law is the counterintuitive way in which he read these ancient texts. He read these sources "against the grain", as one might say today. That is, for this particular project, Melanchthon did not read Demosthenes' speeches as one would expect a humanist to read works of that genre. He was not searching for lessons on style or eloquence, but for information on how the ancient Athenians structured their legal proceedings. In the world of the sixteenth-century Renaissance, when ancient texts were constantly invoked for a wide variety of moral, philosophical, and rhetorical purposes, Melanchthon took the surprising step of reading them as historical sources. In many ways, he anticipated modern approaches to studying Athenian law, which still use Athenian oratory as their main source base, although they also rely on more modern archaeological methods and a wealth of epigraphic sources which were not available in Renaissance Germany.[6]

Considering the fact that Melanchthon's *Comparison* was the first ever European scholarly work to attempt to reconstruct Athenian law, it was remarkably accurate. However, Melanchthon's project was quickly eclipsed by others. Works like Pardoux Duprat's 1559 *Iurisprudentia Vetus*, Carlo Sigonio's *De Republica Atheniensium*, and Samuel Petit's 1635 *Leges Atticae* soon surpassed Melanchthon's work in terms of detail and accuracy.[7] For this reason, the *Comparison* should be considered a pioneering work, but it was also merely a preliminary attempt to solve a problem which later scholars would work out much more successfully.

Besides its originality in the study of Athenian jurisprudence, the *Comparison* is also noteworthy for the way that it illuminates Melanchthon's theory of natural law. The *Comparison* illustrates how Melanchthon thought the inborn ideas of natural law could manifest in the legal systems of antiquity. The overarching principles of natural and divine law are apparent from the organization

6 For modern approaches to literary and epigraphic sources, see Michael Gagarin, *Writing Greek Law* (2008), chs. 1 and 2 and S.C. Todd, *The Shape of Athenian Law* (1993), pp. 7–10, 30–48.

7 See Duprat, *Iurisprudentia vetus, Draconis et Solonis leges* (Lyon, 1559), Sigonio, *De republica Atheniensium libri IIII* (Bologna, 1564), and Petit, *Leges Atticae* (Paris, 1635).

of the work. As the title of the work suggests, the *Comparison* grouped and compared similar Attic and Roman legal actions. But Melanchthon's organizational scheme also compared the ancient legal actions to the natural and divine law; the entire work is organized by the headings of the Ten Commandments. For example, Melanchthon includes the Attic and Roman actions against murder and assault under the heading of the fifth commandment: "You shall not kill." Similarly, religious offenses such as despoiling temples—*crimen sacrilegii* in Rome and *dikē hierosulias* in Athens—were included under the blanket category of the first table of the Decalogue, which included the first three commandments concerning offenses against God.

While the Ten Commandments addressed morality at the highest level of generalization, Melanchthon believed that the Decalogue espoused general principles which formed the bedrock of all concepts necessary for civil life. For example, in his other political writings, Melanchthon frequently interprets the fourth commandment ("Honor your father and mother") quite expansively. Rather than reading this commandment in a strict familial context, Melanchthon saw this commandment as a broad divine institution of authority. Thus, the fourth commandment consecrated not only parental authority, but political and legal authority as well.

This same approach is evident in the *Comparison*. For example, under the heading of the seventh commandment prohibiting stealing, Melanchthon naturally included the basic actions against theft. However, in Melanchthon's mind, this commandment reached beyond mere theft; it established the foundational principles of private property. Thus, under this same commandment, he also included actions on guardianship, on contracts of loan and deposit, and even on the Roman possessory interdicts. As he writes in the preface to the work, "The divine law broadly establishes distinctions of ownership when it says 'You shall not steal' [Exodus 20:15]. Here, the legislator reads the ways in which something becomes a person's property, and he explains the forms of contracts and when a contract should be considered fulfilled or unfulfilled."[8]

This last point demonstrates why the *Comparison* is such a helpful document for understanding Melanchthon's natural law theory. Melanchthon understood the Decalogue as the summary of the divine law, which was identical with the natural law. As he wrote in the preface, "Law is the one chief ruler of human life. It is the eternal wisdom in the divine mind and the unchanging rule of justice which God poured into the minds of men. And he willed that a light be born within us, and afterwards, on Mount Sinai, he proclaimed [it] with

8 See p. 312 below.

a brilliant testimony, so that we might know that it is truly the divine standard for life."[9] Under this framework, the pagan Greeks and Romans took the inborn knowledge of natural law and developed it into complex legal systems. The Attic and Roman actions could be organized under the headings of the Ten Commandments because Attic and Roman law were actually derived from the inborn knowledge of the Decalogue's content. As such, in the *Comparison*, Melanchthon provides a detailed and concrete picture of how he understood the outworking of natural law in history.

Finally, a brief note on the context of the *Comparison* is necessary. On its face, the work seems to be highly theoretical and largely removed from the political exigencies of the day. However, one line at the end of the preface hints that Melanchthon understood the *Comparison* in light of the tumultuous context in which it appeared. The last line of the preface, addressed to Joachim Moller of Hamburg, reads, "I myself pray with my whole heart that God would preserve his Church and their hosts in your homeland and in these lands, that he would guide them, and that he would defend them against the cruelty and tyranny of barbarous and foreign nations."[10] The letter was dated September 1, 1546, nearly two months after the Schmalkaldic War had begun, which suggests that the "cruelty and tyranny of barbarous and foreign nations" was a thinly veiled reference to, among other things, Charles V's Catholic armies.

But what did natural law have to do with the Schmalkaldic War? In 1546, Melanchthon became one of the chief architects of Protestant resistance theory. As Robert von Friedeburg has shown, in the lead-up to the war, Melanchthon began to couch his arguments for resistance in terms of natural law, downplaying the apocalyptic and constitutional elements found in other contemporary Lutheran resistance theories.[11] His short tract *De licita defensione*, likely published sometime in 1546, justified resistance against tyranny on the grounds of natural law.[12] The resistance arguments in the *Summary of Moral Philosophy* reflect this change, as do Melanchthon's revisions to Justus Menius' *Von der Notwehr Unterricht* (Teaching on Self-Defence).[13] The latter text was even translated into Latin, and printed in Wittenberg in 1547 under the title *De defensione concessa humano generi iure naturae* (On Defence Granted to the Human Race by the Law of Nature).[14]

---

9 See p. 311 below.

10 See p. 315 below.

11 See von Friedeburg, *Self-Defence and Religious Strife*, pp. 75–79.

12 This tract can be found in CR 6:150–155. The editors of the CR date the tract to May 1546.

13 See Peterson, "Justus Menius, Philipp Melanchthon".

14 A modern critical edition of that work, in both the German and Latin editions, can be found in Hans-Otto Schneider, ed., *Politischer Widerstand als Protestantische Option*.

The *Comparison* is not explicitly political or polemical like these other resistance tracts were. However, when viewed in this context, it is clear that the *Comparison* was at least intended to reinforce the themes of natural law and divine order within German society.[15] When read alongside Melanchthon's arguments for resistance, the *Comparison* appears as a part of a larger turn towards using natural law to establish and independent Protestant politics. The *Comparison* must be read as a pioneering historical work, a fascinating illustration of Melanchthon's natural law theory, and a neglected piece of Melanchthon's natural law resistance theory during the Schmalkaldic War.

2 Printing History

1546. *Collatio actionum forensium Atticarum & Romanarum praecipuarum. Autore Philippo Melanthone.* (Wittenberg: Veit Kreutzer). [Claus 1546.133 / VD16 M 2732 / USTC 622992]

1548. *Ethicorum Aristotelis primi, II, III, et V. librorum enarratio per Philippum Melanch. Accesserunt eiusdem Oratio de Aristotele. Collatio actionum forensium Atticarum, & Romanarum. In Politicos aliquot Aristotelis libros Commentaria.* (Lyon: Sébastien Gryphe). [Claus 1548.39 / USTC 150025]

1551. *Collatio actionum forensium Atticarum et Romanarum praecipuarum. Autore Philip. Melanth.* (Wittenberg: Heirs of Peter Seitz). [Claus 1551.88 / VD16 ZV 23827 / USTC 622991]

1554. *Collatio actionum forensium Atticarum et Romanarum praecipuarum. Autore Philip. Melanth.* (Wittenberg: Johann Krafft). [Claus 1554.67 / VD16 M 2733]

1562. *Eruditae annotationes Philippi Melanthonis in officia Ciceronis recens editae. Commentarius in primum librum officiorum viri clarissimi Georgii Cracovii I.V. Doctoris & Professoris in Acaemia Witebergensi.* (Wittenberg: Peter Seitz), sigs. [Kvi]^{r}–[Lvii]^{v} [VD16 ZV10753 / USTC 653825] This edition includes an alternate preface (see below), and the text is both revised and shortened.

The *Collatio* was also reprinted in the following seventeenth-century works:

1618. Konrad Rittershausen, *Commentarius novus in quatuor libros institutionum imperialium divi Justiniani* (Strasburg: Heirs of Lazarus Zetzner, 1618), pp. 788–796. [VD17 1:012908D / USTC 2017758]

1649. Konrad Rittershausen, *Commentarius novus in quatuor libros institutionum imperialium divi Justiniani* (Strasburg: Heirs of Lazarus Zetzner). [VD17 3:61471 3H / USTC 2077335]

15 For a fuller discussion of this argument, see Batson, "Sinai and the Areopagus."

1668. Christian Woldenberg, *Principia Juris Romani, i.e. leges Draconis et Solonis, leges Romuli, et leges XII. Tabularum, secundum ordinem a Pardulpho Pratejo, & J. Lipsio observatum: Item Collatio ll. Atticarum et Romanarum Melanchthonis. Quibus accessit introductio utilissima in totum ius canonicum, tam decretum, quam decretales, una cum origine, progressu, et usu eiusdem antehac edita: iam autem in gratiam floridae ll. Iuventutis, quae hoc thesauro carere non potest, iterum publici iuris facta.* (Rostock: Johannis Keil, 1668), pp. 50–62. [VD17 28:724107E / USTC 2692589]

3 A Note on the Text

This translation is based on the first edition of this text, entitled *Collatio actionum forensium Atticarum et Romanarum praecipuarum.* (Wittenberg: Veit Kreuzer, 1546).

While the main text of this work is included in the *Corpus Reformatorum*, a brief explanatory note on that edition is necessary. The preface of the *Collatio*, addressed to Joachim Moller, is included separately in CR 6.225–229 (and MBW 4373). In CR 16.593–596 (fn. 51), the editors insert the alternate preface which was included in Melanchthon's 1562 *Eruditae annotationes Philippi Melanthonis in officia Ciceronis recens editae* (Wittenberg: Peter Seitz, 1562), sigs. [Kvi]^{r}–Liiij^{r}. I have not translated this alternate preface, and the 1562 edition is both shortened and revised. The main text of the 1546 *Collatio* can be found in CR 16.593–614. Melanchthon's two Latin translations of Greek extracts at the end of the work can be found in CR volume 17. The translation of Demosthenes' *Against Timocrates* 149-40 can be found in CR 17.877–880, while his translation of the Solonic elegy quoted in Demosthenes' *On the False Legation* 255 can be found in CR 17.873–876.

4 A Note on the Translation

Because the *Collatio* is a commentary on highly specific legal terms, it was particularly challenging to render this document into readable modern English. In the translation which follows, the following general principles are observed:

Latin and Greek legal terms have been rendered into their approximate English equivalents, but the original language terms have been retained in brackets. Because legal terms carry such specific meanings in the context of their particular legal systems, it is unhelpful to merely translate the Latin and Greek legal actions into modern English. Such translations can never capture the nuanced differences between legal codes separated by such vast cultural, geographic, and temporal gulfs. Moreover, readers can use the original Greek and Latin terms to look up these legal actions in reference works.

I have generally tried to keep footnotes to a minimum. However, since Attic and Roman law are both highly technical subjects, and legal nuances are often material to the substance of the *Collatio*, brief explanations of any relevant technical details are provided in the footnotes. For more technical points of Roman and Athenian law, the footnotes refer the reader to two excellent modern scholarly treatments: Paul du Plessis, *Borkowski's Textbook on Roman Law*. Sixth Edition (Oxford: Oxford University Press, 2020); and S.C. Todd, *The Shape of Athenian Law* (Oxford: Clarendon, 1993).

On Legal Actions (*actio / accusatio / graphē / dikē*): Roman and Attic law relied heavily upon a system of legal actions for resolving disputes between citizens. In Rome, such a procedure was known as an *actio* (Melanchthon also uses the term *accusatio* with no discernible difference), and in Greek it was called *graphē* or *dikē*. Specialists in Greek law recognize subtle differences between the *graphai* and *dikai*: one hypothesis is that a *dikē* was an action against private offenses, while a *graphē* involved cases with a more public dimension (see Todd, pp. 99–112 for a fuller discussion). However, because Melanchthon seems to acknowledge no distinction between *graphai* and *dikai*, no distinctions are made in this translation.

Because actions were complex and highly formal legal procedures, there is no precise English equivalent for these terms. Accordingly, *actio / accusatio / graphē / dikē* are translated generally as "action" and occasionally as "accusation", "suit", or "trial".

On Citations of Pseudo-Demosthenes: Melanchthon's main source for Athenian law is the Demosthenic corpus. Modern scholars have determined that many of the orations belonging to this body are not actually written by Demosthenes, but they are still cited here as part of Demosthenes' corpus, since Melanchthon viewed them as such.

5 Edition

sig. A^v / CR 6.225 / MBW 4373

A Comparison of the Chief Attic and Roman Legal Actions

Prefatory Epistle

Philip Melanchthon to his friend, a man outstanding in erudition and virtue, Joachim Moller of Hamburg.[16]

Law is the one chief ruler of human life. It is the eternal wisdom in the divine mind and the unchanging rule of justice which God poured into the minds of men. And he willed that a light be born within us, and afterwards, on Mount Sinai, he proclaimed [it] with a brilliant testimony, so that we might know that sig. Aij^r it is truly the divine standard for life. |

Because God intends for life to be governed by this law, which shines brightly in every mind by nature, one usually asks about the office of the magistrates. For since the law has already been divinely established, and since to pass other [laws] that depart [from it] is the worst and most atrocious of all crimes, and since this divine law is known to everyone, what do rulers contribute to the peace of human society?

In fact, they are responsible for three functions which are full of dignity. First, they must be the voice of that first and chief law, namely the Decalogue. For although nature shines in the mind, the light of nature must still be stimulated 6.226 / sig. Aij^v by doctrine and by the voice of the magistrates. |

Next, because men are not ruled by doctrine alone, but must be coerced by the fear of punishment, God appointed magistrates over the human race to punish those who violate this law of his. For although God himself is the avenger of trespasses against this standard, still he joined to himself the magistrates, through whom he intended mainly to execute punishments. God punished the wantonness and ambition of [Mark] Antony, but he punished these things through Augustus.[17] And it is no mystery that a law without punishments appears to be just empty noise. For that reason, that saying of Aeschines was so highly

16 Joachim Moller the younger (1521–1588) was a former student of Melanchthon's. He later studied law at various Italian universities and eventually served in various legal and political positions in Celle, Lüneburg, and Hamburg. He was the son of Joachim Moller the elder (1500–1558), the town councillor of Hamburg who was instrumental in adding Hamburg to the Schmalkaldic League in 1534.

17 Octavian (later Caesar Augustus) defeated Mark Antony at the Battle of Actium in 31 BCE. Antony committed suicide when Octavian invaded Egypt in 30 BCE.

esteemed that Demosthenes incorporated it in one of his own orations: "Useless is the state which has no strength [*nervos*] against the wicked."[18] | Therefore, so that the guilty may be brought to trial in an orderly fashion, the names of the crimes were delineated and the forms of actions and accusations were established. sig. Aiij^r

Therefore, these very accusations and actions are the sinews [*nervi*][19] of the laws and of all human society. Because this is the case, not only is it apparent that the force and dignity of the actions is great, but it is also manifest that the magistrates were appointed over the human race mainly on account of the actions. For when [the magistrates] are called the "guardians of the laws", they are not named that merely because they guard some doctrine which is shut up in the libraries, but rather because thereafter, by the severity | of their punishments, they compel the souls of the citizens towards the duties of virtue. sig. Aiij^v

I will further discuss the actions themselves below. But first, I should add the third function of the magistrate. For although it is necessary that the first and foremost of all laws in every government be the ones which are handed down in the Decalogue, rightly understood, nevertheless, God commanded the magistrates to add some other laws, but ones which agree with the Decalogue and account for certain circumstances or special cases. The divine law broadly establishes distinctions of ownership when it says "You shall not steal" [Exodus 20:15]. Here, the legislator enumerates the ways in which something becomes a person's property, and he explains the forms of contracts and when a contract should be considered | fulfilled or unfulfilled. In these expositions, the opinion sig. Aiiij^r of the magistrates is valid both because of probable reasoning in agreement with the Decalogue and because of the authority which God granted to the magistrate, whom [God] commanded in this civic life to add both expositions and supports of the divine laws.

So then, the actions are the guardians of these expositions added by the magistrate. For the legislator's verbal prescriptions about the equal distribution of inheritance would be worthless if he did not then use the authority of legal proceedings to defend that equality | against rapacious and fraudulent heirs, 6.227
who either by force or by fraud would try to exclude the other heirs. | sig. Aiiij^v

18 Melanchthon gives this quote in Greek, followed by a Latin translation. See Demosthenes, *On the False Embassy* 283. I have translated it only once to avoid redundancy.

19 *nervi* generally refers to sinews or muscles in the body. However, here and in the quote above, it can also be used metonymically to refer to strength or power. That is to say, the accusations and actions are the sinews that fill out the laws, and thus they are the strength behind the laws.

Therefore, since the necessity of establishing and distinguishing actions is under consideration, not only should one cherish the doctrine which the wisest men have passed down about [the actions], but one should also seek philosophy within them. For since the actions primarily are the rulers of life, they must be born partly from the Decalogue, and partly from the light of nature which explicates the Decalogue. And it is certainly philosophy, and a thing agreeable to good natures, to consider these sources and, as I would call them, "demonstrations".

So then, whenever we contemplate these sources, it will then certainly be helpful to compare constitutions and to see where serious discipline endured sig. Av[r] for a long time. Initially, the Attic state severely punished | the raving of ungodly men who denied providence, and it restrained lusts with just punishments. But later, once that discipline had become lax, how petulant were both the learned and the ignorant in scorning providence, and how depraved was the general state of morals!

So then, when we consider the ancient constitutions and laws, the decline of laws and discipline, the death of cities and ruin of empires, we see the manifest testimonies of God's presence in the government of this life. For it is not by chance or merely for the sake of bodily necessity that the multitude of men gather together; civil society does not endure by chance. Rather, God joined sig. Av[v] together the union of men and he is the guardian of just society. | And when the careful protection of discipline has died, he overturns and dissipates states and empires as dreadful examples. And since this is a most true and certain fact, we should habituate our souls to reverence for the laws and for discipline, we should rein in our desires, and with moderation of soul we should strive first to please God and then to aid the common good, as far as each is able to do so in his own position.

Devoted students who examine the designs of the ancients who organized the actions in this way will observe how this very philosophy shines forth both in these actions and in the comparison between the two most beautiful states of Athens and Rome. Moreover, I believe that the ancient doctrine of the Athenian sig. [Avi][r] state | was received from Japheth and his sons and was preserved and propagated among his well-mannered descendants.[20] But certainly, if ignorant or rude and barbaric men disparage these monuments, or these bonds of human society and discipline, we should ignore them for precisely that reason. For 6.228 although men's madness in disturbing the political order takes many forms, | I am now solely referring to those who, according to a certain superstition, claim

20 While Melanchthon generally thinks that the laws of Athens are a product of the natural law, it is noteworthy that here he posits a historical process of transmission from Noah's son Japheth to Athens.

that anyone who either seeks his own interest or defends himself in court is acting contrary to the Gospel.[21] Everyone sees that this error is dangerous to communal life. But it is even more atrocious because it is also an insult against God. For the Gospel, | which offers eternal righteousness, in the meantime still (sig. [Avi]v) demands that we spend this life in political society, exhibit the testimonies of our calling, and exercise the duties of many virtues. And not only does [the Gospel] not abolish or disapprove of the ranks of civil life, but it honours them much more than any human wisdom could honour them. For the Gospel affirms that the political order is a gift of God. And although many horrible confusions of governments do exist, stirred up either by human foolishness, or by the devil, who rejoices at misfortune [*epichairekakos*] out of his hate for God and the Church, nevertheless, God alone ensures that human society does not entirely dissolve. For he preserves and always will preserve for his Church certain hosts [*hospitia*], held together with laws and justice, which he | defends. And he com- (sig. [Avii]r) mands us to love these nests, to obey their laws and decisions reverently as if they were the divine voice, and not to disturb the order of life with our desires or our meddling [*polupragmosunē*]. But we have often spoken about this entire question elsewhere, and we have constructed an explication from true and firm foundations, which I have no doubt is now useful and will continue to be useful to good men.

However, although this necessary doctrine previously lay entirely in the shadows, covered over by the filth of the monks, we now see what grace it provides to our churches where these things rightly have been brought to light. But amongst this human depravity, what Pindar says is quite common: "For ancient grace sleeps, and mortals are forgetful."[22] | Nevertheless, God will not (sig. [Avii]v) let his revealed truth be erased, nor will he allow godly labours to be for naught.

Now then, I have recited these things so that, in contemplating them, the students of legal doctrine would not only delight more in their studies, but also direct their labours to this end: that when they understand that political duties please God, they would serve him in this profession of theirs.

But for you, dearest Joachim, I have written this brief and merely rudimentary lucubration, in order to declare to you and to others my fondness for you. Moreover, just as it pleases us to see those who, | having learned right doctrine 6.229
from us, either carry on their studies with great promise or serve the republic successfully, in the same way it is to your great honour | that you are declared to (sig. [Aviij]r) be well-educated by men of pure doctrine and goodwill towards the republic. So

21 A common Anabaptist belief, based on 1 Corinthians 6:1–8, where Paul forbids lawsuits between Christians.

22 Pindar, *Isthmian Ode* VII.16–17.

then, I pray that God, the eternal father of our Lord Jesus Christ, will guide your entire course of life and studies to your own welfare and that of the republic. This I desire both for your sake, and certainly also for the sake of your homeland, the city of Hamburg, which considers the crowning achievement of a city not to be opulence and pleasures, but rather to be the true invocation of God and the sanctity of discipline. For this reason, alongside its other civic distinctions, [that city] also takes care that the Church of God is governed rightly and that the youth learn letters and doctrine that is beneficial for life. Cities like this one deserve honours and | especially deserve this duty: namely that we would ask God to protect them and make them perpetual homes for his doctrine and for true virtue, just as it says in the Psalm: "Pray for the peace of Jerusalem, etc." [Psalm 122:6]. Therefore, I myself pray with my whole heart that God would preserve his Church and their hosts[23] in your homeland and in these lands, that he would guide them, and that he would defend them against the cruelty and tyranny of barbarous and foreign nations.[24]

sig. [Aviij]v

Farewell. September 1, 1546.|

sig. Br / CR 16.593

A Comparison of the Roman and Attic Actions

It is profitable to consider the ancient actions of admirable states. For these states, which passed laws and instituted actions and punishments not only for the sake of peace but for the sake of discipline too, embraced in those actions the doctrine of virtue through good design and order. Therefore, in this way, the Attic and Roman actions should be read as a doctrine about virtue derived from the law of nature, or from the doctrine of the first fathers. These laws are very powerful for ruling morals because they included punishments, the fear of which coerces | ordinary dispositions and inclines them towards virtue. I wanted to advise about the actions in advance so the students would know that they are not just formulas for litigators, but that they are philosophy and the doctrine of virtue.

sig. Bv

So then, we follow the Decalogue in reciting them.

23 *earum hospitia*. Although Melanchthon refers only to *Ecclesiam* in the singular in the preceding clause, *earum* likely refers to an implied plural *ecclesias*, since Melanchthon above refers to governments and states as the *hospitia* (hosts) of the churches.

24 The letter is dated September 1, 1546, nearly two months after the Schmalkaldic War had begun. This last line reflects Melanchthon's apprehension about the war and the possibility that Charles V could crush the German Reformation. It may also be a reference to fears about the invasion of the Ottoman Turks.

The First Table of the Decalogue

sig. Bij^r / [16.597]

The First Accusation

The Romans did not have a name for the action or accusation by which impious speech was prosecuted. But the Athenians did have one, and they named this accusation the "accusation of impiety" [*enklēma asebeias*]. Anaxagoras and Diagoras of Melos were accused and convicted of this because they scorned the received Athenian opinions about the gods.[25] In fact, the city publicly promised a talent as a reward to whoever killed Diagoras, and two talents to whoever brought him in alive. It is similar to that present-day accusation of heresy in the Church. | sig. Bij^v / 16.598

The Second Accusation

Because we have begun from the first commandment and spoken of the charge of impiety, next I will add the charge of sacrilege [*crimen sacrilegii*]. The Athenians called this the "action for temple robbing" [*dikē hierosuleias*]. There was a name for this trial in both cities. Moreover, those who stole sacred things from temples, or who desecrated or profaned sacred places, or who kidnapped suppliants from temples were all prosecuted [for this crime].

There are many famous examples of this throughout history, and great wars often arose on account of such cases. The Spartans dragged the Messenian suppliants out of the temple, and on account of this | it is reported that an earthquake and a war between the Spartans and their slaves followed afterward.[26] Likewise, because a grove had been violated, Pericles started a war that devastated all of Greece. And the Phocaeans were destroyed because they plundered the temple at Delphi, and the generals who had urged this sacrilege perished in various ways.[27] Philomedes[28] hurled himself headlong over a cliff as he fled. His successor Onomarchus was struck down by his own soldiers. When

sig. Biij^r

25 The philosopher Anaxagoras became one of Pericles' leading advisers at Athens. He was accused of impiety for his unorthodox beliefs about the gods. Diagoras of Melos was a poet and philosopher who was widely regarded as an atheist. He was also accused of impiety at Athens.

26 See Thucydides, *History of the Peloponnesian War*, I.128.

27 According to Pausanias, the Phocaeans, under the leadership of Philomelus, plundered the temple at Delphi in order to pay a large tribute to the Amphyctionic League. This ignited the Third Sacred War (356–346 BCE). The events which Melanchthon references in this passage are drawn from Pausanias, *Description of Greece* X.2.1–7.

28 The 1546 edition erroneously reads "Philomedes". The correct name is Philomelus, which appears in the 1554 edition.

Phaylus had dreamed that he resembled a statue of Hippocrates[29] in Delphi, he died of consumption shortly thereafter. For in Delphi, there was a statue of Hippocrates which resembled a decayed body in which the flesh had wasted away and the outlines of the bones appeared to be clothed with thin skin. These sig. Biij^v accounts are in Pausanias, in the section on the Phocaeans. | / 16.599

The Second Table of the Decalogue The Fourth Commandment: Honor Your Father and Mother, etc.

The Third Accusation

The principal crime of the second table is the crime of violated sovereignty [*laesa maiestas*], which occurs namely when either the person of the magistrate or his function suffers an insult.[30] That is, when sedition is incited to overthrow the form of government, or when treason takes place, or betrayal to enemies sig. Biiij^r or other similar crimes which undermine the | form of government occur. For example, in Rome, Manlius was convicted of the crime of violated sovereignty, and the senator Veturius was convicted of the crime of violated sovereignty, for he did not give way to a tribune of the plebs who was crossing the forum, as Plutarch narrates in the life of the Gracchi.[31]

Further, although the Athenians assigned particular names to certain species [of this crime], they still had a general name for them: impeachment [*eisangelia*].[32] This includes all offences recounted under the crimes of violated sovereignty. Impeachment had a peculiar feature: in other crimes, if the accuser did not successfully prove the guilt [of the accused], then he would become legally disgraced [*infamis*] as a calumniator.[33] But in [*eisangelia*], there was no legal disgrace because this accusation was considered a bulwark of public order.

---

29 *statua Hippocratis*. According to Pausanias' account, not a statue depicting Hippocrates, but a votive statue offered by Hippocrates the physician.

30 In D.48.4.1, Ulpian defines violated sovereignty as "an act committed against the Roman people or against its security." See also C.9.8 for further legislation about this crime.

31 For Marcus Manlius Capitolinus, see Livy, *History of Rome* VI.18–20. For Veturius, see Plutarch, *Life of Caius Gracchus* III.3.

32 For the Athenian procedure of *eisangelia*, see Todd, *The Shape of Athenian Law*, pp. 113–115.

33 *Infamia*, or legal disgrace, was a legal status conferred on those who had engaged in shameful conduct such as keeping a brothel, engaging in fraud, or levelling false accusations (D.3.2.1). There were legal consequences to *infamia*, including the inability to hold offices or bring criminal accusations. See *Borkowski's Textbook*, pp. 107–108. Athenian law had a similar penalty known as *atimia*, which was roughly equivalent to disenfranchisement

|**The Fourth [Action]**[34] sig. B

Among the Romans, treason [*proditio*] pertains to the crime of violated sovereignty. The Greeks created a separate accusation and call it "the action for treason" [*dikē prodosias*].[35] iiij^v / 16.600

The Fifth [Action]

Among the Romans, being hired by enemies for money pertains to the crime of violated sovereignty. The Greeks created a separate accusation and call it "the action for bribery" [*dikē dōrodokias*]. In Athens, Timagoras was put on trial for this. When he was sent with Pelopidas as an emissary to the King of Persia, he accepted gifts and did not share the same accommodations as his companion. For these reasons, the citizens killed him after he returned home and his trial concluded, as | Xenophon writes and Plutarch writes in *The Life of Pelopidas*, and Demosthenes recounts many examples in his speech about Aeschines' treachery in the embassy.[36] sig. Bv^r

The Sixth [Action]

Among the Romans, one who deserted the army or fled from battle was prosecuted for violated sovereignty. The Greeks had specific designations—the action for breaking ranks [*graphē leipotaxiou*] and for desertion [*leipostratiou*] —and similar categories were created by the navy. | 16.601

The Fifth Commandment: You Shall Not Kill

The Seventh [Action]

The procedures regarding murder, which are now included under the Cornelian Law, were varied in Athens, and there were various courts of judges.[37] sig. Bv^v

---

and loss of citizen rights pertaining to public life (See Todd, *The Shape of Athenian Law*, pp. 142–143).

34 The previous three headings refer to the first, second, and third "*accusationes*". At this point, Melanchthon stops including the noun and only lists the numbers. Because Melanchthon usually refers in the body of the text to "*actiones*", and because the title of the work is the *Collatio Actionum*, I have chosen to insert the term "Action" in brackets in this heading and those below. In Melanchthon's usage, there is no discernible difference between "*accusatio*" and "*actio*". The terms are interchangeable in this work.

35 See the reference to this in Xenophon, *Hellenika* I.7.22–23.

36 For the charges levelled at Timagoras, see Xenophon, *Hellenika* VII.1.38 and Plutarch, *Life of Pelopidas* 30. In his speech *On the False Embassy*, Demosthenes accused Aeschines of accepting bribes from Philip II of Macedon during a diplomatic mission.

37 A reference to the Cornelian Law Against Murderers and Poisoners (*Lex Cornelia de sicariis et veneficis*), passed ca. 82 BCE during the reign of the dictator Sulla.

For premeditated murder or murder done in the heat of passion, the procedure at the Areopagus was this: First, one had to swear an oath of calumny [*iuramentum calumniae*].[38] Then the facts were narrated without preface and without passion. Then witnesses were called. The judges were not allowed to deliberate together, but they passed their decisions with stones, according to the laws.[39] Further, if the defendant was convicted, he would be subject to capital punishment.

Moreover, two famous trials of the gods took place in the Areopagus. In one of them, Orestes was acquitted even though he killed his mother intentionally.
sig. In another case, Mars was acquitted | after he had killed his daughter's violator,
[Bvi]r Halirrhothius son of Neptune.[40] Antiquity recites these examples to show that
16.602 equity [*epieikeias*] should be derived from a probable cause. |

Killing which was not premeditated, but done for the sake of self-defence, was tried in another place, namely in the Delphinium, and by other judges. And once the necessity of self-defence was established, the defendant was acquitted such that he remained a citizen and kept all the privileges of citizenship. It was there that Theseus pled his case and was acquitted when he had killed the sons of Pallas, who were about to attack him and usurp his rule.[41]

Killing which was not done in self-defence, but by accident, was tried in yet another place, in the Palladium. The penalty for accidental manslaughter was
sig. exile, as is established by many ancient | examples. Telamon was exiled because
[Bvi]v he killed his brother Phocus in a game. So was Patroclus, who killed Clysonymus in a game. There was also Adrastus in Herodotus.[42] And it is worth considering that greater lenience was granted in cases of necessity than in cases of accident, since accidents involve some negligence.

38 That is, an affirmation that the accusation was being brought in good faith.

39 In lawcourts, each juror [*dikastēs*] would cast his vote secretly, by dropping a pebble into one of two urns, labelled for conviction or acquittal. See, for example, Aristophanes, *Wasps*, 986–994.

40 For Orestes, see Aeschylus, *Eumenides*, lines 734–753. For Halirrhothius, see Pausanias, *Description of Greece* I.21.4 and I.28.5.

41 According to Plutarch, *Life of Theseus* 13, the sons of Pallas sought to usurp Theseus' kingship. A group of them lay in wait to attack him, but Theseus ambushed them and killed them.

42 According to Greek myth, Telamon murdered his half-brother Phocus by (perhaps intentionally) striking him in the head with a discus. Patroclus accidentally killed Clysonymus during an argument over a game of dice. Adrastus was exiled for accidentally killing his brother. For Adrastus, see Herodotus, *The Histories* I.35.

The Eighth [Action]

Among the Romans, a single action for injuries [*iniuriarum actio*] includes both severe and minor injuries, and it also covers verbal abuse, assault, and insulting images. | It is distinguished from the accusation of private violence [*vis privata*].[43] But among the Athenians, there are separate actions. The accusation against private violence or atrocious injury is called the "action for *hubris*" [*graphē hubreōs*],[44] | and the penalty was generally legal disgrace [*infamia*], and sometimes even capital punishment, as Lysias explicitly says.[45] Those who are accused in a suit for assault [*verberatio*] are punished with a fine. But those who were convicted of *hubris* could also receive capital punishment, just as in the case of private violence. 16.603 sig. [Bvii]ʳ

Closely related is false litigation [*sukophantia*], when someone was prosecuted who had previously issued a false accusation, circulated false charges about someone else, or committed some fraud which the Romans included in the Cornelian Law concerning frauds.[46] The penalty was legal disgrace. This aligns with the Roman action against calumniators from the Turpilian senatorial decree and the accusation which was established by the Cornelian Law.[47]

Then there are three other, less severe | actions, which are called civil actions, and as the Greeks call them, private actions: The action for assault [*dikē aikias*],[48] when there is a beating which is not serious, and which did not cause a brawl. The penalty was a fine. The action for defamation [*dikē kakēgorias*] covered minor verbal abuses, which, even if they were true, did not cause legal disgrace, and the penalty was left to [the judge's] discretion, excluding the possibility of legal disgrace. The Roman law is harsher, which says that the one found guilty sig. [Bvii]ᵛ

---

43 The Julian Law *De vi privata* established remedies against a category of offenses classified as "private violence". These were often serious offenses, such as gathering a mob which beat a person, but did not kill him (D.48.7.2) See the rest of D.48.7 for additional examples.

44 Although widely agreed to be a form of outrageous assault, the exact nature of the offense of *hubris* is difficult to define. See Todd, *The Shape of Athenian Law*, pp. 270–271.

45 A reference to Lysias' *On the Murder of Eratosthenes*. The speech is a defence of the Athenian Euphiletus, who killed Eratosthenes when Euphiletus found the man in bed with his wife. Throughout the speech, Euphiletus refers to Eratosthenes' crime as *hubris*, and claims that he killed Eratosthenes to fulfil the penalty for *hubris* assigned by the Athenian law. In section 26, before Euphiletus kills Eratosthenes, he says, "It is not I, but the law of the city, which is about to kill you."

46 See Todd, *The Shape of Athenian Law*, pp. 92–94. The Athenian action for *sukophantia* had nothing to do with flattery, as its English cognate suggests. Rather, it was an action brought against those who instigated false accusations.

47 Melanchthon refers here to the *Lex Cornelia de falsis*, passed during the reign of the dictator Sulla. For the laws about calumniators established by the Turpilian senatorial decree, see D.48.16.

48 The 1546 edition incorrectly reads *aitias*, which in 1551 and 1554 is corrected to *aikias*.

in the action of injuries is legally disgraced. The third species, the action for damages [*dikē blabēs*], does not belong here, but to the commandment, "You
16.604 shall not steal". One would only bring this action in order to | restore a loss. This action aligns entirely with the Aquilian Law.[49]

So then, one may ask here: Should a person be punished for making a true
sig. accusation about someone? | The law responds that he should not be punished.
[Bviii]r Here are the words of the law: "It is neither good nor equitable to condemn a person for accusing a harmful man. For it is proper and beneficial that the sins of harmful men be made known."[50] And the preachers in the church should take note of this. For not only may they rebuke the guilty in the case of plainly obvious crimes, but even when a plausible report accuses someone of an action which is not yet entirely proven, the pastors are allowed to admonish the accused such that they drive him to acquit himself, that is, to refute the charge, or indeed that they drive him to correction. Such censures which arise from the office [of pastors] are not unjust, and it especially concerns the Church to guard against
sig. not only fault, but also | against a bad reputation, which provides an opportun-
[Bviii]v ity for despising the Church and ecclesiastical doctrine. And it was rightly said that "I need a good conscience for my own sake, but a good reputation for my neighbour's sake."

The Sixth Commandment: You Shall Not Commit Adultery

The Ninth Accusation

The Romans define the accusation of adultery in the Julian Law.[51] In Greek, it was called the "action for adultery" [*dikē moicheias*], and, as Pausanias writes, the penalty for any adulterer was capital punishment under the ancient Athen-
sig. Cr ian laws.[52] Later, in Solon's law, one who | forcefully violated another man's wife did not receive capital punishment, but was punished with legal disgrace and a
16.605 tortured buttocks.[53] But one | who violated another man's wife by seduction,

49 For the *Lex Aquilia* (3rd century BCE), see D.9.2.

50 D.47.10.18.pr.

51 See D.48.5 and C.9.9. The *Lex Julia* was passed by Augustus in ca. 18 BCE and introduced strict penalties for adultery.

52 Pausanias, *Description of Greece*, IX.36.6–8.

53 A deliberately euphemistic phrase. Melanchthon refers to a punishment for certain sexual crimes, mentioned by Aristophanes in *Clouds* line 1083, whereby the offender would have a radish inserted into his anus and the hair of his buttocks burned off by hot ash. Melanchthon published a Greek edition of *Clouds* in 1521.

without using force, received capital punishment, as Lysias clearly recounts, explaining that a seducer violates both the mind and the body.[54]

The Tenth [Action]

Among the Greeks, the accusation of pimping [*lenocinium*] was called the "action for trafficking" [*dikē proagōgias*], for instance, when a father prostituted his son or daughter, or when anyone prostituted out a young man or woman. Capital punishment was the penalty, as Aeschines shows in reciting that law in *Against Timarchus*.[55] The Roman law | on pimping was less severe. sig. Cv

The Eleventh [Action]

The Romans did not have one single category for *dikē dokimasias*, but among the Athenians, it was a distinguished and honourable censure of morals.[56] For this accusation was set in place against those who defiled themselves through wicked desires contrary to nature, and likewise against deserters and against those who mistreated their parents. The penalty for a defiler [*stuprator*] was capital punishment, but the penalty for the other person was legal disgrace; they could not act as magistrate or serve in the priesthood, nor were they admitted to speak in public or to participate in any decent gatherings. | sig. Cijr

The examples of this accusation are Aeschines' oration *Against Timarchus* and Demosthenes' oration *Against Androtion*.[57] And some write that Timarchus knew that he would die even before the day of his trial.[58]

---

54 cf. Lysias, *On the Murder of Eratosthenes* 26.

55 cf. Aeschines, *Against Timarchus* 14.

56 Melanchthon is technically incorrect here; *dokimasia* was not an action or accusation. In Athens, *dokimasia* [civic examination] was a flexible procedure, but most generally, it was a public investigation before the democratic council (*boulē*) or a court which was used to determine a person's eligibility to hold office or exercise some other privilege. See Todd, *The Shape of Athenian Law*, pp. 115–116.

57 These citations are problematic in two ways. First, Melanchthon mistakenly inferred that a *dokimasia* was a prosecution against sexual crimes because these two cases were about sexual morals. But while *dokimasia* procedures could address sexual morals in their content, they were specifically about one's civic standing and not exclusively about sexual crimes. In *Against Timarchus*, Aeschines uses the procedure of *dokimasia* to try to disqualify his rival Timarchus from bringing a prosecution against him. The particular charge levelled against Timarchus was homosexual prostitution, but the *dokimasia* was not a prosecution for that crime, but an examination into Timarchus' ability to speak in court. Second, Melanchthon is incorrect to cite *Against Androtion* as an example of *dokimasia*. This was a speech given at a *graphē paranomōn*, not a *dokimasia*. The majority of that speech addresses an unlawful proposal of Androtion's, although Demosthenes also accuses Androtion of prostitution (see section 21 of that speech).

58 The ancient *argumentum* to Aeschines' oration *Against Timarchus* reports that some

The Twelfth [Action]

In Greek, the action for divorce is *dikē apopompēs*. In those harsher ancient
16.606 times, this was indeed an action in which the causes of divorce | were explained before the judge with the aim that the injured party would be pronounced free. That this was the custom is apparent from the story about Alcibiades which Lysias and Plutarch recount.[59]

sig. Cijv For when Alciabides' wife, | offended by the wandering lusts of her husband, had gone to live with her brother and intended to get a divorce, Alcibiades requested that she present the divorce petition to the magistrates, and that she do it in person and not through her friends. When the woman appeared in court, Alcibiades and some of his friends came and carried her off forcibly to his house. As a result, she remained with him afterwards as long as she lived.

Accordingly, in the first place, I think that divorce should not be carried out without a judicial investigation [*sine cognitione*], as the Romans later did, and the Turks do now.[60] And I do not believe that divorce should be granted for just any reason whatsoever. In my opinion, the Jews too abused the Law of Moses
sig. Ciijr when they performed divorces for any reason whatsoever. |

Moreover, both Greek and Roman law were in agreement that whenever divorce took place through the fault of the wife, the man would keep the dowry. But if the divorce occurred through no fault of the wife, as often happens, she would keep the dowry, and Demosthenes expressly recites the words of the law in *Against Neaera*.[61] In this matter, those harsher ancient times were in accordance with the Law of Moses. Just as Moses prohibited a man who had divorced his wife from remarrying her again later [Deuteronomy 24:4], so the Greek and Romans laws forbade a woman whose husband divorced her from being remarried. For instance, there was a backlash against Cato's scandalous actions, for after Hortensius died, Cato re-married Marcia.[62] But later, when
sig. Ciijv discipline had been thrown into disorder, the Roman laws allowed | women who had been divorced to remarry. For there was much corruption in the laws

people believed that Timarchus knew, even before the trial took place, that he would eventually be hanged.

59 See Lysias, *Against Alcibiades I*, 28–29 and Plutarch, *Life of Alcibiades* 8.3–5.

60 Roman divorce procedures were largely private and involved minimal judicial interference. See *Borkowski's Textbook*, pp. 128–129.

61 This speech was not given by Demosthenes, but was preserved as part of the Demosthenic corpus.

62 Cato the Younger had divorced his wife Marcia, who then married the much older famous orator Hortensius. After Hortensius died, Cato attempted to marry Marcia again, leading to speculation that Cato was after Hortensius' wealth. See Plutarch, *Life of Cato the Younger* 52.

which the pagans, and now the Turks, passed about marriage. | In every age, 16.607
wandering lusts accumulate into manifold public calamities.

The Thirteenth [Action]

The action against a celibate person was called "the action for celibacy" [*dikē agamiou*]. Presently, Roman law has no penalty for celibacy, and there is no legal action against a celibate person. But formerly, the Roman laws, in a title labelled "On the Ordering of Marriage", punished celibate men by refusing to admit them into the magistracy.[63] | sig. Ciiij^{r}

The Fourteenth [Action]

I will also include under this commandment the accusation of *argia*, that is, of idleness, which was set in place against citizens who were not practicing agriculture or a certain trade. In the ancient laws passed by Draco, legal disgrace was the penalty if someone was convicted of idleness for the first and only time. Afterwards, Solon relaxed it such that a person was disgraced after the third conviction. For he wanted the offender, admonished by the earlier trials, to undertake certain labours in the meantime. If [the offender] failed to do this, then by virtue of his stubbornness, petulance, and confirmed malicious laziness, he would then appear to be in contempt of the laws, and these things deserve a harsher punishment. | sig. Ciiij^{v}

There is no Roman equivalent of this accusation, although prohibiting slothful idleness is certainly most beneficial to discipline. For Cato's saying is true: "Men learn to do evil by doing nothing, and idleness urges many to flee to wicked arts."[64] | 16.608

The Seventh Commandment: You Shall Not Steal

The Fifteenth [Action]

Some thefts are public. Against these thefts, the Julian Law establishes an accusation called the "accusation of embezzlement" [*accusatio peculatus*].[65] In Greek, it was called *phasis*, | that is, "declaration" [*indicatio*] or "denunciation" [*delatio*], sig. Cv^{r}
which encompasses many things. It is the accusation against those who defraud

63 A reference to the *Lex Julia de maritandis ordinibus* (ca. 18 BCE), which, together with the *Lex Papia et Poppaea* (9 CE) encouraged all citizens to marry and imposed certain penalties for celibacy.

64 cf. Columella, *On Agriculture* XI.1.26.

65 See D.48.13.

the treasury, or who unjustly embezzle funds or public revenues, or who tamper with coinage. Among the Romans, this pertains to the crime of fraud [*crimen falsi*].

The Sixteenth [Action]

The Romans have two related actions: the action on mandate [*actio mandati*] and the action on handling another's affairs [*actio negotiorum gestorum*]. The first is granted against a person who did not correctly execute a mandated task.[66] The second was [granted] against a person who [did not correctly execute a task] undertaken of his own initiative.[67]

The Athenians included both of these under one name, which they called
sig. Cvv the "public examinations" [*euthunai*].[68] In fact, the Greeks used this action | not only in civil cases for seeking an account of financial dealings or the administration of funds, but also in public accusations, as when the magistrates who had finished their term in office were called to trial because they had at some point acted contrary to the laws, or when the treachery of ambassadors was prosecuted, as when Demosthenes accused Aeschines of doing many things treacherously in his role as ambassador.[69]

So then, this well-designed action bolsters two virtues which are critically necessary in every government, namely integrity in carrying out one's duties
16.609 and diligence. | Paul talks about both of these things: "As for the rest, this is required: that one be faithful" [cf. 1 Cor. 4:2].

The Seventeenth [Action]

sig. [Cvi]r The action of guardianship [*actio tutelae*] in Greek is called *dikē epitropēs*, which was provided against guardians who mishandled the affairs of their wards. For example, Demosthenes prosecuted his own guardians [for this].[70]

---

66 In Roman law, *mandatum* was a contract in which one party agreed to perform a service for another without pay. See *Borkowski's Textbook*, pp. 284–289; D.17.1; and Inst. 3.26.

67 *negotiorum gestio* was a Roman "quasi-contract" in which party A performed an action that was putatively beneficial to party B, without party B's authorization. For example, if party B was away from his property on business, and his fence was damaged by a fallen tree, Party A could repair the fence without B's authorization and expect reimbursement upon B's return. This action was used when an actor performed such an action in an incorrect, negligent, or harmful way. See du Plessis, *Borkowski's Textbook*, pp. 315–317; D.3.5; and C.2.18.

68 *Euthunai* were examinations into the behaviour of Athenian officials, conducted after they left office, with a particular emphasis on discovering financial misconduct. See Todd, *The Shape of Athenian Law*, pp. 112–113.

69 See Demosthenes, *On the False Embassy*.

70 See, for example, Demosthenes, *Against Aphobus I, II*, and *III*.

The Eighteenth [Action]

The action on deposit, *dikē parakatathēkēs*, was provided against those who had not displayed good faith or due diligence in keeping or returning a deposit.[71] Moreover, a conviction carried two penalties: the convicted would pay for the deposit and any interest, and he would become legally disgraced.

The Nineteenth [Action]

The action for theft, *dikē klopēs*, was a civil action brought either to restore [stolen] property or gain compensation for it. | And the Greeks had three categories of thieves. Petty thieves [*fures*],[72] who stole things without violence, were punished by paying double [of what they stole]. Then there were burglars, who broke into other peoples' homes while armed. We call them burglars [*grassatores*], or in Greek, *toichōruxoi*, that is, "housebreakers", or *lōpodutai*, that is, "clothes-thieves".[73] Then there are robbers [*qui latrocinium exercent*], or *lēstai*. sig. [Cvi]v

These two latter categories received capital punishment. A recent law in our own age is even harsher, as it punishes all thieves with capital punishment. This makes sense in these barbarous nations, where all thieves generally have the same intentions that violent robbers do. | 16.610 / sig. [Cvii]r

Actions Arising from Contract

The Twentieth [Action]

Among the Romans, the actions arising from contract have different names according to their species. The Greeks delineate a few species [of these actions], but the genus is the "action on contract" [*dikē xumbolaiou*].[74] The species are listed: There is the action for an outstanding loan, which they call "action on debt" [*dikē chreous*] or "action on loan" [*dikē daneiou*], that is, when one demands money owed from a loan. Accordingly, there are two orations written in Demosthenes which contain suits arising from a loan.[75] But the action on

71 *depositum* was a form of Roman contract in which the depositor handed over moveable property to a depositee for safekeeping. The depositee had to observe certain standards of good faith and diligence in keeping and returning the deposit. See *Borkowski's Textbook*, pp. 304–306; D.16.3, C.4.34.

72 In the margin, Melanchthon glosses the Latin term *fures* with the Greek *kleptai*.

73 The Greek term literally refers to the theft of clothing, but was also used as a more general term for a thief.

74 As Todd argues (pp. 332–333), this term likely referred to agreements between communities rather than contracts between individuals. *Dikē xumbolaiou* may have also been a synonym for the more common term for an action arising from contracts, *dikē apo sumbolōn*.

75 See *Against Phormio* (oration 34) and *Against Timotheus* (oration 49).

debt [*chreous*] is also applicable to debts incurred from a sale. However, usury is the proper term for when one seeks an amount greater than the principal in
sig. exchange for a loan. |
[Cvii]v The ancients also required the payment of usurious interest if a debt had not been paid by the appointed day, even if the money was owed from a sale. And under both Attic and Roman law, it was legal to practice usury at twelve percent [*centesima*] interest rates, which the debtor was required to pay.[76] But it was illegal to seek or agree to a rate above twelve percent, and a judge would absolve a debtor who was charged any higher rate.

Nevertheless, we ourselves know that the divine law prohibits all usury. But because profane men do not obey the law of God, the magistrates enshrined in these governments a certain limit on usury lest the poor be bled completely
sig. dry. But the rapacity of the usurers does not even keep to this limit. |
[Cviii]r Therefore, because of the great extent of usury, dissensions have often arisen within governments, or great upheavals have followed, as happened in Athens and Rome. However, compensation [*id quod interest*] was sought through the action for damages [*dikē blabēs*]. For it is proper to say that there is compensation [*interesse*] when some party in a contract creates an efficacious cause of
16.611 loss [*efficaciter causam dedit damni*].[77] |

The Action from Sale

The Twenty-First [Action]

Parallel to the Roman action called "action on sale" [*actio ex empto*] is the Attic action called "warranty" [*dikē bebaiōseōs*], that is, guaranteed sale.[78] This action was granted to the buyer against the seller to compel him to deliver goods or
sig. to reimburse in case of eviction. | That is, in a case in which the seller had sold
[Cviii]v

76 The *centesima* interest rate was the rate at which accrued interest would equal the principal after 100 months. It was basically equivalent to a non-compounding twelve percent interest rate.

77 As Melanchthon discusses in the section of the *Summary of Moral Philosophy* entitled "On Contracts", there was a difference between compensation [*id quod interest*] and usury [*usura*]. Usury, or charging money for the service of lending, was clearly immoral. However, compensation [*id quod interest*] was a different, allowable category. Compensation was an amount charged to a borrower if he caused the lender to suffer a loss, that is, if he created an *efficax causa damni*. For example, if party A loaned money to party B, and party B defaulted on the loan, causing some further loss to party A (i.e., if party A could not then pay his own debts), then that additional loss was classified as "compensation".

78 The Roman *actio ex empto* (or *actio empti*) provided buyers some recourse against sellers, i.e. in the case of purchase of defective goods or if the seller failed to deliver the purchased goods. See *Borkowski's Textbook*, pp. 276–279.

someone else's property to an unwitting buyer, then, if necessary, [the seller] would prove that he was the owner of the item sold, or he would reimburse [the buyer] for the sale price.[79] This also encompasses the related actions which are available to buyers.[80]

The Action from the "Interdict *unde vi*"[81]

The Twenty-Second [Action]

The action is called the "action of ejectment" [*dikē exoulēs*], from the verb *exeillō*, that is, "to force out." It was granted either for restoring or retaining possession, or for enjoyment [of possession], if someone prohibits or impedes enjoyment.[82]

The Romans mark off various species with distinct terms, namely the | interdict "*unde vi*" and "*uti possidetis*". But the Athenians included all related actions under the general name [i.e., *dikē exoulēs*] which I mentioned above. So then, just as God intends by means of that law, "You shall not steal", for each person's property to be protected as if by a wall, so he commands the magistrate to execute this law, willing him to protect the citizens so that each may enjoy his own property, keep it, and recover anything that has been unjustly taken from him. There are many obvious examples of this both in history and in daily life. sig. D^r^

Seneca recounts one particularly memorable story.[83] Philip of Macedon had dispatched a soldier to a certain place with firm orders. The soldier was driven aground by a storm, and, exhausted by the ferocity of the tempest, he was rescued by a local peasant. | After recovering for a few days in this man's care sig. D^v^

---

79 If a purchaser was legally deprived (evicted) of his purchased goods by a third party (i.e. if the buyer had unknowingly purchased stolen goods which were then lawfully returned to the rightful owner), the seller was responsible for making good that loss (*praestare evictionem*). See D.21.2.

80 A marginal note here reads "*Redhibitoria. Praescriptis verbis.*" These were the names of actions which buyers could seek against sellers. For returns (*redhibitoria*), see D.21.1. The action of introductory words (*actio praescriptis verbis*) was used to enforce a contract when one party had already performed his duty, but the other had not. See D.19.5.

81 In Roman law, disputes over possession were generally decided by possessory interdicts issued by the praetors. The *interdictum unde vi* (Inst. 4.15.6) was used to restore possession of property which was taken by force. The *interdictum uti possidetis* (D.43.17, C.8.6.1) was generally used to protect the possession of land. The names of the interdicts are taken from the opening words of the praetor's pronouncement.

82 The plaintiff would bring a *dikē exoulēs* to eject an unlawful possessor from real property to which the plaintiff had a lawful claim. See Todd, *The Shape of Athenian Law*, pp. 144–145, 377.

83 See Seneca, *On Benefits* IV.37.

and regaining his strength, the soldier returned to the king and told him of the ordeal, but he did not mention the peasant's kindness. In fact, the soldier asked that the estate located in that area be given to him as a testament to his ordeal, and the king generously granted his request. But when the soldier arrived to
16.612 take possession | of the estate, the peasant went to the king and explained that he had saved the soldier, and that for his kindness he was now being expelled from his own property. At this point, the king retracted his gift and ordered the peasant to keep his own estate, while he ordered the ungrateful soldier to be seared on the forehead with a brand reading "Ungrateful Guest".

The Twenty-Third [Action]

From lease [arises the action] of hire [*misthōseōs*], concerning which the Athen-
sig. Dij^r^ ians also observed | that which is in Roman law: that any property which the tenant brought into the rented house becomes a pledge to the landlord by virtue of the law itself [*ipso iure*], even without any decree from the magistrate, just as it says under the title, "Cases in Which There is a Tacit Contract of Pledge or Mortgage," where it reads, "Everything which is brought or carried in will have been offered in pledge."[84]

The Twenty-Fourth [Action]

There were multiple actions concerning inheritance: *amphisbētēsis*, which was used to determine the heir when someone died intestate and with no children, and *epidikasia*, when the nearest relatives sought the inheritance, even if a will had been made, because they complained that they had been unjustly left out.[85]

---

84 The title is D.20.2.0. The quote is from D.20.2.2. *Locatio conductio* was the Roman contract of hire in which the *locator* [lessor] let out a good or service to the *conductor* [renter] [see Inst.3.24, D.19.2]. Here, Melanchthon refers to a particular feature of such contracts, by which any moveable property which the tenant brought into a rented dwelling or onto rented land became security [*pignus*] for the contract if the tenant did not pay rent. Melanchthon's source for the Greek contract is unclear, although there is mention of a lease [*misthōsis*] contract with deposits in the pseudo-Demosthenic oration *Against Stephanus* I.31–34.

85 Melanchthon is not exactly correct here. *Epidikasia* was the term for a claim to an estate without a direct male heir, while *diadikasia* involved an estate with multiple contested claims. See Todd, *The Shape of Athenian Law*, pp. 216–221.

|The Eighth Commandment: You Shall Not Give False Testimony sig. Dij[v]

The Twenty-Fifth [Action]

One who had given false testimony was tried in the Areopagus, and this was called the "accusation of perjury" [*accusatio pseudomarturiou*]. There were also other actions for those who had claimed to have heard from eyewitnesses, that is, *ekmarturia*.[86] An action for refusing to testify [*actio leipomarturias*] was also granted | against those who, although they could have offered testimony, refused 16.613
to do so, just as there are now laws established for compelling witnesses, since those who know the truth and hide it are unjust just like those who speak falsely, | sig. Diij[r]
and just as Christ does not only condemn those who oppose the truth, but also those who conceal it: "Whoever does not gather with me scatters" [Luke 11:23].

The Twenty-Sixth [Action]

The accusation against an unconstitutional measure [*accusatio paranomōn*], when someone is prosecuted who proposed a law or decree contrary to previously accepted laws, was unknown to the Romans.[87] Moreover, this procedure did not have a name among the Romans precisely because, in Rome, private alteration of the laws was prosecuted under the crime of violated sovereignty, just like the crime of heresy in the contemporary church. But the Athenians distinguished several degrees of laws. They prosecuted those who violated the very bonds of religion | or government through impeachment [*eisangelia*][88] | 16.614
or the accusation of impiety [*accusatione asebeias*]. But they referred viola- sig. Diij[v]
tion of the lower laws to the most general accusation of *paranomōn*, in which the convicted only became legally disgraced, and he would not receive capital punishment. As an example, Aeschines accused Ctesiphon of making a decree that Demosthenes should be granted honours before his accounting was completed.[89]

---

86 In Athenian law, an *ekmarturia* was not a legal action, but a written testimony produced by witnesses who could not appear in preliminary hearings.

87 The *graphē paranomōn* was one of the most well-attested Athenian legal procedures. See Todd, *The Shape of Athenian Law*, pp. 388–389. Demosthenes gave his famous speech *On the Crown* at a *graphē paranomōn*.

88 The text reads ἐισαγγελία (in the nominative case), but the sense in this sentence is ἐισαγγελίᾳ (dative).

89 This accounting likely refers to the *euthunai* (see the sixteenth action above), the requirement that Athenian officials have their tenure examined and approved by an audit after they completed their term. In *Against Ctesiphon* 9–12, Aeschines argued that it was illegal for Ctesiphon to propose conferring honours (in this case, a golden crown) before Demos-

In contrast, one who was unjustly accused could in turn sue his accuser for false litigation [*sukophanteia*], as we have mentioned above, just as in the Roman law one could accuse a calumniator[90] according to the Turpilian senatorial decree. A convicted calumniator would suffer legal disgrace, although that ancient harshness dictated that a calumniator in a capital case should be given the same punishment which would have been applied to his adversary if
sig. Diiij^{r} / [17.877] he were convicted. |

AN EXAMPLE WHICH WARNS AGAINST RASHLY CHANGING THOSE LAWS WHICH HAVE BEEN ACCEPTED BY THE WEIGHTY JUDGMENT OF ONE'S ANCESTORS AND THEREAFTER CONFIRMED BY LONG USE. FROM DEMOSTHENES' SPEECH *AGAINST TIMOCRATES*.

"I will describe to you, judges, a Locrian law, for it will do you no harm to hear
this example, especially one offered by a city rightly established by law. For
these men believe so strongly that the ancient laws should be preserved, that
17.878 their homeland should be maintained as it was founded, | and that new laws
should not be passed either to please the desires of the few or to avoid trials,
sig. Diiij^{v} that | if anyone should present himself in order to seek a new law, he is forced to
propose it with a noose around his neck. If the people approve of his proposed
17.879 law, the speaker | departs unharmed. But if the law is rejected, the speaker is
strangled by the noose. The magnitude of this danger would deter citizens from
passing new laws, and for this reason they obey the ancient laws with greater
zeal and reverence.

And it is said that these people have only passed one new law throughout
many ages. For the city had a law of retaliation, meaning that if someone gouged
out another's eye, in turn his own eye would be gouged out, and there was no
sig. Dv^{r} financial penalty. Now, there was a man who | threatened to gouge out the eye
of a man who only had one eye. The one-eyed man, greatly disturbed by this
17.880 threat, | and considering how miserable his future life of blindness would be,
dared to step forth in the assembly to persuade them to pass a new law stating
that whoever gouged out the remaining eye of a one-eyed man would in turn
have both of his eyes gouged out, to make the punishment equal to the crime.
And the Locrians say that this was the only law passed for two centuries."—
Demosthenes.[91]

---

thenes' time in office had been reviewed and approved. Demosthenes' famous reply in defence of Ctesiphon was his oration *On the Crown*.

90 i.e., one who intentionally makes false accusations.

91 This excerpt is Melanchthon's Latin translation of Demosthenes, *Against Timocrates* 139–141.

|An Elegy of Solon, Quoted by Demosthenes, about the Causes which Bring about Ruin in Kingdoms and Great Cities, Translated by Philip Melanchthon.[92] sig. Dv^v / [17.873]

It is not the gods' desire to overthrow our city;
They favour us, so long as we do not blaspheme their names.
Pallas Athena guards our stronghold,
Eternal care defends our walls.
But citizens with wounded minds
Wantonly try to rip their own country asunder.
For some sell the laws and integrity for a price;
Tormented by their insatiable hunger for gold.
Some practice savagery, grasping at tyranny,
As righteous anger takes up arms against fellow-citizens.
Some try to mend the houses damaged by plundering
When luxury wickedly exhausted the country's wealth. | 17.874
They rip away the public patrimony of our city
And amass their own treasure through force and fraud.
They do not fear the wrath of avenging justice,
The goddess ever-present in the councils of divinity.
She sees every deed with her vigilant eyes,
Let no one think he can deceive the gods. | sig.
Although she may sometimes delay or defer punishment, [Dvi]^r
Wicked deeds still do not escape her mind or memory,
And eventually, she exacts the penalty. Neither kingdoms nor cities
Can escape the dire ruin which they deserve.
Hence a city once proud of wealth and power
Suffers now the sad justice of slavery.
Either the raving citizens draw their swords
For wounding each other, with sedition raging,
Or they provoke strong enemies randomly, for no reason,
They stir the evil which was hitherto slumbering. | 17.875
For the city which provokes its allies with unjust violence
Will soon regret it and meet a sudden death.
By these causes, mighty nations and cities fall,

92 Demosthenes quotes these verses in *On the False Embassy* 255. This was not the first time that Melanchthon published his Latin translation of these verses. See CR 17.873 for additional printing information. This elegy is not included in the 1551 or 1554 Wittenberg editions.

Piety spurned brings a harsh punishment.
Even if some may perhaps survive their country's ruin,
Afterwards, a grave fate awaits them.
Exiles, they wander destitute without hope and home,
Or sell themselves into harsh chains.
Thus, each man is alone when public ruin descends
17.876 And there is no door to keep out evil, |
The hiding places cannot conceal all who flee,
The public chaos even penetrates your bedchambers.
I warn you, citizens: Do not reckon these to be fanciful fables,
Be sure that it is a grave crime to scorn God and the Laws.
But a tranquil peace is kept by reverence for law,
sig. [Dvi]v Which, dispassionate, is not wont to spare the sinner. |
It forbids wicked luxury and restrains rebels,
It does not allow the scattered seeds of evil to grow.
It brings fraud to trial, and prevents
Violent deeds and strife between citizens.
Finally, the life of men will remain peaceful and honourable
As long as pious care for keeping the laws remains.

Printed at Wittenberg by Veit Kreutzer.
1546.

Bibliography

Classical Sources

***Unless otherwise noted, all classical citations refer to the numbering in the Loeb Classical Library series. This bibliography does not include all classical texts referenced by Melanchthon (and identified by the editor in the footnotes). This bibliography only includes those classical editions and translations which are cited or quoted in discussion in the footnotes or introductory essays.

Aristotle. *Aristotelis Ethica Nicomachea.* ed. I. Bywater. Oxford: Oxford University Press, 1894.

Aristotle. *Aristotelis Politica.* ed. W.D. Ross. Oxford: Oxford University Press, 1957.

Aristotle. *Nicomachean Ethics.* trans. H. Rackham. Loeb Classical Library 73. Cambridge: MA, Harvard University Press, 1926.

Aristotle. *Politics.* trans. H. Rackham. Loeb Classical Library 264. Cambridge, MA: Harvard University Press, 1932.

Augustine. *Augustine: Political Writings.* ed. E.M. Atkins and R.J. Dodaro. Cambridge: Cambridge University Press, 2004.

Cicero. *On Invention. The Best Kind of Orator. Topics.* Translated by H.M. Hubbell. Loeb Classical Library 386. Cambridge, MA: Harvard University Press, 1949.

Demosthenes, *Orations, Volume III: Orations 21–26: Against Meidias. Against Androtion. Against Aristocrates. Against Timocrates. Against Aristogeiton 1 and 2.* Translated by J.H. Vince. Loeb Classical Library 299. Cambridge, MA: Harvard University Press, 1935.

Galen. *Claudii Galeni Opera Omnia.* ed. K.G. Kühn. 22 vols. Leipzig: Knobloch, 1821–1833.

Greek Mathematical Works, Vol. I: Thales to Euclid. Translated by Ivor Thomas. Loeb Classical Library 335. Cambridge, MA: Harvard University Press, 1939.

Justinian. *Iustiniani Institutiones.* ed. Paul Krüger. Berlin: Weidmann, 1867.

Justinian. *Digesta Iustiniani Augusti.* ed. Theodor Mommsen. Berlin: Weidmann, 1870.

Justinian. *Codex Iustinianus.* ed. Paul Krüger. Berlin: Weidmann, 1877.

Nicene and Post-Nicene Fathers. *A Select Library of Nicene and Post-Nicene Fathers of the Christian Church,* ed. Philip Schaff and Henry Wace. 28 vols. in 2 series. 1886–1889. [Abbreviated NPNF].

Patrologia Graeca. Ed. J.-P. Migne. 161 vols. Paris: 1857–1886. [abbreviated PG].

Patrologia Latina. Ed. J.-P. Migne. 221 vols. Paris: 1844–1864. [abbreviated PL].

Suda. *Suidae Lexicon.* ed. Immanuel Bekker. Berlin: Reimer, 1854.

Early Modern and Medieval Sources

*** For extensive bibliographies of the texts translated in this volume, see the introductions to each text.

Apel, Johann. *Methodica Dialectices Ratio ad Iurisprudentiam Accomodata*. Nuremberg, 1535.

Baldus de Ubaldus. *Baldi Ubaldi Perusini iurisconsulti … in quartum et quintum Cod. Lib. Commentaria*. Venice: Giunti, 1599.

Boecler, Johann Heinrich. *In Hugonis Grotii jus belli et pacis commentatio*. Strasbourg, 1663.

Budé, Guillaume. *Annotationes Gulielmi Budaei Parisiensis, Secretarii Regii, in quatuor et viginti Pandectarum libros*. Paris: Ioannes Parvus, 1536 (original 1508).

Duprat, Pardoux. *Iurisprudentia vetus, Draconis et Solonis leges*. Lyon: Gulielmus Rovillius, 1559.

Erasmus, Desiderius. *Opera omnia Desiderii Erasmi, Recognita et Adnotatione Critica Instructa Notisque Illustrata*. Amsterdam: Elsevier, 1969–. [abbreviated ASD]

Gratian. *Decretum Magistri Gratiani*, ed. Emil Friedberg. In *Corpus Iuris Canonici*, volume I. Reprint. (Graz: Akademische Druck- u. Verlagsanstalt, 1959). Original, Leipzig: Bernhard Tauchnitz, 1879.

Gerson, Jean. *Oeuvres Complètes*. ed. Mgr. Glorieux, 3 vols. Paris: Desclée & Cie, 1962.

Hemmingsen, Niels. *De lege naturae apodicta methodus*. Wittenberg, 1563.

Hemmingsen, Niels. *On the Law of Nature: A Demonstrative Method*. ed. and trans. by E.J. Hutchinson, introduction by E.J. Hutchinson and Korey D. Maas. Grand Rapids, MI: Christian's Library Press, 2018.

Hooker, Richard. *Of the Laws of Ecclesiastical Polity*, ed. Arthur Stephen McGrade. Cambridge: Cambride University Presss, 1989.

Hostiensis (Henry of Segusio). *Henrici de Segusio Cardinalis Hostiensis Summa Aurea, ad vetustissimos codices summa fide diligentiaque nunc primum collata, atque ab innumeris erroribus, quibus scatebat hactenus, repurgata*. Venice: Giacomo Vitale, 1574.

Innocent IV. *Commentaria Innocentii quarti pont. Maximi super libros quinque Decretalium*. Frankfurt, 1570.

Lagus, Konrad. *Iuris Utriusque Methodica Traditio*. Frankfurt, 1543.

Liber extravagantium decretalium, ed. Emil Friedberg. In *Corpus Iuris Canonici*, volume II. Reprint. (Graz: Akademische Druck- u. Verlagsanstalt, 1959). Original, Leipzig: Bernhard Tauchnitz, 1881.

Luther, Martin. *D. Martin Luthers Werke: kritische Gesamtausgabe*. Weimar: Hermann Böhlau, 1883–2009.

Machiavelli, Niccolò. *The Prince*. ed. Quentin Skinner and Russel Price. Cambridge: Cambridge University Press, 1988.

Melanchthon, Philip. *In Ethica Aristotelis commentarius Philipp. Melanchtho.* Wittenberg: Josef Klug, 1529.

Melanchthon, Philip and Johannes de Sacrobusco. *Liber Iohannis de Sacro Busto, de Sphaera. Addita est praefatio in eundem librum Philippi Melanchthonis ad Simonem Gryneum.* Wittenberg: Joseph Klug, 1531.

Melanchthon, Philip. *De officio principum, quod mandatum Dei praecipiat eis tollere abusus Ecclesiasticos.* Wittenberg: Josef Klug, 1539.

Melanchthon, Philip. *Opera quae supersunt omnia.* Ed. Karl Gottlieb Brettschneider and Heinrich Ernest Bindseil. 28 vols. Halle: Schwetschke et Filium, 1834–1860. [abbreviated CR]

Melanchthon, Philip. *Melanchthons Werke in Auswahl.* ed. Robert Stupperich. 7 vols. Gütersloh: C. Bertelsmann, 1951–1975. [abbreviated MWA]

Melanchthon, Philip. *Melanchthons Briefwechsel: Kritische und Kommentierte Gesamtausgabe im Auftrag der Heidelberger Academie der Wissenschaften.* ed. Heinz Scheible. Stuttgart: Fromann-Holzboog, 1997–. [abbreviated MBW]

Melanchthon, Philip. *Melanchthon deutsch.* ed. Michael Beyer et al. 7 vols. Leipzig: Evangelische Verlagsanstalt, 2011–. [abbreviated MD]

Melanchthon, Philip. *Commentary on Proverbs.* Trans. and ed. by Derek Cooper and Timothy J. Wengert. Grand Rapids, MI: CLP Academic, 2023.

Netter, Thomas. *Doctrinale antiquitatum fidei catholicae ecclesiae contra Wiclevistas et Hussitas libri VI.* Paris: 1521.

Oldendorp, Johann. *Iuris naturalis, gentium, et civilis eisagōgē.* Cologne: Johann Gymnich, 1539.

Panormitanus. *Nicolai Abbatis Panormitani commentaria ad quartum et quintum libros Decretalium.* Tours: Nicolaus Bevilaqua, 1577.

Petit, Samuel. *Leges Atticae.* Paris: Carolus Morellus, 1635.

Postel, Guillaume. *De magistratibus Atheniensium.* Paris: Vascosanus et Galeotus, 1541.

Rittershausen, Konrad. *Commentarius novus in quatuor libros institutionum imperialium divi Justiniani.* Strasburg: Heirs of Lazarus Zetzner, 1618.

Sigonio, Carlo. *De republica Atheniensium libri IIII.* Bologna: Ioannes Rubrius, 1564.

Valla, Lorenzo. *De voluptate ac vero bono libri III.* Basel: Andreas Cartander, 1519.

Woldenberg, *Principia Juris Romani, i.e. leges Draconis et Solonis, leges Romuli, et leges XII. Tabularum.* Rostock: Johannis Keil, 1668.

John Wycliffe. *Iohannis Wycliffe, Tractatus de civili dominio.* ed. R.L. Poole. 4 vols. London, 1885–1904.

Modern Scholarship

Astorri, Paolo. "Early Modern Lutheran Theologians and the Redeemable *Census:* Towards a Reformulation of the Interest Prohibition", *Studia Historica: Historia Moderna* 44.1 (2022): 53–76.

Astorri, Paolo. *Lutheran Theology and Contract Law in Early Modern Germany* (*ca. 1520–1720*). Leiden: Brill, 2019.

Astorri, Paolo. "The Redefinition of Clandestine Marriage by Sixteenth-Century Lutheran Theologians and Jurists", *Law and History Review* 41.1 (2023): 65–92.

Backus, Irena. "Calvin's Concept of Natural and Roman Law", *Calvin Theological Journal* 38 (2003): 7–26.

Baker, Robert C. and Roland Cap Ehlke, eds. *Natural Law: A Lutheran Reappraisal*. St. Louis, MO: Concordia, 2011.

Baschera, Luca. "Shaping Reformed Aristotelianism: Otto Werdmüller's Evaluation of the Nicomachean Ethics in *De dignitate, usu et methodo philosophiae moralis* (1545)", in *Following Zwingli: Applying the Past in Reformation Zurich*, ed. Luca Baschera, Bruce Gordon, and Christian Moser. London: Routledge, 2016, pp. 210–231.

Batson, Alexander. "Calvin and Equity", in *The Oxford Handbook of Calvin and Calvinism*, ed. Bruce Gordon and Carl Trueman. Oxford: Oxford University Press, 2021, pp. 74–87.

Batson, Alexander. "Philip Melanchthon's Humanist Politics: Greek Scholarship in a Time of Confessional Crisis", *Reformation & Renaissance Review* 24.1 (2022): 23–43.

Batson, Alexander. "Sinai and the Areopagus: Philip Melanchthon, Natural Law, and the Beginnings of Athenian Legal History in the Shadow of the Schmalkaldic War", *Journal of the History of Ideas* 85.4 (2024): 713–748.

Batson, Alexander. "Isocrates and the Persian Turks. Ottoman Invasions and Confessional Conflict in the Classical Scholarship of Hieronymus Wolf", *Journal of the Warburg and Courtauld Institutes* 88 (2025).

Bauer, Clemens. "Melanchthons Naturrechtslehre", *Archiv für Reformationsgeschichte* 42 (1951): 64–100.

Bauer, Clemens. "Die Naturrechtsvorstellungen des jüngeren Melanchthon", in Bauer, *Gesammelte Aufsätze zur Wirtschafts- und Sozialgeschichte*. Freiburg: Herder, 1965, pp. 266–276.

Bauer, Joachim, and Michael Haspel, eds. *Jakob Strauss und der reformatorische Wucherstreit. Die soziale Dimension der Reformation und ihre Wirkungen*. Leipzig: Evangelische Verlagsanstalt, 2018.

Baylor, Michael G., ed. *The Radical Reformation*. Cambridge: Cambridge University Press, 1991.

Beck, Andreas J. "Zur Rezeption Melanchthons bei Gisbertus Voetius (1589–1676), namentlich in seiner Gotteslehre", in *Melanchthon und der Calvinismus*, Melanchthon Schriften der Stadt Bretten 9, ed. Günter Frank and Herman J. Selderhuis. Stuttgart-Bad Cannstatt: Frommann-Holzboog, 2005, pp. 317–342.

Beck, Andreas J. "Melanchthon und die reformierte Scholastik", in *Melanchthon und die Reformierte Tradition*, ed. Andreas J. Beck. Göttingen: Vandenhoeck & Ruprecht, 2016, pp. 107–128.

Ben-Tov, Asaph. *Lutheran Humanists and Greek Antiquity: Melanchthonian Scholarship between Universal History and Pedagogy*. Leiden: Brill, 2009.

Berman, Harold. *Law and Revolution II: The Impact of the Protestant Reformations on the Western Legal Tradition*. Cambridge, MA: Belknap Press, 2003.

Bihlmaier, Sandra. *Ars et Methodus: Philipp Melanchthon's Humanist Concept of Philosophy*. Göttingen: Vandenhoeck & Ruprecht, 2018.

Blickle, Peter. *The Revolution of 1525: The German Peasants' War from a New Perspective*, trans. Thomas A. Brady, Jr. and H.C. Erik Midelfort. Baltimore: Johns Hopkins University Press, 1981.

Böttcher, Diethelm. *Ungehorsam oder Widerstand: Zum Fortleben des mittelalterlichen Widerstandsrechtes in der Reformationzeit (1529–1530)*. Berlin: Duncker & Humblot, 1991.

Bourrilly, V.-L. *Guillaume du Bellay, seigneur de Langey, 1491–1542*. Paris, 1905.

Brett, Annabel S. *Changes of State: Nature and the Limits of the City in Early Modern Natural Law*. Princeton: Princeton University Press, 2011.

British Museum, Department of Printed Books. *Short-Title Catalogue of Books Printed in the German-Speaking Countries and German Books Printed in Other Countries: From 1455 to 1600, Now in the British Museum*. London: Trustees of the British Museum, 1962.

Claus, Helmut. *Melanchthon-Bibliographie, 1510–1560*. 4 vols. Gütersloh: Gütersloher Verlagshaus, 2014.

Dauber, Noah. "Deutsche Reformation: Philipp Melanchthon", in *Politischer Aristotelismus: Die Rezeption der Aristotelischen Politik von der Antike bis zum 19 Jahrhundert*, ed. Christoph Horn and Ada Neschke-Hentschke. Stuttgart: J.B. Metzler, 2008.

Dauber, Noah. *State and Commonwealth: The Theory of the State in Early Modern England, 1549–1640*. Princeton: Princeton University Press, 2016.

Deflers, Isabelle. *Lex und ordo: Eine rechtshistorische Untersuchung der Rechtsauffassung Melanchthons*. Berlin: Duncker & Humblot, 2005.

Dilthey, Wilhelm. "Melanchthon und die erste Ausbildung des natürlichen Systems in Deutschland", in *Wilhelm Diltheys gesammelte Schriften, II. Band: Weltanschauung und Analyse des Menschen seit Renaissance und Reformation*. Leipzig: Teubner, 1929, pp. 162–202.

Dingel, Irene. "Melanchthon's Paraphrases of the Augsburg Confession, 1534 and 1536, in the Service of the Smalcald League", in *Philip Melanchthon: Theologian in Class-*

room, Confession, and Controversy, ed. Irene Dingel, Robert Kolb, Nicole Kuropka, and Timothy J. Wengert. Göttingen: Vandenhoek & Ruprecht, 2012, pp. 104–122.

Dingel, Irene. "Melanchthon's Efforts for Unity between the Fronts: the Frankfurt Recess", in *Philip Melanchthon: Theologian in Classroom, Confession, and Controversy*, ed. Irene Dingel, Robert Kolb, Nicole Kuropka, and Timothy J. Wengert. Göttingen: Vandenhoek & Ruprecht, 2012, pp. 123–140.

Dreitzel, Horst. "Von Melanchthon zu Pufendorf: Versuch über Typen und Entwicklung der philosophischen Ethik im protestantischen Deutschland zwischen Reformation und Aufklärung", in *Spätrenaissance-Philosophie in Deutschland 1570–1650*. Berlin: Max Niemeyer Verlag, 2007.

Du Plessis, Paul. *Borkowski's Textbook on Roman Law*. Sixth Edition. Oxford: Oxford University Press, 2020.

Du Plessis, Paul, and John W. Cairns, eds. *Reassessing Legal Humanism and its Claims: Petere Fontes?* Edinburgh: Edinburgh University Press, 2016.

Dunn, James J. "The Reformation of Virtue: The Teaching of Aristotle's *Ethics* at Wittenberg and Helmstedt (1502–1648)". Unpublished Ph.D. diss., Yale University, 2023.

Elert, Werner. *Morphologie des Luthertums. Zweiter Band: Soziallehren und Sozialwirkungen des Luthertums*. 2nd edition. Munich: 1958.

Estes, James. *Peace, Order, and the Glory of God: Secular Authority and the Church in the Thought of Luther and Melanchthon, 1518–1559*. Leiden: Brill, 2005.

Frank, Günter. *Die theologische Philosophie Philipp Melanchthons: 1497–1560*. Leipzig: Benno, 1995.

Frank, Günter. "Die theologische Philosophie Melanchthons (1497–1560): Ein Plädoyer zur Rehabilitierung des Humanisten und Reformators", *Kerygma und Dogma* 42.1 (1996): 22–36.

Frank, Günter. "Fragmentierung und topische Neuordnung der aristotelischen Ethik in der frühen Neuzeit: Ethik bei Viktorin Strigel und Abraham Scultetus", in *Späthumanismus und reformierte Konfession*, ed. Christoph Strohm, Joseph S. Freedman, and Herman J. Selderhuis. Tübingen: Mohr Siebeck, 2006, pp. 153–167.

Frank, Günter. "Melanchthon—der 'Ethiker der Reformation'", in *Der Philosoph Melanchthon*. ed. Günter Frank and Felix Mundt. Berlin: De Gruyter, 2012, pp. 44–76.

Frank, Günter, and Stephan Rhein, eds. *Melanchthon und die Naturwissenschaften seiner Zeit*. Stuttgart: Thorbecke, 1998.

Frank, Günter, with Michael Beyer, eds. *Philipp Melanchthon: Ethicae Doctrinae Elementa et Enarratio Libri quinti Ethicorum*. Stuttgart-Bad Cannstatt: Frommann-Holzboog, 2008.

Fraenkel, Peter, ed. *Natural Theology: Comprising "Nature and Grace" by Professor Dr. Emil Brunner and the reply "No!" by Dr. Karl Barth*. Eugene, OR: Wipf and Stock, 2002.

Gagarin, Michael. *Writing Greek Law*. Cambridge: Cambridge University Press, 2008.

Garnett, George, ed. *Brutus: Vindiciae Contra Tyrannos: Or, Concerning the Legitimate Power of a Prince over the People, and of the People over a Prince.* Cambridge: Cambridge University Press, 1994.

Grabill, Stephen J. *Rediscovering the Natural Law in Reformed Theological Ethics.* Grand Rapids, MI: Eerdmans, 2006.

Grafton, Anthony. "Annius of Viterbo as a Student of the Jews: The Sources of His Information" in Walter Stephens, Earle A. Havens, and Janet E. Gomez, eds., *Literary Forgery in Early Modern Europe, 1450–1800.* Baltimore: Johns Hopkins University Press, 2018, pp. 147–169.

Gregory, Brad S. *The Unintended Reformation: How a Religious Revolution Secularized Society.* Cambridge, MA: Belknap, 2012.

Haakonssen, Knud. *Natural Law and Moral Philosophy: From Grotius to the Scottish Enlightenment.* Cambridge: Cambridge University Press, 2012.

Haakonssen, Knud. "Early Modern Natural Law Theories", in *The Cambridge Companion to Natural Law Jurisprudence*, ed. George Duke and Robert P. George. Cambridge: Cambridge University Press, 2017, pp. 76–102.

Heineck, Hermann, ed. *Die Aelteste Fassung von Melanchthons Ethik.* Berlin: Philosophisch-Historischer Verlag von Dr. R. Salinger, 1893.

Helmholz, Richard. *Roman Canon Law in Reformation England.* Cambridge: Cambridge University Press, 2004.

Herdt, Jennifer. "Natural Law in Protestant Christianity", in *The Cambridge Companion to Natural Law Ethics*, ed. Tom Angier. Cambridge: Cambridge University Press, 2019, pp. 155–178.

Hochstrasser, T.J. *Natural Law Theories in the Early Enlightenment.* Cambridge: Cambridge University Press, 2004.

Höpfl, Harro, ed. *Luther and Calvin on Secular Authority.* Cambridge: Cambridge University Press, 1991.

Hubig, Christoph. "Melanchthon als Interpret der aristotelischen Ethik", in *Werk und Rezeption Philipp Melanchthons in Universität und Schule bis ins 18. Jahrhundert*, ed. Günther Wartenberg and Markus Hein. Leipzig: Evangelische Verlagsanstalt, 1999, pp. 161–177.

Irwin, Terence. *The Development of Ethics: Volume 1: From Socrates to the Reformation.* Oxford: Oxford University Press, 2007.

Jensen, Mads Langballe. "By Convention or by Nature: Melanchthon's Criticism of Late Medieval Ockhamist Political Thought in the *Commentarii in aliquot politicos libros Aristotelis*", *History of Political Thought* 35.1 (2014): 1–28.

Jensen, Mads Langballe. *A Humanist in Reformation Politics: Philipp Melanchthon on Political Philosophy and Natural Law.* Leiden: Brill, 2019.

Jensen, Mads Langballe. "'Without Prophetic and Apostolic Voices': Niels Hemmingsen's *On the Law of Nature According to a Demonstrative Method*", in *Sacred Polities, Natural*

Law and the Law of Nations in the 16th–17th Centuries. ed. Hans Blom. Leiden: Brill, 2022, pp. 56–76.

Karr, Susan Longfield. *Jus Gentium in Humanist Jurisprudence: On Justice and Right.* Leiden: Brill, 2022.

Keen, Ralph, ed. *A Melanchthon Reader*. New York: Peter Lang, 1988.

Keen, Ralph. *A Checklist of Melanchthon Imprints through 1560*. St. Louis: Center for Reformation Research, 1988.

Keen, Ralph. "Defending the Pious: Melanchthon and the Reformation in Albertine Saxony, 1539", *Church History* 60.2 (1991): 180–195.

Keen, Ralph. *Divine and Human Authority in Reformation Thought: German Theologians on Political Order, 1520–1555*. Nieuwkoop: De Graaf, 1997.

Kelley, Donald. *The Foundations of Modern Historical Scholarship: Language, Law, and History in the French Renaissance*. New York: Columbia University Press, 1970.

Kelsen, Hans. *Die philosophischen Grundlagen der Naturrechtslehre und des Rechtspositivismus*. Charlottenburg: Verlag Rolf Heise, 1928.

Kern, Bernd-Rüdiger. "Philipp Melanchthon als Interpret des Naturrechts", in *Werk und Rezeption Philipp Melanchthons in Universität und Schule bis ins 18. Jahrhundert*. ed. Günther Wartenberg and Markus Hein. Leipzig: Evangelische Verlagsanstalt, 1999, pp. 147–160.

Kisch, Guido. *Melanchthons Rechts- und Soziallehre*. Berlin: De Gruyter, 1967.

Koebner, Richard. "Despot and Despotism: Vicissitudes of a Political Term", *Journal of the Warburg and Courtauld Institutes* 14.3/4 (1951): 275–302.

Kolb, Robert. "Melanchthonian Method as a Guide to Reading Confessions of Faith: The Index of the Book of Concord and Late Reformation Learning", *Church History* 72.3 (2003): 504–524.

Kraye, Jill, ed. *Cambridge Translations of Renaissance Philosophical Texts. Volume 1: Moral Philosophy*. Cambridge: Cambridge University Press, 1997.

Kraye, Jill. "Melanchthon's Ethics Commentaries and Textbooks", in *Classical Traditions in Renaissance Philosophy*, ed. Jill Kraye. London: Routledge, 2002, chapter VII (pp. 1–12).

Kristeller, Paul Oskar. *Renaissance Thought: The Classic, Scholastic, and Humanist Strains*. New York: Harper, 1961.

Kristeller, Paul Oskar, F. Edward Cranz, Virginia Brown, and Greti Dinkova-Bruun, eds. *Catalogus translationum et commentariorum: Mediaeval and Renaissance Latin Translations and Commentaries: Annotated Lists and Guides*. 11 vols. Washington, D.C., Catholic University of America Press, 1960–. [abbreviated CTC].

Kuropka, Nicole. *Philipp Melanchthon: Wissenschaft und Gesellschaft. Ein Gelehrter im Dienst der Kirche (1526–1532)*. Tübingen: Mohr Siebeck, 2002.

Kuropka, Nicole. "Melanchthon and Aristotle", in *Philip Melanchthon: Theologian in Classroom, Confession, and Controversy*. ed. Irene Dingel, Robert Kolb, Nicole Kuropka, and Timothy J. Wengert. Göttingen: Vandenhoek & Ruprecht, 2012, pp. 19–28.

Kuropka, Nicole. "Melanchthon und die Ethik", *Zeitschrift für Theologie und Kirche* 113.3 (2016): 235–257.

Kusukawa, Sachiko. *The Transformation of Natural Philosophy: The Case of Philip Melanchthon*. Cambridge: Cambridge University Press, 1995.

Kusukawa, Sachiko. *A Wittenberg University Library Catalogue of 1536*. Binghamton, N.Y., LP Publications, 1995.

Kusukawa, Sachiko., ed. *Philip Melanchthon: Orations on Philosophy and Education*. trans. Christine F. Salazar. Cambridge: Cambridge University Press, 1999.

Lazarus, Micha. "Tragedy at Wittenberg: Sophocles in Reformation Europe", *Renaissance Quarterly* 73.1 (2020): 33–77.

Lotito, Mark. *The Reformation of Historical Thought*. Leiden: Brill, 2019.

MacIntyre, Alasdair, *A Short History of Ethics*. Reprint, Original 1966. New York: Simon & Schuster, 1996.

Manschreck, Clyde Leonard. *Melanchthon: The Quiet Reformer*. New York: Abingdon, 1958.

Maritain, Jacques. *Trois Réformateurs: Luther—Descartes—Rousseau*. Paris: Plon-Nourrit et Cia, 1925.

McGrade, Arthur Stephen. *The Political Thought of William of Ockham: Personal and Institutional Principles*. Cambridge: Cambridge University Press, 1974.

McNeill, John T. "Natural Law in the Teaching of the Reformers", *Journal of Religion* 26 (1946): 168–182.

Methuen, Charlotte. "Lex Naturae and Ordo Naturae in the Thought of Philip Melanchthon", *Reformation and Renaissance Review* 3 (2000): 110–125.

Milton, Anthony. "A Tale of Two Melanchthons: Melanchthon and English Protestantism 1560–1660", in *Melanchthon und die Reformierte Tradition*. ed. Andreas J. Beck. Göttingen: Vandenhoeck & Ruprecht, 2016, pp. 129–138.

Mortimer, Sarah. *Reformation, Resistance, and Reason of State (1517–1625)*. Oxford: Oxford University Press, 2021.

Muller, Richard A., ed. *Dictionary of Latin and Greek Theological Terms, Drawn Principally from Protestant Scholastic Theology*, 2nd edition. Grand Rapids, MI: Baker Academic, 2017.

Muller, Richard A. "Reformation, Orthodoxy, 'Christian Aristotelianism', and the Eclecticism of Early Modern Philosophy", *Nederlands Archief Voor Kerksgeschiedenis / Dutch Review of Church History* 81.3 (2001): 306–325.

Nutton, Vivian. "Wittenberg Anatomy", in *Medicine and the Reformation*, ed. Andrew Cunningham and Ole Peter Grell. London: Routledge, 1993, pp. 11–32.

Osler, Douglas. "The Myth of European Legal History", *Rechtshistorisches Journal* 16 (1997): 393–410.

Pershing, B.H. "The Proposed Mission of Melanchthon to France", *Church History* 3.1

(1934): 41–59.

Peterson, Luther D. "Justus Menius, Philipp Melanchthon, and the 1547 Treatise, *Von der Notwehr Unterricht*", *Archiv für Reformationsgeschichte* 81 (1990): 138–157.

Pinckaers, Servais. *The Sources of Christian Ethics*, translated by Sr. Mary Thomas Noble, 3rd ed. Edinburgh: T&T Clark, 1995.

Potter, D.L. "Foreign Policy in the Age of the Reformation: French Involvement in the Schmalkaldic War, 1544–1547", *The Historical Journal* 20.3 (1977): 525–544.

Rasmussen, Tarald. "Skandinavien", in *Philip Melanchthon: Der Reformator zwischen Glauben und Wissen: Ein Handbuch*. ed. Günter Frank and Axel Lange. Berlin: De Gruyter, 2017, pp. 647–658.

Raunio, Antti. "Divine and Natural Law in Luther and Melanchthon", in *The Lutheran Reformation and the Law*. ed. Virpi Mäkinen. Leiden: Brill, 2006, pp. 21–61.

Rogness, Michael. *Philip Melanchthon: Reformer without Honor*. Minneapolis: Augsburg, 1969.

Ryan, Alan. *On Politics: A History of Political Thought: From Herodotus to the Present*. New York: Liveright, 2012.

Saarinen, Risto. "Die heroische Tugend in der protestantischen Ethik. Von Melanchthon zu den Anfängen der finnischen Universität Turku", In *Melanchthon und Europa. 1 Teilband: Skandinavien und Mittelosteuropa*. ed. Günter Frank and Martin Treu. Stuttgart: Jan Thorbecke, 2001, pp. 129–138.

Scattola, Merio. *Das Naturrecht vor dem Naturrecht. Zur Geschichte des* "ius naturae" *im XVI. Jahrhundert*. Tübingen: Niemeyer, 1999.

Scattola, Merio. "Notitia naturalis de Deo et de morum gubernatione: die Naturrechtslehre Philipp Melanchthons und ihre Wirkung im 16. Jahrhundert", in *Melanchthon und die Marburger Professoren (1527–1627)*. ed. Barbara Bauer, Marburg: Universitätsbibliothek Marburg, 1999, vol. 2, pp. 865–882.

Scheible, Heinz, ed. *Melanchthon in seinen Schülern*. Wiesbaden: Harrassowitz, 1997.

Scheible, Heinz. "Die Bedeutung der Unterscheidung von Gesetz und Evangelium für die theologische Ethik und Praktische Theologie am Beispiel Melanchthons", in *Christentum und Spätmoderne. Ein internationaler Diskurs über Praktische Theologie und Ethik*. ed. W. Gräb et al. Stuttgart: Kohlhammer, 2000, pp. 93–100.

Scheible, Heinz. "Melanchthons Werdegang", in *Aufsätze zu Melanchthon*. Tübingen: Mohr Siebeck, 2010, pp. 28–45.

Scheible, Heinz. *Melanchthon: Vermittler der Reformation: Eine Biographie*. Munich: C.H. Beck, 2016.

Schiffman, Zachary Sayre. *The Birth of The Past*. Baltimore: Johns Hopkins University Press, 2011.

Schneewind, Jerome B. *The Invention of Autonomy: A History of Modern Moral Philosophy*. Cambridge: Cambridge University Press, 1997.

Schneider, Hans-Otto. *Politischer Widerstand als Protestantische Option: Philipp Mel-*

anchthon und Justus Menius: Von der Notwehr (*1547*). Leipzig: Evangelische Verlagsanstalt, 2014.

Schuessler, Rudolf. *The Debate on Probable Opinions in the Scholastic Tradition.* Leiden: Brill, 2019.

Scribner, R.W. "Civic Unity and the Reformation in Erfurt", *Past & Present* 66 (1975): 29–60.

Sinnema, Donald W. "The Discipline of Ethics in Early Reformed Orthodoxy", *Calvin Theological Journal* 28 (1993): 10–44.

Skinner, Quentin. *The Foundations of Modern Political Thought, Volume II: The Reformation.* Cambridge: Cambridge University Press, 1978.

Stiening, Gideon. "'Notitiae principiorum practicorum'. Melanchthons Rechtslehre zwischen Machiavelli und Vitoria", in *Der Philosoph Melanchthon.* ed. Günter Frank and Felix Mundt. Berlin: De Gruyter, 2012, pp. 115–146.

Stillman, Robert E. "The Truths of a Slippery World: Poetry and Tyranny in Sidney's 'Defence'", *Renaissance Quarterly* 50 (2002): 1287–1319.

Stolleis, Michael. "Reichspublizistik—Politik—Naturrecht im 17. und 18. Jahrhundert", in *Staatsdenker in der frühen Neuzeit,* 3rd edition, ed. Michael Stolleis. Munich: C.H. Beck, 1995.

Strauss, Gerald. *Law, Resistance, and the State: The Opposition to Roman Law in Reformation Germany.* Princeton: Princeton University Press, 1986.

Strauss, Leo, and Joseph Cropsey, eds. *History of Political Philosophy.* 3rd ed. Chicago: University of Chicago Press, 1987.

Strohm, Christoph. *Ethik im frühen Calvinismus. Humanistische Einflüsse, philosophische, juristische und theologische Argumentationen sowie mentalitätsgeschichtliche Aspekte am Beispiel des Calvin-Schülers Lambertus Danaeus.* Berlin: De Gruyter, 1996.

Strohm, Christoph. "Zugänge zum Naturrecht bei Melanchthon", in *Der Theologe Melanchthon,* ed. Günter Frank. Stuttgart: Jan Thorbecke, 2000, pp. 339–356.

Strohm, Christoph. "Melanchthon-Rezeption in der Ethik des frühen Calvinismus", in *Melanchthon und der Calvinismus.* ed. Günter Frank and Herman J. Selderhuis. Stuttgart-Bad Cannstatt: Frommann-Holzboog, 2005, pp. 135–157.

Strohm, Christoph. "Melanchthon et l'éthique réformée. Le probleme du statut de droit naturel", in *Crossing Traditions: Essays on the Reformation and Intellectual History: in Honour of Irena Backus,* ed. Maria-Cristina Pitassi and Daniela Solfaroli Camillocci. Leiden: Brill, 2017, pp. 467–491.

Strohm, Christoph. "Jurisprudenz", in *Philipp Melanchthon: Der Reformator zwischen Glauben und Wissen: Ein Handbuch.* ed. Günter Frank, with Axel Lange. Berlin: De Gruyter, 2017, pp. 495–506.

Svensson, Manfred. "Aristotelian Practical Philosophy from Melanchthon to Eisenhart: Protestant Commentaries on the Nicomachean Ethics 1529–1682", *Reformation &*

Renaissance Review 21.3 (2019): 218–238.

Svensson, Manfred. "The Aristotelian Conception of Natural Law and Its Reception in Early Protestant Commentaries on the Nicomachean Ethics", *Perichoresis* 20.2 (2022): 3–18.

Svensson, Manfred. *The Aristotelian Tradition in Early Modern Protestantism: Sixteenth- and Seventeenth- Century Commentaries on the* Ethics *and* Politics. Oxford: Oxford University Press, 2024.

Sytsma, David S. "John Calvin on the Intersection of Natural, Roman, and Mosaic Law", *Perichoresis* 20.2 (2022): 19–41.

Todd, S.C. *The Shape of Athenian Law*. Oxford: Clarendon, 1993.

Troje, Hans Erich. "Konrad Lagus (ca. 1500–1546): Zur Rezeption der Loci-Methode in der Jurisprudenz", in *Melanchthon in seinen Schülern*, ed. Heinz Scheible. Wiesbaden: Harrassowitz, 1997, pp. 255–284.

Tuck, Richard. *Natural Rights Theories: Their Origin and Development*. Cambridge: Cambridge University Press, 1979.

Tuck, Richard. *The Rights of War and Peace: Political Thought and the International Order from Grotius to Kant*. Oxford: Oxford University Press, 1999.

VanDrunen, David. *Natural Law and the Two Kingdoms: A Study in the Development of Reformed Social Thought*. Grand Rapids, MI: Eerdmans, 2010.

von Friedeburg, Robert. *Self-Defence and Religious Strife in Early Modern Europe: England and Germany, 1530–1680*. London: Routledge, 2002.

von Kaltenborn, Karl. *Die Vorläufer des Hugo Grotius auf dem Gebiete des ius naturae et gentium im Reformationszeitalter*. 2 vols. Leibzig: Gustav Mayer, 1848.

Wartenberg, Günther. "Melanchthon als Politiker", in *Der Theologe Melanchthon*, ed. Günter Frank. Stuttgart: Jan Thorbecke, 2000, pp. 153–168.

Watt, J.A. "Spiritual and Temporal Powers", in *The Cambridge History of Medieval Political Thought, c. 350–c. 1450*. ed. J.H. Burns. Cambridge: Cambridge University Press, 2008, pp. 367–423.

Weaver, William. *Homer in Wittenberg: Rhetoric, Scholarship, Prayer*. Oxford: Oxford University Press, 2023.

Wengert, Timothy. *Law and Gospel: Philip Melanchthon's Debate with John Agricola of Eisleben over* "Poenitentia". Grand Rapids, MI: Baker, 1997.

Wengert, Timothy. "Philip Melanchthon and a Christian Politics", *Lutheran Quarterly* 17.1 (2003): 29–62.

Whitman, James Q. *The Legacy of Roman Law in the German Romantic Era: Historical Vision and Legal Change*. Princeton, NJ: Princeton University Press, 1990.

Wiersma, Hans. "Luther on Lending: A Pastoral Response Regarding the Subject of Usury", *Word & World* 30.2 (2010): 191–199.

Witte, John. "The Reformation of Marriage Law in Martin Luther's Germany: Its Significance Then and Now", *Journal of Law and Religion* 4.2 (1986): 293–351.

Witte, John. *Law and Protestantism: The Legal Teachings of the Lutheran Reformation.* Cambridge: Cambridge University Press, 2009.

Wolin, Sheldon S. *Politics and Vision: Continuity and Innovation in Western Political Thought.* Expanded edition. Princeton: Princeton University Press, 2004.

Classical Author Index

Author Index (Post-Classical)

Scripture Index

Subject Index